Study Guide

Bukatko/Daehler

CHILD DEVELOPMENT
A Topical Approach

Michael Vigorito
Seton Hall University
South Orange, New Jersey

Carolyn Greco-Vigorito
St. John's University
Staten Island, New York

HOUGHTON MIFFLIN COMPANY   BOSTON   TORONTO

DALLAS   GENEVA, ILLINOIS   PALO ALTO   PRINCETON, NEW JERSEY

Senior Sponsoring Editor: Michael DeRocco
Development Editor: Suzanne Morris
Ancillary Coordinator: Tracy Theriault
Manufacturing Coordinator: Holly Schuster
Marketing Manager: Diane McOscar

Cover photograph by James Scherer

Printed in the U.S.A.

ISBN: 0-395-48145-7

BCDEFGHIJ-HS-99876543

Library of Congress Catalog Card Number: 91-72007

CONTENTS

TO THE STUDENT

This *Study Guide* is designed to help you master the material in *Child Development: A Topical Approach* by Bukatko and Daehler. The *Study Guide* is intended to supplement the textbook—not replace it. If used properly, you will be able to increase your understanding of the key concepts and issues discussed in the text. For each chapter in the textbook there is a corresponding chapter in the *Study Guide* that is divided into the following sections:

- A list of **Learning Objectives** to help you master the material by focusing your attention on the key concepts in each chapter. These concepts form a detailed map of the general ideas and major points made in the text chapter. Page numbers that correspond to the location of the objectives in the textbook are included to encourage you to use the *Study Guide* and the textbook together.

- A **Chapter Outline** that presents the topics in each chapter, organized by major headings and subheadings. All the key terms are included and page numbers corresponding to each segment of the outline are provided. The outline is excellent for review purposes, but it should not be used as a replacement for reading the chapter.

- A section called **Key Terms Review,** a fill-in-the-blank type quiz on the key terms and concepts covered in the chapter. The answers are conveniently provided at the end of the section.

- **Multiple-Choice Questions** that test your knowledge of the material in the chapter. Twenty fact/concept questions test your understanding of the concepts, definitions, and theories covered in the chapter. Ten application questions test your ability to apply the information you have learned to everyday situations or problems. Answers to the questions, along with explanations about why each choice is correct or incorrect, are included at the end of the tests. The correct choice is followed by the page number in the textbook where the information can be found.

Please keep in mind that the material in the *Study Guide* does not cover the concepts and research findings presented in the textbook with the same depth of detail. Therefore, it should not be used as a substitute for a careful reading of the textbook. However, the *Study Guide* does provide a structured approach to learning that will enhance your ability to successfully complete your course in child development. Good luck!

M. V.
C. G.-V.

CHAPTER 1

STUDYING CHILD DEVELOPMENT

LEARNING OBJECTIVES

1. Define development and discuss the goals of developmental psychology. (pp. 3–4)

2. Discuss how the view of childhood changed from medieval and Renaissance times to the Age of Enlightenment. (pp. 5–8)

3. Discuss the origins of developmental psychology by comparing and contrasting the approaches used by the early scholars to study developmental issues. (pp. 8–12)

4. Describe developmental psychology in the twentieth century. (pp. 12–13)

5. Discuss current concerns about the disappearance of childhood in contemporary psychology. (pp. 14–15)

6. Discuss the role of theories in scientific research. (pp. 15–16)

7. Identify the requirements for scientifically measuring attributes and behaviors. (pp. 16–17)

8. Compare and contrast the four methods available to developmental psychologists to collect data. (pp. 17–23)

9. Compare and contrast the three basic research designs utilized by developmental psychologists to learn about development. (pp. 24–30)

10. Discuss the advantages and disadvantages of the three strategies for assessing developmental change. (pp. 30–35)

11. Explain the goals of cross-cultural studies of development. (pp. 35–36)

12. Discuss the ethical concerns that arise in human developmental research. (pp. 36–38)

CHAPTER OUTLINE

Development is a term used to describe all of the physical and psychological changes that an individual undergoes in a lifetime. *Developmental psychologists* describe and explain these changes by relying on scientific research methods—systematic, objective, and verifiable fact-finding procedures. (pp. 3–4)

I. **THE SCIENTIFIC STUDY OF THE CHILD IN WESTERN SOCIETY** (pp. 4–13)
   In the last century, developmental psychology as a field has grown at a rapid rate. Attitudes toward children have shifted considerably during this time, a fact that has created an emphasis on children as the objects of scientific study.

A. **Historical Perspectives on the Nature of Childhood** (pp. 5–8)
   In contemporary American society children are viewed as distinct from adults and are protected and nurtured. This view of childhood is relatively recent. Children of the Middle Ages in Europe, although recognized as different and possessing special needs, were incorporated into the adult world as soon as they were physically able to contribute to the economy. The changes in attitudes toward children began to occur in the sixteenth century, when child labor was no longer essential for economical survival as the economy became trade-based rather than agrarian.

   The changing view of childhood was reinforced by seventeenth- and eighteenth-century philosophers who emphasized the child as a developing being. John Locke's belief that the newborn's mind was a *tabula rasa*, or "blank slate," emphasized the idea that the individual is shaped by environmental experiences. Locke's philosophy, called *empiricism*, conveyed the need to provide children with proper experience through good rearing practices and education. Jean Jacques Rousseau described the child as a "noble savage" and argued that children require adult guidance to bring their natural instincts in line with the social environment.

B. **The Origins of Developmental Psychology** (pp. 8–12)
   Charles Darwin and Wilhelm Preyer studied their children not to understand child development but to support the emerging views about the evolution of human beings. Although their observational procedures had many methodological problems, they stimulated interest in the systematic study of the child.

   G. Stanley Hall, considered by historians to be the father of developmental psychology, has many "firsts" attached to his name. Among Hall's many contributions was his adoption of the questionnaire method to systematically collect data on large groups of children. Hall was a strong supporter of evolutionary theory and maintained that the child's behavior was largely based on instincts, but that by adolescence these instincts could be shaped to provide a wide range of human potentials.

Alfred Binet developed the first intelligence assessment scale. The use of this scale to identify unique patterns in the mental capabilities of each child led to the important study of *individual differences*.

Unlike the other major figures in the birth of developmental psychology, James Mark Baldwin did not provide methodologies for studying children but instead contributed important theoretical issues. Baldwin presaged many current ideas, such as development as a mutual dynamic between the child and others.

C. **Developmental Psychology in the Twentieth Century** (pp. 12–13)
During the first forty years of the twentieth century, developmental psychologists primarily gathered descriptive information on children. Many major institutes or research centers devoted to the study of child development were founded. Today scholars interested in child development comprise a variety of disciplines and subareas of psychology.

   Controversy: Is Childhood Disappearing from Contemporary Society? (pp. 14–15)
   Some observers warn that the distinction between childhood and adulthood is beginning to blur again, as it once did in pre-Enlightenment times. The merging of adults' and children's clothing styles, eating habits, and modes of entertainment are provided as evidence of such concerns. The push to achieve new levels of proficiency at early ages and the increasing number of children experiencing adult problems such as alcoholism and sexual abuse further support the concern over disappearing childhood.

II. **RESEARCH METHODS IN DEVELOPMENTAL PSYCHOLOGY** (pp. 15–38)
As in other research disciplines, developmental psychologists rely on the *scientific method* to evaluate predictions of specific *theories* or to determine the applicability of theory to real-world settings. Researchers must identify the variables of interest, choose a method for collecting data on children, and choose a research design to test hypotheses generated by their theories.

A. **The Role of Theories** (pp. 15–16)
Theories are important for any scientific endeavor because they serve several functions. Theories organize large amounts of information that have been obtained by previous research, explain the observations, and provide predictions about behaviors that can be tested in the form of clearly stated hypotheses. If hypotheses about the cause of or influence on behavior fail to be supported following systematic and objective tests, then the theories that gave rise to the hypotheses must be modified or rejected.

B. **Measuring Attributes and Behaviors** (pp. 16–17)
When conducting research, scientists examine *variables* such as attributes and behaviors that may vary between and within individuals. The ultimate goal of scientific research is to determine the causal relationship among variables. To attain this goal variables must be *operationally defined*, that is, precisely specified in measurable terms. Variables must demonstrate *validity*, that is, the variable must actually measure what it was intended to measure. The measurement of a variable must also be *reliable* when administered repeatedly, and when measured by several observers it should show *inter-rater reliability*.

C. **Collecting Data** (pp. 17–23)
Researchers have several approaches to measuring variables or collecting data; which approach is used depends on the specific questions and goals that they have. Scientists who use *naturalistic observations* do not manipulate variables directly but simply attempt to discern important relationships among variables of interest. A well-designed naturalistic observation will have operationally defined all relevant variables, avoided *subject reactivity* (the tendency of subjects who know that they are being observed to alter their behavior), and minimized the effects of *observer bias* (the tendency of researchers to interpret the behaviors being measured to be consistent with their research hypotheses). Naturalistic observations are particularly useful in examining antecedents and consequences of behaviors in previously unexplored areas of child development. A disadvantage of this research method is that cause-and-effect relationships among variables are difficult to establish.

Structured observations are research situations in which the experimenter devises ways to elicit those behaviors of interest that normally would not be displayed consistently in a natural setting. This form of observation under highly structured situations, usually a laboratory, provides the researcher with control over the precise nature of the variables of interest. Structured observations focus on a wide variety of behaviors, such as memory strategies, time to learn a task, and emotional displays, and on *physiological measures* such as heart rate. A disadvantage of this approach is that children may not react in a research laboratory in the same way they would in their natural setting.

Sometimes the best way to learn what children know or how they behave is to ask them or their parents rather than to observe them. With *structured interviews* a child is asked a predetermined sequence of questions. The *questionnaire* is a standard set of items to which children provide written responses. Although questionnaires may be difficult for some children to understand, and some may not respond truthfully, a major advantage of the method is that it can be given to a large number of children at the same time and the responses can be scored quickly. The *clinical method* is a flexible, open-ended questioning technique that permits the researcher the flexibility to follow a child's train of thought. The disadvantages of this method include difficulties in making systematic comparisons between subjects and the possibility of biased questioning.

When a large number of studies are available in the same area and the results are inconsistent or in conflict, a *meta-analysis* can be conducted. With meta-analysis the results of previously published research are statistically analyzed in order to assess if the central variable in all of the studies has an important effect. One disadvantage of this procedure is that the variables of concern may not have been defined identically across all studies in the pool being analyzed.

D. **Research Designs** (pp. 24–30)
The type of research design chosen by an experimenter determines whether a variable will be manipulated (experimental design) or not (correlational design), whether many or only a few subjects will be studied, and other features of the research process.

Correlational studies are used to look for systematic relationships between variables of interest. The direction and strength of the relationship between two variables is described with the statistical tool known as the *correlation coefficient* (r). The sign of r indicates whether the variables change in the same direction (*positive correlation*) or in the opposite direction (*negative correlation*). The value of r, which ranges from 0 to 1, provides an indication of the strength of the relationship, with 0.0 signifying no relationship between variables and 1.0 indicating a perfect one-to-one relationship between variables. The correlation method is useful when it is not possible for the researcher to manipulate the variables of interest. However, because variables are not manipulated in correlational studies, it is not possible to determine cause-and-effect relationships.

The major strength of the *experimental design* is that it can isolate cause-and-effect relationships between variables. The variable suspected of being the cause of a behavior is called the *independent variable*. The *dependent variable* is the behavior being measured or the suspected outcome. To accurately make a cause-and-effect statement it is important to avoid any systematic variation other than that provided by the independent variable. Thus, experimental studies provide control for factors other than the independent variable that can potentially influence the dependent variable. A common control procedure is to *randomly assign* subjects to different treatment groups, one of which is usually a control group that receives no treatment. When subjects cannot be randomly assigned to groups, the researcher must be cautious in making cause-and-effect statements. Such is the case with *quasi-experiments*, where the independent variable is not directly manipulated but occurs as a result of the subject's natural experiences. In *field experiments*, experimental manipulations are carried out in a natural setting, such as the child's home or school.

The *single-subject design* provides an in-depth examination of one or a few children. *Case studies* involve intensive descriptions of the child. Sigmund Freud and Jean Piaget are well known for utilizing this design. The *single-case design* manipulates an independent variable and notes any change in behavior over time. Cause-and-effect statements concerning the independent and dependent variables in single-case designs are more difficult to make, since factors concurrent with the independent variable might have actually changed the behavior. In addition, the ability to generalize the results of single-subject designs to larger populations may be limited.

E. **Strategies for Assessing Developmental Change** (pp. 30–35)
The developmental psychologist relies on two approaches to record changes in behavior that occur over time—the longitudinal study and the cross-sectional study.

When the same sample of subjects is repeatedly observed over time, typically over years, a *longitudinal study* is being used. Although costly and time consuming, this type of research is the only strategy that can be utilized to determine the stability of human characteristics. The longitudinal study does have several methodological drawbacks, such as changes that may occur in the composition of the group being studied due to sample attrition and *age-history confound* (alterations in the originally defined variables due to historical changes).

In the *cross-sectional study*, children of different ages are observed or tested at the same point in time. Such studies are more economical than longitudinal studies and provide a means of rapidly assessing changes in behavior with age. Cross-sectional studies cannot be used to determine the stability of the child's characteristics and are subject to *cohort effects*, the generational differences between children of different ages as a result of the cultural and historical climate in which they were reared. Thus, any observed differences between ages attributed to the treatment manipulated by the experimenter may in fact be due to cohort effects.

The *sequential study* can be described as a compromise between the longitudinal and cross-sectional approaches; groups of children at different ages are repeatedly observed or tested for only a few years. The sequential study gains the advantages of both the longitudinal and cross-sectional studies but suffers the same problems as the longitudinal study, although to a lesser degree.

F. **Cross-Cultural Studies of Development** (pp. 35–36)
Cross-cultural studies, which compare children from different cultural groups, are very useful in addressing the issues of whether certain behaviors or abilities are determined by biological or experiential factors. Similar developmental features seen across cultures imply biological or genetic influences, whereas variations suggest experiential influences on development.

G. **Ethical Issues in Developmental Research** (pp. 36–38)
The American Psychological Association has established guidelines for the use of human subjects in psychological research. Subjects must provide *informed consent* before participating in a study, have the right to decline or stop at any time, and must be *debriefed* at the conclusion of the study if they were deceived about the true nature of the study. In addition all data must be kept confidential. The same guidelines apply to children, but the implementation of these guidelines is often difficult because children may not understand the nature of the study and may be especially sensitive to the effects of participating in a research study.

Key Terms Review

1. In the experimental design the _____ variable is suspected of causing a change in the _____ variable.

2. In the _____ an experiment is conducted in a "natural" real-world setting such as the child's home.

3. _____ of subjects to groups avoids systematic bias in experimental designs.

4. _____ is the degree to which a measure will yield the same results if administered repeatedly, whereas _____ is the degree to which an assessment procedure actually measures what it was intended to measure.

5. A(n) _____ is a factor having no fixed or constant value in a given situation.

6. _____ is the theory that experiences shape the individual, that all knowledge is derived from sensory experiences.

7. In the _____ only one or a few children are studied over a period of time.

8. A(n) _____ is a set of ideas or propositions that help organize or explain observable phenomena.

9. The _____ is a statistical procedure that summarizes the strength and direction of the relationship between two variables in a(n) _____ study.

10. The _____ study compares subjects in different cultural settings.

11. The degree to which two or more observers agree in their observations is called _____ .

12. In longitudinal studies _____ , or changes in originally defined variables due to changes in sociohistorical context, may affect the generalizability of the findings.

13. Subjects' tendency to alter their natural behavior because they know that they are under observation is called _____ .

14. A(n) _____ describes systematic changes between two variables that are in opposite directions; in a(n) _____ the changes in the two variables are in the same direction.

15. To formally acknowledge that a subject understands the purpose, procedures, and risks of a study she is about to participate in, the subject provides _____ .

16. A(n) _____ is a research method in which assignment of subjects to groups is determined by their natural experiences.

17. The _____ uses objective, measurable, and repeatable techniques to gather information.

18. In the _____ the experimenter manipulates one or more independent variable to determine the effect on the dependent variable.

19. _____ is a term used to describe the physical and psychological changes in an individual over a lifetime.

20. A(n) _____ is a set of standardized questions that are administered to subjects in written form.

21. The tendency of researchers to interpret ongoing events as consistent with their research hypotheses is called _____ .

22. In the _____ a standardized set of questions is administered orally to subjects, whereas in the _____ the investigator modifies questions in reaction to the child's response.

23. In the _____ subjects of different ages are examined at the same point in time.

24. _____ translates literally as "blank slate," the belief that infants are born with no innate knowledge or abilities.

25. The _____ involves an in-depth description of the psychological characteristics and behaviors of an individual.

26. _____ are those unique characteristics that distinguish a person from other members of a larger group.

27. The _____ specifies variables of interest in terms of measurable properties.

28. _____ is the systematic and scientific study of changes in human behaviors and mental activities over time.

29. In a(n) _____ the same subjects are repeatedly tested over a period of time, usually years.

30. _____ involves observing naturally occurring behaviors in real-life settings, while _____ involves observing behaviors as they occur within a situation constructed by the experimenter, usually in a laboratory.

31. The _____ examines groups of children of different ages over a period of time.

32. _____ is a statistical approach used to analyze the results of published studies to assess the effect of the common central variable.

33. The _____ describes characteristics shared by individuals growing up in a given sociohistorical context that can influence developmental outcomes.

34. A(n) _____ is a measure of heart rate, brain activity, respiration rate, or other bodily responses to stimulation.

35. A(n) _____ provides a subject who was deceived about the purpose of the study that he participated in with the true goals of the study.

Answers to Key Terms Review

1. independent, dependent
2. field experiment
3. Random assignment
4. Reliability, validity
5. variable
6. Empiricism
7. single-case design
8. theory
9. correlation coefficient (r), correlational
10. cross-cultural
11. inter-rater reliability
12. age-history confound
13. subject reactivity
14. negative correlation, positive correlation
15. informed consent
16. quasi-experiment
17. scientific method
18. experimental design
19. Development
20. questionnaire
21. observer bias
22. structured interview, clinical method
23. cross-sectional study
24. Tabula rasa
25. case study
26. Individual differences
27. operational definition
28. Developmental psychology
29. longitudinal study
30. Naturalistic observation, structured observation
31. sequential study
32. Meta-analysis

33. cohort effect
34. physiological measure
35. debriefing

Multiple-Choice Questions

Fact and Concept Questions

1. The term used to describe all the psychological and physical changes a human being undergoes in a lifetime is
    a. learning.
    b. ethology.
    c. development.
    d. maturation.

2. The Age of Enlightenment describes the period of time when
    a. the writings of important thinkers such as Locke and Rousseau shaped the popular understanding of childhood.
    b. the social structure shifted from an agrarian to a trade-based economy.
    c. the scientific method was first used as a method of study in developmental psychology.
    d. European methods of research were brought to the United States to provide researchers with new ways to study development.

3. Who described the child as a "noble savage"?
    a. John Locke
    b. Sigmund Freud
    c. James Mark Baldwin
    d. Jean Jacques Rousseau

4. G. Stanley Hall, the father of modern developmental psychology, maintained that
    a. the majority of the child's behavior had to be learned through experience.
    b. the child's behavior was largely based on instinct but could be shaped by the individual during specific periods of development.
    c. the child's behavior is primarily a result of instinct with minimal environmental influences.
    d. the field of developmental psychology should include the study of individual differences.

5. G. Stanley Hall was the first to develop an instrument that could be used to
   a. administer questionnaires to children.
   b. conduct naturalistic observational research.
   c. conduct detailed examination of individual children.
   d. study individual differences in mental capacities.

6. The scientific method is employed whenever
   a. a scholar discusses or gathers information on a topic of interest.
   b. a scholar gathers data that are objective, measurable, and capable of being replicated.
   c. a scholar formulates a theory that describes and explains a behavior of interest.
   d. a scholar observes behavior in the laboratory.

7. The ultimate goal of the scientific researcher is to
   a. determine the causal relationship among variables.
   b. describe relationships between variables.
   c. publish in scientific journals.
   d. provide an accurate description of the variables of interest.

8. The degree to which a measure will yield the same result if administered repeatedly is called
   a. validity.
   b. inter-rater reliability.
   c. reliability.
   d. consistency.

9. One of the disadvantages of naturalistic observations is that
   a. children may not always respond truthfully or accurately.
   b. children will not react to situations as they would in real life.
   c. cause-and-effect relationships are difficult to establish.
   d. they are worthwhile only for topics that have been under intense research.

10. An advantage of the clinical method of interviewing over the structured interview is that with the clinical method the interviewer
    a. can modify the questions in response to the child's responses to follow the child's train of thought.
    b. can gain knowledge about what children know by asking them directly.
    c. can gain information from many children at the same time.
    d. can determine the reasons why the children know what they know.

11. The meta-analysis technique is particularly useful when
    a. a researcher wishes to determine cause-and-effect relationships between variables.
    b. a researcher wants to determine the reliability of a measurement procedure.
    c. a researcher wants to determine the validity of a measurement procedure.
    d. the results of studies in the same area are inconsistent or in conflict with each other.

12. Studies that look for systematic relationships between two or more characteristics of subjects are called
    a. correlational studies.
    b. experimental studies.
    c. single-subject studies.
    d. longitudinal studies.

13. As the correlation coefficient approaches _____ the relationship between the two variables becomes weaker.
    a. a positive value
    b. a negative value
    c. 0
    d. a number greater than 1

14. The experimental design involves
    a. examining whether a change in one variable is accompanied by a change in another variable.
    b. the manipulation of one or more independent variables.
    c. the manipulation of one or more dependent variables.
    d. testing an individual many times over several years.

15. One of the advantages of using the experimental research design to study development is that
    a. the observations made are personal and subjective.
    b. the results of the research are always straightforward and unequivocal.
    c. cause-and-effect relationships among variables can be identified.
    d. it is usually exhaustive, examining every important aspect of development.

16. The text describes an experiment that investigated whether infants change their emotional responses based on the facial expressions of their mothers. The mother's facial expression was the
    a. base-line variable.
    b. experimental variable.
    c. independent variable.
    d. dependent variable.

17. A researcher who is conducting a field experiment probably
    a. tests subjects in their own home.
    b. tests subjects in a well-controlled laboratory setting.
    c. observes subjects in a natural setting without manipulating any variables.
    d. examines subjects for correlations between two variables of interest.

18. In longitudinal studies an investigator tests
    a. different subjects at different ages.
    b. different subjects at the same ages.
    c. the same subjects at different ages.
    d. different behaviors in the same subjects.

19. Which of the following is most likely to provide researchers with a rapid assessment of changes in behavior that occur with age?
    a. The longitudinal study
    b. The cross-sectional study
    c. The sequential study
    d. The single-subject study

20. To ensure that developmental psychologists comply with ethical guidelines when conducting experiments with children, most institutions in which research is conducted require
    a. informed consent from the participating subjects and their parents.
    b. a debriefing of all subjects and their parents at the end of the experiment.
    c. that all subjects receive both treatment and control conditions.
    d. that institutional review boards evaluate research proposals containing potential risks to subjects before the research is conducted.

Application Questions

1. Griffith believes that his newborn daughter's future abilities will be determined by her experiences in life and not by her genetic inheritance. Griffith's beliefs are similar to the philosophy espoused by
   a. Charles Darwin.
   b. Jean Jacques Rousseau.
   c. John Locke.
   d. G. Stanley Hall.

2. Professor Torrez studies helping behavior in toddlers. She had two of her undergraduate assistants independently analyze the same videotape of toddlers engaging in play activity for the frequency of helping behavior. The results tabulated by both students were very similar, suggesting that they achieved
   a. low inter-rater reliability.
   b. high inter-rater reliability.
   c. low inter-rater validity.
   d. high inter-rater validity.

3. Miguel would like to systematically compare the responses of children of various ages to questions related to death and dying. Miguel should probably use the _____ method to gather data.
   a. structured interview
   b. clinical
   c. experimental
   d. naturalistic observation

4. When reviewing the literature on the effects of moderate alcohol consumption by pregnant mothers on the behavioral development of infants, Harlene was frustrated to find that the results were inconsistent and in conflict. Harlene should
   a. probably abandon this area of research.
   b. consider conducting a correlational study.
   c. consider conducting a meta-analysis.
   d. consider conducting an observational study.

5. While conducting her master's thesis research on children's play behavior, Sheena discovered that as a child got older the amount of imaginary play decreased. The relationship between age and imaginary play can be described as
   a. a positive correlation.
   b. a negative correlation.
   c. zero correlation.
   d. causal correlation.

6. Tonya believes that playing adventure video games can actually enhance problem-solving abilities in seven-year-olds. To best test her hypothesis Tonya should
   a. conduct a correlational study.
   b. conduct a natural observational study.
   c. design and conduct an experiment.
   d. conduct structured interviews with seven-year-olds who play adventure video games.

7. Stephen believes that he can toilet train toddlers at an earlier age by having them view films of children successfully learning to use the toilet. To test his idea Stephen randomly assigns toddlers who are not yet toilet trained to two groups. One group of toddlers views short films of young children who are praised for successfully going to the "potty." The other group views short films of children playing with no reference to toilet training. Stephen then notes the number of toddlers who are successfully toilet trained by the end of the experiment. The independent variable in this experiment is
   a. whether or not the toddlers are toilet trained by the end of the experiment.
   b. the type of film viewed by the toddlers.
   c. the random assignment of subjects to groups.
   d. the number of toddlers in each group.

8. Ardella travels to young infants' homes to test their memories for a simple task. On the first day Ardella teaches the infants to kick their feet in order to make a colorful mobile hanging over the crib shake. The next day the infants are tested again to see if they remember the kicking task. Ardella is conducting a
   a. correlational study.
   b. cross-sectional study.
   c. field experiment.
   d. naturalistic observation.

9. Since their birth sixteen years ago, Mark and Martin have participated in a research study on twins and their development. They fill out a questionnaire twice a year and are visited by a psychologist who gives them standardized intelligence tests once a year. Mark and Martin have been participating in a
   a. cross-sectional study.
   b. longitudinal study.
   c. quasi-experimental study.
   d. cohort study.

10. Georgine has volunteered to have her two-year-old participate in a perception experiment at a nearby university. When she arrives at the laboratory with her child the first thing that she will probably do is
    a. undergo a debriefing on the real purpose of the experiment.
    b. sign an informed consent form.
    c. have her child tested before she begins to get fussy and cry.
    d. receive a small sum of money to cover her travel expenses.

Answers to Multiple-Choice Questions

The correct answer appears first and is preceded by an asterisk.

Answers to Fact and Concept Questions

1. *c. Psychologists use the term *development* to describe all the physical and psychological changes that occur throughout an individual's lifetime. (p. 3)
   a. Although learning is an important part of the changes that occur during development, it does not account for all of the psychological and physical changes.
   b. Ethology is the scientific study of animal behavior.
   d. Although maturation is an important part of the physical changes that occur during development, it does not account for all of the psychological and physical changes.

2. *a. It was during the eighteenth-century Age of Enlightenment that the sweeping social changes that had begun in the sixteenth and seventeenth centuries were solidified by the writings of Locke and Rousseau. (pp. 6–8)
   b. The social changes that resulted from a change in the economy occurred in the sixteenth and seventeenth centuries, before the Age of Enlightenment.
   c. Although the scientific method was being used in this age, developmental psychology was not yet an established discipline of study.
   d. The use of European methods in American developmental research first occurred in the nineteenth century, when G. Stanley Hall brought over the questionnaire method.

3. *d. Jean Jacques Rousseau defined the child as a "noble savage" as a way of endorsing the nurturance of natural tendencies and curiosity. (p. 7)
   a. John Locke is known for his description of the newborn's mind as a *tabula rasa*.
   b. Sigmund Freud, the founder of psychoanalysis, developed a comprehensive theory of psychosocial development.
   c. James Mark Baldwin is viewed by historians as one of the most important American developmental psychologists in the twentieth century.

4. *b. Hall was a believer of evolutionary theory and thus stressed the role of instinct in the behavior of the child. (p. 10)
   a. John Locke's philosophy of empiricism holds that all knowledge must be learned. Hall did not promote the philosophy of empiricism.
   c. Although Hall emphasized the importance of biology in behavior, he believed that during adolescence the individual could shape her behavior despite the constraints imposed by instinct.
   d. Hall's questionnaire method encouraged research on large groups of children. It was Alfred Binet who emphasized the importance of individual differences.

5. *a. G. Stanley Hall was the first American psychologist to use the questionnaire in developmental research. (p. 10)
   b. Naturalistic observation research could be conducted without the questionnaires developed by Hall.
   c. Previous approaches emphasized the examination of individual children, but Hall's work allowed researchers to collect group data and compare groups of children for the first time.
   d. Alfred Binet developed the first formal assessment scale for intelligence, which was used to identify patterns in mental capacities that were unique in each child.

6. *b. Any research project that utilizes the scientific method will collect data objectively and in a manner that could be reproduced by other investigators. (p. 15)
   a. The gathering and discussion of information do not define the scientific method; many scholars from nonscientific disciplines discuss the information that their studies yield.

c. Although theories are important for the success of scientific research, they do not suffice. For research to follow the scientific method, data must be collected in a measurable way that can be replicated.

d. There is no guarantee that research conducted in the laboratory is scientific. If the researcher fails to objectively measure behavior in a way that can be replicated by others, the laboratory research is not scientific.

7. *a. Ultimately researchers hope to determine what variables cause the occurrence of other variables. (p. 16)

b. Identifying whether there is any relationship between two variables is an important step in research, but ultimately a researcher will want to know if there is a cause-and-effect relationship between two related variables.

c. Although scientists need to publish their findings in scientific journals so that other scientists know of their work, it is not the ultimate goal of scientific research.

d. Providing an accurate description of the variable under study is essential for good science, but it is not the ultimate goal of scientific research.

8. *c. If a measure is made repeatedly and each time the same result is obtained, then the measure is said to have reliability. (p. 16)

a. Validity refers to the degree to which a measure actually measures what the researcher intended it to measure.

b. Inter-rater reliability refers to the degree to which two or more observers agree in their observations.

d. Although consistency sounds like a correct choice, this is not the standard term used in psychology.

9. *c. Because the experimenter does not manipulate variables during naturalistic observations, causal relationships between variables cannot be determined. (p. 17)

a. In the naturalistic observation approach to collecting data, children are not approached with questions; researchers simply observe and record data from a real-world setting.

b. As long as the researcher is inconspicuous while making his or her observations, there is no reason to believe that a child will not act normally when in his usual surroundings.

d. In fact, the opposite is true. Naturalistic observations are especially useful when a topic has not been extensively researched.

10. *a. Unlike the structured interview, which sticks to a rigid protocol of predetermined questions, the clinical method allows the investigator to modify questions in reaction to the child's response. Piaget was well known for using this method. (p. 21)

b. All interview methods gain information about what a child knows by asking the child directly rather than by simply observing her.

c. Because the interview method involves talking with individual subjects, the interview cannot be administered to a group of children simultaneously. The questionnaire can be administered to a large number of children at the same time.

d. The question of why children know what they know is a cause-and-effect question. Although the interview method could provide some possible reasons why children have a certain piece of knowledge, the interview cannot determine the actual cause of the knowledge.

11. *d. Meta-analysis is conducted on a body of previously published research on a specific topic. The studies that are analyzed usually concern a controversial topic. (p. 22)
a. The experimental method must be used to determine cause-and-effect relationships between variables.
b. Reliability refers to the degree to which a measure will yield the same result if it is administered repeatedly. Meta-analysis is not used to test for reliability.
c. Validity refers to the degree to which empirical data that were collected are actually a measure of what the experimenter intended to measure. Meta-analysis is not performed on data that were actually collected by an investigator.

12. *a. In correlational studies the relationship between two variables is examined; the variables are not manipulated by the experimenter in this type of research design. (p. 24)
b. In the experimental design, cause-and-effect relationships are investigated by manipulating one or more independent variables.
c. In order to systematically look for relationships between two or more variables, many subjects must be examined. The single-subject design examines a single subject or just a few subjects.
d. The longitudinal study is a strategy for assessing developmental change that occurs over time, not a research design for examining relationships between variables.

13. *c. A correlation coefficient of 0 indicates that there is no relationship between the two variables. (p. 24)
a. A positive correlation indicates that as one variable changes, the other variable changes in the same direction. It does not indicate the strength of the relationship.
b. A negative correlation indicates that as one variable changes, the other variable changes in the opposite direction. It does not indicate the strength of the relationship.
d. A correlation coefficient of 1.0 indicates a perfect correlation. It is not possible to get a correlation greater than +1.0 or smaller than −1.0.

14. *b. The experimental design examines causal relationships among variables by manipulating the independent variables, which are the suspected causes of behavior. (p. 25)
a. The correlational design is utilized to examine systematic relationships between two variables.
c. The dependent variable is the behavior being measured, which is assumed to be affected by the independent variable. Dependent variables are not manipulated by the investigator.

    d. Although a subject can be tested many times in an experimental design if necessary, repeated testing is not a required feature of the design.

15. *c. As a result of random assignment in experimental designs, a distinct advantage is that cause-and-effect relationships among variables can be identified. (p. 25)
    a. One of the criteria for scientific experimental research is that all data must be collected objectively and in an unbiased manner.
    b. Although a major advantage of experimental research is that it can provide cause-and-effect relationships between variables, results obtained from a scientific study are not always easily interpreted.
    d. One of the criticisms of experimental research designs is that they do not capture the complexities of the changes that occur during development.

16. *c. The mother's facial expression was the independent variable because it was assumed to influence the infant's emotional response. (pp. 25–26)
    a. Establishing a base line of behavior is important for single-subject designs, but *base-line variable* is not a term used in an experimental design.
    b. There is no term called *experimental variable* in an experimental design.
    d. The infant's emotional response was the dependent variable because it was assumed to be affected by the mother's facial expression.

17. *a. In the field experiment the experimental manipulations of a variable are made in a natural setting, such as a child's home or school. (p. 27)
    b. Field experiments are conducted when there is some concern that a child may not act normally in a strange situation like an unfamiliar laboratory.
    c. Although the field experiment is conducted in a natural setting, variables are still manipulated by the experimenter.
    d. The field experiment investigates causal relationships rather than just correlations, since one or more variables are manipulated by the experimenter.

18. *c. In longitudinal studies the same subjects are tested several times as they age. (p. 30)
    a. The cross-sectional study measures different subjects at different ages.
    b. Longitudinal studies are used for studying changes in behavior that occur with changes in age. A longitudinal study, therefore, would not test children of only one age.
    d. Longitudinal studies are used to determine how behaviors and abilities change with age. A longitudinal study, therefore, would not change the behavior being measured with age.

19. *b. The cross-sectional study tests many children of varying ages at the same point in time; therefore, it takes less time than the longitudinal study. (p. 32)
    a. The longitudinal study requires time, usually years, to complete; therefore, it would not provide a rapid assessment of behavior.
    c. The sequential study combines features of the longitudinal study and the cross-sectional study. So it would take an intermediate amount of time to

complete—more time than the cross-sectional study and less time than the longitudinal study.

    d. If a single-subject design is used to assess changes in an individual's behavior with increasing age, then it would obviously take a considerable amount of time to complete the study.

20. *d. The institutional review board evaluates both potential risks to the subjects of experiments and the researchers' compliance with ethical practices. (p. 37)

    a. Although the experimenter is required to obtain informed consent, the consent does not ensure that the experimenter is following ethical guidelines.

    b. Although the experimenter is required to debrief subjects when they were misled about the purpose of the experiment, the debriefing does not ensure that the experimenter is following ethical guidelines.

    c. Although some research designs permit all subjects to get both treatment and control conditions, in most designs subjects can receive only one of the two conditions.

Answers to Application Questions

1. *c. It was Locke who espoused empiricism and described the child as a *tabula rasa*. (p. 7)

    a. Griffith's view reflects the philosophy of empiricism. Darwin introduced the world to the theory of evolution, which emphasizes the importance of genetics in behavior.

    b. Rousseau believed that instincts present at birth had a strong influence on a child's development.

    d. Hall was not an empiricist but a strong believer in evolutionary theory. He suggested that early development was primarily governed by biology.

2. *b. A high inter-rater reliability would indicate that the students were reliably measuring the same behavior. (p. 17)

    a. A low inter-rater reliability would indicate that the two students had very different results.

    c. Validity refers to the extent to which a measure actually assesses a condition under consideration. Validity cannot be assessed by comparing two raters' scores.

    d. Validity refers to the extent to which a measure actually assesses a measure under consideration. Validity cannot be assessed by comparing two raters' scores.

3. *a. In the structured interview each child is given the same sequence of questions; thus, it is ideal for Miguel's research. (p. 20)

    b. Although it is useful, open-ended question of the clinical method makes it difficult to compare responses between children.

    c. The experimental method is not appropriate, since Miguel does not need to manipulate any variables and is not considering causal factors.

    d.   Naturalistic observation is unlikely to yield much information concerning children's attitudes toward death and dying. It would be better to ask the children questions directly.

4. *c. A meta-analysis of all of the previously published research can be very useful in determining if moderate alcohol consumption has an important effect on infant behavioral development. (p. 22)
    a.   Harlene should not abandon this area of research since there are still many unanswered questions that need to be addressed. The business of science is to provide answers to questions of interest.
    b.   Given the topic, the studies that Harlene reviewed were probably mostly correlational. Another correlational study is unlikely to resolve the issue.
    d.   Observing mothers in their normal environment is unlikely to provide any useful information concerning the effects of alcohol on infant development.

5. *b. As age increases, imaginary play changes in the opposite direction (it decreases). This relationship describes a negative correlation. (p. 24)
    a.   A positive correlation would suggest that as age increases, imaginary play also increases.
    c.   A zero correlation would suggest that there is no relationship between the two variables, but there clearly is a negative relationship.
    d.   There is no such term as *causal correlation*; causality cannot be determined from correlations.

6. *c. Tonya needs to manipulate exposure to video games (the independent variable) and measure problem-solving ability (the dependent variable) in order to determine if there is a causal relationship between the two variables. (p. 25)
    a.   A correlational study would indicate if video game playing is related to better problem-solving abilities, but it would not be able to indicate if there was a causal relationship between the two variables.
    b.   To test her hypothesis Tonya needs to manipulate the children's exposure to video games. A naturalistic observation study does not permit manipulation of variables.
    d.   Simply interviewing children who play video games is unlikely to provide support for her hypothesis. Tonya needs to manipulate children's exposure to video games and measure problem-solving ability in order to determine if there is a causal relationship between the two variables

7. *b. The type of film viewed (the independent variable) is suspected of influencing toddlers' successful use of the toilet (the dependent variable). (p. 25)
    a.   The number of children who are toilet trained by the end of the study is the dependent variable.
    c.   Random assignment of subjects to groups is an important method of control, but it is not the independent variable.
    d.   The number of toddlers per group is not a variable in an experiment.

8. *c. Since Ardella is working with infants in their homes, she is conducting a field experiment. (p. 27)
   a. A correlational study examines the systematic relationships between two variables. Only one variable is being measured in this study—the kicking behavior.
   b. A cross-sectional study tests children of different ages at the same point in time. The study described does not indicate that age is a variable of interest.
   d. Ardella is not conducting a naturalistic observation, since teaching a child to kick (a manipulation) involves more than just observing a naturally occurring behavior.

9. *b. Longitudinal studies are conducted to examine the same subjects repeatedly over a period of time, usually years, in order to determine the stability of human characteristics. (p. 30)
   a. Cross-sectional studies are studies in which subjects of different ages are examined at the same point in time.
   c. A quasi-experiment is a study in which the assignment of subjects to experimental groups is determined by their natural experience. No information is given about the nature of group assignment in this example.
   d. A cohort effect is the result of characteristics shared by individuals growing up in a given sociohistorical context that influences their developmental outcomes.

10. *b. A subject (or the subject's parent) must sign an informed consent form before participating in a study. (p. 37)
   a. The debriefings occur at the completion of a study, not at the beginning.
   c. Although this may sound like a good idea, the informed consent form must be signed before participating in an experiment.
   d. Some researchers do provide subjects with a small sum of money to cover travel expenses after participating in the study, but that is unlikely to be the first order of business when they arrive at the laboratory.

CHAPTER 2

THEMES AND THEORIES

LEARNING OBJECTIVES

1. Discuss what theories are designed to do and why they are vital to science. (pp. 41–42)

2. List and describe six key themes in development. (pp. 42–48)

3. Describe the learning theory approach to development. (pp. 48–49)

4. Discuss the principles of classical and operant conditioning. (pp. 49–50)

5. Compare and contrast social learning theory's process of observational learning with traditional learning theory. (pp. 50–53)

6. Define and discuss the key concepts in Piaget's cognitive-developmental theory, including schemes, assimilation, accommodation, and equilibration. (pp. 53–57)

7. Compare the neo-Piagetian theories of Fischer and Case with Piaget's theory. (pp. 57–59)

8. Describe the information-processing approach to development. (pp. 59–62)

9. Describe Freud's psychoanalytic theory of development. (pp. 62–63)

10. List and discuss Freud's three components of the personality. (pp. 63–65)

11. List and describe Freud's psychosexual stages of development and the resolution of conflict at each stage. (pp. 65–66)

12. Compare and contrast Erikson's psychosocial stages of development with Freud's psychosexual stages. (pp. 66–69)

13. Define and describe contextual approaches to development (pp. 69–70)

14. List and describe the levels of Bronfenbrenner's ecological systems theory. (pp. 70–72)

15. Describe and discuss Vygotsky's sociohistorical theory. (pp. 72–73)

16. Describe and discuss transactional theory. (pp. 73–74)

17. Define ethology and describe how ethological theories have contributed to our understanding of development. (pp. 74–75)

18. Discuss the implication of mother-infant bonding immediately after birth. (pp. 76–77)

CHAPTER OUTLINE

I. **SIX MAJOR THEMES IN DEVELOPMENTAL PSYCHOLOGY** (pp. 42–48)
Theories serve to organize facts about a particular subject of study, and they guide further research, but most importantly theories serve to explain research findings in an orderly and predictable fashion. Specific theories that have been developed to study child psychology typically center around several basic themes in development. The chapter presents six such themes and describes how each theory addresses them.

A. **What Roles Do Nature and Nurture Play in Development?** (p. 43)
The *nature-nurture debate* is concerned with whether behavior is the result of innate, genetic influences (nature) or the history of environmental stimulation to which each individual is exposed (nurture). The importance of the debate is in its implications for developmental outcomes. If behavior is inherited, then no amount of environmental influence or learning will change its course. If, on the other hand, behavior is largely influenced by experience, it becomes critical that all children get exposure to those experiences that will maximize their chances for positive developmental outcomes.

B. **How Does the Sociocultural Context Influence Development?** (pp. 43–44)
Human development occurs within a larger social group. The influences of the values and resources of that social group on development are wide and varied. Each theory of development has a separate view on how integral a part the sociocultural context plays in an individual's development.

C. **How Does the Child Play an Active Role in Development?** (pp. 44–45)
The question of whether the child is a passive receiver of incoming information or takes an active role in acquiring his behaviors is a controversial one in modern psychology. Today, most psychologists adopt the position that the child is an active participant in his own growth and development. Characteristics of the child appear to dictate which aspects of the world he chooses to be engaged in, and consequently, the reactions each receives from others.

D. **Is Development Continuous or Stagelike?** (pp. 45–46)
Children change dramatically as they grow and develop. A debate revolves around how to explain the dramatic changes that are observed. Do children go through a series of *stages*, sudden changes in unique developmental qualities? Or is the process of change a more gradual, continuous one? The stage view suggests that at different periods of development children exhibit qualitative differences in how they perceive, think, feel, and behave. Alternatively, the continuous view sees development as consisting of small, gradual, quantitative advances in the way the child perceives, thinks, and feels about the world.

E. **Are There Sensitive Periods in Development?** (pp. 46–47)
The concept of *sensitive periods* in development refers to instances when a child is most responsive to, and influenced by, certain types of environmental events. These experiences can be either detrimental, as in the case of drugs during certain weeks of pregnancy, or necessary and even enhancing, as in the case of exposure to language during early childhood. Disagreement about the importance of sensitive periods stems from the evidence that many children appear to be resilient regarding the effects of environmental influences on their development. Most psychologists continue to adopt the position that there are sensitive periods for certain kinds of experiences. The challenge they face is identifying which experiences and at what times children are vulnerable to these events.

F. **How Do the Various Domains of Development Interact?** (pp. 47–48)
Although the different domains of development are often discussed separately, psychologists recognize that they do not operate in isolation. Advances in physical development, for example, can lead to changes in social and cognitive development. To date, theories of development have not devoted much time to questions regarding the interactions between domains of development. The authors point out, however, that in order to understand and explain the behavior of the whole child, theories of development will have to explain how each domain contributes to the other during the developmental process.

II. **LEARNING THEORY APPROACHES** (pp. 48–53)
Learning is the relatively permanent change in behavior as a result of experience. Extreme learning theory, such as that proposed by John B. Watson, holds that all behavior can be explained by the experiences that a person has encountered.

A. **Behavior Analysis** (pp. 49–50)
Behavior analysis is a theoretical concept that relies on the principles of *classical* and *operant conditioning* to explain behavioral development. Ivan Pavlov was the first to observe the classical conditioning of a salivation response in dogs. He found that a neutral stimulus (such as a tone) repeatedly paired with a stimulus that elicits a reflexive response (such as food eliciting salivation) could then elicit the reflexlike response by itself. Operant conditioning, or instrumental conditioning, is a learning process through which behaviors increase if they are followed by rewarding outcomes. Behavior modification, sometimes referred to as applied behavior analysis, is concerned with how the principles of conditioning can be applied to bring about desired changes in behavior. Even though classical and operant conditioning are believed to play a large role in development, critics suggest that behavior cannot be completely understood without accounting for the presence of internal, psychological structures, such as emotions and motivations.

B. **Social Learning Theory** (pp. 50–51)
Social learning theory stresses the importance of learning others' behavior in the absence of reinforcement. Many psychologists have documented that humans learn via *observational learning*, the acquisition of behaviors from watching and listening to others. Albert Bandura, a primary proponent of social learning theory, emphasizes that complex language, social and moral customs, and other achievements cannot be learned solely by conditioning. Observing and imitating a model allows for new skills to be acquired quickly and efficiently in a social context. Bandura's theory, expanded to include cognitive processes, is known as social cognitive theory.

C. **Learning Theory and Themes in Development** (pp. 51–53)
Although both are learning theory approaches, behavior analysis and social learning theory emphasize different aspects of the six themes in development outlined in this chapter. Behavior analysis emphasizes the role of the external environment in rewarding or punishing behavior. The social learning theories rely more heavily on the roles of biology and other internal factors that interact with experience to affect development. Behaviorists theorize that the principles of learning are universal and, therefore, less subject to sociocultural differences. Social learning theory, on the other hand, recognizes the importance of learning in a social context and, consequently, places great emphasis on cultural differences for learning. According to behaviorists such as B. F. Skinner, the person is a passive receiver of environmental consequences to behavior. Social learning theory, however, incorporates mental and motivational constructs in learning, which presumes an active role on the part of the child, who adjusts and reacts to the environment. Behaviorists and social learning theorists both agree that development is a continuous process in which changes in behavior are gradual and can be measured quantitatively. Neither position theorizes sensitive periods because all experiences are important throughout the development of the individual. Lastly, behaviorists do not consider interactions among domains of development; the principles of conditioning are presumed to apply across all domains. Social learning theory stresses the reciprocal interactions among domains, recognizing that what is observed and imitated is a consequence of the physical, cognitive, and social status of the child.

III. **COGNITIVE-DEVELOPMENTAL APPROACHES** (pp. 53–59)

The *cognitive-developmental* theories stress the emergence of psychological structures, which are organized ways of thinking that affect the way the child interprets experience. An important aspect of cognitive-developmental theories is that all normal children show similar mental, social, and emotional capacities at roughly the same ages regardless of their varying experiences. Jean Piaget is the most well-known cognitive-developmental theorist. His view emphasizes that development is action oriented and that mental structures change with qualitative reorganization at different stages.

A. **Piaget's Theory** (pp. 53–55)

Piaget's theory of how children acquire knowledge about the world focuses on two basic processes, *adaptation*, the tendency to adjust to the conditions of the environment, and *organization*, the tendency for knowledge structures to become more systematic and coherent. The basic mental structure for Piaget is the *scheme*. Schemes are coordinated and systematic ways of acting on and reasoning about the world. Schemes are applied and exercised at all stages of development, and they become increasingly complex and sophisticated with development. The processes that permit the changes in schemes with development are called *assimilation* and *accommodation*. Assimilation refers to the process of acting on, or understanding, new information through existing schemes. Accommodation occurs when new information does not fit into an existing scheme and therefore the scheme must change to accommodate the new information. For Piaget, assimilation and accommodation are the complementary processes that maintain mental equilibrium. As new experiences are encountered, the individual's understanding of the world is thrown out of balance. Balance is restored either by assimilating the new experience into an existing scheme or by accommodating the new experience by construction of a new, modified scheme. This process, called *equilibration*, brings about more organized and powerful schemes for thinking over the course of development. When schemes undergo substantial reorganization, a qualitatively distinct stage of development, a new level of knowledge, has been reached. Piaget proposed four major stages of intellectual development: sensorimotor, preoperational, concrete, and formal.

B. **Piaget's Theory and Themes in Development** (pp. 56–57)

Piaget was largely influenced by biological theories. He emphasized the process of *maturation*, the gradual unfolding over time of genetic programs for development. The inherent roles of action and equilibration also point to Piaget's slant toward the nature side of the nature-nurture debate. However, Piaget stressed that these biological factors must interact with experience for knowledge development to proceed. Piaget minimized the influence of sociocultural differences in the development of knowledge. He believed that sociocultural dissimilarities might affect the speed and ultimate level of development in some instances, but for the most part all children progress through the stages at roughly similar ages. According to Piaget, the child is very much an active participant in her own cognitive development. Knowledge is constructed, created by the continuous revision and reorganization of mental structures. Although he recognized that development was an ongoing process, Piaget stressed that children proceed through a series of qualitatively distinct stages of development that represent major reorganizations in the way they think about the world. Piaget did not discuss sensitive periods in his theory, but he did suggest that different levels of thinking would permit a certain "readiness" for various kinds of experiences. Piaget's theory was primarily one of cognitive development; consequently, he did not discuss physical or social development. Others since Piaget have adopted his theory to explain developmental changes in many domains including social cognition, the child's understanding of thoughts, feelings, and interactions with others.

C. **Neo-Piagetian Views** (pp. 57–59)
Piaget's theory has had great influence in developmental psychology and education. His views have been extended by others to encompass social and moral development. However, Piaget's theory has also been criticized, particularly his concept of stagelike transformations in thinking. Several theorists have modified and expanded Piaget's theory to handle these criticisms. Kurt Fischer suggests that transitions in thinking occur in specific domains or skills, not across the board simultaneously. Robbie Case also created a theory based on Piagetian ideas. Case's theory also has four stages of development, but it differs in the explanation of transitions from one stage to the next. According to Case, developmental change occurs through maturation and organization of efficient and automatic actions, not equilibration.

IV. **INFORMATION-PROCESSING APPROACHES** (pp. 59–62)
There are numerous developmental theories that stem from an *information-processing* approach. The central focus of most information-processing models is on how the mind processes incoming information and how information moves from one place in the system to the next. A primary assumption is that the human mind, like the computer, has a limited capacity for processing information. With development, changes in capacities, skills, and strategies help the child process information more effectively. The human mind is theorized to possess cognitive structures, such as a sensory store, short- and long-term memory, executive systems, and response systems. Moreover, the mind uses strategies and rules to guide information processing and responding. Developmental improvements in memory, concept formation, language, and problem solving are the result of changes in the rules and strategies used to process the information entering the system.

A. **Information-Processing Approaches and Themes in Development** (pp. 61–62)
Information-processing theories have not specifically addressed the nature-nurture debate. A few basic capacities are presumed to be present at birth, but these interact with experience to produce changes in strategies, rules, etc. The sociocultural context has been ignored, because the models assume that all cognitive systems, regardless of specific cultural differences, operate according to the same principles. Information-processing approaches accept that the child is an active processor of information and therefore selects the information to which he attends and processes. These approaches also typically depict development as continuous and quantitative in the way changes are characterized. Little emphasis has been placed on sensitive periods for information processing. The interaction among domains had also been largely ignored until recently,

when new theories have added social cognition and information-processing perspectives to peer relationships, language, and personality development.

V. PSYCHOANALYTIC APPROACHES (pp. 62–69)

Psychoanalytic models of development are concerned with emotional and personality development. Their emphasis is on unconscious motivations that contribute to behavior. Sigmund Freud was the founding father of psychoanalytic theory, but others, such as Erik Erikson, have modified and expanded psychoanalytic theory, and it continues to influence our understanding of development today.

A. Freud's Psychosexual Theory (pp. 63–66)

As a clinical neurologist, Freud pioneered the use of free association as a way of relieving the symptoms of certain mental disorder by letting a patient report whatever came into his or her mind. From his observations of clinical patients, Freud developed his *psychosexual theory of development*, which suggests that personality development originates from conflicts in early childhood. The energy of psychological behavior comes from the libido. Tension builds and must be released, or conflict and anxiety arise. The pleasure principle guides the desire to reduce the built-up libidinal energy quickly through immediate gratification, whether the action is socially acceptable or not. With development, the individual acquires means of reducing tension in rational, socially appropriate ways, and thus the personality begins to operate according to the reality principle. Freud theorized three main structures of the personality that develop and operate to reduce the build-up of libidinal energy.

At birth, and for much of infancy, the baby's personality is dominated by the *id*—the innate, primitive, unconscious part of the mind ruled by the pleasure principle. The *ego* gains control of the personality in early childhood. The ego is the rational, conscious part of the mind, and it operates according to the reality principle. The *superego*, which monitors both the id and ego, is the final structure of the personality to develop. The superego searches for ways to reduce anxiety through socially acceptable means. It develops following the resolution of the Oedipal complex in boys and the Electra complex in girls.

According to Freud, children between three and six years of age develop sexual fantasies about the parent of the opposite sex. The desire to have an intimate relationship with the mother for boys, or with the father for girls, leads to great anxiety and fear of punishment from the rival parent. The child reduces the anxiety by adopting the characteristics of the parent of the same sex, a process Freud called identification. In this way, identification leads to gender identity and internalization of the moral values of the parents. The superego, made up of the *conscience* and the *ego ideal*, comprise the child's ideas about wrong or punishable behavior, and positive, rewarded behavior.

Freud stressed that the structures of the personality develop through a series of five stages. Libidinal energy becomes focused on specific areas of the body during each successive stage of development. The stages are the *oral stage*, the *anal stage*, the *phallic stage*, a period of *latency*, and the *genital stage*. Tension at each stage is reduced by activities focused on the area of the body that requires gratification. Tension reduction at each stage leads to resolution of that stage and movement to the next stage. However, lack of gratification at any stage could lead an individual to become fixated at that stage for the rest of her life.

Freud's theory has been criticized by many other psychological theorists. Many have been particularly critical of his failure to recognize sociocultural influences on development and his emphasis on innate, biological drives. Erik Erikson developed a psychoanalytic theory of personality development that accounts for the influence of social factors on the individual.

B. **Erikson's Psychosocial Theory** (pp. 66–68)
Erikson modified Freud's psychoanalytic theory to emphasize the importance of society in shaping reality for the child. His eight-stage theory stresses the role of the ego in resolving conflicts at each stage within the demands of the society in which a person lives. Thus, for Erikson, development is *psychosocial*. The individual has the opportunity to resolve the crisis at the time it arises or later in life. A common theme in Erikson's theory is the individual's search for *identity*, the acceptance of one's self and society.

C. **Psychoanalytic Theories and Themes in Development** (pp. 68–69)
Both Freud and Erikson stress the biological component of the development of behavior, yet both also recognize the importance of specific experiences for resolution of conflicts and crises throughout development. They differ in their views of the sociocultural influences on development. Freud's theory is restricted to the child's immediate, familial environment, whereas Erikson speaks more about the broader sociocultural demands on the child. For Freud, the child is more the passive receiver of biological urges, or, at most, someone who reacts to conflict and tension. For Erikson, the child is more active in seeking his identity within the society. Freud and Erikson view development as a series of stages, with behavior at one stage laying the foundation for behavior at the next stage. Freud, however, viewed the passage from one stage to another as critically dependent on key experiences and therefore placed greater emphasis on sensitive periods in development than Erikson. As far as the interaction among domains of development, both Freud and Erikson saw the intricate relationship among thought, emotions, and social interactions as necessary and important for normal development.

VI. **CONTEXTUAL APPROACHES** (pp. 69–78)
Children develop within a complex set of overlapping environments—the family, the community, the political system, and the culture. *Contextual models* of development address the broad range of biological, physical, and sociocultural settings that influence development.

A. **Ecological Systems Theory** (pp. 70–72)
Urie Bronfenbrenner's *ecological systems theory* focuses on the broad range of situations that children encounter and are influenced by during their development. The *microsystem*

includes the immediate environment that impacts on the child—family, school, friends, and neighborhood. The *mesosystem* encompasses interactions among various contexts within the microsystem. The *exosystem* includes the larger contexts of social, economic, political, and religious settings. The broadest context is the *macrosystem*, which comprises societal and cultural values and practices that ultimately impact on the individual.

B. **Vygotsky's Sociohistorical Theory** (pp. 72–73)
Culture refers to the historical, human-generated aspect of the environment, which has great influence on the experiences the child receives. Lev Vygotsky's *sociohistorical theory* emphasizes the unique cultural and social contexts within which every child develops. As children grow and participate in their own culture, they acquire the language, practices, and ways of thinking specific to that culture. According to Vygotsky, language is a particularly important tool because it can influence the child's thinking and problem-solving abilities.

C. **Transactional Theory** (pp. 73–74)
Transactional theory views development as a dynamic, continual process that involves reciprocal exchange. The child is transformed by the surrounding people and environment, and in turn affects changes in the people and environment surrounding her, which in turn produces changes in the child. Transactional theory attributes much of a child's development to the active role that the child plays in creating the environment within which she develops. The importance of transactional theory becomes evident when attempting to apply theories to interventions that might affect the course of development. Interventions will necessarily involve both the child and people and contexts surrounding her.

D. **Ethological Theory** (pp. 74–75)
Ethology is the discipline concerned with how adaptive behaviors have evolved and how they function to help a species survive. Konrad Lorenz and Niko Tinbergen were zoologists who first studied the contributions of the inherited, biological bases of behavior and how those behaviors interact with particular environments. Behaviors such as aggression, courtship, and competition have been studied by ethologists. Ethological theory proposes that there are certain species-specific behaviors common to all members of a species. In humans these are reflexes, babbling, smiling, and orientation to interesting events. Ethologists also posit that certain kinds of learning may occur only during sensitive periods in development. *Imprinting*, for example, is the behavior of newly born birds and some other animals to follow and remain near a particular stimulus, usually the mother. The particular stimulus must make certain movements or sounds within a short time after the young are born or imprinting will not occur. Although human infants do not become imprinted to their mothers, John Bowlby and others have suggested that the species-specific behaviors of newborns, such as crying and smiling, form the basis for attachment, the mutual system of physical, social, and emotional support between caregiver and infant.

Controversy: How Important Is Bonding? (pp. 76–77)

Marshall Klaus and John Kennell reported that the events occurring within the first few hours following birth are extremely important for the development of a positive relationship between a mother and her infant. This position had serious implications for hospital practices throughout the United States, leading doctors and nurses to encourage early and frequent contact between mothers, as well as fathers, and their newborns. Klaus and Kennell's research, however, has been challenged by other researchers, who have argued that early bonding is not necessary for the establishment of positive infant-caregiver relationships, although the opportunity for early bonding may encourage a parent's participation in caregiving and provides parents with an immediate involvement with their infants.

E. **Contextual Approaches and Themes in Development** (pp. 77–78)

With the exception of ethological theories that stress biological contributions, contextual theories emphasize nurture in the developmental process. Most contextual theories are concerned with sociocultural influences on development; ethological theories, however, are assumed to be applicable in all cultures. Contextual models view the child as an active participant in the environment; at times the relationship between the two is assumed to be bidirectional, each influencing the other. Contextual models view development as a gradual and continuous process without reference to any major qualitative changes that occur with age. Ethological theories place great emphasis on sensitive periods; however, other contextual models do not include sensitive periods in their approach. Contextual models, including ethological approaches, are concerned with the interactions among all domains of development.

Key Terms Review

1. In Piagetian theory, _____ is the inborn tendency to adjust to the environment.

2. A form of learning that occurs during a sensitive period in development in which an organism tends to remain close to a particular stimulus is called _____ .

3. Incorporating evolutionary theory into an understanding of the origins of behavior, _____ is the discipline concerned with the survival value of certain behaviors.

4. _____ is the gradual unfolding over time of genetic programs for development that are not affected by experience.

5. _____ explains the development of behavior by the principles of classical and operant conditioning.

6. _____ is a relatively permanent change in behavior that results from exploration, observation, practice, and other forms of experience.

7. In Piagetian theory, the process of interpreting an experience in terms of current ways of understanding is called _____ , whereas the process of modifying current ways of understanding when they no longer fit is called _____ .

8. _____ is a type of learning in which the frequency of a behavior increases as a result of rewarding or desired outcomes that the behavior produces.

9. In Bronfenbrenner's ecological system theory, _____ describes the environmental settings that indirectly affect the child by influencing his or her immediate environment.

10. In Piagetian theory, the mental structure underlying a coordinated and systematic pattern of thinking applied across similar objects or situations is called a(n) _____ .

11. In Freudian theory, the _____ operates according to the pleasure principle and the _____ operates on the reality principle.

12. The _____ is the ongoing theoretical controversy over whether development is the result of the child's genetic endowment or experiences.

13. In Bronfenbrenner's ecological systems theory, the _____ describes the major historical events and the broad values, practices, and customs promoted by a culture.

14. The _____ approach views the human, much like a computer, as having a limited ability to process information.

15. Piaget used the term _____ to describe the inborn tendency for structures and processes to become more systematic and coherent.

16. In the _____ stage of development, libidinal energy is focused on the mouth, whereas in the _____ stage, libidinal energy is focused on control of defecation.

17. In Freudian theory, the _____ is the part of the superego that defines unacceptable behaviors and actions.

18. _____ are a set of theories that emphasize the importance of unconscious motivations in determining personality development and behavior.

19. A(n) _____ is a developmental period during which the organization of thought and behavior is qualitatively different from an earlier or later period.

20. In Piagetian theory, _____ is an innate self-regulatory process that begins with the discovery of a discrepancy between a child's schemes and results in more organized and powerful schemes for thinking about and adapting to the environment.

21. _____ is a type of learning in which a neutral stimulus repeatedly paired with another stimulus that elicits a reflexive response eventually begins to elicit the response by itself.

22. The _____ , in Freudian theory, is part of the superego that describes the positive standards for which an individual strives.

23. The _____ is a theoretical orientation that recognizes an individual's environment as consisting of a wide range of biological, physical, and sociocultural settings.

24. The _____ in Freudian theory is the final stage, in which sexual energy is directed to peers of the opposite sex.

25. _____ emphasizes the importance of learning through observation and imitation of behaviors modeled by others.

26. According to Freud's _____ , many aspects of an individual's personality originate in an early and broad form of childhood sexuality, while according to Erikson's _____ , personality development proceeds through eight stages.

27. In Freudian theory, the _____ is a mental structure that monitors socially acceptable and unacceptable behavior.

28. In Bronfenbrenner's ecological system theory, the immediate environment provided in such settings as the home, school, workplace, and neighborhood is called the _____ ; the interrelationships among these various settings is the _____ .

29. In Eriksonian psychosocial theory, _____ is the acceptance of both self and society that must be achieved at every stage of development.

30. _____ , which was formulated by Vygotsky, emphasizes the historical (cultural) and social processes that are part of the context of development for every child.

31. During the _____ stage in Freud's psychosexual theory, libidinal energy is suppressed and energy is focused on intellectual, athletic, and social achievements.

32. The _____ is a brief period during which specific kinds of experiences have significant positive or negative consequences for development and behavior.

33. _____ is a theoretical orientation that explains development in terms of the active construction of psychological structures concerned with the interpretation of experience.

34. _____ is Bronfenbrenner's theory that development is the joint outcome of individual and experiential events.

35. According to Freudian theory, it is during the _____ that the superego is established as a result of the resolution of unconscious conflict with the parent of the same sex.

36. _____ is a form of learning that takes place by simply observing another person's behavior.

37. _____ is a theoretical perspective that highlights the reciprocal relationship between child and environment.

Answers to Key Terms Review

1. adaptation
2. imprinting
3. ethology
4. Maturation
5. Behavior analysis
6. Learning
7. assimilation, accommodation
8. Operant conditioning
9. exosystem
10. scheme
11. id, ego
12. nature-nurture debate
13. macrosystem
14. information-processing
15. organization
16. oral, anal
17. conscience
18. Psychoanalytic models
19. stage
20. equilibration
21. Classical conditioning
22. ego ideal
23. contextual model
24. genital stage
25. Social learning theory
26. psychosexual, psychosocial
27. Superego
28. microsystem, mesosystem
29. identity
30. Sociohistorical theory
31. latency
32. sensitive period
33. Cognitive-developmental theory
34. Ecological systems theory

35. phallic stage
36. Observational learning
37. Transactional theory

Multiple-Choice Questions

Fact and Concept Questions

1. Most psychologists would agree that
   a. nature is all important for development.
   b. nurture is all important for development.
   c. the nature-nurture debate is no longer an important theme in development.
   d. both nature and nurture contribute to a certain degree to different aspects of development.

2. Some theories of development propose that behavior changes during development occur in rapid, sudden transitions with major reorganization of underlying mechanisms. This describes the concept of
   a. continuity in development.
   b. stages in development.
   c. equilibration in development.
   d. sensitive periods in development.

3. The existence of sensitive periods in development suggests that
   a. children are more sensitive when they are younger.
   b. there are qualitative changes in the way children think about the world.
   c. exposure to or lack of certain environmental events affects development more at certain times than at others.
   d. development is gradual and continuous.

4. The learning process that predicts that behaviors that are followed by rewarding or desired outcomes will increase in frequency is
   a. classical conditioning.
   b. applied conditioning.
   c. operant conditioning.
   d. punishment.

5. The theoretical approach to development that emphasizes the importance of learning through observation and imitation of others is called
   a. learning theory.
   b. social learning theory.
   c. ecological systems theory.
   d. ethological theory.

6. According to B. F. Skinner, children
   a. can only learn information commensurate with their cognitive level.
   b. are unaffected by conditioning.
   c. have an active role creating their own experiences.
   d. are passive receivers of reinforcers and punishers that control behavior.

7. _____ theories support the notion that children acquire knowledge through the emergence of organized patterns of thinking that change at comparable ages.
   a. Learning
   b. Psychoanalytic
   c. Cognitive-developmental
   d. Sociohistorical

8. The most comprehensive and well-known cognitive-developmental theory was formulated by
   a. Konrad Lorenz.
   b. Jean Piaget.
   c. Lev Vygotsky.
   d. Sigmund Freud.

9. The basic mental structure in Piaget's theory of cognitive development is a(n)
   a. cognition.
   b. stage.
   c. action.
   d. scheme.

10. According to Piaget, changes in thinking over development are _____ and represent _____ differences in knowledge.
    a. stagelike, quantitative
    b. stagelike, qualitative
    c. gradual, quantitative
    d. gradual, qualitative

11. The _____ approach describes thinking as the flow of information from one mental structure to the next.
    a. cognitive-developmental
    b. cognitive-information
    c. information-processing
    d. transactional-processing

12. The founder of the psychoanalytic school of thought was
    a. Erik Erikson.
    b. Konrad Lorenz.
    c. Jean Piaget.
    d. Sigmund Freud.

13. According to Freud, the set of biological instincts that powers human behavior by producing psychological tension is called
    a. ego.
    b. unconscious.
    c. libido.
    d. superego.

14. According to psychoanalytic theory, the personality is made up of
    a. the id, ego, and superego.
    b. the oral, anal, and phallic psychosexual stages of development.
    c. pleasure and reality.
    d. assimilation and accommodation.

15. In his psychoanalytic theory, Erikson stressed the importance of _____ for the development of the individual's personality.
    a. libidinal energy
    b. societal influences
    c. innate behavior patterns
    d. sensitive periods

16. _____ believed that development must be studied not only in the home but also in the schools, neighborhoods, and communities.
    a. Erik Erikson
    b. Urie Bronfenbrenner
    c. Lev Vygotsky
    d. Konrad Lorenz

17. Which of the following theorists emphasized the historical and social processes that are part of the context of development for every child?
    a. Urie Bronfenbrenner
    b. Lev Vygotsky
    c. Konrad Lorenz
    d. Robert Hinde

18. Traits that improve the survival of a species are more likely to be found in succeeding generations. This is the premise behind which theory?
    a. Psychoanalysis
    b. Learning theory
    c. Evolution
    d. Ecological systems theory

19. According to ethologists, species-specific behaviors are
    a. learned.
    b. innate.
    c. culturally specific.
    d. dependent on experience.

20. A form of learning that occurs during a sensitive period in development in which an organism stays close to a particular stimulus, such as its mother, is called
    a. conditioning.
    b. attachment.
    c. imprinting.
    d. accommodation.

Application Questions

1. Dr. Jefferson has written a book for parents entitled *How to Toilet Train Your Child Quickly and Easily*. In the book she instructs parents to give the child a small gift each time he or she uses the toilet successfully. Dr. Jefferson's technique for toilet training is most obviously influenced by a(n) _____ approach to development.
    a. cognitive-developmental
    b. learning theory
    c. psychoanalytic
    d. ethological

2. Each time Tommy hits his baby sister, his mother punishes him with a spanking. According to social learning theory, Tommy's punishment is likely to
    a. result in an increase in Tommy hitting his sister.
    b. result in Tommy no longer hitting his sister.
    c. have no effect on Tommy's behavior.
    d. result in an advancement to the next stage of cognitive development.

3. Duane went to see a karate movie. Now he moves around his house attempting to kick his siblings. Duane's behavior is easily explained by the process of
    a. libido.
    b. classical conditioning.
    c. imprinting.
    d. observational learning.

4. When Marissa's infant gets an object in her hand, she puts it in her mouth and tries to suck it. Marissa's infant is _____ new objects according to her sucking scheme.
    a. adapting
    b. organizing
    c. assimilating
    d. accommodating

5. In an effort to uncover the source of his anxiety, Hugo's psychologist had him report whatever thoughts or ideas came into his mind. The psychologist's method is called
    a. equilibration.
    b. reminiscence.
    c. free association.
    d. hypnosis.

6. When Neal was five he became extremely attached to his mother and didn't want his father around for any reason. According to Freud, Neal was in the midst of a(n)
   a. identity crisis.
   b. Oedipal complex.
   c. Electra complex.
   d. fixation anxiety.

7. Lucia has an overeating problem. A psychoanalytic interpretation of her behavioral problem would suggest that Lucia
   a. is fixated at the oral stage of development.
   b. is suffering from an Oedipal complex.
   c. finds food reinforcing.
   d. has a genetic disorder.

8. Ludmila had difficulty learning to read when she began formal schooling. This was most probably because she did not have access to any books and was never read to by her parents. Contextual models of development would suggest that problems within the _____ were responsible for her reading difficulties.
   a. microsystem.
   b. mesosystem.
   c. exosystem.
   d. macrosystem.

9. Brigitte, the youngest of three children, is allowed many more freedoms than her older siblings had been given at the same age. This is most likely the case because as their children grew, Brigitte's parents also changed their style of parenting. Which theoretical approach best explains the mutual effects parents and children have on each others' development?
   a. Learning theory
   b. Psychoanalytic theory
   c. Ethological theory
   d. Transactional theory

10. Ricky lives on a farm and frequently feeds the ducks that live in a pond near the house. Recently, he found duck eggs that had been abandoned by the mother duck and brought them home to hatch. He kept them warm and, when they hatched, Ricky was the first thing that the ducks saw. Since then, the ducks follow Ricky everywhere around the farm. The ducks follow Ricky because
    a. they have become imprinted to him.
    b. they are reinforced for following the person who feeds them.
    c. they are searching for their mother.
    d. they are learning to fly.

Answers to Multiple-Choice Questions

The correct answer appears first and is preceded by an asterisk.

Answers to Fact and Concept Questions

1. *d. Most psychologists agree that both biology and experience interact and influence the development of the individual. (p. 43)
   a. Although there may be biological constraints on development, experience is also important for development.
   b. Although experience contributes to development, biology has been shown to place constraints on development.
   c. The nature-nurture debate continues to be an important theme for the study of development.

2. *b. The concept of stages in development implies that there are periods when there are sudden transitions with major reorganizations in the underlying capacities of the child. (p. 45)
   a. The concept of continuity in development implies that changes in the child's behavior are the result of small, gradual advances rather than major reorganization of underlying abilities.
   c. Equilibration is the process of maintaining a balance between new information and existing schemes through the processes of assimilation and accommodation.
   d. A sensitive period in development is a period of time when specific experiences can have dramatic positive or negative consequences for development.

3. *c. Experiences that occur during a sensitive period of development have significant positive or negative consequences for development and behavior. (p. 47)
   a. Although sensitive periods do occur more frequently in younger organisms, there is no stipulation that they occur only in younger as opposed to older individuals.
   b. According to some theories of development, there are qualitative changes in the way children think, but this does not describe the concept of sensitive periods.
   d. According to some theories of development, it is a gradual and continuous process, but this does not describe the concept of sensitive periods.

4. *c. Operant conditioning describes the learning process that predicts that behaviors followed by rewarding outcomes will increase in frequency. (p. 49)
   a. Classical conditioning occurs when a previously neutral stimulus becomes associated with a stimulus that elicits a reflexive response and eventually can elicit the reflexlike response by itself.
   b. The term *applied conditioning* does not exist; applied behavior analysis is the therapeutic means of changing behavior through the use of conditioning procedures.
   d. Punishment predicts that behaviors followed by negative or aversive consequences will decrease in frequency.

5. *b. Social learning theory emphasizes the importance of observational learning and imitation of the behaviors of models for the acquisition of and changes in behavior that occur with development. (p. 50)
   a. Learning theory, in its extreme, stresses the importance of conditioning for the acquisition of and changes in behavior that occur with development.
   c. Ecological systems theory emphasizes that development is the joint outcome of experiences that occur within the context of the child's immediate surroundings and the larger social and cultural environment.
   d. Ethological theory stresses the importance of the evolutionary origins of behaviors and their adaptive value for the survival of the species.

6. *d. B. F. Skinner, a learning theorist, claimed that the individual plays a passive role in development, responding to the environment according to the reinforcers and punishers that control behavior. (p. 52)
   a. Piaget's theory, not Skinner's, is concerned with the cognitive level of the child.
   b. B. F. Skinner, a learning theorist, held the view that the child is very much affected by the principles of conditioning.
   c. B. F. Skinner, a learning theorist, held the view that the child is a passive recipient of environmental experiences.

7. *c. Cognitive-developmental theories explain development as the emergence in children of organized patterns of thinking that change in predictable ways during their development. (p. 53)
   a. Learning theories explain development as the acquisition of behavior through the processes of conditioning.
   b. Psychoanalytic theories explain development as the resolution, or lack thereof, of conflicts that arise from unconscious motivations during development.
   d. Sociohistorical theories explain development as the result of cultural and social processes that impact on the child during development.

8. *b. Jean Piaget was the psychologist who developed the most well-known and comprehensive theory of cognitive development; his theory continues to influence psychology today. (p. 53)
   a. Konrad Lorenz, a zoologist, was influential in developing ethological theories of development.
   c. Lev Vygotsky developed the sociohistorical theory of child development.
   d. Sigmund Freud is best known for his psychoanalytic theory of personality development.

9. *d. A scheme is the basic mental structure in Piaget's theory; it underlies a coordinated and systematic pattern of behaviors and is applied across similar objects or situations. (p. 54)
   a. Although Piaget was concerned with the development of cognition, this is not the basic mental structure in his theory.
   b. Stages are important in Piaget's theory, but they are not the basic mental structure that guides thinking.

    c. Actions are important for the development of knowledge according to Piaget, but this is not the term used to describe the basic mental structures.

10. *b. Piaget believed that development is stagelike and that thinking is qualitatively different at each stage. (p. 55)
    a. Piaget did believe that development is stagelike, but according to his theory, thinking is qualitatively different at each stage.
    c. Piaget did not believe that developmental changes in thinking are gradual and quantitative; according to his theory, changes in thinking occur in stages with qualitative differences observed at each stage.
    d. Piaget did not believe that developmental changes in thinking are gradual, although he did consider them to be qualitatively different at various stages of development.

11. *c. The information-processing approach explains thinking as the flow of information from one mental structure to the next within a system. (p. 59)
    a. The cognitive-developmental approach explains thinking as the active construction of psychological structures that are established at comparable ages by all children.
    b. There is no theoretical approach called the cognitive-information approach. The correct term is *information-processing approach*.
    d. There is no theoretical approach called the transaction-processing approach. Transactional theories stress the dynamic interaction between the child and the environment during development.

12. *d. Sigmund Freud is considered the founder of the psychoanalytic school of thought in psychology. (p. 62)
    a. Erik Erikson was a member of the psychoanalytic school, but he was not its founder. He stressed the psychosocial influences on development.
    b. Konrad Lorenz was a zoologist who greatly influenced the field of ethology.
    c. Jean Piaget propounded cognitive-developmental theories of knowledge development.

13. *c. The libido is the set of biological instincts that make demands on the mind by initiating a form of tension. (p. 63)
    a. In Freud's theory, the ego is the component of the personality that is rational and operates according to the reality principle.
    b. The unconscious is that portion of the mind of which we are not aware or do not have access to.
    d. The superego is the component of the personality that monitors acceptable and unacceptable behavior.

14. *a. The id, ego, and superego make up the structures of the personality, which, according to Freud, influence how libidinal energy is expressed. (p. 63)
    b. The oral, anal, and phallic stages are the first three stages of Freud's psychosexual stages of development.

c. The pleasure and the reality principles are the irrational and rational ways, respectively, that libidinal urges are satisfied, according to Freudian theory.

d. Assimilation and accommodation are the two processes that help maintain a mental equilibrium between new information and existing schemes in Piaget's cognitive-developmental theory.

15. *b. Erikson stressed the importance of society in shaping and forming reality for the child. (p. 66)

a. Freud stressed the importance of libidinal energy in the behavior of the individual.

c. Ethological theories stress the importance of innate patterns of behavior for development.

d. Erikson did not stress sensitive periods as essential for the advancement of the child from one stage to the next. Conflicts not resolved early in life could be resolved later on, according to Erikson.

16. *b. Bronfenbrenner believed that development must be studied by examining the many levels of the sociocultural context within which the child exists. (p. 70)

a. Erikson did acknowledge the importance of society in the development of the child, but his theory focuses on the individual's resolution of conflicts at various stages of development.

c. Vygotsky emphasized the historical context of the child for development.

d. Lorenz was interested in studying the inherited behavior patterns that contribute to development of the individual.

17. *b. Vygotsky emphasized the historical and social context of the child, which dictates the views and skills necessary for him or her to acquire. (p. 72)

a. Bronfenbrenner stressed the importance of many levels of the contextual environment of the child for development, such as the family, schools, neighborhood, religion, and government.

c. Lorenz stressed the importance of innate biological behavior patterns that are passed to the individual as a result of their survival value.

d. Hinde is a well-known ethologist who has studied the mutual interchange between inherited behaviors and the environment in which the behavior is exhibited.

18. *c. Evolution is the theory, proposed by Darwin, that states that traits which improve the survival of offspring are more likely to be found in succeeding generations. (p. 74)

a. Psychoanalysis is the therapeutic approach to uncovering the unconscious sources of anxiety.

b. Learning theory posits that behaviors are determined solely by the environmental experiences of the individual and the history of rewards and punishments that he has experienced.

d. Ecological systems theory proposes that development must be studied within each level of the child's sociocultural context.

19. *b. Ethologists believe that there are species-specific behavior patterns that are the result of evolutionary processes and are inherited from previous, successful generations. (p. 75)
    a. Ethologists identify species-specific behavior as inherited behavior, not learned behavior.
    c. Ethologists would not agree that species-specific behaviors are influenced by cultural differences.
    d. Ethologists would not agree that species-specific behaviors are completely dependent on environmental experiences.

20. *c. Imprinting is a form of learning that takes place during a brief period early in life in which the offspring of some animals remain close to a moving stimulus, usually the mother. (p. 75)
    a. Conditioning is the learning process whereby associations are formed between environmental stimuli, responses to those stimuli, and the consequences of the responses.
    b. Attachment is the mutual system of physical, social, and emotional support between caregiver and offspring.
    d. In Piaget's cognitive-developmental theory, accommodation is the modification of an existing scheme in order to understand new information that cannot be understood using the old scheme.

Answers to Application Questions

1. *b. Learning theory would suggest that reinforcement of the desired behavior (in this case, the gift) will lead to an increase in the frequency of the behavior. (p. 49)
    a. A cognitive-developmental approach to toilet training would suggest that you must wait until the child has attained a certain stage of maturity in order for learning to occur.
    c. Psychoanalytic theory does not discuss the role of reinforcement.
    d. Ethological theory would suggest that innate, biological predispositions are responsible for behavior, and would not discuss the role of environmental reinforcement.

2. *a. Social learning theory would predict that children learn by observation and imitation; therefore, if Tommy's mother hits him, he is likely to learn that hitting is acceptable behavior and increase the frequency with which he hits his sister. (p. 50)
    b. Social learning theory would not predict that Tommy's hitting behavior will disappear; instead, he will imitate his mother's behavior.
    c. Social learning theory would predict that observed behavior of a model is likely to be imitated; thus, Tommy will be affected by his mother's behavior.
    d. Social learning theory does not incorporate a concept of stages.

3. *d. Observational learning is the social learning concept that describes how behaviors can be learned simply by watching a model perform them, which is typically what happens when children watch favorite characters on TV or in the movies. (p. 50)

a. Libido is the Freudian concept for the psychological energy of the personality.
b. Classical conditioning is the learning process whereby neutral stimuli that have been associated with reflex-eliciting stimuli come to elicit responses by themselves.
c. Imprinting is a form of learning that takes place during an early sensitive period in development, when some species of animals will follow the closest object that moves, usually the mother.

4. *c. Assimilation is the process of applying an existing scheme to new objects or situations, which is what Marissa is doing. (p. 54)
a. Adaptation is the Piagetian concept referring to the processes of assimilation and accommodation by which the individual adjusts to the environment.
b. Organization is the Piagetian concept referring to increased coherence in the knowledge structures.
d. Accommodation is the process of modifying schemes to adjust to new information. Marissa is not accommodating her sucking scheme to adjust to various objects.

5. *c. Free association is the Freudian therapeutic practice of letting the individual say whatever comes to mind in order to get at the source of his or her anxiety. (p. 63)
a. Equilibration is the Piagetian concept whereby mental balance is maintained through the processes of assimilation and accommodation.
b. Reminiscence is a process of recall, but it is not the procedure that Freud developed to reduce anxiety.
d. Freud did use hypnosis, but it requires that the person be placed in an altered state of consciousness; free association is possible only in an awake individual.

6. *b. Oedipal complex is the term used to describe the intimate relationship that three- to six-year-old boys want to establish with their mothers. (p. 64)
a. *Identity crisis* is the term Erikson used to explain the conflict of adolescence.
c. Electra complex is the term used to describe the desires that three- to six-year-old girls have for their fathers.
d. *Fixation* is the term Freud uses to describe an adult who is preoccupied with actions associated with an early stage of psychosexual development.

7. *a. A Freudian interpretation of overeating would be to say that the person is fixated at the oral stage of development and therefore continues to derive pleasure from actions associated with the mouth. (p. 65)
b. The Oedipal complex refers to boys who, during the phallic stage of development, develop an intense attraction to their mothers.
c. Lucia may very well find food reinforcing, but this would be a learning theory explanation of an overeating problem, not a psychoanalytic interpretation.
d. Lucia may have a genetic predisposition for being overweight, but this is not the explanation a psychoanalytic theorist would provide.

8. *b. The mesosystem refers to interactions between settings within the microsystem, such as experiences in the home and how they affect performance in school. (p. 70)

a. The microsystem refers to the immediate impact on the child by family and other people close to the child.

c. The exosystem makes up the wider context of social, economic, religious, and political settings that have indirect bearing upon the child.

d. The macrosystem is the broadest context; it includes all the major historical, political, and cultural practices of a society.

9. *d. Transactional approaches to development assert that change occurs in both the parent and the child; development is viewed as a dynamic, never-ending process involving a continual reciprocal exchange. (p. 73)

a. Learning theory posits that the child is controlled by the environment and not vice versa; there is no mutual interaction between parent and child.

b. Psychoanalytic theory suggests that the child must resolve conflicts arising from psychological tension. The theory does not discuss the mutual effect of parents and children upon each other.

c. Ethological theory is concerned with the innate behaviors that are displayed and modified as a result of interaction with the environment. The theory does not address the issue of mutual change in parent and child with development.

10. *a. Ethologists have observed that some species of animals learn during a sensitive period in early life to follow the first stimulus they encounter, a process called imprinting, which typically keeps them close to their mother. (p. 75)

b. There is no indication that Ricky was feeding the ducks. This is a classic example of imprinting, which does not require reinforcement.

c. There is no way to measure if the ducks know that their mother is missing.

d. There is no mention of the ducks flying.

CHAPTER 3

GENETICS AND HEREDITY

LEARNING OBJECTIVES

1. Distinguish between an individual's genotype and phenotype. (pp. 85–86)

2. Describe the basic structure and functions of the chromosomes, genes, and DNA. (pp. 86–89)

3. Describe the process of cell division and chromosome duplication in mitosis and meiosis. (pp. 89–91)

4. Describe how genetic information is expressed in the traits and behavior of individuals. (pp. 91–94)

5. Discuss the role of the genotype and environment in producing the phenotype, using PKU as an example. (pp. 94–97)

6. List, describe, and discuss some of the more common gene disorders, autosomal anomalies, and sex chromosome abnormalities. (pp. 97–109)

7. Describe the role of genetic counselors. (pp. 109–110)

8. Discuss the alternatives available to couples who risk having children with genetic defects and the legal, medical, and social controversy that these options have engendered. (pp. 110–111)

9. Describe and discuss how behavior geneticists investigate the hereditary and experiential basis of individual differences by examining resemblances among family members. (pp. 112–113)

10. Discuss how concordance rates and correlation coefficients are used to estimate the degree of resemblance among family members. (pp. 113–114)

11. Discuss how genotypic and environmental factors interact to influence phenotypic expression. Distinguish among the concepts of canalization, passive correlation, evocative correlation, and niche picking. (pp. 114–119)

12. Discuss the influence of nature and the environment on human traits such as intelligence, temperament, mental illness, and other behavioral characteristics. (pp. 119–126)

CHAPTER OUTLINE

I. **PRINCIPLES OF HEREDITARY TRANSMISSION** (pp. 85–97)
The genetic potential that a person inherits is called the *genotype*. A person's observable characteristics and behavior are called the *phenotype*. The phenotype is determined by a complex interaction of the genotype with environmental experiences. The genotype is formed when human reproductive cells called *gametes* (egg and sperm) combine during fertilization to provide the newly created offspring with basic units of heredity called *genes*. The genes code for the production of proteins and enzymes, which provide biochemical reactions critical for development and body functioning. The genes comprise segments of larger units called *chromosomes*. Research in the 1990s may result in a map of the entire *human genome*, the identification of the genes and complex molecules that make up the genetic information contained in all forty-six chromosomes.

A. **The Building Blocks of Heredity** (pp. 86–89)
Each chromosome is made up of a long, spiral, ladderlike staircase called *deoxyribonucleic acid*, or *DNA*. Each rung of the DNA ladder is constructed of pairs of *nucleotides*. Human beings have forty-six chromosomes organized into twenty-three homologous pairs. Twenty-two of the paired chromosomes are similar in males and females and are called *autosomes*. In the female the twenty-third pair consists of two X chromosomes. In the male the twenty-third pair consists of one X chromosome and one Y *chromosome*. A *karyotype* is a pictorial representation of an individual's chromosomes.

B. **Cell Division and Chromosome Duplication** (pp. 89–91)
The fertilized egg, or *zygote,* begins as one cell containing forty-six chromosomes and grows by *mitosis*, a process of cell division that produces new cells containing duplicates of all forty-six chromosomes. The gametes are formed by a process of cell division called *meiosis*. In meiosis one chromosome from each pair is randomly selected for each cell. The random segregation of the paired chromosomes and the phenomenon of *crossing over* in meiosis, as well as the joining of genes from an egg and sperm, ensure that each offspring (with the exception of identical twins) is genetically unique.

C. **Gene Expression** (pp. 91–94)

Each characteristic, or trait, is coded by at least one pair of genes on an autosome, one inherited from the mother and the other from the father. These alternate forms of a specific gene are called *alleles*. If two alleles of a gene are identical, the trait that they code for is said to be *homozygous*. If two alleles contain a different sequence of nucleotide pairs, the trait that they determine is said to be *heterozygous*. In heterozygous genotypes the phenotype is determined by the way the two allelic forms interact. When only one of the two alleles affects the phenotype, the allele whose characteristic is observed is called *dominant;* the weaker allele is called *recessive. Codominance* is the condition in which the phenotype reflects both alleles of a heterozygous genotype. Many traits are *polygenic,* determined by more than one gene.

D. **Gene Functioning and Regulation of Development** (pp. 94–97)

Genes are also classified in terms of their general function. *Structural genes* code for the production of enzymes and other proteins. *Regulator genes* control structural genes, turning them on or off when the appropriate environmental signals are present. Proteins are produced in the cytoplasm of a cell through a process initiated by RNA. Sometimes the nucleotide sequence of a gene is modified and an enzyme fails to be produced. This is what happens in *phenylketonuria*, or *PKU*, a condition in which the amino acid phenylalanine cannot be metabolized.

II. **GENE AND CHROMOSOMAL ABNORMALITIES** (pp. 97–109)

Mutations, or sudden changes in genetic material, occur often and provide genetic diversity between individuals. Mutations can occur in a single gene, in a large section of autosomal chromosomes, or in the sex chromosomes. Some mutations have little or no impact; others can lead to severe disruption in physical and behavioral development.

A. **Gene Disorders** (pp. 97–103)

There are many known gene disorders. Some are caused by the inheritance of a dominant gene, such as *Huntington's disease,* while others are caused by the inheritance of recessive alleles, as in *sickle cell anemia* and PKU. Many disorders are *sex-linked* because they are associated with genes on the twenty-third pair of chromosomes. Sex-linked disorders such as hemophilia, red-green color blindness, and Duchenne muscular dystrophy are associated with alleles on the X chromosomes that often have a dominant-recessive relationship.

B. **Autosomal Anomalies** (pp. 103–106)

Occasionally, an extra autosomal chromosome is inherited. This condition is called *trisomy. Down syndrome*, or *trisomy 21*, is the most common genetic cause of mental retardation. Mutations also occur when large sections of chromosomes are deleted or duplicated. Such structural aberrations of autosomes often lead to mental retardation and severe physical deformities.

C. **Sex Chromosome Abnormalities** (pp. 106–109)
A varying number of sex chromosomes may be inherited, leading to anomalies displaying a wide variety of phenotypic expressions. Early studies suggested that the presence of an extra Y chromosome was linked to antisocial behaviors, since the XYY pattern was found in an unusually high number of prison inmates. The higher percentage of the XYY pattern among inmates, however, is probably related to lowered intelligence and increased physical stature rather than to increased aggression. Studies also suggest that children with sex chromosome abnormalities may be more vulnerable to environmental stressors than children with the normal number of sex chromosomes. Structural defects in sex chromosomes, such as in *fragile X syndrome*, can also result in physical and behavioral disorders.

III. **GENETIC COUNSELING** (pp. 109–110)
Prospective parents at risk for children with a genetic disease because of a family history of disorders or because of other factors can receive *genetic counseling. Genetic screening* can indicate if couples planning to conceive a child are heterozygous or homozygous for a genetic disorder.

A. **Prenatal Screening** (p. 110)
Amniocentesis and chorionic villus sampling are two of the many prenatal tests available to determine if a fetus has a known genetic disorder.

Controversy: When is a Mother a Mother and a Father a Father? (pp. 110–111)
Couples who are at risk for children with a genetic disease or who are unable to conceive have many options in addition to adoption. When the male is at risk the couple may elect artificial insemination by donor. When the female is at risk or unable to conceive, options include surrogate motherhood and in vitro fertilization. Advances in the field of genetic engineering should provide additional options in the future. Although these methods offer hope for couples at risk or couples unable to conceive, the legal, medical, and social implications have shrouded these procedures in a storm of controversy.

IV. **BEHAVIORAL AND DEVELOPMENTAL GENETICS** (pp. 112–125)

A. **The Methods of Behavioral Geneticists** (pp. 112–114)
Behavior geneticists often conduct selective breeding experiments in animals to learn more about the influence of genetics and the environment on behavior. The study of twins provides a means of determining the role of nature and nurture in humans. When *monozygotic (identical) twins* are observed to be more similar in a trait than *dizygotic (fraternal) twins*, one possible interpretation is that the trait is determined by the common genotype. Because most twins also share common environments, researchers study the similarities between twins who have been adopted or otherwise raised in different environments. The degree of resemblance among monozygotic and dizygotic twins, siblings, and adopted children is estimated using *concordance rates* and correlation coefficients.

B. **Conceptualizing the Interaction Between Genotype and Environment** (pp. 114–119)
The nature of the contributions made by the genotype and the environment is complex because they often interact. An interaction occurs when the influence of one variable on development is affected by, or depends on, the value of the second variable. The nature of interactions is exemplified by the concept of a *range* (or *norm*) *of reaction*. For example, the effects that different environments have on intellectual development depends on the genotype. Similarly, the influence of the genotype on intellectual capacity depends on whether the environment is stimulating or unstimulating. With some attributes a *canalization* process ensures that the genotypic influence on the phenotype dominates, and only extreme variations in the environment can alter the phenotypic expression.

The interactions that occur between genotype and environment make it difficult to estimate to what degree each variable contributes to development. Accurate estimates of their contributions are also complicated by passive, reactive (or evocative), and active (or *niche-picking*) correlations that exist between the genotype and the environment.

C. **Hereditary and Environmental Influences on Behavior** (pp. 119–125)
Studies of family resemblances demonstrate that both the genotype and the environment impact on many aspects of human behavior. Indications that heredity contributes to intelligence come from studies showing that correlations in performance on intelligence tests increase as genetic relationships increase. Similar correlations are seen between genetic relationships and personality characteristics, *temperament*, abnormal behavior, and other characteristics. That the environment also contributes to human behavior is revealed by research showing greater similarities among identical twins reared together (who share genotype and environment) than among identical twins reared apart (who share genotype only). The child's active role in the environment may also contribute to how the environment influences development. For example, passive correlations between the genotype and the environment may have greater impact on intelligence in infancy, but niche picking may have greater impact later in development. Moreover, environmental factors within families may promote differences among individual children.

Much has been learned about how the genotype and environment influence each other, but assessing the *heritability* for intelligence and other traits may not be possible because of the complex nature of genotype-environment interactions.

V. **THEMES IN DEVELOPMENT: GENETICS AND HEREDITY** (p. 126)
What roles do nature and nurture play in development? The genome that an individual inherits from his or her parents plays a major role in determining the way in which the human body and behavioral traits develop. However, the phenotype that is expressed is a product of a complex interaction between genotype and environment.

How does the child play an active role in the effects of heredity on development? The traits and behaviors displayed by children is in part a result of social, cultural, and other environmental influences. The child, however, also plays an active role by selecting environments that are compatible with her genotype.

Key Terms Review

1. The threadlike structures of DNA that form a collection of genes are called _____ .

2. The division process for most cells, which results in a full complement of chromosomes, is called _____ . The sex cells, or _____ , divide by the process of _____ , which results in twenty-three chromosomes in each human egg and sperm cell.

3. The twenty-two different pairs of homologous chromosomes are called the _____ .

4. Genetic variability is ensured partly by the phenomenon of _____ , a process during the first stage of meiosis when genetic material is exchanged between autosomes.

5. The _____ is a product of the interaction between the genotype and the environment, resulting in an individual's observable and measurable characteristics.

6. A person who inherits two alleles of a gene that are identical is said to be _____ for that trait. A person who inherits two alleles that are different is said to be _____ for that trait.

7. The allele whose characteristics are observed in the phenotype is considered _____ ; the allele whose characteristic is not evident is considered _____ .

8. _____ is a genetic condition in which the amino acid phenylalanine is not metabolized. This condition can lead to mental retardation.

9. _____ is a dominant genetic disorder characterized by involuntary movements of the limbs, mental deterioration, and premature death.

10. _____ disorders are associated with genes carried on the X chromosome.

11. A disorder that is associated with a pinched or broken region of the X chromosome is _____ syndrome.

12. _____ provides prospective parents with estimates of the likelihood of having children with a genetic disorder.

13. The concept that development of certain attributes is governed primarily by the genotype is the principle of _____ .

14. _____ twins come from the same zygote, whereas _____ twins come from two separate fertilized eggs.

15. Unlike ethologists, _____ study the hereditary and experiential basis of individual differences.

16. The _____ and the _____ are two statistical measures used to estimate the degree of resemblance among family members.

17. The concept of a(n) _____ describes the scope of phenotypic differences that are possible as a result of the environment and the limits imposed by the genotype.

18. A child may play an active role in seeking out experiences compatible with his or her genotype. This tendency is called _____ .

19. _____ is the proportion of variability in the phenotype that can be accounted for by genetic influences.

20. A set of personality traits evident in infancy and early childhood and theorized to have some genetic basis is referred to as _____ .

21. A(n) _____ is a large segment of nucleotides within a chromosome that codes for the production of proteins and enzymes.

22. _____ is caused by an extra copy of chromosome 21 and is associated with a distinct set of physical features and mental retardation.

23. A sudden change in the molecular structure of a gene is a(n) _____ . It may occur spontaneously or be caused by an environmental event.

24. _____ are alternate forms of a specific gene that provide a genetic basis for individual differences.

25. A(n) _____ characteristic is influenced by two or more genes.

26. The condition in which individual, unblended characteristics of two alleles are reflected in the phenotype is called _____ .

27. The _____ is the entire inventory of nucleotide base pairs comprising the genes and chromosomes of humans.

28. The pictorial representation of an individual's chromosomes is called the _____ .

29. _____ is a long, spiral, staircase-like sequence of molecules created by the nucleotides.

30. _____ are repeating basic building blocks of DNA that consist of nitrogen-based molecules of adenine, thymine, cytosine, and guanine.

31. The systematic search for certain genotypes using a variety of tests is called _____ . This procedure can detect individuals at risk for developing genetic abnormalities, bearing offspring with potential chromosome or gene defects, or having genetic susceptibility to environmental agents.

32. _____ genes switch other genes on and off.

33. The fertilized egg cell is called the _____ .

34. The _____ is shown by those possessing a heterozygous genotype for sickle cell anemia.

35. _____ genes are responsible for the production of enzymes and other protein molecules.

36. _____ is a condition in which an extra chromosome is present in an individual.

37. The total genetic endowment inherited by an individual is called his _____ .

38. The _____ chromosome is the larger of the two sex chromosomes; females generally have two, and males have only one. The _____ chromosome is smaller; males normally have one, and females have none.

39. In regions of the world where malaria is found, and among descendants of these regions, a genetic blood disorder called _____ is common.

Answers to Key Terms Review

1. chromosomes
2. mitosis, gametes, meiosis
3. autosomes
4. crossing over
5. phenotype
6. homozygous, heterozygous
7. dominant, recessive
8. Phenylketonuria (PKU)
9. Huntington's disease
10. Sex linked
11. fragile X
12. Genetic counseling

13. canalization
14. Monozygotic (identical), dizygotic (fraternal)
15. behavior geneticists
16. concordance rate, correlation coefficient
17. range of reaction
18. niche picking
19. Heritability
20. temperament
21. gene
22. Trisomy 21 (*or* Down syndrome)
23. mutation
24. Alleles
25. polygenic
26. codominance
27. human genome
28. karyotype
29. Deoxyribonucleic acid (DNA)
30. Nucleotides
31. genetic screening
32. Regulator
33. zygote
34. sickle cell trait
35. Structural
36. Trisomy
37. genotype
38. X, Y
39. sickle cell anemia

Multiple-Choice Questions

Fact and Concept Questions

1. The contribution of nature to the individual is evident in
   a. eye color.
   b. height.
   c. gender.
   d. all of the above.

2. Biologists believe that genetic diversity is important for
   a. mutations.
   b. eye color.
   c. survival of the species.
   d. behavior.

3. The observable characteristics and behavior of a person are referred to as the
   a. phenotype.
   b. human genome.
   c. genotype.
   d. alleles.

4. Chromosomes are made up of regions called _____ , which are composed of _____ .
   a. nucleotides, genes
   b. DNA, genes
   c. genes, DNA
   d. genes, RNA

5. Each gamete has _____ chromosomes.
   a. 46
   b. 23
   c. 96
   d. an unknown number of

6. The process by which most cells divide is called
   a. crossing over.
   b. mitosis.
   c. meiosis.
   d. mutation.

7. It has been estimated that structural genes account for about _____ of the human genome.
   a. 100 percent
   b. 90 percent
   c. 33 percent
   d. 3 percent

8. Which of the following disorders is caused by a single gene on an autosome?
   a. Duchenne muscular dystrophy
   b. Trisomy 21
   c. Huntington's disease
   d. Fragile X syndrome

9. Sex-linked disorders are found
   a. more frequently in males than in females.
   b. more frequently in females than in males.
   c. equally often in females and males.
   d. only in animals.

10. Which of the following statements concerning Down syndrome is *incorrect?*
    a. Down syndrome is the most common cause of mental retardation.
    b. Down syndrome is caused by the inheritance of an extra twenty-first chromosome.
    c. The probability of a mother giving birth to a Down syndrome baby increases with age.
    d. Most children born with Down syndrome do not live beyond thirty years.

11. If the male member of a couple carries a genetic disorder or is infertile, the couple may elect
    a. surrogate motherhood.
    b. artificial insemination by donor.
    c. in vitro fertilization.
    d. genetic screening.

12. The Baby M case poignantly illustrates that
    a. current advances in reproductive technology are unreliable.
    b. genetic screening procedures represent an invasion of privacy.
    c. selective breeding studies are unethical.
    d. advances in reproductive technology are making it difficult to define motherhood legally.

13. The degree of resemblance among family members is estimated with the statistical measure(s)
    a. concordance rate.
    b. correlation coefficient.
    c. interaction.
    d. both a and b.

14. A behavior geneticist studying monozygotic twins who are being raised in different surroundings is probably trying to evaluate
    a. the effects of the genotype on behavior.
    b. the effects of the environment on behavior.
    c. the effects of the phenotype on behavior.
    d. all of the above.

15. How different environments affect a child's intellectual development depends on the child's genotype. This relationship between the genotype and phenotype is an example of
    a. an interaction.
    b. a correlation.
    c. canalization.
    d. heritability.

16. People bearing the genotype that causes PKU can minimize the repercussions of the disorder by
    a. maintaining a diet high in phenylalanine.
    b. maintaining a diet low in phenylalanine.
    c. maintaining a diet high in ketones.
    d. undergoing genetic screening.

17. A highly canalized attribute
    a. is easily influenced by the environment.
    b. is minimally influenced by the genotype.
    c. strongly resists environmental influences.
    d. is a result of a rare mutation.

18. According to Scarr and McCartney, as a young child grows older and gains greater independence, the correlation between the genotype and environment is likely to
    a. change from active to passive.
    b. remain passive.
    c. remain active.
    d. change from passive to active.

19. According to the text, the combined findings of 111 studies investigating the influence of the genotype and the environment on intellectual development indicate that
    a. environmental factors make the primary contribution to intelligence.
    b. genetic factors make the primary contribution to intelligence.
    c. both environmental and genetic factors make contributions to intelligence.
    d. it is not possible to determine whether environmental or genetic factors contribute to intelligence.

20. Current research on mental illness indicates that
    a. the concordance rate for manic depression is greater among identical twins than among fraternal twins.
    b. the likelihood of suffering manic depression is the same for adopted children whose biological parents have the disease and for children whose biological parents do not have the disease.
    c. schizophrenia is caused primarily by stressful environmental conditions.
    d. schizophrenia is 100 percent concordant in identical twins.

Application Questions

1. Joe's gender was determined at fertilization by his _____ sex chromosome.
   a. mother's
   b. father's
   c. grandfather's
   d. grandmother's

2. Maria has red hair; both of her parents have brown hair. The gene for red hair
   a. must be dominant.
   b. must be heterozygous.
   c. must be recessive.
   d. is not possible to know with the information given.

3. Maxine and Stephen's mother is a carrier of a sex-linked recessive disorder. Maxine and Stephen are twins. Which of the following statements is accurate?
   a. Maxine and Stephen are equally likely to have the disorder.
   b. Maxine is more likely to have the disorder.
   c. Stephen is more likely to have the disorder.
   d. Neither Maxine nor Stephen is likely to have the disorder.

4. Ellen has a family history of Huntington's disease. Before she decides to have children she may want to consult
   a. a psychologist.
   b. a doctor.
   c. a genetic counselor.
   d. her family members.

5. Karen and Carl gave birth to a child with a genetic disorder. He has a long, narrow face, large ears, large testes, and is likely to have attentional problems and be mentally retarded. The child probably has
   a. fragile X syndrome.
   b. Down syndrome.
   c. PKU.
   d. Huntington's disease.

6. Celeste is thirty-nine years old and is planning to have a fourth child. She is a good candidate for
   a. artificial insemination by donor.
   b. surrogate motherhood.
   c. in vitro fertilization.
   d. amniocentesis.

7. The Garcias have elected surrogate motherhood to have their first child. The most likely reason they were advised to undergo this procedure is that
   a. Mr. Garcia is at risk for having a child with a genetic disorder.
   b. Mrs. Garcia is at risk for having a child with a genetic disorder.
   c. Mr. Garcia is infertile.
   d. Mrs. Garcia is over thirty-five years of age.

8. Dr. Jackson, a behavior geneticist, is interested in determining if creativity is more similar among identical twins or among fraternal twins. Which statistical measure should Dr. Jackson use?
   a. Correlation coefficient
   b. Concordance rate
   c. Dominant-recessive analysis
   d. Interactional analysis

9. Clorinda, who is larger and stronger than most other girls her age, chose soccer as an after-school activity instead of arts and crafts. Her choice is consistent with the concept of
   a. niche picking.
   b. passive correlations.
   c. polygenic traits.
   d. homozygous traits.

10. Pauline, an experienced babysitter, has noticed that Chin, a Chinese infant, is easier to comfort than George and Diana, who are American infants. Such ethnic differences among infants have been attributed to
    a. environmental influences on personality development.
    b. genetic influences on temperament.
    c. sociocultural influences on infant behavior.
    d. none of the above.

Answers to Multiple-Choice Questions

The correct answer appears first and is preceded by an asterisk.

Answers to Fact and Concept Questions

1. *d. All three traits—eye color, height, and gender—are contributions of nature. (p. 83)
   a. Eye color is a contribution of nature, but this is only part of the answer.
   b. Height is a contribution of nature, but this is only part of the answer.
   c. Gender is a contribution of nature, but this is only part of the answer.

2. *c. Genetic diversity increases the chances that at least some members of a population will adapt to a sudden change in the environment. (p. 84)
   a. A mutation is a sudden change in the molecular structure of a gene caused spontaneously or by an environmental event. It contributes to genetic diversity, but it doesn't explain why genetic diversity is important.
   b. Eye color does vary in a population, but this variation doesn't explain why genetic diversity is important.
   d. Behavior does vary in a population, but this variation doesn't explain why genetic diversity is important.

3. *a. The phenotype refers to the characteristics and traits that a person actually displays. (p. 85)
   b. The human genome refers to the estimated 100 million nucleotide pairs that are possible in human DNA, a portion of which is inherited by an individual.
   c. The genotype is the total genetic potential inherited by an individual. Not all of the genetic information is translated directly into a particular trait.
   d. An allele is a distinctive form of a specific gene. How two alleles interact determines whether the trait they code for will be observable.

4. *c. Chromosomes are a collection of genes, which consist of DNA. (p. 86)
   a. Chromosomes are made up of nucleotides, but the nucleotides are not made up of genes.
   b. Chromosomes are made up of DNA, but the DNA is not made up of genes.
   d. Chromosomes are a collection of genes, but they do not consist of RNA. RNA is a molecule that conveys information from the DNA to the cytoplasm of a cell.

5. *b. The gametes, egg and sperm cells, have twenty-three chromosomes; when they combine during fertilization the zygote will have the normal forty-six. (p. 89)
   a. There are forty-six chromosomes in nearly all normal human body cells *except* the gametes.
   c. There are no body cells that have ninety-six chromosomes.
   d. We do know the number of chromosomes in each body cell.

6. *b. Mitosis occurs in most cells of the body and yields forty-six chromosomes in each cell. (p. 90)
   a. Crossing over is a process that occurs during the first stage of meiosis, which produces the gametes.
   c. Meiosis forms the gametes, which results in twenty-three chromosomes in each egg and sperm cell.
   d. A mutation is a sudden change in the molecular structure of a gene; it is not a process of cell division.

7. *d. The current estimate of the percentage of structural genes in the human genome is 3 percent (p. 96)
   a. The human genome contains at least two types of genes, structural and regulator genes; thus, structural genes cannot make up 100 percent of the genome.

b. Structural genes have been estimated to account for less than 90 percent of the human genome.

c. Structural genes have been estimated to account for less than 33 percent of the human genome.

8. *c. Huntington's disease is caused by the inheritance of one dominant autosomal gene. Its symptoms include personality changes, depression, and loss of motor control. (p. 97)

a. Duchenne muscular dystrophy is a sex-linked disorder caused by a gene usually found on the X chromosome.

b. Trisomy 21 is an autosomal anomaly resulting from the inheritance of an extra chromosome, which contains many genes, not just one.

d. Fragile X chromosome is a result of a structural defect in the X chromosome.

9. *a. Most sex-linked disorders are carried on the X chromosome. Because the male has only one X chromosome while the female has two, recessive alleles are more likely to be expressed in the male than in the female. (p. 102)

b. The second X chromosome in females can counter a recessive gene in the first chromosome, thus reducing the likelihood of the disorder being expressed. The lack of the second X chromosome in the male makes him more likely to get the disorder.

c. The lack of a second X chromosome in the male, which would be needed to dominate a recessive allele in the first chromosome, makes the chances of inheriting the disorder greater in males.

d. Sex-linked disorders are fairly common in humans.

10. *d. This statement is incorrect. Better medical and physical care has increased the life span of Down syndrome children; more than 50 percent live over thirty years. (p. 104)

a. This statement is correct. Down syndrome, or trisomy 21, is the most common cause of mental retardation in the United States and other countries.

b. This statement is correct. Down syndrome is an autosomal disorder; the majority of cases are caused by the presence of an extra twenty-first chromosome.

c. This statement is correct. Mothers over the age of thirty-five give birth to over half of the Down syndrome infants, suggesting that the chances of giving birth to a Down syndrome baby increase with age.

11. *b. When the male is unable to conceive or is a carrier of a genetic disease, the female can be artificially inseminated with sperm provided by a donor. (p. 110)

a. Surrogate motherhood is an option available to couples who wish to have a child but the female is unable to conceive or is a carrier of a genetic disease.

c. In vitro fertilization is an option available to couples who wish to have a child but the female is unable to conceive or is a carrier of a genetic disease.

d. Genetic screening can be used to identify people at risk for having children with potential gene or chromosome defects; it is not an option that will help couples to have a child.

12. *d. The courts were asked to rule whether Baby M's legal parent was the surrogate mother (who was impregnated by artificial insemination) or the genetic father (who provided the sperm). The courts ruled in favor of the father, but the court hearing was long and controversial. (p. 111)
    a. Current reproductive technology has been very effective in providing couples with several options to have children.
    b. There are concerns that genetic screening may invade people's privacy, but the Baby M case did not deal with this issue.
    c. Selective breeding studies are conducted with animals and are within current ethical guidelines. Nevertheless, the Baby M case did not deal with this issue.

13. *d. Both concordance rate and correlation coefficients are statistical measures used to determine the degree of resemblance among family members. (p. 113)
    a. Concordance rate is a statistical measure that determines the percentage of twins who have the same specific trait; it is used to estimate the degree of resemblance among family members. This choice is correct, but it's only part of the answer.
    b. A correlation coefficient is a statistical measure used to determine the relationship among individuals on traits or characteristics that vary on a continuous scale, such as intelligence or height. This choice is correct, but it's only part of the answer.
    c. An interaction is not a statistical test but a conditional relationship between two variables, such as genotype and environment.

14. *b. Since monozygotic twins have the same genotype, any observed differences would be attributed primarily to environmental factors. (p. 114)
    a. Monozygotic twins have the same genotype. A behavior geneticist interested in the effects of the genotype on behavior would more likely study individuals who did not share an identical genotype.
    c. The phenotype, which includes behavior, is a product of the genotype and environment; the phenotype cannot be a cause of behavior.
    d. Examining the effects of different environments on individuals sharing the same genotype (monozygotic twins) reveals the influence of the environment on human traits and characteristics, not the influence of the genotype or the phenotype.

15. *a. Whenever the effect of one variable on behavior depends on a second variable, an interaction between the two variables is said to have occurred. For example, because the effect of environment on intelligence depends on the child's genotype, the environment is said to interact with the genotype. (p. 115)
    b. A correlation describes the relationship between two variables, but, as always, correlation does not imply causation. The statement that the environment's influence depends on the genotype implies a causal relationship.
    c. Although canalization can be described as an interaction between the genotype and environment, the term identifies a specific principle whereby the genotype resists all but extreme environmental influences on the phenotype.
    d. Heritability is the estimated contribution that heredity or the genotype makes to the phenotype; environmental influences are excluded from this estimate.

16. *b. PKU can lead to severe mental retardation as a result of the buildup of phenylalanine. Because phenylalanine is a product of diet, consuming a diet low in phenylalanine greatly minimizes mental retardation. (p. 115)
    a. PKU is caused by the inability to metabolize the amino acid phenylalanine. Thus, a diet high in phenylalanine will most likely hasten the illness.
    c. PKU is a result of the inability to metabolize phenylalanine, not ketones. Adjusting the level of ketones in the diet is not a method of treatment for the disorder.
    d. Genetic screening can be utilized to identify individuals carrying the gene for PKU, but it cannot be used to reduce the effects of the disorder.

17. *c. An attribute that is influenced primarily by the genotype and strongly resists all but extreme environmental influences is said to be highly canalized. (p. 116)
    a. The environment modifies the genotype's influence on a highly canalized trait only under extreme conditions.
    b. A highly canalized trait is primarily under the influence of the genotype.
    d. Highly canalized traits are not rare mutations but common to all members of a species.

18. *d. Experiences in a young child's life are determined primarily by caregivers, and so the correlations between the genotype and environment are primarily passive. As the child gains more independent control of his environment, the correlations are more likely to be active. (p. 119)
    a. Initial correlations are likely to be passive rather than active since infants' experiences are determined by their caregivers. As a child grows older and gains greater control over the environment, the correlations are more likely to be active.
    b. Although the young child's initial experiences are primarily passive, they are unlikely to remain passive as the child becomes more independent and gains greater control over the environment.
    c. Active factors are likely to increase with age as the child becomes more independent and gains greater control over his environment; however, the young child is more likely to experience passive factors.

19. *c. Environmental and genetic factors interact to influence intellectual development. (p. 120)
    a. Although environmental factors make an important contribution to intelligence, so do genetic factors.
    b. Although genetic factors make an important contribution to intelligence, so do environmental factors.
    d. Although it may not be possible to identify to what degree genotype and environment contribute to intelligence, studies make it clear that both factors do contribute.

20. *a. The concordance rate for manic depression in identical twins is 70 percent; for fraternal twins the concordance rate is 15 percent. (p. 124)
    b. The frequency of manic depression is greater among children whose parents have the illness than among children whose parents do not have the illness.

c. Although it is likely that environmental factors contribute to schizophrenia, evidence is very strong that there is a genetic basis for schizophrenia.

d. No mental disorder has been found to be 100 percent concordant in identical twins, suggesting that environmental influences contribute to mental illness.

Answers to Application Questions

1. *b. Joe's father can contribute either an X or a Y chromosome; it is the Y chromosome that determines if the individual will develop as male. (p. 88)

   a. Joe's mother can contribute only an X chromosome to the zygote; this chromosome does not distinguish males from females.

   c. Although many traits may be passed along from Joe's grandfather, Joe's sex will be determined by his father's sex chromosomes.

   d. Although many traits may be passed along from Joe's grandmother, Joe's sex will be determined by his father's sex chromosomes.

2. *c. The gene must be recessive and can be expressed in the phenotype only if both genes (one from mother, one from father) contain the instructions for red hair. (p. 93)

   a. If the gene for red hair was dominant, at least one of Maria's parents would also have red hair, given that Maria inherited the gene for red hair from one of her parents.

   b. The term *heterozygous* refers to a genotype in which two alleles of a gene are different. A single gene cannot itself be heterozygous, but it can be part of a heterozygous genotype.

   d. With the information given it is possible to determine that both of Maria's parents must carry the recessive gene for red hair. Maria received both recessive genes and thus has red hair in her phenotype.

3. *c. Males are more likely to have a recessive disorder than females; therefore, Stephen is more likely to have the illness. (p. 103)

   a. If Maxine and Stephen were identical twins, then they would be equally likely to have the disorder; however, since they are of the opposite sex they must be fraternal twins. Males are more likely to have a recessive disorder than females.

   b. Males are more likely to have a recessive disorder than females; therefore, Maxine is less likely to have the illness.

   d. Because males have only one X chromosome, they are more likely to have a recessive disorder than females, who have a second allele to mask the recessive one. Therefore, Stephen, the male twin, is more likely to have the disorder.

4. *c. A genetic counselor can provide an analysis of the genotype of prospective parents and provide estimates of the likelihood of bearing a child with a genetic disorder. (p. 109)

   a. Although a psychologist may be helpful to Ellen if she wants to discuss her distress over her family history, a psychologist could not discover Ellen's genotype.

b. A general medical doctor would not be likely to do genetic screening.
d. Family members can be understanding and supportive, but they cannot provide Ellen with an accurate analysis of her genotype.

5. *a. Fragile X syndrome is the second most common cause of mental retardation. Males with this disorder commonly have long, narrow faces, large ears, and large testes. (p. 109)
   b. Down syndrome babies are characterized by an epicanthal fold of the eye, flattened facial features, short stature, and short, broad hands.
   c. PKU can lead to mental retardation if the child is not placed on a low-protein diet. Infants with PKU do not have any discernible physical features that would indicate the presence of the disorder.
   d. The symptoms of Huntington's disease usually have a late onset; children who have inherited genes for this disorder do not have any discernible features that would indicate its presence.

6. *d. Because Celeste is over thirty-five years of age, she is at risk for giving birth to a child with trisomy 21. To determine if the fetus she is carrying has trisomy 21 Celeste can undergo amniocentesis. (p. 110)
   a. Although Celeste is already a mother, she is above thirty-five years of age and therefore is at risk for giving birth to a child with trisomy 21. Artificial insemination by donor is not an option for women at risk for trisomy 21.
   b. Given that Celeste is above thirty-five years of age she is at risk for giving birth to a child with trisomy 21. However, surrogate motherhood is not an option for women at risk for trisomy 21.
   c. In vitro fertilization is not an option for women of Celeste's age who are at risk for trisomy 21.

7. *b. When the female is at risk for having children with a genetic disorder, the couple can elect surrogate motherhood to become parents. (p. 111)
   a. When the male is at risk for having children with a genetic disorder, the couple would be likely to elect artificial insemination by donor to become parents rather than surrogate motherhood.
   c. When the male is infertile, the couple would be likely to elect artificial insemination by donor to become parents rather than surrogate motherhood.
   d. When the female is above thirty-five years of age, she is at risk for giving birth to a child with trisomy 21 and is a good candidate for amniocentesis or chorionic villus sampling, not surrogate motherhood.

8. *b. Concordance rate is a statistical measure that determines the percentage of twins who share a similar trait. (p. 113)
   a. Although the correlation coefficient is a statistical measure for examining degree of similarity among individuals, it is more appropriate in cases where two variables that vary along a continuum are being examined.

c. Dominant-recessive relationships describe the complex ways in which alleles interact to determine the phenotype; analysis of these relationships is not a statistical procedure.

d. There is no statistical procedure called interactional analysis.

9. *a. Clorinda is larger and stronger than most girls her age and therefore is likely to be athletically inclined. Her choice of soccer as an after-school activity is consistent with her genotype and therefore is a good example of niche picking. (p. 118)

b. Passive factors are usually provided by caregivers and are not a result of the child's actions. Clorinda's role in choosing soccer is active, not passive.

c. Clorinda's large stature is most likely a result of polygenic influences; however, the term *polygenic* ("many genes") does not define the tendency to actively select an environment that is consistent with a genotype.

d. A person's genotype is said to be homozygous when both genes have the same allelic form. This would not have any direct effect on Clorinda's choice of soccer as an after-school activity.

10. *b. Studies on infants of different ethnic groups have implicated genetic differences in temperament. (p. 122)

a. Studies that have investigated differences in behavioral characteristics among infants of different cultures have attributed such differences to the genotype, not the environment.

c. Although sociocultural factors certainly influence behavioral development, studies examining behavioral differences among infants of various cultural groups have implicated genetic factors.

d. Studies on infants of different ethnic groups *have* implicated genetic differences in temperament.

CHAPTER 4

THE PRENATAL PERIOD AND BIRTH

LEARNING OBJECTIVES

1. Identify and describe the three stages of prenatal development. (p. 130)

2. Describe the process of fertilization and the formation, implantation, and differentiation of the blastocyst. (pp. 130–132)

3. Describe the development of the body organs and systems during the embryonic period and the principle of cephalocaudal development. (pp. 133–136)

4. Identify the characteristics of the transition from the embryonic period to the fetal period and describe development during the second and third trimesters of pregnancy. (pp. 136–138)

5. Identify and describe the various procedures that are available for the detection and diagnosis of genetic disorders. (pp. 138–139)

6. Identify and describe the structures present in the prenatal environment that maintain and support the developing embryo and fetus during pregnancy. (p. 140)

7. Identify the principles of teratology and describe how each contributes to our understanding of the environmental factors that affect development. (pp. 140–144)

8. List and describe drugs and diseases that are known teratogens and explain the effects of each on development. (pp. 144–154)

9. List and describe the environmental hazards that can be teratogenic and the effects they have on development. (pp. 154–156)

10. Describe the various maternal conditions that can have an effect on the developing individual. (pp. 156–160)

11. Describe the prepared childbirth techniques that are available and their influence on the perinatal environment. (pp. 160–164)

12. Describe the stages of labor and discuss the differences between a vaginal delivery and a caesarean birth. (pp. 164–165)

13. Describe and discuss the problems of low–birth weight infants and the interventions that may help them. (pp. 165–170)

14. Describe the newborn and discuss the available assessment techniques for determining his or her status at birth. (pp. 170–172)

15. List and describe the newborn's sleep and waking states. (pp. 172–174)

CHAPTER OUTLINE

I. **THE STAGES OF PRENATAL DEVELOPMENT** (pp. 130–139)
Prenatal development is the period of time from conception to birth when the developing individual undergoes a series of transformations from a single-celled *zygote*, to an *embryo*, and to a *fetus*. Prenatal development takes place in three stages: the *germinal period* (from fertilization to 10–14 days after conception), the *embryonic period* (about 2–8 weeks after conception), and the *fetal period* (about 8 weeks to birth). The prenatal period ends at birth. The events surrounding the beginning of birth and the setting into which the newborn enters is called the *perinatal environment*. *Postnatal development* begins once the baby is born.

A. **Fertilization** (pp. 130–131)
Fertilization can take place when a mature egg cell, or ovum, is released from the female's ovary into the Fallopian tube and male sperm cells are present. The sperm cells, which enter through the vagina and travel to the uterus and then into the Fallopian tubes, are attracted to the ovum. A successful sperm cell will penetrate the egg cell, and the chromosomes of the sperm and egg will combine to form a fertilized egg, called the zygote, which contains the full forty-six chromosomes necessary for further development. If no sperm cells are present in the Fallopian tube, then the mature ovum will traverse the Fallopian tube and exit the female's body through the uterus.

B. **The Germinal Period** (pp. 131–132)
Within a day of fertilization, the newly formed zygote begins a series of mitotic cell divisions called *cleavages* to form the *morula*, a solid sphere of sixteen cells. Each cell has

the identical ability to become a separate organism because at this early stage the cells are undifferentiated. The cells begin to differentiate when they segregate into an outer and an inner layer of cells collectively called the *blastocyst*. The blastocyst implants itself in the lining of the uterus ten days following conception.

C. **The Embryonic Period** (pp. 132–136)
Following implantation of the blastocyst a three-layered embryo is formed. The endoderm will become the lining of most inner organs, the mesoderm will become the skeletal, muscular, and cardiovascular systems. A group of cells from the ectoderm forms the *neural tube*, which will develop into the spinal cord, nerves, and the brain. During the fourth week after conception, the neural tube closes, first at the cephalo (head) end, forming the brain, and then, a few days later, at the caudal (tail) end, forming the spinal cord. This sequence conforms to the cephalocaudal principle of development: organ systems near the head develop more rapidly than those in the lower end of the body. Anencephaly and spina bifida are abnormal conditions in which the cephalic or the caudal region of the neural tube, respectively, fail to close, resulting in death or severe nervous system damage.

D. **The Fetal Period** (pp. 136–138)
The fetal period begins at eight weeks, when bone starts to form, and ends at birth. The fetus is recognizably human early in this stage, and most structures and organs have already formed. The second trimester, or second three months of the pregnancy, is characterized by such rapid growth in body size that the mother can now feel fetal movements, called quickenings. During the final three months of pregnancy, the third trimester, the brain continues to undergo considerable development. Sensory systems develop such that the fetus is now capable of smelling, tasting, hearing, seeing, and feeling. It is in the third trimester that the fetus attains *viability*, the ability to survive outside of the womb. *Gestational age* is counted from the first day of the mother's last menstrual period. Most babies are born between 269 and 274 days gestational age.

E. **Prenatal Diagnosis** (pp. 138–139)
There are several prenatal screening procedures available that can detect over two hundred defects in the developing embryo and fetus. In *amniocentesis*, which can be performed between sixteen and eighteen weeks, a small amount of amniotic fluid is extracted via a needle inserted through the mother's abdomen in order to examine the chromosomes in the fetal cells that are present in the fluid. In *chorionic villus sampling*, which can be performed between eight and twelve weeks, a sample of the membrane surrounding the embryo (the chorion) is cultured to examine the chromosomal makeup of the cells. *Ultrasonography* is a nonintrusive procedure that produces a picture of the embryo or fetus with sound waves that pass through the mother's abdominal wall and reflect off the fetus. Ultrasound provides information about head size, body size, neural tube status, and gestational age.

II. ENVIRONMENTAL FACTORS INFLUENCING PRENATAL DEVELOPMENT (pp. 140–159)

The prenatal period is characterized by an amazing sequence of events that must proceed in an intricately precise way. Certainly the genetic information present in the chromosomes guides this development, but we now know that the condition of the prenatal environment is also critical for normal development to occur.

A. Support Within the Womb (p. 140)

The *placenta* is a network of blood vessels and capillaries, some originating from the mother and some from the fetus. It is the site where nutrients and waste products are exchanged between the maternal and fetal blood systems. Oxygen, carbon dioxide, and other chemicals can pass through the capillaries, but not the blood cells themselves because they are too large. The *umbilical cord* transports the nutrients and waste products between the fetus and the placenta. The amniotic sac is the fluid-filled membrane surrounding the fetus, protecting it from bumps and shocks.

B. Teratogens (pp. 140–144)

Teratology is the study of birth defects that result from environmental causes. Environmental agents causing such disruptions are known as *teratogens*. The first conclusive evidence of the effects of environmental agents on the developing embryo and fetus came from mothers who used thalidomide during pregnancy. Thought to be a harmless drug, thalidomide caused severe malformations of the arms and legs in infants who had been exposed during early prenatal development. This demonstrated conclusively that many environmental agents cross what was previously believed to be the placental barrier. Research has revealed several principles of teratology:

The principle of susceptibility states that different species as well as different individuals within a species are differentially affected by the same teratogens. (For example, developing rats are unaffected by thalidomide.)

The principle of critical or sensitive periods states that the effects of a teratogen depend on the period of time during development when the fetus is exposed.

The principle of access states that factors affecting the access of a teratogen to a developing individual influence the extent of the damage.

The principle of dose-response relationships states that the dosage level of a teratogen influences the extent of the damage to the developing individual.

The principle of teratogenic response states that teratogens do not show uniform effects on all aspects of prenatal development.

The principle of interference with specific mechanisms states that teratogens affect prenatal development by interfering with biochemical processes that are responsible for the basic functioning of cells.

The principle of developmental delay and "sleeper effects" states that some teratogens may cause only temporary delays in development. In other cases, the effects are not seen for many years after birth.

C. **Drugs as Teratogens** (pp. 144–150)

Prenatal exposure to alcohol, in its most severe form, causes *fetal alcohol syndrome (FAS)*, which results in infants born with some physical abnormalities and mild to moderate mental retardation. Even casual use of alcohol has been found to lead to less severe fetal alcohol effects (FAE) such as hyperactivity, short attention span, growth problems, and learning and language problems. Cigarette smoking has been linked to increased rates of fetal and infant mortality. The most consistent effect of smoking on the developing fetus is to lower birth weight. Spontaneous abortions, stillbirths, and neonatal deaths have also been consistently linked to smoking. Reduced oxygen to the embryo and fetus probably accounts for the teratogenic effects of nicotine and the many other pharmacological agents found in cigarette smoke. The effects of over-the-counter and prescription drugs on prenatal development are less clear-cut. Medical professionals recommend that pregnant women take no drugs. The effects of illegal drugs such as heroin, marijuana, and cocaine on the developing human embryo and fetus have not been conclusively demonstrated largely because of methodological problems inherent in this area of research. It is difficult to determine why children of addicted mothers are at risk because drug-abusing mothers often are malnourished, smoke, drink alcohol, receive poor prenatal care, and provide an inadequate postnatal environment for their infant. Well-controlled research with animals provides some evidence that prenatal exposure to drugs significantly impairs development and behavior.

D. **Diseases as Teratogens** (pp. 150–154)

We now know that numerous diseases and parasitic bacteria that pregnant women may be exposed to can cause serious birth defects. Exposure to rubella (German measles) during the first trimester can result in growth retardation, cataracts, hearing deficits, heart defects, and mental retardation. Toxoplasmosis is caused by a parasite that can be found in cat feces or raw and partially cooked meats. The effects of the disease on the fetus are most devastating if it is contracted early in the pregnancy. Cytomegalovirus results in a swelling of the salivary glands. It is the most common source of infection for newborns. Sexually transmitted diseases such as herpes, chlamydia, gonorrhea, syphilis, and AIDS either disrupt conception or pregnancy or are transmitted to the fetus. In the case of AIDS, infants who acquire the disease during prenatal or perinatal exposure to HIV show poor growth and motor and mental retardation. Many die within a matter of months after birth.

E. **Environmental Hazards as Teratogens** (p. 154)

Many environmental substances have been found to be teratogenic. Radiation, lead, carbon monoxide, and many other chemicals cause birth defects, particularly if the embryo or fetus is exposed during early prenatal development.

Controversy: Should Companies Bar Women from Jobs with Environmental Hazards?
(pp. 155–156)
There is a great deal of controversy concerning whether women of childbearing age should be banned from occupations where they might come in contact with potentially teratogenic substances even before they may be aware that they are pregnant. Many companies that manufacture or utilize hazardous materials want to establish fetal protection policies so that they are not liable for damage to the unborn. Opponents of fetal protection policies fear that such policies may be used to keep women from attaining certain jobs.

F. **Maternal Conditions and Prenatal Development** (pp. 156–160)
In addition to teratogens, a number of maternal conditions are associated with prenatal risk factors. Maternal age has been correlated with increased risk in pregnancy. The likelihood of having a child with Down syndrome, a premature infant, and a difficult labor increases as maternal age advances past thirty-five. Teenage mothers are at an even greater risk because they are less likely to receive adequate prenatal care. Adequate nutrition is extremely important for prenatal physical and brain development. Malnutrition early in pregnancy can lead to spontaneous abortions, stillbirths, and nervous system damage. When occurring later in pregnancy, malnutrition is associated with reduced fetal growth and low birth weight. A clear picture has not emerged regarding the relationship between maternal stress and prenatal development. According to some research, maternal stress may complicate a pregnancy by affecting hormone levels and blood flow to the placenta and by increasing the use of cigarettes, alcohol, and drugs, resulting in low birth weight and respiratory difficulties.

G. **A Final Note on Environment and Prenatal Development** (p. 160)
It is important to note that although many environmental and maternal factors may be teratogenic, between 90 and 95 percent of babies in the United States are born well developed and apparently normal.

III. **BIRTH AND THE PERINATAL ENVIRONMENT** (pp. 160–170)
With the onset of labor, the fetal period ends and the birth process begins. During labor the fetus begins its journey from the safe confines of the amniotic sac, down through the birth canal, and out into the world. Within minutes of birth the newborn must begin breathing, sucking, and swallowing in order to survive in its new environment. The self-sustaining uterine environment is replaced by the social environment of parents, grandparents, siblings, and others on whom the infant must depend for its survival.

A. **Childbirth Techniques** (pp. 161–163)
Societal rituals and techniques of childbirth vary and affect how it is perceived and how easily it progresses. Concerns over the effects of drugs on fetal development have led to methods of prepared childbirth, which aim to teach mothers to relax and to understand the changes that occur during labor and childbirth, and encourage a cooperative relationship between doctor and mother during the childbirth experience. The methods founded by Grantley Dick-Read and Fernand Lamaze emphasize the supportive role of

the father or another companion to reduce the mother's anxiety and, consequently, her pain. Women who have companions present during labor spend significantly less time in labor (nine vs. nineteen hours), require less drugs, and have babies who show less fetal distress than women who have routine nursing care.

>*Controversy: Is Medication During Childbirth Harmful?* (p. 162)
>A major controversy exists over the use of medication during childbirth. The issue is whether drugs used to alleviate maternal pain during childbirth have negative or teratogenic effects on the infant who is exposed to them via the placenta. Although the available research findings are equivocal, to be safe, obstetricians recommend that conservative amounts of pain-relieving drugs be used during labor and childbirth.

B. **Birth Settings** (pp. 163–164)
The overwhelming majority of infants in the United States are born in hospital settings. A desire to create a more relaxed and natural setting for childbirth has led to more and more infants being born at home or in free-standing birthing centers (FSBC). The problem with nonhospital birth settings is the concern with safety. In most cases, mothers considered at risk for any potential perinatal problems are encouraged to use hospitals for their deliveries.

C. **Labor and Delivery** (pp. 164–165)
Labor begins with the onset of regular, increasingly frequent contractions. There are three stages of labor. In the first stage, uterine contractions and dilation of the cervix permit descent of the baby down the birth canal. Continued descent and birth of the baby occur in the second stage, and expulsion of the placenta occurs in the final stage. A caesarean birth is delivery through a surgical incision made in the mother's abdomen and uterus. In the past, caesarean birth was recommended for breech babies. The availability of *fetal monitoring devices* to monitor fetal stress, concerns about birth trauma such as anoxia, and risk of infection from sexually transmitted diseases have contributed to the increase of the caesarean rate in the last decade, particularly in the United States.

D. **Low Birth Weight** (pp. 165–170)
Infants born weighing less than 5½ pounds are considered to be low birth weight. As birth weight decreases, the likelihood of death in the first few weeks of life increases significantly. In the United States, low birth weight is a common problem because of the number of teenage mothers and the lack of prenatal resources for some members of the population. Low–birth weight infants are at risk for respiratory difficulties, hyperactivity, greater frequency of illness, and disruption of family functioning. In the long term, however, low–birth weight infants who survive show few intellectual and developmental effects from their birth-weight status. A distinction is made between low–birth weight infants who are preterm (less than thirty-five weeks gestational age) and those born nearer to term (thirty-eight to forty weeks), but who are small for gestational age (SGA). Efforts to reduce the problems associated with low birth weight have been aimed at improved monitoring of infants' perinatal status and improved prenatal care, particularly for mothers at risk. Various attempts have been made to give low–birth weight

infants either compensatory experience to duplicate conditions in the womb or enriching stimulation, which would be similar to the experiences of the healthy newborn. Studies have reported at least temporary benefits from both types of extra stimulation, the most consistent of which is increased weight gain. The long-term effects of added stimulation are unclear, however, because the social and rearing conditions of the infant once he or she leaves the hospital have a powerful influence on later development.

IV. THE NEWBORN (pp. 170–174)

The newborn infant, if delivered vaginally, will have a flattened nose and misshapen head as a result of the pressure on the bones of the skull during the passage through the birth canal. The skin is covered with vernix caseosa, an oily, cheeselike substance that protects against infections. The first task of the newborn is to begin breathing with its lungs. Initially, a newborn's respiration is shallow and erratic. Within thirty to ninety minutes after birth, however, the normal infant will show deep, regular breathing. The umbilical cord will be cut, severing the connection between the newborn and the placenta. Next, the newborn must regulate its body temperature. The low fat reserves of newborns in relation to their large body surface makes it difficult for them to retain heat. An external heat source or close contact with the mother can help them to maintain their body temperature.

A. Assessing Newborns (pp. 171–172)

The newborn is assessed immediately after birth using the Apgar Scale, which provides a measure of the baby's vital signs. The Neonatal Behavioral Assessment Scale (NBAS) provides an evaluation of the baby's behavior on a variety of dimensions, such as interaction with the tester, responsiveness to objects, reflex motor capacities, and ability to control behavioral state. The NBAS is used to assess the newborn's neurological condition and can predict developmental outcomes in the first few months of life.

B. Newborn Sleep States (pp. 172–174)

The newborn, who spends a great deal of the day sleeping, displays a wide range of states, from drowsiness to regular or irregular sleep, alert activity, alert inactivity, and crying. Initially the baby changes from sleeping to waking states frequently. As they get older, infants change states less often, but sleep for longer periods of time, so that by three to four months they may sleep through the night. The sleep patterns of infants are dictated to a certain extent by cultural differences. Infants display two distinct sleep states. REM (rapid eye movement) sleep is an active sleep that includes muscle jerks and irregular breathing and heart-rate activity. NREM (non-REM) sleep is a quiet sleep in which few movements and more regular heart rate and breathing are present. Compared to adults, infants spend proportionally more time in REM sleep. The autostimulation theory suggests that REM sleep provides the infant's central nervous system with what may be essential amounts of stimulation that the infant may miss by not being awake for long periods of time.

V. **THEMES IN DEVELOPMENT: THE PRENATAL PERIOD AND BIRTH** (pp. 174–176)
What roles do nature and nurture play in prenatal development and birth? Prenatal development is influenced by parents' genetic programs, the condition of the mother and her exposure to drugs, chemicals, hazardous living conditions, and other environmental influences. Development obeys principles established by genetics and biochemical and physiological processes, but exposure to various maternal conditions can radically alter the normal path.

How does the sociocultural context influence prenatal development and birth? An expectant mother's actions are influenced by her surrounding community and culture. Although scientific and technological advances may be available, parents may not have the resources or the desire to access them. Societal support can be a major factor contributing to the successful development of low–birth weight infants.

Is development before and after birth continuous or stagelike? The process of birth is a major transition, and the dramatic changes associated with birth match stagelike descriptions of development. The processes governing the proliferation, differentiation, and emergence and functioning of organs are conceptualized as continuous.

Are there sensitive periods in prenatal development and shortly after birth? Yes. There are periods when the embryo is far more susceptible to specific kinds of insults than at other times. Early experience, too, may be important for low–birth weight infants.

Key Terms Review

1. _____ development takes place from the moment of conception to the beginning of labor, while _____ development is the period following birth.

2. The events occurring immediately before, during, and after the birth of an infant, including the medical, physical, and social setting, are called the _____ environment.

3. The _____ period of prenatal development begins about the eighth week after conception and ends at birth.

4. The _____ is a spherical cell mass that is formed about the forth day after conception and embeds in the uterine lining.

5. Failure of the _____ to close can cause spina bifida or no brain growth.

6. _____ refers to the ability of a baby to survive outside the mother's womb.

7. The _____ is the age of the fetus derived from the onset of the last menstrual period of the mother.

8. In _____ a sample of the fluids surrounding the developing fetus is withdrawn through a syringe inserted through the abdominal wall.

9. _____ involves the biopsy of hairlike projections from the chorion, the outer wall of the membrane in which the embryo develops.

10. The support organ formed by cells from both the blastocyst and the uterine lining is called the _____ ; it serves to provide oxygen and nutrients to the developing embryo.

11. _____ are environmental agents that, when present during the prenatal period, can cause birth defects and behavioral deficits.

12. Heavy consumption of alcohol by the mother can lead to _____ , a cluster of abnormalities, including retardation of growth and intellectual development.

13. In order to estimate gestational age and to look for physical abnormalities in the fetus a physician may utilize the procedure called _____ .

14. The fluid-filled protective membrane surrounding the fetus is called the _____ .

15. _____ refers to the mitotic cell division of the zygote that occurs within twenty-four to thirty hours after conception.

16. The period of prenatal development in which major biological organs and systems are formed is called the _____ period.

17. The _____ is used to measure fetal heartbeat during delivery.

18. The _____ period lasts about ten to fourteen days following conception, before the fertilized egg becomes implanted in the uterine wall.

19. The solid ball of cells formed by the cleavage of the zygote is called the _____ .

20. Oxygen, nutrients, and waste products are transported between the placenta and the embryo via the _____ .

Answers to Key Terms Review

1. Prenatal, postnatal
2. perinatal
3. fetal
4. blastocyst

5. neural tube
6. viability
7. gestational age
8. amniocentesis
9. Chorionic villus sampling
10. placenta
11. Teratogens
12. fetal alcohol syndrome (FAS)
13. ultrasonography
14. amniotic sac
15. Cleavage
16. embryonic
17. fetal monitoring device
18. germinal
19. morula
20. umbilical cord

Multiple-Choice Questions

Fact and Concept Questions

1. The period of the embryo lasts from about
   a. fertilization to the eighth week.
   b. the second to the eighth week.
   c. the eighth week to birth.
   d. the second week to birth.

2. The correct order of the stages of prenatal development is
   a. zygote, embryo, fetus.
   b. fetus, embryo, zygote.
   c. zygote, fetus, embryo.
   d. fertilized ovum, zygote, fetus.

3. Fertilization can take place
   a. in the womb.
   b. in the Fallopian tube.
   c. at any time during the menstrual cycle.
   d. in the absence of sperm.

4. The fertilized ovum undergoes cell divisions called
   a. meiosis.
   b. morulas.
   c. cleavages.
   d. fermentation.

5. The developing embryo is differentiated into three layers. One of these layers, the ectoderm, will develop into the
   a. organs.
   b. skeletal muscles.
   c. cardiovascular system.
   d. central nervous system.

6. The principle of cephalocaudal development explains why
   a. the neural tube closes to form the brain before it closes to form the spinal cord.
   b. the neural tube closes to form the spinal cord before it closes to form the brain.
   c. the legs of a developing fetus are formed before the arms.
   d. the reproductive system of a developing fetus is formed before the nervous system.

7. It is during the third trimester that the fetus
   a. can be detected by the mother for the first time.
   b. begins to have a functional nervous system.
   c. shows a dramatic improvement in viability.
   d. begins forming the major organ systems.

8. The procedure that involves extracting a small amount of the fluid surrounding the fetus for the purpose of chromosomal examination is called
   a. ultrasonography.
   b. chorionic villus sampling.
   c. karyotyping.
   d. amniocentesis.

9. The network of blood vessels and capillaries where nutrients and waste products are exchanged between mother and fetus is called the
   a. placenta.
   b. umbilical cord.
   c. amnion.
   d. chorion.

10. Teratology is the study of
    a. genetic influences on behavior.
    b. birth defects caused by the environment.
    c. sociocultural influences on behavior.
    d. maternal-fetal blood exchange.

11. The extent of a teratogen's effect will depend on the precise time that the developing embryo or fetus is exposed to the substance. This describes the principle of
    a. developmental delay.
    b. dose-response relationships.
    c. access.
    d. critical or sensitive periods.

12. A drug that was determined to have a "sleeper effect" on children was
    a. thalidomide.
    b. alcohol.
    c. heroin.
    d. DES.

13. Prenatal exposure to rubella during the first trimester can result in an infant who has
    a. FAS.
    b. DES.
    c. mental retardation.
    d. liver dysfunction.

14. According to the text, who is most likely to have a healthy, normal infant?
    a. A teenager having her first child
    b. A thirty-seven-year-old woman having her first child
    c. A twenty-three-year-old woman having her first child
    d. A thirty-six-year-old woman having her second child

15. The rate of infants born with some type of birth defect is
    a. between 0 and 1 percent.
    b. between 5 and 10 percent.
    c. between 10 and 20 percent.
    d. between 20 and 30 percent.

16. Research on the effects of medication administered during childbirth
    a. suggests that pain-lessening drugs and sedatives do not pass readily through the placenta.
    b. suggests that heavy use of drugs during labor is not associated with learning disorders in school-age children.
    c. has been criticized as being methodologically inadequate.
    d. suggests that pain-lessening drugs that reduce maternal stress during labor are associated with reduced fetal abnormalities.

17. Newborns who are born small for gestational age (SGA) are more likely to suffer from _____ than infants who are born preterm.
    a. congenital anomalies
    b. respiratory distress
    c. Down syndrome
    d. anoxia

18. Premature babies given extra nonnutritive sucking while in the hospital
    a. had greater eating problems up to one year of age than premature babies not given the opportunity for nonnutritive sucking.
    b. gained weight more rapidly than premature babies not given the opportunity for nonnutritive sucking.
    c. gained weight less rapidly than premature babies not given the opportunity for nonnutritive sucking.
    d. stayed in the hospital longer than premature babies not given the opportunity for nonnutritive sucking.

19. To assess the physical condition of a newborn shortly after birth a pediatrician would use
    a. the NBAS.
    b. the autostimulation scale.
    c. a fetal monitoring device.
    d. the Apgar Scale.

20. Autostimulation theory proposes that
    a. the infant's nervous system stimulates her to wake up several times a day.
    b. the infant's nervous system provides stimulation of the immature respiratory system to ensure continued breathing.
    c. REM sleep provides the infant's nervous system with periods of powerful stimulation.
    d. the newborn engages in self-stimulation in order to maintain a brief time of wakefulness.

Application Questions

1. Cheryl has delivered a baby with anencephaly. This would indicate that during prenatal development the baby's
   a. arms and legs did not develop properly because of a drug that Cheryl took while she was pregnant.
   b. spinal cord did not develop properly because Cheryl had a viral infection while she was pregnant.
   c. brain did not develop properly because the neural tube failed to close during the embryonic period.
   d. sexual organs did not develop properly because of prenatal exposure to excess hormones.

2. MaryJo has just found out that she is pregnant. Her doctor will ask her which of the following dates in order to determine the gestational age of her child?
   a. The date she believes fertilization took place
   b. The date of her last menstrual period
   c. The date of her pregnancy test
   d. The date two weeks after her last menstrual period

3. Hilda is pregnant and has just felt her baby move for the first time. This fetal movement is referred to as
   a. quickening.
   b. myelinization.
   c. viability.
   d. gestation.

4. Inez, a heavy smoker, has continued to smoke throughout her pregnancy. There is a good chance that her baby will
   a. be mentally retarded.
   b. be perfectly healthy and normal.
   c. have a much lower birth weight than a normal infant.
   d. have hearing and visual defects.

5. Annette is a healthy, nonsmoking forty-two-year-old who is pregnant with her first child. Annette's baby is at increased risk for
   a. low birth weight.
   b. spina bifida.
   c. toxoplasmosis.
   d. Down syndrome.

6. Mariko is in labor and is connected to a fetal monitoring device. Her doctor has determined that the fetal heart rate is showing that the baby is undergoing severe distress. The doctor is most likely to recommend a
   a. caesarean birth.
   b. vaginal birth.
   c. breech birth.
   d. freestanding birthing center.

7. Jerry was born preterm. This means he was born at
   a. forty-three weeks conceptual age.
   b. forty weeks conceptual age.
   c. thirty-six weeks conceptual age.
   d. thirty-two weeks conceptual age.

8. Greg was in the delivery room when his son was born. He was upset at the baby's appearance because he was covered with vernix caseosa. The doctor most likely told Greg
   a. not to be concerned because all normal infants are born covered with this substance, which protects the baby against infection.
   b. not to be concerned because all normal infants are born covered with this substance, which helps regulate their breathing after birth.
   c. not to be concerned because all normal infants are born covered with this substance, which helps regulate their body temperature.
   d. they should be concerned because this substance is a sign of respiratory distress.

9. At birth, Nicole receives Apgar scores of 7 and 9. These scores indicate that
   a. she is in severe respiratory distress.
   b. she should be sent to neonatal intensive care.
   c. she has poor muscle tone.
   d. she is normal and healthy.

10. While Paula is watching her newborn baby sleep, she notices that he is twitching and breathing irregularly. On closer inspection she can see the baby's eyes moving under the closed eyelids. The baby is probably in
    a. quiet sleep.
    b. REM sleep.
    c. NREM sleep.
    d. alert sleep.

Answers to Multiple-Choice Questions

The correct answer appears first and is preceded by an asterisk.

Answers to Fact and Concept Questions

1. *b. The embryonic period begins about the tenth to fourteenth day after fertilization, when implantation occurs, and ends at about the eighth week, when bone begins to form. (p. 130)
   a. During the first ten days after fertilization, the growing fertilized egg is called the zygote, morula, and blastocyte, respectively; it is not an embryo until implantation occurs.
   c. The embryo becomes a fetus beginning eight weeks after conception and lasting until birth.
   d. From two weeks after conception to birth includes the embryonic and the fetal periods.

2. *a. The zygote develops into the embryo, which then develops into the fetus. (p. 130)
   b. The zygote is the fertilized egg and, therefore, is the first stage of prenatal development, not the last.
   c. The embryonic stage occurs before the fetal stage.
   d. The fertilized ovum and the zygote are not different stages of prenatal development, but the same initial stage.

3. *b. The egg, or ovum, is released into the Fallopian tube; if sperm are present, fertilization will occur. (p. 131)
   a. The womb, also known as the uterus, is where the fertilized egg is implanted; fertilization does not occur here.

    c. The opportunity for fertilization usually begins about fourteen days after the start of the menstrual cycle, when an egg is released into the Fallopian tube. Fertilization cannot occur at any other time during the menstrual cycle.

    d. The fertilization process requires the presence of sperm.

4. *c. Cleavage is a mitotic division of the zygote. (p. 131)

    a. Meiosis describes the process by which the sex cells, sperm and ovum, are produced, not the development of a fertilized egg.

    b. The morula is a ball of sixteen cells that results from a process of cell division, but it does not describe a cell-division process.

    d. Fermentation is a chemical reaction caused by living organisms; it is not involved in prenatal development.

5. *d. The central nervous system arises from a small collection of ectodermal cells. (p. 133)

    a. The organs arise from the endoderm, or lower layer.

    b. The skeletal muscles arise from the mesoderm, or middle layer.

    c. The cardiovascular system arises from the mesoderm, or middle layer.

6. *a. The cephalocaudal principle states that the development of organs and systems occurs more rapidly near the head than in lower regions of the body; therefore, the neural tube should close to form the head before it closes to form the spinal cord. (p. 136)

    b. The cephalocaudal principle states that the development of organs and systems occurs more rapidly near the head than in lower regions of the body; therefore, one should not expect the neural tube to close to form the spinal cord before closing to form the brain.

    c. This statement is incorrect, but even if it were true, it could not be explained by a principle that describes development as proceeding in a head-to-tail direction.

    d. This statement is incorrect because the nervous system begins to form before the reproductive system.

7. *c. It is during the third trimester that viability, or the ability of the baby to survive outside the mother's womb, dramatically improves. (p. 137)

    a. Fetal movement is usually detected by the mother in the second trimester; these first movements are subtle fetal kicks known as quickening.

    b. The nervous system begins to function about the fifth week after conception—in the first trimester, not the third.

    d. The major organ systems begin to form early in fetal development, during the embryonic period, which ends at about eight weeks after conception.

8. *d. In amniocentesis a syringe is used to extract a small sample of the amniotic fluid surrounding the developing fetus. (p. 138)

    a. Ultrasonography is a nonintrusive procedure that uses sound waves to create a picture of the developing fetus.

b. Chorionic villus sampling is an intrusive prenatal screening procedure that involves a biopsy of chorionic tissue, not the extraction of fluid.

c. Karyotyping is not a prenatal screening procedure but a method used to develop photomicrographs of an individual's chromosomes.

9. *a. It is at the placenta that oxygen, essential nutrients, and waste products are exchanged between the fetus and the mother. (p. 140)

b. The umbilical cord transports the blood containing oxygen and nutrients from the placenta to the embryo, but it is not the site of exchange for these substances.

c. The amnion is a thin, tough sac that contains the embryo and the amniotic fluid; it is not the site of exchange for nutrients and waste products.

d. The chorion is the outer wall of the membrane in which the embryo develops; it is not the site of exchange for nutrients and waste products.

10. *b. Teratology is the study of birth defects and behavioral disturbances caused by environmental factors present during the fetal period. (p. 141)

a. The study of genetic influences on behavior is called behavioral genetics.

c. Sociocultural factors play an important role in the access to teratogens (principle of access), but the study of such factors is not called teratology.

d. In order to study how teratogens may affect the fetus it is important to understand that there is a maternal-fetal blood exchange, but the study of the mechanism of this exchange is not called teratology.

11. *d. The extent to which a teratogen will have negative consequences on the fetus depends on whether exposure to the teratogen occurred during a sensitive or critical period. (p. 142)

a. Developmental delay is one of the principles of teratology that describes effects of teratogens that are temporary or that do not appear until late in development.

b. Dose-response relationship is a principle of teratology that describes the importance of dosage level of a teratogen in producing fetal damage.

c. The principle of access states that the accessibility of a teratogen to a fetus or embryo influences the degree of damage.

12. *d. A "sleeper effect" refers to a teratogen, such as DES, whose impact goes unnoticed until childhood or later. Children of women who took the hormone DES during pregnancy have a high rate of genital-tract cancers later in life. (p. 144)

a. Thalidomide is a teratogen with devastating consequences, but the deformities that occur are immediately apparent at birth.

b. The teratogenic effects of alcohol can take many forms, since the effects are dose-related. The most severe case leads to fetal alcohol syndrome, which is immediately apparent at birth.

c. Infants born to heroin-addicted mothers often undergo withdrawal symptoms at birth, such as tremors and high-pitched cries; the drug clearly has immediately noticeable effects.

13. *c. Rubella can cause a variety of physical and mental problems including mental retardation. (p. 151)
   a. Fetal alcohol syndrome, or FAS, occurs in babies born to alcoholic mothers. It is not caused by rubella.
   b. Diethylstilbestrol, or DES, is a teratogenic drug that produces a "sleeper effect." It is not a cause of rubella.
   d. Liver dysfunction is not a primary problem associated with rubella.

14. *c. Teenage mothers and mothers over the age of thirty-five are at greater risk for delivering less healthy babies than mothers between these two age groups. (p. 156)
   a. A teenager is at considerable risk for delivering an unhealthy baby primarily because the teenage population is least likely to seek adequate prenatal care.
   b. Babies of mothers over thirty-five have an increased risk of Down syndrome, prematurity, and mortality, primarily because heath-related problems generally accompany aging.
   d. Babies of mothers over thirty-five have an increased risk of Down syndrome, prematurity, and mortality, primarily because heath-related problems generally accompany aging.

15. *b. The percentage of healthy babies born in the United States is between 90 and 95 percent. (p. 160)
   a. The percentage of healthy babies born in the United States is between 90 and 95 percent; thus, the percentage born with birth defects is greater than 1 percent.
   c. The percentage of healthy babies born in the United States is between 90 and 95 percent; thus, the percentage born with birth defects is less than 20 percent.
   d. The percentage of healthy babies born in the United States is between 90 and 95 percent; thus, the percentage born with birth defects is less than 30 percent.

16. *c. The influence of maternal medication on fetal development is difficult to establish because many factors, such as poor health and labor difficulties, are associated with the use of medication during childbirth, making many of these studies methodologically inadequate. (p. 162)
   a. Most drugs, including sedatives and pain-lessening drugs, readily pass through the placenta and enter the baby's circulatory system.
   b. Heavy use of drugs during labor has been associated with an increased frequency of learning disorders in school-age children.
   d. There is no evidence that the use of drugs during childbirth reduces fetal abnormalities. The uncertainties concerning the effects of maternal medication on fetal development have led most obstetricians to suggest a minimal amount of drug administration during labor.

17. *a. Congenital anomalies are somewhat more likely to occur in SGA infants than in preterm infants. (p. 167)
   b. Respiratory distress is more likely among preterm infants than among SGA infants.

c. Down syndrome is caused by an extra twenty-first chromosome; it is not related to low birth weight.

d. Anoxia occurs as a result of damage to the umbilical cord or head during birth; it is not related to low birth weight.

18. *b. Studies show that extra stimulation, such as nonnutritive sucking, provides premature infants with several benefits, including rapid weight gain. (p. 169)

a. Preterm infants given extra nonnutritive sucking had fewer eating problems later on.

c. Preterm infants given extra nonnutritive sucking gained weight more rapidly.

d. Preterm infants given extra nonnutritive sucking stayed in the hospital fewer days.

19. *d. The Apgar scale is widely used to diagnose the physical state of the newborn. (p. 171)

a. The NBAS is a scale that assesses newborns' behavior on a variety of dimensions, not just physical characteristics.

b. Autostimulation is not a scale but a theory of the function of REM sleep in newborns.

c. The fetal monitoring device is used to monitor the physical condition of the baby before birth, not after birth.

20. *c. Autostimulation theory states that the stimulation of the nervous system that occurs during REM sleep compensates for the brief amount of time each day that the infant is awake. (p. 173)

a. A newborn infant does wake up several times a day, but the autostimulation theory does not try to explain this sleep-wake pattern.

b. Healthy, full-term infants can breath on their own efficiently, while premature infants often need assistance with respiration, but autostimulation theory does not describe an infant's response to respiratory difficulties.

d. The brief period of time that the newborn is awake is not due to any self-stimulating behavior.

Answers to Application Questions

1. *c. The term *anencephaly* is used to refer to a child born with an abnormally developed brain, which results when the cephalic (head) region of the neural tube fails to close. (p. 136)

a. Deformed arms and legs have been associated with the use of thalidomide during pregnancy, but such physical deformities are not called anencephaly.

b. A viral infection may cause abnormal development of the spinal cord, but anencephaly describes brain disorders, not spinal cord disorders.

d. Anencephaly describes a condition of abnormal brain growth, not abnormal growth of sexual organs.

2. *b. Gestational age is the common reference for prenatal development; it is based on the first day of the mother's last menstrual period. (p. 137)

a. The mother is probably the most likely to know approximately when fertilization took place; nevertheless, such estimates are not very accurate and therefore are not used to estimate gestational age.

c. A pregnancy test can determine whether or not a woman is pregnant, but it cannot provide an estimate of the baby's age.

d. Although conception usually occurs approximately two weeks *after* the onset of the last menstrual period, it has become standard procedure to estimate gestational age using the onset of the last menstrual period.

3. *a. In the second trimester the mother is likely to feel fetal kicks called quickening. (p. 137)

b. Myelinization is the process of neural growth during which myelin forms around neurons to insulate and speed the conduction of the neural impulse.

c. Viability refers to the ability of the developing fetus to survive outside the mother's womb.

d. Gestation refers to the period of carrying a developing embryo and fetus—that is, the period of pregnancy.

4. *c. The more a mother smokes while pregnant, the lower the newborn baby's average weight. (p. 146)

a. Although deleterious effects of maternal smoking on the developing infant do occur, studies have failed to uncover any consistent mental deficits or long-term consequences in infants born to smoking mothers.

b. Babies born to smoking mothers are usually smaller and lighter in weight, not perfectly healthy and normal. Smoking is also associated with increased stillbirths and neonatal deaths.

d. Studies have consistently failed to find any evidence that smoking causes congenital defects such as hearing and visual problems.

5. *d. The likelihood of giving birth to a child with Down syndrome increases with age; women over the age of thirty-five are particularly at risk. (p. 156)

a. Healthy mothers over thirty-five have no more complications during pregnancy than younger mothers, and since Annette doesn't smoke there is no reason to expect that she is at risk of having a low–birth weight baby.

b. Spina bifida is a disorder in which the spinal cord fails to develop properly. This disorder is not related to maternal age.

c. Toxoplasmosis results from infection by a parasite found in the feces of small animals like cats and in raw or partially cooked meats. A forty-two-year-old woman is at no higher or lower risk of getting this disease than anyone else.

6. *a. A caesarean birth permits a quick delivery, which is critical if the baby is in severe distress. The baby is delivered through an incision in the mother's abdomen and uterus. (p. 164)

b. It is critical that birth occur as quickly as possible when a baby is in severe distress during labor. Since vaginal birth may take many minutes, the doctor is unlikely to recommend this method of birth.

c. A breech birth describes the situation where the baby is in a foot-first position in the uterus; it is not a method of birth.

d. Freestanding birthing centers provide a more natural and relaxed setting, but they are not equipped to handle complications that may arise during labor.

7. *d. Jerry would be less than thirty-five weeks conceptual age, which is the criterion for a preterm classification. (p. 167)

a. Preterm babies are defined as those born less than thirty-five weeks conceptual age.

b. Preterm babies are defined as those born less than thirty-five weeks conceptual age.

c. Preterm babies are defined as those born less than thirty-five weeks conceptual age.

8. *a. Vernix caseosa is an oily, cheeselike substance that covers the newborn and helps protect against infection. (p. 170)

b. All normal newborns are born covered with this substance, but it does not play a role in regulating breathing.

c. All normal newborns are born covered with this substance, but it does not play a role in regulating body temperature.

d. There is no need to be concerned because this substance covers all normal newborns and is not related to any form of distress.

9. *d. An Apgar score of 7 or better usually indicates that the baby is healthy and not at risk. (p. 171)

a. An Apgar score of 7 or better usually indicates that the baby is healthy and not at risk; therefore, it is unlikely that Nicole would have difficulties with her breathing.

b. An Apgar score of 7 or better usually indicates that the baby is healthy and not at risk; therefore, there is no need to provide Nicole with neonatal intensive care.

c. An Apgar score 7 or better indicates that Nicole's muscle tone is normal.

10. *b. During REM (rapid eye movement) sleep, muscle jerks are frequent, breathing and heart rate are irregular, and the eyes move rapidly under the closed eyelids. (p. 173)

a. During quiet, or NREM, sleep few movements are observed, and breathing is regular.

c. During quiet, or NREM, sleep few movements are observed and breathing is regular.

d. There is no stage of sleep called alert sleep.

CHAPTER 5

PHYSICAL GROWTH AND MOTOR SKILLS

LEARNING OBJECTIVES

1. Describe the patterns of physical growth and the methods for determining the norms of growth and development. (pp. 181–186)

2. Discuss the measures of physical maturity. (pp. 186–189)

3. Describe the genetic, neural, and hormonal determinants of physical growth and development. (pp. 189–192)

4. Discuss the importance of nutrition and the physical environment for physical growth and development. (pp. 192–193)

5. Discuss the impact of social and emotional factors on physical development. (pp. 193–195)

6. Describe secular trends as an important environmental determinant of physical growth and development. (pp. 195–196)

7. Describe how physical characteristics such as height and weight influence people's perceptions of others, as well as their own sense of worth. (pp. 196–197)

8. Discuss the possible causes of obesity and other eating disorders that are prevalent in modern society. (pp. 198–200)

9. Describe the social and emotional consequences of early and late maturity. (pp. 200–202)

10. Describe the pattern of growth of the brain and its neurons during the prenatal and postnatal periods. (pp. 202–205)

11. Identify the two types of neural plasticity and their relationship to sensitive periods. (pp. 206–207)

12. Explain the differences between the right and left hemispheres of the brain, and discuss the issues concerning lateralization. (pp. 207–208)

13. Describe the different types of primitive and postural reflexes. (pp. 208–211)

14. Describe sudden infant death syndrome (SIDS) and its associated risk factors. (p. 212)

15. Discuss the significance of rhythmical stereotypes, postural control, locomotion, and manual control. (pp. 212–217)

16. Describe the ways in which motor skills develop in preschool and later-childhood years. (p. 217)

17. Describe and discuss the research on the biological and environmental determinants of motor development. (pp. 217–222)

CHAPTER OUTLINE

I. **HOW THE BODY GROWS AND DEVELOPS** (pp. 181–189)
Physical growth and development of motor skills influence cognitive, social, and other dimensions of development. Cognitive and social factors, such as how an individual is perceived by others, in turn can influence the physical growth and development of motor skills.

A. **Norms of Growth** (pp. 181–183)
Growth is part of the more broadly defined concept of development and refers specifically to the increase in physical size of the body. To determine the rate of growth of the average person, physical characteristics such as weight and height are measured quantitatively in a sample of the population to establish *norms*. Such normative data indicate that while males and females grow at the same rate in infancy and childhood, an adolescent growth spurt occurs in girls about two years earlier than it occurs in boys.

B. **Patterns in Physical Growth** (pp. 183–186)

The pattern of development for individual systems of the body often is *cephalocaudal*—parts of the body near the head grow more rapidly than parts more distant from the head—or *proximodistal*—parts of the body near the middle develop before those near the periphery. The rate of growth for different body systems also differs and depends on the functional importance of the particular system. Thus, the brain grows rapidly early in infancy, whereas maturity of the reproductive system is delayed until adolescence.

C. **Individual and Group Differences in Physical Growth** (p. 186)

There is considerable variability in the rate of physical growth and development among individuals within a group as well as among ethnic and cultural groups.

D. **Measuring and Defining Physical Maturity** (pp. 186–189)

Large variations in physical development both within and between individuals make the estimation of physical maturity difficult. The most reliable measure of growth is *skeletal maturity,* which is determined by x-rays of the size, shape, and position of bones and provides an estimate of how much additional growth will take place in the individual. Other observable indicators of maturity are developmental milestones in sexual maturity, such as spontaneous ejaculation in males and *menarche* in females, that are associated with *puberty.* But indexes of sexual maturity, as in the case of physical size, are quite variable both within and between individuals.

II. **WHAT DETERMINES PHYSICAL GROWTH AND DEVELOPMENT?** (pp. 189–196)

A. **Biological Determinants** (pp. 190–192)

Genetic influences on physical growth are strongly implied by similarities in height and body proportion among family members and significant differences between cultural and racial groups. The hypothalamus, a small but complex region at the base of the brain, is believed to contain the genetic code for height and is presumed to regulate the rate of growth until the genetically determined height is attained. The hypothalamus makes possible the *catch-up growth* and *lagging-down growth* that occur when environmental factors that interfere with normal growth are removed. This brain structure regulates the *pituitary gland* to release human growth hormone (HGH) and stimulates the adrenocortex to release additional hormones necessary for growth. Other gonadotropic hormones released by the pituitary gland contribute to the production of sperm and elevate the production of *testosterone* in boys; they also regulate the menstrual cycle and stimulate the production of *estrogens* and *progesterone* in girls.

B. **Environmental Determinants** (pp. 192–196)

The environment plays an important role in physical growth and maturation in many ways. The effects of the nutritional environment on growth can be positive, as when dietary supplements increase weight in children at risk for malnourishment, or negative, as in the case of marasmus and kwashiorkor, forms of severe malnutrition. Seasonal variation, light, and high altitude are some of the characteristics of the environment known to influence the rate of physical growth.

Inadequate or abusive caregiving can lead to retardation of physical growth and emotional development as indicated by *failure to thrive* and *deprivation dwarfism*. The power of the environment on maturation is also evident when examining *secular trends*, consistent patterns of change in the environment that occurs over generations.

III. THE SOCIAL-EMOTIONAL CONSEQUENCES OF BODY CHANGE (pp. 196–202)

A. **Height** (pp. 196–197)
People's perceptions of each other are often influenced by observable physical characteristics. Taller boys, for example, are seen as more competent than shorter boys.

   Controversy: *When Should Human Growth Hormone Be Made Available to Foster Growth?* (pp. 197–198)
   Society's stereotypical attitudes about height have led some parents to seek human growth hormone treatment to augment their child's height, a procedure that raises many ethical questions. The long-term health risks of this treatment are unknown.

B. **Obesity and Other Eating Disorders** (pp. 198–200)
An individual's weight can influence the way others respond to him or her. Our society and other industrialized societies view obesity negatively. Despite the negative attitudes toward people with excess weight, there has been a substantial increase in obesity over recent decades. An increase in the time spent in sedentary activity, limited physical activity, and shifts to higher-calorie diets all contribute to the increase in obesity in our culture. Genetic predispositions for obesity may interact with the environment to produce obese individuals who have greater numbers of fat cells, greater sensitivity to external, food-related stimuli, and decreased responsiveness to internal hunger cues than normal-weight people. The perceived social and cultural pressures to maintain an ideal weight also contribute to eating disorders such as anorexia nervosa and bulimia nervosa.

C. **Early versus Late Maturity** (pp. 200–202)
Most teenagers are concerned about their changing bodies and attractiveness. Teenagers' attitude toward their physical appearance depends on many factors such as maturity, sex, whether they are prepared for the physical changes that occur at puberty, and other sociocultural factors. In females, having knowledge concerning the changes that occur at puberty decreases the likelihood of viewing menarche as a negative event. Early maturity enhances a male's satisfaction with his appearance but increases dissatisfaction in females. In general, early maturity is beneficial for males; the effects in females are less clear but may involve some conflict. The greater tendency of early maturing females to be involved in norm-breaking activities and unacceptable behaviors may stem from pressures to conform to older peers.

IV. HOW THE BRAIN AND NERVOUS SYSTEM DEVELOP (pp. 202–208)

A. The Developing Brain (pp. 203–205)
The brain grows at a rapid rate prenatally and continues to grow after birth, though at a slower rate. Different brain areas grow at different rates—the brain stem and midbrain are almost complete at birth, while the *cerebral cortex* continues to develop postnatally. The brain consists of 10 to 20 billion *neurons* and *glial cells,* which outnumber neurons by a factor of ten. Parts of many neurons become surrounded by *myelin,* a sheath of fatty material that insulates and speeds neural impulses. Neuron proliferation, neuron migration, and neuron differentiation guide the brain development that occurs prenatally. After birth, additional brain development is largely due to neuron differentiation, which increases the number of connections between neurons and possibly causes cell death. Experiments on visual processing in developing kittens exemplifies the important role that the environment plays in the cell-differentiation process.

B. Plasticity and Sensitive Periods in Brain Development (pp. 206–207)
Certain brain areas and the individual neurons within these brain areas possess *plasticity.* Plasticity describes changes in the nervous system following damage, such as the ability of a brain structure to replace the functions normally controlled by other brain areas that have been damaged. This form of plasticity is most evident in young children. Plasticity also describes the differentiation process during development. Some neurons differentiate only during critical periods in development and are sensitive to experience-expectant information, as in the development of pattern vision in many animals. Other neurons can undergo differentiation throughout development and are sensitive to experience-dependent information. Animal studies show that exposure to enriched environments increases size of neurons, connections between neurons, and number of glial cells early in development and in adults.

C. Brain Lateralization (pp. 207–208)
The cerebral cortex is divided into right and left hemispheres. In general, each hemisphere has specialized functions. The process of one hemisphere dominating the other is called *lateralization.* For example, in most right-handed people the left hemisphere is especially involved in language while the right hemisphere is involved in spatial processing. Studies suggest that infants display behaviors suggestive of lateralization at birth; however, researchers are still uncertain whether lateralization is a progressively developing process.

V. HOW MOTOR SKILLS DEVELOP (pp. 208–217)
The immature motor abilities of the newborn infant improve with development as the skeletal, muscular, and nervous systems mature. However, not all motor development follows cephalocaudal and proximodistal patterns. Differentiation and integration of motor abilities also occur with development. The earliest movements of the newborn are *reflexes*—involuntary responses to environmental stimuli such as touch, sound, and light.

A. **The First Actions: Reflexes** (pp. 209–211)

The earliest reflexes are classified as *primitive* and *postural*. Primitive reflexes are necessary for survival and include reflexes that provide nourishment, such as rooting and sucking. Postural reflexes maintain body orientation and include stepping and body righting. Most of these early reflexes disappear as the nervous system matures and some of the postural reflexes are incorporated into voluntary behaviors. Although reflexes are innate and involuntary, some can be modified with experience.

B. **Sudden Infant Death Syndrome** (p. 212)

The ability to modify reflexes and integrate them with voluntary motor skills is an important developmental process. It has been suggested that *sudden infant death syndrome (SIDS)*, the sudden, unexplained death of an otherwise healthy infant, may be a result of an unsuccessful integration of reflexive and voluntary control of breathing.

C. **Motor Milestones** (pp. 212–217)

During the first year of life, infants exhibit *rhythmical stereotypes*, repeated sequences of movement that do not appear to be goal-directed but that may be integrated into later voluntary behavior. Directed, voluntary behaviors gradually emerge in the first year. Some of these behaviors can be described as motor milestones because they provide the infant with a new way to interact with the environment. The ability to maintain postural control is one of the first milestones. Locomotion, or the ability to walk independently, is a major milestone that gradually develops from motor achievements that precede walking such as crawling, creeping, and cruising. Learning about the many objects in the world improves when progress in eye-hand coordination and prereaching behavior develops into the ability to control objects manually.

D. **Motor Skills in Preschool and Later-Childhood Years** (p. 217)

Differentiation and integration of motor and sensory skills continue to develop into preschool and later-childhood years. Toddlers and young preschoolers engage primarily in large-muscle activity. Older preschoolers engage in a greater number of small-muscle activities such as coloring, drawing, and cutting. Throughout childhood motor skills are performed more quickly and efficiently, providing children with increasing competence in their interactions with the environment. Greater competence allows children to attain greater social status.

VI. **WHAT DETERMINES MOTOR DEVELOPMENT?** (pp. 217–222)

The development of motor skills most likely is a result of maturation, a biological unfolding of genetically preadapted responses, and experiential factors.

A. **Biological Determinants** (p. 218)

Evidence consistent with a maturational view of motor development is provided by several studies. Cross-cultural studies describe a similar cephalocaudal and proximodistal pattern of motor skill growth in many varied cultures. Developmentally disabled babies achieve milestones in the same sequence as normal babies. Greater concordance in motor skills with increasing genetic similarity also supports a genetic influence on motor development.

B. **Environmental Determinants** (pp. 218–222)
The serious developmental delays seen in institutionalized children who are severely deprived of experience with motor activity demonstrate that environmental factors are crucial for proper motor development. But what role does experience play in the normally developing child?

One approach used to learn if environmental factors influence the development of motor skills is to manipulate an infant's experience and compare his or her motor development with a nonmanipulated infant's. One study, using twins as subjects, provided one twin with extra practice of a specific motor skill, while the other twin did not receive any extra training. Another study examined Hopi Indian infants, whose motor experiences were limited by the cultural practice of swaddling. These early studies were interpreted as providing evidence for maturational processes since the environmental manipulations did not alter motor development. As is often the case, however, separating genetic influences from environmental influences is a difficult task. The twin and Hopi Indian studies may not have succeeded in significantly altering the infants' experiences. The nontrained twins (who were not always monitored outside the experimental situation) may have gained substantial practice on their own. The Hopi Indians, although swaddled, may have gained important postural orientation experience that could promote walking skills. More recent studies indicate that practice of motor skills can produce early walking. Cross-cultural differences in the onset of motor milestones also provide evidence for environmental influences. But genetic differences between cultures cannot be ruled out as a contributor to such cultural dissimilarity.

VII. **THEMES IN DEVELOPMENT: PHYSICAL GROWTH AND MOTOR SKILLS** (pp. 222–224)
What roles do nature and nurture play in physical growth and motor skill development? Development is influenced by genetic programs combined with hormonal factors and various maturational principles of skill acquisition. Physical development is also influenced by environmental factors such as stimulation by caregivers.

How does the sociocultural context influence physical growth and motor skill development? Caregivers' attitudes toward development are influenced by cultural resources, standards, and settings. Advances in knowledge of nutrition, views about appearance, and education have also affected secular trends for many aspects of development. Finally, the extent to which a culture promotes specific skills affects children's efforts to acquire these skills.

How does the child actively contribute to the process of physical growth and the development of motor skills? Babies' efforts to exercise rudimentary motor skills may contribute to the organization of more voluntary motor behaviors. Also, the child's acquisition of locomotion skills provokes reactions from caregivers. The child's activity in general undoubtedly contributes to further improvements in motor skills.

Are physical growth and motor skill development continuous or stagelike? Spurts in physical development often give rise to conceptions of stagelike development. But even dramatic changes such as those during puberty are grounded in prior continuous changes.

Are there sensitive periods in physical growth and motor skill development? Brain development exhibits sensitive periods for the processing of certain kinds of information.

How do physical growth and motor skills interact with other domains of development? A child's size and improvement in motor skills dramatically influence the responses and expectations of caregivers, peers, and others. Similarly, the young adolescent's status with peers is often influenced by physical growth, coordination, and skill.

Key Terms Review

1. Organs, systems, and motor movements near the head tend to develop earlier than those near the feet. This is the principle of _____ development.

2. The hormone produced by the ovaries that helps to prepare the uterus for implantation of the zygote is _____ .

3. The _____ is the outer, largest portion of the brain that undergoes rapid differentiation during the last few months of prenatal development and the first few years of life.

4. During _____ the individual is transformed from a state of immaturity to one who is capable of reproduction.

5. An increase in the rate of growth of an individual following a period of illness or poor nutrition is referred to as _____ .

6. _____ is a condition in which a child fails to grow at a normal rate due to an emotionally inadequate environment.

7. The hormone _____ , which is produced by the ovaries, contributes to pubertal changes and helps prepare the uterus for implantation of a zygote.

8. A condition in which growth in height or weight is substantially below normal and is associated with inadequate social-emotional relationships with caregivers is called _____ .

9. _____ cells within the brain form myelin and help protect and nourish neurons.

10. In most individuals the left hemisphere is more involved with language processing and the right hemisphere is more involved in spatial information. This describes the concept of _____ .

11. _____ is the first occurrence of menstruation.

12. In order to insulate and speed neural impulses, a sheath of fatty cells called _____ surrounds some neurons.

13. _____ are cells in the nervous system that transmit information to other cells through an electrochemical process.

14. Hormones affecting physical growth and development are released by a structure located near the hypothalamus called the _____ .

15. Organs and systems of the body near the middle develop earlier than those in the periphery. This pattern of growth describes _____ development.

16. Repeated movements such as leg kicking and hand waving that seem to have no apparent goal are referred to as _____ .

17. The _____ refers to the consistent pattern of change that is observed over generations, such as increasing height and earlier onset of sexual maturity.

18. The extent to which cartilage has ossified to form bone provides an accurate measure of _____ .

19. A(n) _____ is a measure of average values and variations in some aspect of development in relation to age.

20. The sudden, unexplained death of an infant as a result of failure to continue breathing during sleep is called _____ .

21. _____ reflexes are associated with maintaining a particular, usually upright, orientation; these reflexes disappear or become incorporated into voluntary behavior.

22. _____ reflexes are identified with survival and protection of the individual; these reflexes usually disappear during the first year of life.

23. _____ growth is a condition in which, after periods of rapid acceleration because of congenital or hormonal disorders, growth is slowed so that subsequent increases in height conform to those normally expected for the individual.

24. The capacity of immature systems to take on different functions as a result of experience is called _____ .

25. The testes of the male produce the hormone _____ , which contributes to fetal sex differentiation and also triggers the emergence of puberty changes.

26. _____ are involuntary movements in response to touch, light, sound, and other forms of stimulation. They are controlled by subcortical neural mechanisms.

Answers to Key Terms Review

1. cephalocaudal
2. progesterone
3. cerebral cortex
4. puberty
5. catch-up growth
6. Deprivation dwarfism
7. estrogen
8. failure to thrive
9. Glial
10. lateralization
11. Menarche
12. myelin
13. Neurons
14. pituitary gland
15. proximodistal
16. rhythmical stereotypes
17. secular trend
18. skeletal maturity
19. norm
20. sudden infant death syndrome (SIDS)
21. Postural
22. Primitive
23. Lagging-down
24. plasticity
25. testosterone
26. Reflexes

Multiple-Choice Questions

Fact and Concept Questions

1. The broad term that describes the changes in physical size of the body, accompanying orderly patterns, and increasingly complicated levels of functioning is
   a. growth.
   b. development.
   c. evolution.
   d. maturity.

2. An adolescent growth spurt occurs
   a. only in children deprived of adequate nutrition during childhood.
   b. in boys approximately four years before it occurs in girls.
   c. in boys approximately two years before it occurs in girls.
   d. in girls approximately two years before it occurs in boys.

3. Physical growth trends observed in many parts of the body
   a. are primarily cephalocaudal.
   b. are primarily proximodistal.
   c. are either cephalocaudal or proximodistal.
   d. do not always conform to cephalocaudal or proximodistal principles.

4. Cross-cultural studies on physical growth show that
   a. there is great variability in the rate of growth among individuals but not between groups.
   b. there is great variability in the rate of growth between groups but not among individuals within a group.
   c. there is great variability in the rate of growth among individuals and between groups.
   d. great variability in the rate of growth among individuals occurs only in some groups.

5. The scientific standard for determining physical maturity is
   a. skeletal age.
   b. individual size.
   c. onset of the growth spurt.
   d. onset of puberty.

6. The first menstrual period is called
   a. puberty.
   b. ovulation.
   c. menarche.
   d. spontaneous ejaculation.

7. Researchers have theorized that the brain area that serves as a "growth center" is the
   a. adrenal gland.
   b. hypothalamus.
   c. marasmus.
   d. hindbrain.

8. Human growth hormone promotes growth by
   a. directly stimulating bones to grow.
   b. stimulating the hypothalamus to release several growth-related hormones.
   c. stimulating the liver to release the hormone somatomedin.
   d. stimulating the release of insulinlike growth factor from the brain.

9. Studies on the effects of nutrition on the developing individual have indicated that the nutritional environment
   a. if substantially inadequate may have negative influences on children's physical growth, but adequate nutrition has minimal positive influences.
   b. if adequate may have positive influences on children's physical growth, but if substantially inadequate it has surprisingly minimal negative influence.
   c. may exert negative (if inadequate) or positive (if adequate) influences on children's physical growth.
   d. has little effect on children's physical growth, indicating the resilience of the developing child.

10. A sufferer of failure to thrive syndrome is defined as any
    a. premature infant.
    b. stillborn infant.
    c. child whose growth is slightly below the norm for that child's age group.
    d. child whose growth is substantially below the norm for that child's age group.

11. Nonorganic failure to thrive syndrome is
    a. probably initiated or further aggravated by the caregiver's interaction with the child.
    b. caused primarily by the genetic makeup or characteristics of the child.
    c. characterized by stunted growth in otherwise perfectly normal children.
    d. caused by endocrine or gastrointestinal illness in many cases.

12. The tendency of each new generation to experience puberty earlier than the preceding one is called
    a. menarche.
    b. catch-up growth.
    c. secular trend.
    d. skeletal maturity.

13. Studies show that mothers of small children perceive taller boys as _____ than smaller boys.
    a. more competent
    b. less competent
    c. more aggressive
    d. less aggressive

14. Neuron proliferation and migration occur
    a. prenatally.
    b. postnatally.
    c. prenatally and postnatally.
    d. throughout the entire lifetime of an individual.

15. Research on the development of the visual system in cats indicates that
    a. differentiation of the visual system proceeds with little influence from sensory stimulation.
    b. sensory experience guides the differentiation of the visual system.
    c. the visual system is fully developed at birth.
    d. neural differentiation will proceed only when sensory stimulation is provided.

16. The form of plasticity that is sensitive to experience-expectant information
    a. can occur throughout an individual's lifetime.
    b. can occur only during sensitive or critical periods.
    c. can occur prenatally but not postnatally.
    d. is more likely to occur after five years of life than during the first five years of life.

17. The concept of _____ is illustrated by the fact that in most individuals language is dominated by one of the two hemispheres.
    a. plasticity
    b. sensitive periods
    c. neuron differentiation
    d. lateralization

18. The sucking reflex in infants is
    a. involuntary and cannot be modified by experience.
    b. initially involuntary but can be modified by experience.
    c. really not a reflex but the earliest type of voluntary behavior.
    d. one of the most important postural reflexes.

19. The text suggests that rhythmical stereotypes
    a. may eventually become recruited and integrated into voluntary actions.
    b. are caused by brain damage that results from a significant period of anoxia during birth.
    c. increase the chances of learning disabilities later in childhood.
    d. may significantly delay the appearance of some major motor milestones.

20. Cross-cultural studies have found that
    a. children in many cultures achieve milestones at similar ages, but the order of milestones achieved may differ.
    b. children in all cultures achieve milestones in the same order and at the same ages.
    c. children in many cultures achieve milestones at different ages and may differ in the order of the milestones achieved.
    d. motor milestones are achieved at similar ages and in consistent order in many cultures.

Application Questions

1. Kristie and Peter, who have been close friends since they were toddlers, are now celebrating their tenth birthday together. Although they are equal in height and weight, it is likely that in the next few years Kristie will
    a. grow taller and heavier than Peter.
    b. grow taller but not heavier than Peter.
    c. be shorter and not as heavy as Peter.
    d. continue to grow at the same rate as Peter.

2. Eleven-year-old Stuart broke his wrist when he fell off a bicycle. While examining the x-rays of the broken wrist, the doctor noticed that a considerable amount of Stuart's bones had not yet ossified. This means that
    a. the injury was more serious than originally believed.
    b. Stuart should expect to show considerably more physical growth.
    c. Stuart will probably be shorter than most children his age.
    d. Stuart is most likely suffering from a serious bone disorder.

3. Manuela has just experienced her first menstrual period. This means that she is
    a. sexually mature and capable of reproduction.
    b. sexually mature but is not necessarily capable of reproduction.
    c. capable of reproduction but is not yet sexually mature.
    d. not necessarily sexually mature or capable of reproduction.

4. Rachel was normal size at birth, but grew to be only four and a half feet tall. It is likely that Rachel's
    a. pituitary gland does not produce enough HGH.
    b. adrenal gland does not produce enough HGH.
    c. pituitary gland produces excess levels of HGH.
    d. adrenal gland produces excess levels of HGH.

5. Leslie has always been extremely concerned about her weight and is now very thin and reporting that she is no longer having menstrual periods. Leslie is most likely suffering from
   a. bulimia nervosa
   b. anorexia nervosa.
   c. cancer.
   d. failure to thrive syndrome.

6. Although he is a college sophomore, Jason often displays childish, attention-getting behavior, which often disrupts his relationship with his professors and his peers. Jason may have
   a. been a late-maturing child.
   b. been an early maturing child.
   c. been a child who matured within the normal age range.
   d. not yet matured.

7. Luther is a newborn. His brain will increase in size over the next two years as a result of an increase in
   a. the number of neurons.
   b. the size and complexity of neurons.
   c. the size of glial cells.
   d. the number and size of neurons.

8. Marya, an excellent student, is often impressed by the amount of new information that she can retain in order to do well in her classes. This remarkable capability would not be possible if it were not for the brain's ability to be sensitive to
   a. critical periods.
   b. experience-expectant information.
   c. experience-dependent information.
   d. experience-independent information.

9. Cal is holding a pail with one hand and using the other hand to fill it with sand. In order to perform this task, Cal must have developed
   a. neat pincer grasp.
   b. functional asymmetry.
   c. ballistic reaches.
   d. prereaching.

10. Elissa is a toddler. She is likely to engage in play such as
    a. pulling and pushing things.
    b. coloring and drawing.
    c. cutting and pasting.
    d. sculpting with clay.

Answers to Multiple-Choice Questions

The correct answer appears first and is preceded by an asterisk.

Answers to Fact and Concept Questions

1. *b. *Development* is a general term describing broad changes in body size, pattern of growth, and functional complexity of the growing individual. (p. 181)
   a. *Growth* refers specifically to the increase in the physical size of the body.
   c. *Evolution* describes changes in the physical characteristics of individuals that occur across generations.
   d. *Maturity* describes the state or quality of being fully grown; it does not describe the broad changes that occur during growth.

2. *d. Although the age of onset of the growth spurt varies a great deal among individuals, it usually occurs approximately two years earlier in girls. (p. 182)
   a. A growth spurt is a normal process of development and occurs in all healthy adolescents.
   b. In general, the growth spurt occurs earlier in girls.
   c. In general, the growth spurt occurs earlier in girls.

3. *d. Not all physical growth patterns conform to the cephalocaudal and proximodistal principles of development. (p. 184)
   a. Although some growth trends are cephalocaudal, this pattern of growth does not dominate physical development.
   b. Although some growth trends are proximodistal, this pattern of growth does not dominate physical development.
   c. Although both cephalocaudal and proximodistal development do occur, they are not the only patterns of development that are observed.

4. *c. The many biological and environmental influences on physical development contribute to the variability in growth seen between groups and among individuals within a group. (p. 186)
   a. There is considerable variability between groups as a result of cultural and possible biological differences.
   b. All groups show variability in growth among their members.
   d. All groups show variability in growth among their members.

5. *a. Skeletal age, the extent to which cartilage has ossified, is an excellent index of maturity. (p. 188)
   b. The large variability in individual size makes it a poor indicator of maturity.
   c. Although the growth spurt is an indicator of maturity, it is also quite variable and, therefore, is not the scientific standard for physical maturity.
   d. The onset of puberty varies enormously from one individual to another and, therefore, is a poor indicator of physical maturity.

6. *c. Menarche, or the first menstrual period, is one of the indicators of sexual maturity in females. (p. 189)
   a. Puberty refers to a series of physical changes that occur during the adolescent years; one of these changes in females is the first menstrual period.
   b. Ovulation refers to the release of an egg during the middle of the menstrual cycle.
   d. Spontaneous ejaculation is an indicator of sexual maturity in males.

7. *b. The hypothalamus is located at the base of the brain and is believed to monitor and regulate physical growth. (p. 191)
   a. The adrenal gland releases hormones that influence growth, but it is not part of the brain.
   c. Marasmus is a disease that results from malnutrition; it is not a brain structure.
   d. The hindbrain is a brain area necessary for important survival functions, but it is not the area of the brain believed to be a "growth center."

8. *c. Human growth hormone stimulates bone growth indirectly by activating the release of somatomedin from the liver. (p. 191)
   a. Although human growth hormone promotes bone growth it does not do so by directly stimulating the bones.
   b. The hypothalamus causes human growth hormone to be released, but it does not release growth hormones in response to human growth hormone.
   d. Human growth hormone does not stimulate the release of insulinlike growth factor.

9. *c. Studies show that malnutrition can have a substantial negative impact and that dietary supplements can have a positive influence on children's physical growth. (p. 192)
   a. The nutritional environment can have a negative or positive influence on the developing individual's physical growth.
   b. The nutritional environment can have a negative or positive influence on the developing individual's physical growth.
   d. Studies on nutrition and physical growth show that malnutrition can have a substantial negative impact and that dietary supplements can have a positive influence on children's physical growth.

10. *d. A child who is *substantially* below the norm is perceived as having failure to thrive syndrome. (p. 193)
    a. The premature infant is immature and small in size because of an early birth, not as a result of failure to thrive syndrome.
    b. A stillborn infant is dead at birth; this is not the failure to thrive syndrome.
    c. There is great variability in growth among individuals; a child who is below the norm does not necessarily have the failure to thrive syndrome.

11. *a. Studies suggest that failure to thrive is most likely a result of the caregiver's misperceptions of the child's behavior, indifference, and less positive interactions with the child. (p. 194)

b. Although failure to thrive syndrome may be partly a result of the child's genetic makeup, the condition is most likely a result of how the caregiver responds to the child.

c. Infants with failure to thrive syndrome are not normal in many respects, including physical growth and responsiveness to stimulation.

d. By definition, failure to thrive syndrome describes cases where no specific organic or other cause can be identified.

12. *c. The earlier onset of maturity and greater height seen among children relative to their parents reflects a pattern of change in the environment that occurs over generations called secular trend. (p. 195)

a. Menarche is the first menstrual period, which marks the onset of maturity in girls.

b. Catch-up growth describes the increase in growth seen in an individual following a period of disrupted growth.

d. Skeletal maturity is a measure of how much additional growth will occur in a developing individual.

13. *a. Mothers perceive taller boys as better able to get along with others and less likely to cry when frustrated. (p. 196)

b. Mothers tend to treat smaller boys as younger (and therefore less competent) than taller boys the same age.

c. Although there may be reason to believe that taller boys are perceived as more aggressive than smaller boys, the studies cited in the text did not describe any results on perceived aggression.

d. The studies cited in the text did not describe any results on perceived aggression.

14. *a. Neuron proliferation refers to the growth of new nerve cells; neuron migration refers to the movement of neurons to other locations. Both of these processes occur prenatally. (p. 204)

b. Neuron proliferation ends approximately one to two months before birth and therefore does not occur postnatally.

c. Neuron proliferation ends approximately one to two months before birth and therefore does not occur postnatally.

d. Neuron proliferation is complete by the first to second month before birth.

15. *b. During the neural differentiation process, the specific visual experiences of a kitten produce neurons that are more selective and tuned to specific kinds of visual stimulation. (p. 205)

a. The neuron differentiation process is strongly influenced by the developing individual's sensory experience.

c. Although all of the neurons of the visual system are present at birth, the visual system is not fully developed, since the differentiation process continues after birth.

d. The visual system will develop even in the absence of sensory stimulation, but the differentiation process will not be influenced by various kinds of environmental stimuli.

16. *b. This form of plasticity occurs during critical periods when the neurons are expected to receive a certain kind of information that is important to their functioning. (p. 206)
   a. Neurons are sensitive to experience-expectant information during critical periods and thus plasticity cannot occur throughout an individual's lifetime.
   c. Most of the experience that shapes the developing brain occurs postnatally.
   d. Plasticity is most evident in the nervous system of infants and very young children.

17. *d. The process of one hemisphere dominating the other in terms of a particular function is called lateralization. (p. 207)
   a. Plasticity refers to changes in brain function that result from experience or damage to other brain structures. Hemispheric dominance is not an example of plasticity.
   b. Some forms of plasticity occur during sensitive periods. Hemispheric dominance is not an example of a sensitive period.
   c. Although neuron differentiation is necessary for the hemispheres to develop their particular function, hemispheric dominance is not an example of neuron differentiation.

18. *b. Studies show that infants can learn to modify different components of the sucking reflex. (p. 211)
   a. The sucking response in newborns is reflexive, but studies show that infants can learn to modify this behavior.
   c. Sucking is a primitive reflex that ensures intake of potential nutrients, but with experience a child gains voluntary control of this behavior.
   d. Sucking is a primitive reflex, not a postural reflex.

19. *a. Although rhythmical stereotypes have no apparent goal, they can be recruited and integrated into more complex voluntary behavior. (p. 213)
   b. Rhythmical stereotypes are seen in all normally developing infants; they are not a sign of pathology.
   c. Rhythmical stereotypes are seen in all normally developing infants; they are not a sign of future behavioral difficulties.
   d. Rhythmical stereotypes are seen in all normally developing infants; they do not produce delays in motor development.

20. *d. Although individual differences exist, children in many cultures achieve milestones at similar ages and in a consistent order. (p. 218)
   a. The ages at which motor milestones are achieved differ among some cultures, but the order of motor milestones achieved is similar across cultures.
   b. The order of the motor milestones achieved is consistent across cultures, but the ages that they are achieved may differ, depending on cultural and social influences.
   c. The ages at which motor milestones are achieved differ among some cultures, but the order of motor milestones achieved is similar across cultures.

Answers to Application Questions

1. *a. The growth spurt occurs approximately two years earlier in girls, so Kristie is likely to grow taller and heavier than Peter. (p. 186)
   b. The growth spurt, which occurs earlier in girls, includes increases in height and weight.
   c. Although adult males tend to be taller and heavier than adult females, adolescent girls are often taller than adolescent boys because of the girls' earlier growth spurt.
   d. The earlier growth spurt usually seen in girls is likely to make Kristie taller and heavier than Peter during the next few years.

2. *b. Incomplete ossification indicates that the bones are still increasing in size; therefore, Stuart should expect to continue to grow. (p. 188)
   a. Incomplete ossification of bones in children is not a sign of pathology but an indication that the bones are still growing.
   c. Incomplete ossification indicates further growth. Since Stuart is still growing, we really can't determine whether he will be shorter than most children his age.
   d. Incomplete ossification of bones in children is not a sign of pathology but an indication that the child is still growing.

3. *b. Although Manuela is sexually mature, she is not necessarily capable of reproduction because the first ovulation may not occur until up to one and a half years after the first menstrual period. (p. 189)
   a. Although Manuela is sexually mature, she is not necessarily capable of reproduction because the first ovulation may not occur until up to one and a half years after the first menstrual period.
   c. To be capable of reproduction a female must be sexually mature.
   d. Sexual maturity is indicated by the first menstrual period (menarche); therefore, Manuela would be considered sexually mature.

4. *a. Rachel's stunted growth is most likely a result of the pituitary gland's failure to produce HGH. (p. 191)
   b. It is the pituitary gland, not the adrenal gland, that produces HGH.
   c. Reduced levels—not excess levels—of HGH stunt growth.
   d. It is the pituitary gland, not the adrenal gland, that produces HGH.

5. *b. Anorexia nervosa is a self-imposed form of starvation in which the individual becomes dangerously thin and may have disrupted menstrual periods. (p. 199)
   a. Although bulimia nervosa is an eating disorder, individuals suffering from this disorder appear to be normal in weight.
   c. Although an individual suffering from cancer may be extremely thin and may have disrupted menstrual periods, the fact that Leslie was always extremely concerned about her weight suggests that she is suffering from an eating disorder.
   d. Failure to thrive is a term applied to young children who are extremely low in weight.

6. *a. Late-maturing boys tend to report more negative feelings about themselves and tend to display more attention-getting behavior. (p. 201)
   b. Early maturity enhances status and self-confidence in boys; they are, therefore, less likely to display childish, attention-getting behavior.
   c. It is the late-maturing boys who are more likely to display childish, attention-getting behavior.
   d. Boys mature between nine and seventeen years of age; therefore, it is unlikely that Jason has not yet matured.

7. *b. Postnatal brain growth is largely a result of an increase in the size of neurons and complexity of connections between neurons. (p. 204)
   a. Neuron proliferation stops approximately one to two months before birth; therefore, postnatal brain growth cannot be due to an increase in the number of neurons.
   c. Postnatal brain growth is largely a result of an increase in the size and complexity of neurons, not glial cells.
   d. Postnatal brain growth results from an increase in neuron size, not in neuron number.

8. *c. An individual is able to learn because the brain is sensitive to experience-dependent information throughout life. (p. 206)
   a. The ability to learn new information does not occur during a critical period but progresses throughout an individual's lifetime.
   b. Individuals are sensitive to experience-expectant information during critical periods. Ability to learn new information is not limited to critical periods.
   d. There is no type of information called experience-independent information.

9. *b. A child who can coordinate both hands to perform a complex task has developed functional asymmetry. (p. 216)
   a. Neat pincer grasp describes the ability to make fine grasping movements with the fingers.
   c. Ballistic reaching describes the ability to retrieve objects in the visual field rapidly and accurately.
   d. Prereaching describes a newborn infant's attempt to reach and make contact with nearby objects.

10. *a. Toddlers are more likely to engage in large-muscle activities such as pulling and pushing things rather than in small-muscle activities. (p. 217)
   b. Toddlers are more likely to engage in large-muscle activities than in small-muscle activities such as coloring and drawing.
   c. Toddlers are more likely to engage in large-muscle activities than in small-muscle activities such as cutting and pasting.
   d. Toddlers are more likely to engage in large-muscle activities than in small-muscle activities such as sculpting with clay.

CHAPTER 6

LEARNING AND PERCEPTION

LEARNING OBJECTIVES

1. Explain the basic learning processes present in infancy, including classical and operant conditioning, imitation, and habituation. (pp. 228–233)

2. Discuss the social and cultural context of learning, particularly the process of scaffolding. (pp. 233–235)

3. Describe the roles of caregivers and teachers as models for learning. (pp. 235–236)

4. Discuss the debate concerning when children should learn to read. (pp. 236–237)

5. List and describe the methods used to study infant sensory and perceptual capacities. (pp. 237–241)

6. Describe and discuss infant visuomotor skills. (pp. 241–244)

7. Describe infant visual perception capacities, including depth perception, pattern and form perception, and object perception. (pp. 244–250)

8. Describe and discuss infant auditory capacities such as sound perception, musical pattern perception, and speech perception. (pp. 250–254)

9. Describe the perceptual capacities of smell, taste, and the cutaneous senses. (pp. 254–258)

10. Discuss the coordination of sensory and perceptual information from two senses, such as audition and vision, and vision and touch. (pp. 258–261)

11. Describe perceptual process development in childhood, particularly how part-whole perception and attention develop. (pp. 261–265)

12. Explain how environmental experience can have serious effects on perceptual development. (pp. 265–268)

CHAPTER OUTLINE

I. **LEARNING IN INFANCY AND CHILDHOOD** (pp. 228–237)
Learning is usually defined as a way of acquiring new skills and behaviors from experience. This process permits continual adaptation to a changing environment, increases survival, and helps the individual solve problems encountered in the environment. Learning stresses the "nurture" side of the nature-nurture theme because it is concerned with how experience affects the individual, but the text also explains how biology can set limits on what the child can or cannot learn.

A. **Basic Learning Processes in Infancy** (pp. 228–232)
Developmental psychologists have found evidence for a number of basic learning processes in early infancy. In classical conditioning a neutral stimulus, called the *conditioned stimulus (CS)*, becomes associated with a stimulus that spontaneously elicits an inborn response. It is the *unconditioned stimulus (UCS)* that normally elicits the *unconditioned response (UCR)*. Following a number of pairings of the CS with the UCS, the CS alone will come to elicit a response similar to the UCR. The response that is elicited by the CS alone is called the *conditioned response (CR)*. For example, touching the infant's cheek (UCS) will elicit a head turn (UCR). If music is played each time the infant's cheek is touched, the infant will turn her head in response to music alone. The music is the CS that comes to elicit the head turn, the CR. Infants as young as two hours have been shown to exhibit classical conditioning. Newborn infants' limited behaviors, however, restrict the CRs they can learn. They easily learn CRs to feeding stimuli, but not to aversive stimuli, which would require defensive behaviors.

Operant conditioning involves changes in behavior as a result of the positive or negative consequences that follow the behavior. In general, behaviors increase in frequency when followed by a *positive reinforcement* or by the removal of an aversive stimulus (*negative reinforcement*). Behaviors decrease in frequency when they are followed by absence of rewards or the presentation of an aversive event, a *punishment*. Experimental evidence also exists for operant conditioning in newborns within a few hours of birth.

Imitation is the process whereby infants will repeat a response that another individual, the model, has made. Some researchers have reported that one- or two-day-old newborns can imitate facial expressions. Other psychologists have questioned whether the infants' behaviors are true imitations or biologically programmed responses to any external stimulation. During the second six months of life, infants show that they can imitate a wide variety of modeled behavior, and they become much more precise in their imitative abilities. Beginning around eighteen to twenty-four months of age, the infant demonstrates *deferred imitation*—the ability to imitate a model's behavior hours, days, or even weeks later. Thus, infants and children appear able to acquire many behaviors by watching others.

Habituation is the gradual decline in responding following repeated occurrences of the same stimulus. Habituation in infants has adaptive value because the infant can learn to ignore stimuli with little informational value and attend instead to stimuli that provide new information. Once habituated to a stimulus, the infant will respond to any observable change in the stimulus. This process is called *recovery from habituation* (sometimes referred to as *dishabituation*). Recovery from habituation can be used to discover the sensory capacities of the infant. Nearly all infants demonstrate habituation, but premature, brain-damaged, and younger infants show less rapid habituation and less rapid recovery from habituation than older, more mature infants.

B. **Learning Throughout Childhood** (pp. 233–236)
The increasing richness and complexity of the child's behaviors is partly a result of the parents' direct manipulation of reinforcers in order to promote desired behaviors in their children. Children respond by increasing their socially desirable behaviors, such as chores and self-care. Observational learning becomes an important way for children to learn. Much of what children have to learn is culturally prescribed. Initially, parents and teachers provide culturally specific and general problem-solving information to children.

Vygotsky's concept of social activity highlights this view. He suggests that a child's knowledge is cultivated by formal and informal interactions with caregivers, peers, and tutors, who convey all the knowledge a culture has accumulated. One way this difficult job is accomplished is by *scaffolding*. A scaffold provides external support for the child by offering skills and techniques in which the child is deficient. As the child's abilities increase, the scaffold is slowly removed. The *zone of proximal development*, a key concept of Vygotsky's theory of development, stresses that the most effective help the child can receive from an expert is that which is just slightly beyond the child's capacities, thereby building on the child's current level of competence. Both teachers and parents provide the child with this expert assistance.

Controversy: When Should Children Learn to Read? (pp. 236–237)
Most children do not learn to read until they are five or six years old, when they enter a formal schooling program. Critics such as Glen Doman of the Better Baby Institute suggest that children should be taught to read at age two or three so they will have an advantage when they get to school. The controversy surrounds the deleterious effects this push for early reading performance may have on the very young child. In most cases toddlers do not have the physical or perceptual skills required for sustained attention to the printed words. If they experience frustration and lack of progress on these premature attempts at reading, they may learn that reading is an unpleasant

activity rather than an enjoyable one. For this reason most psychologists and reading specialists encourage parents to promote reading by reading to their young children and making books and reading a familiar, interactive, and enjoyable activity for the preschool child.

II. **SENSORY AND PERCEPTUAL CAPACITIES IN INFANTS** (pp. 237–261)
Psychologists distinguish between *sensation*, the registration of basic information such as sights or sounds by the sensory receptors and the brain, and *perception*, the organization and interpretation of sensations. Developmental psychologists are interested in studying the sensory and perceptual capacities of the young child, particularly infants, in order to determine the earliest appearance of these abilities.

A. **Studying Infant Sensory and Perceptual Capacities** (pp. 238–241)
Most of the techniques that researchers have developed to study infant sensation and perception involve measures of *attention*. Attention is the alertness or arousal that is focused on a selected aspect of the environment. Infants will display attentional differences as a function of the differences among stimuli that they can perceive in the environment. Initially, studies explored preferential looking behaviors in infants. In this situation the infant is shown two stimuli simultaneously and the experimenter records the amount of time the infant looks at each stimulus. These studies revealed that infants prefer complex visual patterns such as faces or bull's eye patterns over solid-colored circles. The limitation of this procedure is that in the absence of a measurable preference it is unclear whether infants cannot perceive the difference between the stimuli or if they simply have no preference for one over the other.

Another technique involves *habituation*, the decrement in responding to repeated stimulation. The logic of this procedure for studying infant perception is that infants presented with the same stimulus for repeated trials will decrease their attention to that stimulus. If the stimulus is then changed in some way, and the infant can perceive the change, then the infant will demonstrate recovery from habituation—that is, renew his attention to the altered stimulus.

Operant conditioning procedures have also been employed to study infant perception. Infants are rewarded with food or other pleasant events for the production of a response, such as sucking or head turning, in the presence of a particular stimulus.

Other procedures, such as those utilizing physiological responses like heart rate or neurological brain activity, have also been used to examine the sensory and perceptual abilities of infants.

B. **How Vision Develops** (pp. 241–250)
More than just a passive receiver of sensory information, the human infant is an active perceiver of the visual information in the environment. Developmental psychologists have spent much of their time investigating the visuomotor skills of the infant. In order to see clearly, the lens of the eye must refract, or bend, the light that enters the eye and

project that light onto the retina, the surface at the back of the eye that contains the sensory receptors for light.

Accommodation is the process whereby the lens changes its shape so that objects at different distances from the eye can be brought into focus on the retina. Newborns have fairly good accommodation for objects located approximately eight to twenty inches away.

Saccades, the rapid movements of the eye for inspection of objects or viewing in the periphery, occur immediately after birth. However, the newborn's saccadic eye movements are slow and range over small distances. By one month infants' saccades are similar to those of adults. *Smooth visual pursuit* consists of following a slowly moving target with smooth, continuous movements of the eyes. Infants younger than two months do not show reliable *vergence* (the rotation of the eyes to focus on withdrawing and approaching objects), but by three months they demonstrate this skill more reliably. How well an infant can see is the question answered by measures of *visual acuity*, which is the ability to make discriminations between contours, borders, and edges in the visual array.

The Snellen chart visual acuity is measured in older children and adults. Procedures that rely on preferential looking have been primarily used to measure infants' visual acuity. If the infant prefers one pattern of wider black and white stripes over a pattern of narrower stripes, the conclusion would be that the infant cannot perceive the narrower stripes and see instead an uninteresting gray field. In this way the exact width of stripe that the infant can discriminate can be determined, providing a measure of visual acuity. Visual acuity improves rapidly in the first six months after birth.

Brightness contrast, the difference in brightness of light and dark contours, is another ability that improves rapidly and reaches adultlike levels by six months.

By two months of age, and possibly before, infants possess color vision. The retina contains rods and cones, the two types of receptor cells for light energy. Rods are sensitive to intensity of light, whereas cones are sensitive to wavelengths of light that are responsible for color perception.

Interpreting depth. The ability to perceive depth is partly a result of binocular vision, the reception of slightly different visual input by the two eyes. The synthesis of these two images into a single three-dimensional percept is called *stereopsis*. Depth perception is also made possible by *kinetic cues* that come from eye movements, head or body movements, and movement of objects in the environment. Studies using the *visual cliff* have found that infants who are able to crawl will not crawl from the shallow to the deep side of the cliff. These results suggest that infants two to three months old can detect the cues from the deep side of the visual cliff that signal depth. At five to seven months, infants appear able to detect pictorial depth cues (which can be perceived by one eye) such as relative size, shadows, interposition of surfaces, and linear perspective. It is not certain whether the perception of these cues is innate or very quickly learned.

Interpreting patterns and form. Most psychologists believe that infants construct perceptions of integrated, holistic, and meaningful visual figures through repeated experience with contours, angles, and shading. There is some evidence, however, that visual information processing in infants under two months of age is governed by basic responses of the visual system to relatively simple elements such as contours, angles, and motion. After two months of age, scanning becomes more systematic. The *externality effect* refers to the fact that infants less than two months old tend to look at only the outer contours of a complex stimulus. Older infants, however, will scan the internal features of a complex stimulus, thereby processing the entire pattern. The recognition of "subjective" contours is another source of evidence that by three to four months of age, infants perceive patterns, not isolated angles or features. The face is a visual pattern that is obviously important to the infant. By two months of age, infants appear able to distinguish and prefer a pattern whose features are organized into a face rather than scrambled. By three months of age, infants can discriminate their mothers from strangers, as well as discriminating facial expressions such as sad, angry, and happy.

Interpreting objects. How does the infant distinguish one object from another even when many objects can be found in contact with one another? The use of kinetic cues are helpful in identifying objects. Four-month-olds, but not newborns, will perceive a partially occluded object as a unified whole, if the visible pieces of the object are seen moving together. Kinetic cues are also used in the perception of biological motion. When a pattern of lights is programmed to simulate a person walking, five-month-olds, but not three-month-olds, react to a greater degree when the display is changed to one in which the pattern of lights no longer resembles a person walking.

C. How Hearing Develops (pp. 250–254)

Babies begin responding to sound stimuli several weeks before birth. Remarkably, newborns prefer sounds they heard prenatally. In one study, pregnant women read aloud a passage of *The Cat in the Hat*. After birth, their newborn infants were willing to suck on a specially designed pacifier in order to turn on a recording of their mother reading the same passage. Prenatal familiarity helps to explain why newborns prefer to listen to a recording of their mother rather than to a stranger speaking. Although infants can detect sound before birth, their hearing improves after birth. By six months, babies can distinguish between high-frequency sounds as well as adults do. The ability to hear low-frequency sounds, however, improves until ten years of age.

Newborns display *sound localization*, the ability to locate a sound by turning the head or eyes in the direction of the sound; however, they are less precise in locating the position of a noise than children or adults. Infants of two to three months begin to recognize changes in sound patterns, such as the duration of intervals between bursts of sound. Six-month-olds can distinguish more complex rhythms and melodies. The importance of sound pattern perception applies not only to music appreciation but to the phrasing and perception of the sound rhythms that underlie speech.

Understanding speech is an important accomplishment for the infant. It begins in the second half of the first year of life, but researchers have discovered that infants under six months have the perceptual capacities to discriminate the basic distinctive speech sounds called phonemes. Phonemes differ by less than 20/1000th of a second in the onset or transition of a frequency of sound. By six months infants can discriminate among all of the phonemes in any of the hundreds of languages spoken around the world. Theoretical accounts of these findings suggest that either infants are born with a "speech module," an innate capacity to detect and process speech sound, or they make use of general auditory capacities and quickly learn to utilize these auditory abilities in order to process speech sounds.

Evidence for innate speech perception comes from studies that show that even when phonemes are different acoustically, we treat them as the same phoneme. Related support comes from studies on *categorical perception*. Categorical perception occurs when we do not perceive small changes in voice onset time (VOT) of a phoneme such as *ba*, but do detect the change in VOT when it occurs across a category boundary such as *ba* vs. *pa*. Infants as young as one month old demonstrate categorical perception for many speech sounds. Counterevidence to the innate view of speech perception is revealed in findings that monkeys and even chinchillas show categorical speech perception. Moreover, categorical perception occurs with some sounds other than speech.

There appears to be a sensitive period for detection of phonemes. Infants older than eleven to thirteen months seemingly lose the ability to distinguish speech sounds from languages other than the primary language, discriminations they were able to detect when they were younger. Thus, acoustic experience continues to have an impact on speech perception.

D. **How Smell, Taste, and the Cutaneous Senses Develop** (pp. 254–258)
Developmental psychologists have spent less research time investigating smell, taste, and the cutaneous senses, which are the receptors of the skin responsible for detecting touch, pressure, pain, and temperature. Newborns can detect many odors, as measured by their facial expressions to odor stimuli. By five days of age, breast-fed infants will prefer their own mother's breast pad over another mother's breast pad. Extended experience with a particular odor leads to preferences for that odor within forty-eight hours of birth. In addition, reliable sex differences have been observed; at all ages, females are more sensitive to odors than males.

Infants respond to taste stimuli differentially shortly after birth, making a relaxed facial response to sweet, lip pursing to sour, and mouth openings to bitter. Innate taste preferences may help infants meet nutritional needs and avoid harmful substances.

Stimulation of the skin of newborns elicits a variety of reflexes, such as crying in response to painful stimuli. Newborns have difficulty responding to extremes of hot and cold. Regulation of their body temperature is difficult because newborns cannot sweat. They do make some responses to increases in their body temperature by reducing their activity, sleeping, and extending their extremities.

E. **How Intermodal Perception Develops** (pp. 258–261)

Information about the world can be processed from several senses at once. The coordination of information from multiple sensory systems is called *intermodal perception*. According to James and Eleanor Gibson, infants are "amodal" at birth; that is, they may not be able to differentiate stimulation from the different sense organs. As they gain experience, infants and children learn to distinguish between information originating from their various senses. This process is called *perceptual differentiation*. Alternative theoretical perspectives posit that infants can identify separate sensory inputs but must learn (through enrichment, for example) to coordinate the relationships between them. Research has revealed that infants as young as three and a half months old demonstrate intermodal perception. The evidence comes from studies in which infants show a preference to look at a film that matches the audio track being played to them. They will also prefer to look at a film of one parent, a mother or father, when that parent's voice is being played through a speaker. When visual and auditory cues conflict, infants under six months are more likely to attend to auditory cues, but by ten months visual cues strongly influence intermodal perception. Infants also appear able to coordinate vision and touch information. Six-month-olds who manipulate an object with their hand can then recognize the object by visual inspection alone. The evidence is not conclusive regarding the innate or learned coordination of sensory information; there may be some truth to both perspectives.

F. **Drawing Conclusions about Infant Perceptual Development** (p. 261)

Infants appear to possess sophisticated sensory and perceptual systems at birth and shortly after. They are able to detect and discriminate sensory inputs and interpret them. They interpret and organize sensory inputs and coordinate them in ways that are highly similar to the older child and adult.

III. **PERCEPTION IN CHILDHOOD** (pp. 261–268)

Although infants show remarkable perceptual abilities at birth or shortly after, perception does change with further development. Children become faster and more efficient at perceptual discrimination as their attention to features of the environment becomes more focused and organized.

A. **How Perceptual Learning Develops** (pp. 262–263)

Eleanor Gibson's theory of perceptual learning emphasizes three developmental changes: increased specificity in perception, improved attention, and more economical and efficient acquisition of perceptual information. Learning to read, for example, requires attention to new kinds of visual discriminations. Older children are significantly better at selecting identical letterlike figures from variations of the standard figure than are younger children. The younger child is more likely to mistake rotations and reversals of the standard as identical to the standard. Gibson believes that improved perceptual discriminations such as these come from the increased experience with and inspection of letterlike forms that children have as they begin to read and write. This exposure affords the child the opportunity to recognize critical, distinguishing features of such figures.

B. **How Part-Whole Perception Develops** (pp. 264–265)
Preschoolers' perception is frequently influenced by the whole; that is, they have difficulty analyzing objects according to specific features and attributes. This finding may not mean that they can't detect the parts or feature, but it may depend on the complexity of the stimuli. The simpler the stimuli the more likely it is that children as young as three years old report seeing both parts as well as the integrated whole.

C. **How Attention Develops** (p. 265)
As children develop, their attention to aspects of the environment becomes more organized, systematic, and selective. Older children are more likely to explore an unfamiliar object thoroughly and are therefore more likely to recognize it later. In studies with four- and five-year-olds, the five-year-olds were more thorough in visually inspecting pictures of houses that were either identical or discrepant in some way. Five-year-olds were also more systematic is comparing the two houses before deciding if they were identical or different. The increased abilities of older children may be due to cognitive as well as perceptual sophistication.

D. **The Interaction of Experience and Perceptual Development** (pp. 266–268)
Although the child is born with many sensory capacities, research with animals and humans has revealed that experience is very important for maintaining perceptual capacities. Sensory deprivation, for example, has serious detrimental consequences for the developing infant. Infants born with cataracts show a gradual and permanent loss of their ability to discriminate objects over time. There are as well, sensitive periods, such as for binocular vision, during which perceptual capacities may be lost if specific external stimulation is limited. Perception also appears to be influenced by the sociocultural experiences of the child.

IV. **THEMES IN DEVELOPMENT: LEARNING AND PERCEPTION** (pp. 268–270)
What roles do nature and nurture play in learning and perceptual development? The basic mechanisms of learning are ready to influence development at or shortly after birth. Newborns have rudimentary capacities to see, hear, feel, taste, and smell. Sensory and perceptual capacities do, however, improve substantially as a result of maturation and a rich variety of experiences.

How does the sociocultural context influence learning and perceptual development? In all cultures the actions of caregivers and models provide knowledge of what is socially accepted and expected within a community. Specific cultural demands, such as "carpentered environments," may also have considerable bearing on perceptual development.

How does the child play an active role in learning and perceptual development? What the child learns contributes to the kind of interactions he or she will be exposed to and the kinds of opportunities for further learning she or he will have. Gibson's theory highlights the important role that the activity of the child plays in perception and its development.

Are there sensitive periods in learning and perceptual development? Perception of patterns, forms, depth, and perhaps sound, which begins in the first months of life, appears to be heavily dependent on experience. In the absence of some types of stimulation, infants do not acquire or may lose certain perceptual capacities.

How do learning and perceptual development interact with development in other domains? The child learns social skills, labels and acceptable ways to express thoughts and feelings, and numerous other behaviors through the basic principles of learning. Through perceptual development, the child recognizes the stimuli and events that are important for his or her world. And gains in perception throughout infancy and childhood are substantially influenced by physiological and neural advances.

Key Terms Review

1. The visuomotor process by which small, involuntary muscles change the shape of the lens of the eye so that images of objects seen at different distances are brought into focus on the retina is called _____ .

2. _____ is the gradual decline in a response following repeated presentations of the same stimulus.

3. Rapid movements of the eye to inspect an object are called _____ .

4. A(n) _____ is a rewarding stimulus that will strengthen a response when it follows that response.

5. A(n) _____ is a learned response that is exhibited to a previously neutral stimulus as a result of pairing a conditioned stimulus with an unconditioned stimulus.

6. Psychologists have used the _____ to test depth perception by measuring whether infants will cross the surface of a glass-covered table, one of whose sides is made to appear well below the other.

7. We fail to distinguish between sounds that vary on some basic physical dimension except when those sounds lie on opposite sides of a critical juncture point. This process is known as _____ .

8. A(n) _____ is an aversive stimulus that, when removed, serves to strengthen a response.

9. _____ occurs when we perceive a single image of an object even though the perceptual input is binocular and differs slightly for each eye.

10. The ability to imitate a model's behavior hours, days, and even weeks after it has been observed is referred to as _____ .

11. In order to fixate objects at different distances, we must rotate our eyes in opposite directions. This visuomotor ability is called _____ .

12. A(n) _____ is a neutral stimulus that begins to elicit a response similar to the unconditioned stimulus with which it has been paired.

13. _____ refers to the neural receptors' processing of the basic information in the external world.

14. _____ arise from the movement of the eyes, head, or body, or from movement of objects in the environment, and are a source of information about depth.

15. An individual will show _____ , a return of the intensity, frequency, or duration of a response, following a change in the experienced stimulus.

16. _____ decreases the frequency of a response by following the response with an aversive stimulus or the removal of a pleasant stimulus.

17. The _____ is automatically elicited by the unconditioned stimulus.

18. A state of alertness that allows the individual to focus on a selected aspect of the environment is called _____ .

19. Infants younger than two months of age are more likely to focus on the external features of a complex stimulus. This is called the _____ .

20. _____ refers to the ability to coordinate information from more than one sensory modality to perceive an object.

21. _____ is the process of interpreting sensory information as meaningful experiences.

22. The temporary assistance by a person to encourage and support a lesser-skilled person in completing a task or problem is called _____ .

23. _____ is the ability to determine the point of origin of a sound.

24. The consistent, unbroken tracking by the eyes that serves to maintain focus on a moving target is called _____ .

25. A(n) _____ , without prior training, elicits a reflexlike response.

26. _____ is the theoretical process proposed by Eleanor and James Gibson in which experience contributes to the ability to make increasingly finer perceptual discriminations and to distinguish among sensory modalities for the source of the stimulation.

27. The _____ is the range of support and assistance provided by an expert that helps children to carry out activities that they cannot yet complete themselves.

28. The ability to make fine discriminations among features and elements in a visual array is one way of measuring _____ .

Answers to Key Terms Review

1. accommodation
2. Habituation
3. saccades
4. positive reinforcer
5. conditioned response
6. visual cliff
7. categorical perception
8. negative reinforcer
9. Stereopsis
10. deferred imitation
11. vergence
12. conditioned stimulus
13. Sensation
14. Kinetic cues
15. recovery from habituation (or dishabituation)
16. punishment
17. unconditioned response
18. attention
19. externality effect
20. Intermodal perception
21. Perception
22. scaffolding
23. Sound localization
24. smooth visual pursuit
25. unconditioned stimulus
26. Perceptual differentiation
27. zone of proximal development
28. visual acuity

Multiple-Choice Questions

Fact and Concept Questions

1. A stimulus that elicits a response in the absence of any learning is called a(n)
   a. conditioned stimulus.
   b. unconditioned stimulus.
   c. unconditioned response.
   d. unlearned stimulus.

2. The process of _____ involves changes in responding as a function of the positive or negative consequences that follow.
   a. operant conditioning
   b. classical conditioning
   c. habituation
   d. imitation

3. In operant conditioning, negative reinforcement
   a. increases responses by administering desired stimuli.
   b. decreases responses by removing desired stimuli.
   c. increases responses by removing aversive stimuli.
   d. decreases responses by administering aversive stimuli.

4. Infants' ability to imitate facial expressions
   a. does not occur until about one year after birth.
   b. is poor during the first few weeks of life but improves after six months of age.
   c. is very good beginning shortly after birth.
   d. is very good during the first few weeks of life but deteriorates slightly after six months of age.

5. The young child's ability to reproduce a modeled activity after some delay is called
   a. habituation.
   b. scaffolding.
   c. deferred imitation.
   d. operant conditioning.

6. According to Vygotsky, social activity is critical for learning. By this he means that
   a. reinforcement is necessary for learning to occur.
   b. neutral stimuli can come to elicit responses after being paired with stimuli, which reflexively lead to a response.
   c. formal and informal interactions with other people lead to knowledge acquisition.
   d. the absence of social stimulation leads to severe and permanent perceptual deficits.

7. The most effective assistance a child can receive is on a task just slightly ahead of her capacities. This concept is referred to as
   a. social activity.
   b. the externality effect.
   c. categorical learning.
   d. the zone of proximal development.

8. According to most psychologists and reading specialists
   a. preschool reading programs lead to greater success in school and long-lasting literacy benefits.
   b. children learn to read best when they are drilled with flash cards from the time they are infants.
   c. children may suffer a sense of failure and a decrease in their self-esteem if they are forced to read at too early an age.
   d. children rarely show an interest in reading materials prior to formal schooling.

9. _____ is the detection of environmental stimulation via the neural receptors in the sense organs.
   a. Sensation
   b. Perception
   c. Dishabituation
   d. Categorical perception

10. In one research procedure used to study infant perception, infants are given a special nipple that records their sucking rate in response to various stimulations. This procedure is called
    a. imitation.
    b. vergence.
    c. high-amplitude sucking.
    d. classical conditioning.

11. A saccade is
    a. the process of bringing objects at various distances into focus on the retina.
    b. the rapid movement of the eyes to inspect an object or to view a stimulus in the periphery.
    c. fixation on a slowly moving target.
    d. the rotation of the eyes in opposite directions in order to focus on objects as they approach or recede.

12. Research has revealed that by two to three months of age, infants can see color. This is supported by the finding that _____ by this time.
    a. the rods begin to function
    b. the cones begin to function
    c. the retina begins to function
    d. accommodation is well developed

13. The visual cliff has been used to study
    a. depth perception.
    b. color perception.
    c. the externality effect.
    d. pattern and form perception.

14. Visual scanning studies have revealed that
    a. infants under two months of age prefer to visually explore the edges and contours of a complex stimulus.
    b. infants under two months of age prefer to visually explore the internal features of a complex stimulus.
    c. infants over two months of age prefer to visually explore the edges and contours of a complex stimulus.
    d. infants over two months of age show no preferences for any particular part of a complex stimulus.

15. In a study of prenatal auditory abilities, DeCasper and Spence found that
    a. newborns could not discriminate between their mother's voice and their father's voice.
    b. newborns could discriminate between a recording of their mother's voice reading a passage she had read aloud repeatedly during her pregnancy and one she had not read while she was pregnant.
    c. newborns failed to discriminate between a recording of their mother's voice reading a passage she had read aloud repeatedly during her pregnancy and one she had not read while she was pregnant.
    d. newborns could not discriminate between their mother's voice and a stranger's voice.

16. Shortly after birth, infants will turn their head or eyes in the direction of a sound source. This auditory process is called
    a. sound localization.
    b. phonemic localization.
    c. voice onset time discrimination.
    d. sound vergence.

17. Categorical perception is the best evidence for the theoretical perspective that posits that
    a. speech perception requires many years to develop.
    b. there is an innate capacity for speech perception.
    c. infants cannot discriminate between voice onset times.
    d. speech is probably perceived by infants in the same manner as all other auditory stimuli.

18. Within a few days of birth
    a. mothers can identify their own infants on the basis of odor alone.
    b. mothers cannot identify their own infants on the basis of odor alone.
    c. fathers cannot identify their own infants on the basis of odor alone.
    d. males are more sensitive to odors than females.

19. The fact that a baby will turn toward the door to look for her mother when she hears her mother's voice from another room is explained by the process of
    a. dishabituation.
    b. perceptual differentiation.
    c. amodal perception.
    d. intermodal perception.

20. Research with adults and children over six months indicates that
    a. auditory cues dominate visual cues when the two are in conflict.
    b. visual cues dominate auditory cues when the two are in conflict.
    c. neither auditory cues nor visual cues dominate when they are in conflict.
    d. auditory cues dominate visual cues only when the auditory sounds are meaningful to the listener.

Application Questions

1. Each time Trish's mother fed her a bottle, she would sing "Rock-a-Bye Baby" to her. Now, when Trish hears her mother singing "Rock-a-Bye Baby," she starts sucking, even if the bottle is not present. The song is a(n)
    a. positive reinforcer.
    b. unconditioned stimulus.
    c. conditioned stimulus.
    d. conditioned response.

2. Whenever Colin kicked his feet while he was in his crib, his mobile would shake. Colin learned to kick his feet hard to make the mobile shake vigorously. This kind of learning is referred to as
    a. classical conditioning.
    b. operant conditioning.
    c. imitation.
    d. observational learning.

3. When Cassy was brought home from the hospital, the family dog barked, which startled Cassy and made her cry. After hearing the dog bark many times, however, Cassy no longer startles when the dog barks. This illustrates the process of
    a. habituation.
    b. classical conditioning.
    c. operant conditioning.
    d. imitation.

4. Carl, who is nine months old, has been crawling for about a month. When Carl's mother places him on the bed while she is cleaning the floor, Carl crawls to the edge of the bed and most likely will
   a. crawl off the edge of the bed because he has not developed a fear of crawling.
   b. crawl off the edge of the bed even though he may be frightened by the drop.
   c. stop at the edge and not crawl off of the bed because he can perceive the drop and has developed a fear of falling.
   d. stop at the edge, look down, and then continue to crawl because he has not yet developed the binocular perception necessary to perceive the drop to the floor.

5. Matthew is one month old. When he looks at his mother, he most likely looks at her
   a. eyes.
   b. mouth.
   c. smile.
   d. hair.

6. Jessica is three weeks old. When a neighbor comes to visit and picks her up, Jessica begins to cry. When Jessica's mother takes her, she stops crying. It is likely that Jessica can identify her mother because she is familiar with her
   a. facial features.
   b. voice.
   c. hairline.
   d. touch.

7. Peter is four years old. Which of his senses is probably not fully developed?
   a. Vision
   b. Smell
   c. Touch
   d. Hearing

8. When Karen was three weeks old she developed an infection and had to take an oral medication that was somewhat bitter tasting. Karen most likely
   a. took the medicine without problem.
   b. sucked the medicine vigorously.
   c. spit the medicine out.
   d. took the medicine in her mouth and made a facial expression that resembled disgust.

9. Janet is four years old and although she can identify some of the letters of the alphabet, she has trouble distinguishing between *b* and *d*. Most likely Janet
   a. has a learning disability and will always have trouble reading.
   b. will learn to distinguish between reversals of letters with repeated experience.
   c. was not reinforced for distinguishing between reversals of letterlike figures prior to this time.
   d. has a visual perception deficit.

10. Daryl is four and his brother is nine years old. They were both working in an activity book where they had to pick the two pictures out of six that were identical to each other. Daryl is most likely to
   a. be better than his brother at identifying the pair of identical pictures.
   b. be worse than his brother at identifying the pair of identical pictures.
   c. be equal to his brother at identifying the pair of identical pictures.
   d. be better than his brother at first, but then lose interest quickly and become frustrated with the game.

Answers to Multiple-Choice Questions

The correct answer appears first and is preceded by an asterisk.

Answers to Fact and Concept Questions

1. *b. Unconditioned stimuli elicit inborn responses in the absence of any learning. (p. 228)
   a. A conditioned stimulus will produce a response only after it has been paired with an unconditioned stimulus a sufficient number of times.
   c. Unconditioned responses are the behaviors that are elicited by unconditioned stimuli.
   d. *Unlearned stimulus* is not an accepted term for stimuli that elicit inborn responses.

2. *a. In operant conditioning the frequency of behaviors followed by positive consequences increases, while the frequency of behaviors followed by negative consequences decreases. (p. 229)
   b. Although positive events (such as food) and negative events (such as loud noise) are used in classical conditioning, they usually precede, not follow, the behavior that they elicit.
   c. Habituation refers to the decrease in behavior as a result of the repeated presentation of the stimulus that elicits the behavior.
   d. Imitation describes a form of learning that occurs without reinforcement (positive or negative consequences).

3. *c. Negative reinforcement increases responses by removing the aversive stimulus that follows the response. (p. 230)
   a. Desired stimuli that increase the responses they follow are called positive reinforcers.
   b. When behaviors decrease as a result of the removal of desired stimuli, punishment is said to have occurred.
   d. When behaviors decrease as a result of an aversive stimulus, punishment is said to have occurred.

4. *b. Imitations are very fragile and easily disrupted in young infants, but by six
        months of age, they become more frequent and precise. (p. 231)
    a. Some researchers have been able to observe imitation in very young infants.
    c. Imitation is very fragile in very young infants.
    d. Imitations become more frequent and precise beginning at about six months of age.

5. *c. When a child observes a behavior and then repeats the behavior later on, he is
        displaying deferred imitation. (p. 232)
    a. Habituation refers to the decrease in behavior as a result of the repeated
        presentation of the stimulus that elicits the behavior.
    b. Scaffolding describes the temporary support provided by a person to encourage
        further development of skills in a lesser-skilled person.
    d. Operant conditioning requires reinforcement; modeling is learning without
        reinforcement.

6. *c. Vygotsky stressed the importance of interactions with other people for learning.
        (p. 235)
    a. Skinner stressed the importance of reinforcement for learning (operant
        conditioning).
    b. It was Pavlov who discovered how neutral stimuli come to elicit responses
        through classical conditioning.
    d. This statement may be true, but it is not what Vygotsky's theory emphasizes.

7. *d. The zone of proximal development describes support provided by an expert to
        help a nonexpert (such as a child) learn to complete a task that is slightly beyond
        her current ability. (p. 235)
    a. Social activity was emphasized by Vygotsky as an important form of learning.
    b. The externality effect is the tendency of young infants to focus on outer elements
        of complex figures.
    c. Categorical perception involves the ability to perceive categories of speech sounds.

8. *c. Failure to show progress in reading when forced to learn at an early age may
        lead to a decrease in the child's self-esteem and increased reading problems later.
        (p. 237)
    a. There is little evidence that early reading programs lead to greater success in
        school.
    b. There is little evidence that flash card drills are effective. Such drills may give
        parents inappropriate expectations.
    d. Most children show an interest in reading materials such as letters and books
        before formal schooling begins.

9. *a. Sensation is the process by which the receptors detect stimuli in the environment.
        (p. 237)
    b. Perception is the process of organizing and interpreting sensations into
        meaningful experiences.

    c. Dishabituation describes a specific phenomenon whereby a habituated response returns following a change in stimulation.

    d. Categorical perception involves the ability to perceive categories of speech sounds.

10. *c. When reinforced with interesting stimuli such as sounds, high-amplitude sucking can be a very effective tool for studying infant perception. (p. 240)

    a. Imitation is not a research procedure but a form of learning that appears early in development.

    b. Vergence is the ability to rotate the eyes in opposite directions, not a procedure for studying infant perception.

    d. Classical conditioning is a form of learning whereby neutral stimuli come to elicit responses.

11. *b. Saccades are rapid eye movements used to inspect an object or view a stimulus in the periphery. (p. 242)

    a. The process of focusing an image on the retina is called accommodation.

    c. Fixation on a slowly moving object is called smooth visual pursuit.

    d. Vergence describes the rotation of the eyes in opposite directions in response to approaching and receding objects.

12. *b. The cone receptors underlie color vision; they begin to function two to three months after birth. (p. 244)

    a. Rods are not sensitive to color and therefore are not involved in color vision.

    c. The retina contains many types of cells, most of which are already functioning at birth.

    d. Accommodation is important for focusing the image on the retina, but it is not involved in color vision.

13. *a. Visual cliff studies indicate that young infants can perceive depth. (p. 245)

    b. Visual cliff studies have not been used for color perception.

    c. Visual scanning techniques, not the visual cliff apparatus, are used to study the externality effect.

    d. Preferential looking and habituation procedures, not the visual cliff apparatus, have been used to study pattern perception.

14. *a. Very young infants visually explore the external features of a complex figure rather than the inside features. (p. 247)

    b. Very young infants generally do not explore the internal features of a complex stimulus.

    c. Older infants tend to visually explore the internal features of a complex figure.

    d. Older infants prefer to visually explore the internal features of a complex figure.

15. *b. When mothers read *The Cat in the Hat* to their unborn babies, the babies later preferred to hear them read the familiar passage rather than an unfamiliar one. (p. 251)

    a. Studies show that infants can distinguish their mother's voice from other voices.

c. Infants were able to discriminate between the familiar and unfamiliar passages.

d. Studies show that infants can distinguish their mother's voice from other voices.

16. *a. The ability to determine a sound's point of origin, called sound localization, appears to be present shortly after birth. (p. 252)

b. Phonemes are the basic sound units of speech; they are not involved in sound localization.

c. Voice onset times allow the infant to discriminate phonemes.

d. There is no auditory process known as sound vergence.

17. *b. The phenomenon of categorical perception is consistent with the view of an innate capacity for speech perception. (p. 254)

a. Infants as young as one month can discriminate some speech sounds.

c. Infants can discriminate between voice onset times that cross categorical boundaries; this is called categorical perception.

d. The phenomenon of categorical perception is not consistent with a general auditory capacity explanation of speech perception.

18. *a. Mothers as well as other family members can identify their infant by smell alone. (p. 256)

b. Mothers quickly learn to identify their baby by smell alone.

c. Fathers can identify their infant on the basis of smell alone.

d. Evidence suggests that, at all ages, females are more sensitive to odors than are males.

19. *d. Intermodal perception is the ability to coordinate information from at least two senses, which this baby is clearly doing. (p. 258)

a. Dishabituation is the recovery of a response that had undergone habituation; it does not involve the coordination of hearing and vision.

b. The baby is coordinating two separate senses; perceptual differentiation refers to an infant's ability to distinguish between two senses.

c. Amodal perception refers to the inability to differentiate between sensory systems being stimulated; since the baby is coordinating vision and hearing, her perception is clearly not amodal.

20. *b. Research shows that after six months of age, visual cues dominate when they conflict with auditory cues. (p. 260)

a. Visual cues dominate when they are in conflict with auditory cues.

c. When auditory and visual cues conflict, the visual cues dominate.

d. The dominance of visual cues over auditory cues does not depend on the meaning of the stimuli.

Answers to the Application Questions

1. *c. The song was at one time a neutral stimulus, but after repeated pairings with the bottle, it has become a conditioned stimulus. (p. 228)
   a. This scenario describes a classical conditioning procedure. "Positive reinforcer" is an incorrect answer because it is an operant conditioning term, not a term describing classical conditioning.
   b. The unconditioned stimulus is the food in the bottle.
   d. The conditioned response is the sucking elicited by the conditioned stimulus.

2. *b. Operant behaviors are those that, when followed by desired consequence (a positive reinforcer), increase in frequency. A moving mobile appears to be desired by Colin and, therefore, he has learned to kick to get the mobile to move. (p. 230)
   a. In classical conditioning, conditioned and unconditioned stimuli occur *before* the responses. Colin's behavior does not match the behavior elicited by classical conditioning since he is making a response in order to receive stimulation.
   c. Imitation is a form of learning that does not require reinforcement. There is no reason to believe that Colin is imitating someone's behavior.
   d. Observational learning occurs without reinforcers. There is no reason to believe that Colin learned to kick by observing someone else kicking.

3. *a. Habituation is a learning process that involves a gradual decline in a response following repeated presentations of a stimulus. Cassy has become habituated to the dog's barking and is no longer startled by it. (p. 232)
   b. In classical conditioning, responses come to be elicited more frequently by a neutral stimulus that has been paired with an unconditioned stimulus. The dog's bark is not eliciting a response from Cassy any longer; therefore, it has not become a conditioned stimulus.
   c. In operant conditioning, the individual would have to make a response and have that response followed by a reward or the removal of an aversive stimulus in order for the response to increase in frequency. The baby's response was initially a reflexive response to the loud noise and was not followed by any consequences that would lead to an increase in her crying responses.
   d. Imitation involves the observational learning of a model's behavior. Cassy has not learned to imitate the dog's bark.

4. *c. Infants demonstrate the ability to perceive depth shortly after birth and develop a fear of falling once they begin to crawl, so Carl is not likely to crawl off the bed. (p. 245)
   a. Once infants have been crawling for some time, research indicates that they develop a fear of falling. It is not likely Carl will crawl off the edge of the bed because he is capable of perceiving the depth to the floor and is afraid of falling.
   b. Carl is not likely to crawl off the bed, because he has developed a fear of falling.
   d. Binocular depth perception, or stereopsis, develops during the first six months of life. Carl, a nine-month-old, has binocular perception and perceives the depth to the floor from the edge of the bed; therefore, he is not likely to crawl off the bed.

5. *d. The hair or outer contour of the face and head are typically the aspects of a stimulus that a one-month-old is likely to scan; this is referred to as the externality effect. (p. 247)
   a. Eyes are an internal component of the face stimulus; infants under two months of age do not typically scan the internal features of a complex stimulus.
   b. The mouth is an internal component of the face stimulus; infants under two months of age do not typically scan the internal features of a complex stimulus.
   c. The smile is an internal component of the face stimulus; infants under two months of age do not typically scan the internal features of a complex stimulus.

6. *b. It is very likely that Jessica can identify her mother's voice. Infants are able to distinguish their mother's voice from a stranger's almost immediately after birth. (p. 252)
   a. It is not likely that Jessica can identify and recognize her mother by her facial features at this early age because infants under two months of age do not scan the internal features of the face and, therefore, do not recognize faces until that time.
   c. Although very young infants are likely to scan the external edges of the face, such as the hairline, there is no evidence that they use this information to recognize individuals such as their mother.
   d. Very young infants are sensitive to touch stimulation, but there is no evidence that they can recognize their mother's touch at such an early age.

7. *d. Some aspects of auditory development may take as long as ten years to develop; thus, hearing is the last of the senses to become fully developed. (p. 252)
   a. Visual abilities become adultlike by six to eight months of age.
   b. Smell appears to be very well developed at birth.
   c. Infants become increasingly sensitive to touch, particularly painful events, within a month after birth.

8. *d. Newborns typically respond to bitter-tasting substances with a mouth opening and a facial expression classified as disgust. (p. 256)
   a. The receptors for taste are well developed before birth. Bitter-tasting stimuli will yield a disgust reaction in newborns; thus, Karen most likely did not take the medicine without a problem.
   b. Infants will suck sweet stimuli vigorously, but not bitter stimuli.
   c. Newborns do not have the voluntary ability to spit out something in the mouth even if that stimulus is unpleasant.

9. *b. With repeated experience and inspection of the letters of the alphabet, the regularities and differences of such stimuli are recognized by the child. (p. 263)
   a. Research on perceptual learning reveals that younger children do not discriminate certain perceptual changes in letterlike stimuli until they have had experience with such stimuli. These early perceptual difficulties are normal and do not necessarily indicate a learning disability.

    c. Systematic reinforcements of parents or teachers do not enable the child to distinguish among perceptual events; only repeated experience and exposure to these events leads to perceptual learning.

    d. There is no evidence in this example that Janet has a visual perception deficit; her responses are normal for her age.

10. *b. Daryl is not likely to systematically and exhaustively search the stimuli when comparing them and, therefore, is likely to be much worse at this task than his nine-year-old brother. (p. 265)

    a. Research on attention and perception reveals that preschool children are not systematic in their comparison of perceptual stimuli and, therefore, are not very good at finding identity or differences when comparing visually complex stimuli. Daryl is not likely to be better than his nine-year-old brother at this task.

    c. Daryl is likely to be much worse at systematically comparing visually complex pictures.

    d. Even though Daryl may lose interest in this difficult task more quickly than his older brother, he is not likely to be good at it initially.

CHAPTER 7

LANGUAGE

LEARNING OBJECTIVES

1. Differentiate among phonology, semantics, syntax, and pragmatics. (pp. 274–275)

2. Describe the infant's ability to respond to elements of human speech. (pp. 275–277)

3. Describe the infant's prelinguistic utterances and discuss the role of experience in the development of these utterances. (pp. 277–279)

4. Discuss the young child's use of gesture as a communication tool. (pp. 279–281)

5. Describe the general trends in the acquisition of first words and individual differences in children's acquisition of language. (pp. 281–284)

6. Discuss the ways in which children derive meaning from words, particularly the role of parent-child interaction and the influence of the child's emerging conceptual skills. (pp. 284–286)

7. Describe the acquisition of syntax as the child progresses from the two-word stage to mature speech. (pp. 286–289)

8. Discuss the parent's role in guiding the child's acquisition of pragmatics and how the acquisition of language is related to social development. (pp. 290–293)

9. Describe the changes in metalinguistic awareness, including the child's increasing appreciation of humor. (pp. 293–294)

10. Describe behavior theory's account of language acquisition and its difficulty in explaining many aspects of children's language. (pp. 295–298)

11. Discuss the extent to which biological structures contribute to the development of language. (pp. 298–300)

12. Discuss the evidence for and against the view of a critical period for the acquisition of first and second languages. (pp. 300–302)

13. Compare and contrast the linguistic, cognitive, and social-interaction perspectives of language development. (pp. 302–308)

14. Describe the evidence demonstrating how language influences cognition, self-regulation of behavior, and cultural socialization. (pp. 308–313)

CHAPTER OUTLINE

I. **THE COURSE OF LANGUAGE ACQUISITION** (pp. 274–295)
Language is multifaceted, consisting of complex verbal and nonverbal skills that are learned in a relatively short period of time. The newborn infant must first learn the *phonology* of her language—the rules for combining the fundamental sound units of the language. Next, the child must learn *semantics*, or the meaning of words, and then, in order to learn to combine words correctly or grammatically, she must determine the principles of *syntax*. The child's language finally becomes adultlike when she realizes *pragmatics*, the social rules for employing language effectively and appropriately, at about four or five years of age.

A. **From Sound to Meaning: Phonological and Other Prelinguistic Skills** (pp. 275–281)
The first task of the newborn infant is to develop phonological skills in order to receive and produce messages. Considerable evidence indicates that the infant is sensitive to sounds made by other humans at birth. Very young infants can discriminate among different *phonemes* categorically. Infants prefer the high-pitched "baby talk" that mothers usually use, indicating that they are sensitive to the *prosodic features* of speech, the patterns of intonation, stress, and rhythm that communicate meaning. It is also apparent that infants can detect differences in language, since habituation studies show that they prefer their native language to another language.

The production of language emerges in the form of crying. By six to eight weeks, the child begins to produce *cooing* sounds, vowel-like utterances occasionally accompanied by consonants. At about three to six months of age, the child produces consonant-vowel combinations (*babbling*) and shortly thereafter his vocalizations feature *reduplicated babbling*. Although it is clear that the child's prelinguistic utterances are linked to physiological changes in the vocal apparatus and the central nervous system, debate has centered around the role the child's surroundings plays in prelinguistic utterances. The discovery of cultural differences in babbling and of differences in the preverbal utterances of deaf and normal-hearing infants provide support for the interactional hypothesis of preverbal utterance development. Gestures are also an important communicative tool for infants, as indicated by their use of *protodeclarative* gestures to call an adult's attention to an object and *protoimperative* gestures to get an adult to perform an action. Although gestures develop along with verbal skills in infancy, they eventually drop out by the second year.

B. **Content: The Acquisition of Semantics** (pp. 281–286)
Children begin to speak one word at a time at twelve to twenty months. The words most frequently used during this one-word stage are *nominals*, which label objects, people, or events. The first few words are acquired slowly, but at about eighteen months most children show a *vocabulary spurt*. Several changes occur in this one-word stage such as changes in the proportion of different word types in the children's vocabulary and in the degree to which words are bound to a specific context. The child's comprehension of language, or *receptive language*, far exceeds his *productive language*. In general, children show common trends in the way they acquire language. But considerable individual differences are seen as well. Children vary in terms of the age of the first word uttered, whether or not a vocabulary spurt is seen, and whether their one-word speech displays a *referential style* (mostly object words) or *expressive style* (words that direct the behaviors of others). Researchers have speculated that individual differences may result from variations in neurological structure, inborn differences in temperament, and parental influences.

Children derive the meaning of words in a variety of ways. Parents help children increase their vocabulary by labeling objects in their environment, particularly objects that the child actively points to. As the child becomes proficient in speaking, the parents provide her with more information by affording *linguistic contrast* in the form of corrections. The child also plays an active role in learning the meaning of new words by using the context to provide clues to the meaning of an unfamiliar spoken word (a process called *fast-mapping*) and by being predisposed to the *mutual exclusivity bias*, the tendency to treat unfamiliar words as labels for new objects in the child's immediate environment rather than as synonyms for words she already knows. The child's emerging conceptual skills also influence the acquisition of word meaning. The *semantic feature hypothesis* suggests that the child uses perceptual features to label objects, while the *functional theory* suggests that the child uses the function of the objects to label objects. These conceptual processes lead to errors such that labels may be applied to a broader (*overextension*) or a narrower (*underextension*) class of objects than the term signifies.

C. **Form: The Acquisition of Syntax** (pp. 286–289)
Two-word utterances begin at about twenty-four months of age, and shortly thereafter the child combines more than two words to express relations among objects and events in the world. An analysis of the child's average number of *morphemes* per utterance, or *mean length utterance (MLU)*, shows a rapid growth between one and a half and four years

of age. The child's grammar during the two-word stage has been described as *telegraphic*, consisting of combinations of nouns, verbs, and adjectives without modifiers. The two-word utterances are highly ordered. For instance, the utterance "more milk, more cookie" contains *pivot grammar* that makes use of a *pivot word* (more) as an anchor for *open words* (milk, cookie). Other grammars have also been observed in the two-word stage. By two and a half years of age, children begin to fill in utterances with adjectives, pronouns, and prepositions, and include *inflections* to signal plurals and verb tense. During this stage children produce predictable changes in the use of negatives and in forming questions. In general children gradually acquire the rules of syntax as they approach the more adult form in a systematically and orderly manner.

D. **Context: The Acquisition of Pragmatics** (pp. 290–293)
The acquisition of pragmatics—the proper use of speech in a social context—is also important for the proper use of language. Parents play an important role in teaching their children pragmatics by giving direct instructions ("say thank you") and by acting as models of politeness. It is unclear how children learn the more subtle social conventions that accompany socially skilled communication. *Referential communication* tasks have been used to examine children's awareness of the requirements needed to effectively communicate a novel topic or item to others. These studies show that young children are limited in their abilities to describe novel objects to other people. It is unlikely that this limited ability is a result of egocentricism, the inability to understand the perspective of others, since preschool children adjust their speech to a simpler form when speaking to a younger child. Older children also show *comprehension monitoring*—the ability to evaluate the adequacy of a communication.

E. **Abstraction: The Acquisition of Metalinguistic Awareness** (pp. 293–294)
Language learning is rapid from about eighteen months to five years, but *metalinguistic awareness*, children's ability to understand and be aware of their own competency with grammatical rules, does not occur until the early school years. Nevertheless, there are some early indicators of metalinguistic awareness. Children as young as two years can identify grammatically incorrect passages, although they cannot correct them. Children's appreciation of humor based on semantic ambiguities and their understanding of *metaphors* further demonstrate their metalinguistic awareness. These developing abilities are most likely tied to advances in cognition.

F. **The Sequence of Language Acquisition: An Overview** (pp. 294–295)
The study of the child's acquisition of language has shown language development to be orderly and very rapid.

II. **HOW DO WE EXPLAIN LANGUAGE ACQUISITION?** (pp. 295–308)
Children's use of language is *generative*—that is, they express thoughts through the novel and creative combinations of words. Several hypotheses have been proposed to explain the pattern of language acquisition seen in children.

A. **The Behaviorist Perspective** (pp. 296–298)
Behavior theory accounts for language acquisition through selective reinforcement of the child's vocalization and through imitation of a competent speaker of the language. Although reinforcement and imitation certainly play a role in language development, they cannot account for many aspects of children's language. There is little evidence that parents directly reinforce their children for grammatically correct speech, although they will indirectly provide feedback about the correctness of their child's speech, such as providing *expansions* of the child's verbalizations. Behavior theory is unable to account for *overregularizations* that result in the incorrect application of grammatical rules to words that are exceptions to the rules. Such errors are best explained by viewing the child as an active player, as extracting abstract rules from the language that he is exposed to and applying them to new situations.

B. **The Biological Perspective** (pp. 298–300)
The biological approach emphasizes the maturation of brain structures and the role of lateralization in language development. In most people, the left hemisphere controls language ability. Examination of brain-damaged adults has led to the discovery of localized brain structures in the left hemisphere that control speech production and comprehension. *Expressive aphasia*, the inability to speak fluently, occurs when *Broca's area* is damaged, and *receptive aphasia*, the inability to understand spoken speech, results from damage to *Wernicke's area*. Language impairments resulting from brain damage show a similar pattern in children and adults, although children are more likely to recover language. The greater brain plasticity seen in children has been attributed to the delay in the lateralization of the brain until two years of age. However, recent research has found evidence of lateralization by the first few months of life, suggesting that greater brain plasticity in children may be independent of lateralization. The predictable emergence of language milestones seen in all children (even in deaf children not exposed to a formal language) and the common features that are shared by all languages (such as phonology, semantics, and syntax) suggest that language may result from an innate biological mechanism. Because many different languages exist all over the world, it is clear that nurture also play an important role in language acquisition.

Controversy: Is There a Critical Period for Second-Language Learning? (pp. 300–302)
There has been considerable debate concerning whether humans display a critical period for the acquisition of language. Evidence for critical periods includes greater recovery of language in brain-damaged children when brain damage occurs before puberty, cases of defective language in abused children exposed to language late in life, and deficits in language acquisition by deaf people exposed to American Sign Language after twelve years of age. Some investigators cite the observation of a decreasing ability to learn a second language with increasing age as additional evidence for a critical period. However, others have warned that there are many problems in interpreting the research used to support the critical period hypothesis. For instance, many adults do become proficient in a second language. Thus, the available evidence does not support a strong version of the critical-period hypothesis for first- or second-language learning.

C. **The Linguistic Perspective** (pp. 302–303)

In his attack on the behaviorist theory of language acquisition, Noam Chomsky proposed that language is generative and that the child is biologically prepared to extract grammatical rules from language through an innate grammatical processor called the Language Acquisition Device (LAD). Evidence in support of the linguistic perspective includes the very rapid acquisition of words and syntactic rules during the first five years, the application of those rules to new words never seen before, and the overuse of such rules, as in overregularizations. The linguistic perspective falls short, however, in explaining the development of semantics and how the hypothetical LAD functions.

D. **The Cognitive Perspective** (pp. 303–304)

Some cognitive theorists describe language as arising from the child's thinking achievements. For Jean Piaget, language is possible only when the *semiotic function*, the ability to symbolize, emerges. Eve Clark and Katherine Nelson argue that language is preceded by conceptual understanding based on shared perceptual or functional features. Recent studies that relate specific cognitive skills to language development suggest that the cognitive and language domains tend to develop at the same time. The *specificity hypothesis* describes children as developing specific semantic attainments consistent with certain cognitive skills present at a given stage in development. *The rare event learning mechanism (RELM)* model views language as similar to any complex, rule-based skill that children master as they advance cognitively. When adults repeat a child's utterance but embed it in a more complex syntactic structure, they are using a *recast*. By doing so, they are highlighting discrepancies between the child's simple utterance and a more advanced one.

E. **A Social Interaction Perspective** (pp. 304–308)

The social interaction perspective views language as a social activity. Although this view recognizes the child's innate predisposition for language, her need for support and for models of appropriate speech are emphasized. Parents, who are generally motivated to communicate with their young children, often speak to them in a simplified version of spoken language called *motherese*. In this form of communication, questions are often used as a way to encourage *turn-taking*, alternating vocalization by parent and child, and as *turnabouts* to explicitly request a response from the child. Motherese may serve to assist the child's acquisition of word meaning, facilitate the acquisition of syntax, and provide lessons in pragmatics such as conversational turn-taking. Studies show that mothers who engage their children in conversation increase their children's rate of language acquisition. But cross-cultural studies that have examined cultures in which mothers do not use motherese to communicate with their young children suggest that verbal interaction between parent and child is not essential for the emergence of language. Children may also develop language by learning to adjust to conversations with their fathers, siblings, peers, and other members in their society.

III. **THE FUNCTIONS OF LANGUAGE** (pp. 308–313)

A. **How Language Influences Cognition** (pp. 309–310)
Several experimental results have been reported showing the powerful influence of language on cognitive accomplishments. Children who employ verbal rehearsal strategies are more likely to recall information following a time delay than children who do not. Children are more successful in categorizing groups of objects if they are provided with the name of one category member from each group. Linguistic labels may improve categorization by helping children attend to different features of the groups being categorized. The influence of language on thought is also illustrated by the better performance of bilingual children on problem-solving tasks compared to monolingual children.

B. **How Language Influences Self-Regulation** (pp. 310–312)
Language influences self-regulating behavior. Lev Vygotsky saw a child's *private speech* as guiding her observable behavior and her *inner speech* as directing the nature of her thoughts. A. R. Luria proposed three stages of the verbal regulation of behavior that progress from more overt to more internalized private speech. In the first stage (eighteen months to three years) the words of others stimulate the child's motor behavior but rarely inhibit behavior. In the second stage (three to five years) the child's own verbalizations and the words of others can increasingly initiate and inhibit behavior. In the final stage (five years) the child's thoughts and actions are controlled by the qualities and content of speech that has become internalized. Research by American psychologists has provided some empirical support for the ideas of their Russian colleagues.

C. **How Language Influences Cultural Socialization** (pp. 312–313)
Language also plays an important role in the socialization of children by helping them learn their culture's values and beliefs. For instance, in many languages the words used for speaking with individuals with greater authority differ from the words used to speak to individuals of equal status.

IV. **THEMES IN DEVELOPMENT: LANGUAGE** (pp. 313–315)
What roles do nature and nurture play in language development? Many factors indicate that nature sets early human dispositions to develop language; for example, the fact that certain portions of the brain are devoted to language functions. Nurture interacts with biological tendencies in the form of the child's experiences with more mature language users.

How does the sociocultural context influence language development? The use of motherese; the elements of phonology, semantics, syntax, and pragmatics; and the content and structure of a specific language all vary from culture to culture. Language thereby plays a role in the child's socialization.

How does the child play an active role in the process of language development? The child often influences which objects or people caregivers will label when he looks at or points to specific items. The child actively employs context and the mutual exclusivity bias to derive the meanings of words and abstracts out the regularities in language to generate his own verbalizations.

Is language development continuous or stagelike?   Early language production, in particular, seems stagelike; however, recent studies suggest that there are more continuities than previously thought. For example, infant babbling is related to the language the child will eventually speak.

Are there sensitive periods in language development?   It is widely believed that the entire period from infancy to adolescence is a sensitive period for the acquisition of language. However, there is no firm evidence that the ability to learn language drops off dramatically at adolescence. Adults often learn a second language with nativelike proficiency.

How does language development interact with development in other domains?   The child's early ability to produce spoken language parallels the maturation of the vocal apparatus and the central nervous system. The emergence of language also coincides with the onset of certain cognitive skills, such as memory. Language itself is nurtured largely within the context of social interactions with caregivers. By the same token, language has an impact on other domains, such as analytic thinking and mental flexibility.

Key Terms Review

1. The grammatical rules that dictate how words can be combined are known as _____ .

2. A(n) _____ is the smallest unit of sound that changes the meanings of words.

3. Patterns of intonation, stress, and rhythm that communicate meaning in speech are known as _____ .

4. The child's vocalized speech to himself that directs behavior is called _____ speech.

5. Vowel-like utterances called _____ and consonant-vowel utterances called _____ characterize the infant's first attempts to vocalize.

6. The fundamental sound units and combinations of units in a given language are known as _____ .

7. In _____ grammar, one word is repeated and a series of other words fills the second slot. The repeated, or anchor, word is called the _____ word, and the variable word that accompanies it is the _____ word.

8. The use of a gesture to call attention to an object or event is called _____ ; the use of a gesture to issue a command or request is called _____ .

9. _____ is the meaning of words or combinations of words.

10. A(n) _____ , which is the first type of word most children produce, labels an object, person, or event.

11. The _____ hypothesis suggests that early concepts are based on the child's perception of the shared features of objects.

12. _____ is the tendency to apply a label to a broader category than the term actually signifies. _____ is the application of a label to a narrower class of objects than the term signifies.

13. The portion of the cerebral cortex that controls expressive language is _____ ; the part that controls language comprehension is _____ .

14. The smallest unit of meaning in speech is a(n) _____ .

15. The child's ability to comprehend spoken speech is _____ language; the child's ability to say and use words herself is _____ language.

16. _____ children tend to have mostly object labels in their vocabulary, while _____ children use words to direct the behavior of other people or to comment on them.

17. In _____ , meanings of words are derived from the context in which they are spoken.

18. _____ is the repetition of simple consonant-vowel combinations in the early stages of language development.

19. Children profit from _____ , the correction of their incorrect utterances by pointing out both the error and the correct term.

20. _____ theory suggests that early concepts are based on the child's perception of the uses of objects.

21. The average number of morphemes per utterance is known as _____ .

22. _____ speech contains few modifiers, prepositions, or other connective words.

23. _____ is an alteration to a word, such as tense or plural form, that indicates its syntactical function.

24. The ability to evaluate the adequacy of a communication is called _____ .

25. The _____ is the tendency for children to assume that unfamiliar words label new objects.

26. In _____ , a term is transferred from the object it customarily designates to describe a comparable object or event.

27. _____ language is a unique and novel combination of words and sentences that speakers produce without having heard them before.

28. An adult's repetition and elaboration of a child's utterance is called _____ .

29. _____ is the inappropriate application of syntactic rules to words and grammatical forms that show exceptions.

30. The loss of the ability to speak fluently is called _____ aphasia; the loss of the ability to comprehend the speech of others is called _____ aphasia.

31. _____ is the ability to symbolize objects.

32. The _____ hypothesis suggests that specific cognitive achievements precede specific language achievements.

33. The _____ postulates the development of attention, memory, and other cognitive processes as a prerequisite to language achievements.

34. _____ is the repetition of a child's utterance along with some new elements.

35. The simple, repetitive, high-pitched speech of caregivers to young children is known as _____ .

36. _____ consists of alternating vocalization by parent and child.

37. _____ are elements of conversation that request a response from the child.

38. The interiorized form of private speech is known as _____ speech.

39. A period of rapid word acquisition, or _____ , typically occurs early in language development.

40. _____ are rules for using language effectively within a social context.

41. _____ is used in situations that require the speaker to describe an object to a listener or to evaluate the effectiveness of a message.

42. _____ is the ability to reflect on language as a communication tool and on the self as a user of language.

Answers to Key Terms Review

1. syntax
2. phoneme
3. prosodic features
4. private
5. cooing, babbling
6. phonology
7. pivot, pivot, open
8. protodeclarative communication, protoimperative communication
9. Semantics
10. nominal
11. semantic feature
12. Overextension, Underextension
13. Broca's area, Wernicke's area
14. morpheme
15. receptive, productive
16. Referential, expressive
17. fast-mapping
18. Reduplicated babbling
19. linguistic contrast
20. Functional
21. mean length utterance
22. Telegraphic
23. Inflection
24. comprehension monitoring
25. mutual exclusivity bias
26. metaphor
27. Generative
28. expansion
29. Overregularization
30. expressive, receptive
31. Semiotic function
32. specificity
33. rare event learning mechanism (RELM)
34. Recast
35. motherese
36. Turn taking
37. Turnabouts
38. inner
39. vocabulary spurt

40. Pragmatics
41. Referential communication
42. Metalinguistic awareness

Multiple-Choice Questions

Fact and Concept Questions

1. The phonology of a given language refers to
   a. the correct order of words.
   b. the rules for using language effectively.
   c. the fundamental sound units and the rules for combining them.
   d. the meaning of the words of a language.

2. Word order is an important component of a language. The rules for combining words comprise the principles of
   a. phonology.
   b. pragmatics.
   c. pivot grammar.
   d. syntax.

3. During the infant's first year, the emphasis on language acquisition occurs in the area of _____ development.
   a. semantic
   b. pragmatic
   c. syntax
   d. phonological

4. Research with infants has shown that soon after birth, they
   a. prefer music over human voices.
   b. cannot distinguish speech sounds from other sounds.
   c. prefer human voices over other sounds.
   d. prefer a stranger's voice over their own mother's voice.

5. The quality of "baby talk" that seems to make it attractive to infants is its
   a. loudness.
   b. rhythm.
   c. simplicity.
   d. higher pitch.

6. The role of nurture in human language ability is indicated by the infant's
   a. ability to babble.
   b. ability to distinguish among phonemes in many languages.
   c. ability to distinguish between her native language and other languages.
   d. preference for high-pitched speech.

7. The first vocal ability that infants demonstrate is
   a. cooing.
   b. crying.
   c. babbling.
   d. reduplicated babbling.

8. Proponents of the independence hypothesis believe that
   a. babbling is independent of cooing.
   b. specific babbling patterns are learned for each language.
   c. the language environment of the child influences his babbling patterns.
   d. babbling is under maturational control and is not influenced by the native language.

9. Psychologists have compared the babbling of deaf infants with hearing infants and found that
   a. deaf infants don't babble.
   b. deaf infants' babbling is noticeably different from the babbling of hearing infants.
   c. deaf infants' babbling is identical to the babbling of hearing infants.
   d. deaf infants' babbling is lower in pitch than that of hearing infants.

10. The average child will have a ten-word vocabulary by the time she is
    a. six months old.
    b. twelve months old.
    c. eighteen months old.
    d. twenty-four months old.

11. Children who demonstrate a(n) _____ style in their early language use words to direct the behavior of others.
    a. referential
    b. expressive
    c. communicative
    d. receptive

12. The endings of some words, such as -ed or -s, which change the meaning of the word are examples of
    a. morphemes.
    b. polyphemes.
    c. phonemes.
    d. pivot words.

13. Behaviorists explain language acquisition as the result of
    a. biological predispositions for language.
    b. brain lateralization.
    c. reinforcement and imitation of selected vocalizations.
    d. the cognitive level of the child.

14. If a child applies a rule of grammar to a word that is an exception to a rule, he is demonstrating
    a. fast-mapping.
    b. overregularization.
    c. overextension.
    d. protoimperatives.

15. Most individuals with damage to _____ of the brain show language impairments.
    a. the left hemisphere
    b. the right hemisphere
    c. both lateralizations
    d. the brainstem

16. Damage to Broca's area leads to
    a. receptive aphasia.
    b. expressive aphasia.
    c. incomprehensible speech.
    d. a failure to understand speech.

17. Support for the hypothesis that there is a critical period for language comes from
    a. studies of syntax errors in preschoolers.
    b. studies of adults with physical damage to the left hemisphere.
    c. studies of infant lateralization of speech.
    d. studies of children who were first exposed to language late in life.

18. Which of the following is a characteristic of motherese?
    a. Parents' use of turnabouts
    b. Parents' use of positive reinforcement
    c. Parents' use of inflections
    d. Parents' use of pivot words

19. Cross-cultural studies on child-parent interactions have shown that
    a. use of motherese is unique to American parents.
    b. use of motherese is universal, used by parents of all cultures.
    c. motherese, although used by parents of many cultures, is not essential for the emergence of language.
    d. children of cultures where the parents do not use motherese show severely disrupted language acquisition.

20. According to Vygotsky, the child's internalized voice that guides her thoughts is called
   a. private speech.
   b. inner speech.
   c. telegraphic speech.
   d. generative speech.

Application Questions

1. Lauren, who is six months old, can detect the difference between *ma* and *pa*. The sounds that distinguish *ma* and *pa* are called
   a. prosodic features.
   b. pragmatics.
   c. phonemes.
   d. semantics.

2. Ten-month-old Carlton has started to say "dadadadada." This vocalization is called
   a. a word.
   b. reduplicated babbling.
   c. categorical perception.
   d. spectral analysis.

3. Eduardo, who is just beginning to say words, has learned the names for many objects. He is displaying a(n) _____ style in his vocabulary.
   a. referential
   b. expressive
   c. action
   d. pragmatic

4. The first time Abigail saw a tiger at the zoo she said, "Kitty." According to the _____ hypothesis, Abigail said "Kitty" because she noticed the similarity between the appearance of a tiger and a cat.
   a. functional
   b. fast-mapping
   c. expressive
   d. semantic feature

5. While Frank was helping his mother bake cookies, she asked him for the rolling pin. Even though Frank had never seen a rolling pin before, he correctly handed it to her, probably because it was the only object on the table he had never seen before. Frank's successful interpretation of his mother's words is an example of
   a. the mutual exclusivity bias.
   b. the semantic feature hypothesis.
   c. referential style.
   d. expressive style.

6. Brooke has reached the two-word stage of language development. Her utterances include such phrases as "Want cookie," "Doggie run," and "Go bye-bye." Brooke's speech can be categorized as
   a. prosodic.
   b. telegraphic.
   c. reflective.
   d. metalinguistic.

7. "Why did the boy throw butter out the window? Because he wanted to see butter-fly." Stephen finds this joke to be very funny, but his little brother, Stuart, who is four years old, does not, probably because
   a. Stuart does not understand phonological ambiguities.
   b. Stuart does not understand syntactic ambiguities.
   c. Stuart does not understand semantic ambiguities.
   d. Stuart is too young to appreciate any form of humor.

8. Larissa's grandfather recently had a stroke. Although he clearly can understand what people are saying, he has great difficulty forming sentences. Larissa's grandfather most likely suffered damage to
   a. Wernicke's area in the right hemisphere.
   b. Wernicke's area in the left hemisphere.
   c. Broca's area in the right hemisphere.
   d. Broca's area in the left hemisphere.

9. Toshiko has recently shown evidence of the cognitive ability to symbolize. According to Piaget, Toshiko
   a. should already have a vocabulary of at least ten words.
   b. should shortly begin to develop the semiotic function.
   c. should shortly begin to learn her first words.
   d. should no longer exhibit telegraphic speech.

10. Hannah's mother spent considerably more time conversing with her when she was an infant than Sheila's mother did with Sheila. At two years of age, Hannah is likely to
    a. have a larger vocabulary than Sheila.
    b. have a smaller vocabulary than Sheila.
    c. have a vocabulary similar in size to Sheila's.
    d. understand more words than Sheila, but produce fewer words.

Answers to Multiple-Choice Questions

The correct answer appears first and is preceded by an asterisk.

Answers to Fact and Concept Questions

1. *c. Each language has a certain number of sounds, called *phonemes*. These phonemes and the rules for combining them in a given language make up that language's phonology. (p. 274)
   a. The rules for combining words and placing them in the correct order are called the rules of syntax, not phonology.
   b. Pragmatics are the rules for using language effectively according to social convention.
   d. Semantics refers to the meaning of words or combination of words.

2. *d. The grammatical rules that dictate how words can be combined are called syntax. (p. 275)
   a. The rules of phonology dictate how the phonemes of a language, not the words, are combined.
   b. Pragmatics are the rules for using language effectively according to social convention.
   c. Although pivot grammar is a rule for combining words, it is unique to the child in the two-word stage; it is not a term describing the general rules for combining words.

3. *d. Before language can be learned, the young child must first learn phonology, the units of sounds used in a language. (p. 275)
   a. Semantics are the principles for determining word meaning. A one-year-old child is just beginning to learn language; therefore, he must first learn the sounds or phonemes of the language before meaning can be discerned.
   b. Pragmatics are the rules for correctly using language within a social context. A one-year-old child is just beginning to learn language; he must learn the rules of phonology, semantics, and syntax before pragmatics can be acquired.
   c. Syntax is the rules for combining words. A one-year-old child is just beginning to learn language; he must first learn phonology and then the meaning of some words before learning to combine the words.

4. *c. Studies show that newborns prefer to listen to human voices over other sounds. (p. 276)
   a. Studies show that newborns prefer to listen to human voices over other sounds such as music.
   b. Because newborns prefer to listen to human voices over other sounds, they must be able to discriminate these two forms of auditory stimuli.
   d. Studies show that given a choice between a stranger's voice or their mother's voice, infants prefer to listen to their mother's voice.

5. *d. Research indicates that it is the high pitch of "baby talk" that makes it attractive to infants. (p. 276)
   a. Although the loudness of "baby talk" may vary, research indicates that variation in loudness is not what makes it attractive to the infant.

b. Research indicates that the rhythm of "baby talk" is not what makes it attractive to the infant.

c. Although "baby talk" is simplistic, this simplicity is not what makes it attractive to infants.

6. *c. The young infant's ability to distinguish her own language from other languages that she is not exposed to demonstrates that the child can learn to differentiate among languages. (p. 276)

a. Because all infants, even deaf infants, begin to babble at about the same time, this ability is most likely inborn.

b. Evidence indicates that even very young infants can discriminate between phonemes, indicating that this ability is inborn.

d. The very young infant's preference for high-pitched speech is most likely innate.

7. *b. The infant is able to cry at birth; thus, crying is the infant's first vocalization. (p. 277)

a. Cooing does not emerge until six to eight weeks after birth.

c. Most children begin to babble at about three to six months.

d. Reduplicated babbling doesn't occur until after the child has already begun to babble, at about nine or ten months.

8. *d. The independence hypothesis argues that babbling is primarily a result of biological underpinnings. (p. 278)

a. The independence hypothesis addresses the nature-nurture influence on babbling; it does not state that babbling occurs independently of cooing.

b. In order for babbling patterns to vary along with the different languages, the child's native language would have to influence his babbling. The independence hypothesis denies any influence of nurture on babbling.

c. The independence hypothesis argues that the development of babbling is largely independent of environmental influences.

9. *b. Even though deaf infants babble, they do not reach the stage of reduplicated babbling by ten months, whereas hearing infants do. (p. 279)

a. Even deaf infants babble.

c. Although for many years psychologists thought that the babbling of deaf and hearing children was very similar, recent studies indicate that there are differences, particularly in reduplicated babbling.

d. There is no evidence that the babbling of deaf and hearing infants differs in pitch.

10. *c. Once the child learns her first word, she adds one to three words per month; thus, the average child attains a ten-word vocabulary by about eighteen months. (p. 281)

a. Most children do not produce their first word until ten to twelve months of age; therefore, they could not have a vocabulary of ten words at six months.

b. At about twelve months, most children are just beginning to speak their first words; therefore, they cannot have a vocabulary of ten words by twelve months.

d. A vocabulary growth spurt occurs in most children after eighteen months; thus, by twenty-four months the child will have a vocabulary considerably larger than ten words.

11. *b. Children with expressive styles more frequently use words that have social functions, often directing the behavior of others. (p. 284)
   a. Children with referential styles have large vocabularies of words used to label objects.
   c. Although any use of words by children is a form of communication, *communicative style* is not a term used to describe children's speech.
   d. *Receptive style* is not a term used to describe children's speech.

12. *a. Morphemes are the smallest units of meaning in speech. The morpheme *-ed* changes a word's meaning to indicate past tense; the morpheme *-s* changes a word's meaning to indicate more than one (plural). (p. 287)
   b. *Polyphemes* is not a real term.
   c. Phonemes are the smallest units of sound in a language, not the smallest units of meaning.
   d. Pivot words are semantic regularities unique to children in the two-word stage of language acquisition; they are not a component of normal adult language.

13. *c. Behaviorists assume that the acquisition of language can be accounted for by such basic principles of learning as reinforcement and imitation. (p. 296)
   a. Behavior analysis emphasizes the role of nurture rather than nature on language acquisition.
   b. The role of brain lateralization in language acquisition has been addressed by researchers advocating the biological perspective of language development.
   d. The behaviorist approach to understanding language acquisition does not address the cognitive abilities of the developing child.

14. *b. Young children often overuse grammatical rules—for example, saying *runned* to express the past tense of *run*. This phenomenon is called overregularization. (p. 297)
   a. Fast-mapping is a process by which children use the context to determine the meaning of an unfamiliar word. It is not a rule of grammar.
   c. Overextension is the tendency to apply a label to a broader category than the term implies.
   d. Protoimperative communication is a form of gesture intended to make a demand or request.

15. *a. In most people the left hemisphere controls language; therefore, any damage to this hemisphere usually causes language impairment. (p. 298)
   b. In most people it is the left hemisphere that controls language; thus, language impairment is not expected following damage to the right hemisphere.
   c. Lateralization is not a brain structure and therefore cannot be damaged.

d. The brainstem is involved in the control of essential reflexes such as breathing; it is not involved in language comprehension or production.

16. *b. Damage to Broca's area causes expressive aphasia, the inability to produce fluent speech. (p. 298)
a. Receptive aphasia is the inability to comprehend speech; it is caused by damage to Wernicke's area.
c. People with damage to Broca's area find it very difficult to produce words. People with damage to Wernicke's area produce speech that appears to be fluent but is incomprehensible.
d. Damage to Wernicke's area causes the inability to understand speech (receptive aphasia); damage to Broca's area results in poor speech production.

17. *d. The fact that language deficits are seen in children who are not exposed to a formal language until late in life suggests that there is a critical period for language. (p. 300)
a. The observation of syntax errors made by children has provided important information concerning the child's active role in language acquisition, but it does not provide evidence for the critical period hypothesis.
b. Studies of adults with damage to the left hemisphere has led to the understanding of brain lateralization, but it does not provide evidence for the critical period hypothesis.
c. Recent studies show that lateralization of the hemispheres occurs in the first few months after birth; thus, lateralization is unlikely to be related to critical periods for language.

18. *a. Motherese includes the use of turnabouts, elements of a conversation that explicitly request a response from the child. (p. 305)
b. Reinforcement is certainly used by parents to teach their children some aspects of language, but it is not a component of the conversational style called motherese.
c. Inflections, ends to words that signal plurals or verb tense, are a normal part of the English language, not just of motherese.
d. Pivot words are a unique feature of the verbalizations of a child in the two-word stage, not of motherese.

19. *c. Motherese does not seem to be essential for the emergence of language because the children of parents from cultures that do not use features seen in motherese eventually become proficient users of their language. (p. 307)
a. Features of motherese have been observed in fourteenth other languages; thus, it is not unique to American parents.
b. Not all cultures use motherese to communicate to their children; some cultures adopt a very different style of communicating with their children.
d. The children of parents from cultures that do not use features seen in motherese become proficient users of their language.

20. *b. According to Vygotsky, inner speech dictates the direction of the child's thoughts. (p. 311)
    a. According to Vygotsky, private speech is the overt, audible speech that the child produces to guide her observable behavior.
    c. Telegraphic speech is a characteristic of the two-word stage of language acquisition.
    d. Language in general is described as generative—novel and creative combinations of words to express unique ideas; this is not a unique component of Vygotsky's theory.

Answers to Application Questions

1. *c. The sounds *ma* and *pa* differ because of the phonemes *m* and *p*. (p. 276)
   a. Prosodic features are the patterns of intonation, stress, and rhythm that communicate meaning, not the sounds, or phonemes, of a language.
   b. Pragmatics are the rules for using language.
   d. Semantics are the meaning of words, not sounds.

2. *b. The repetition of the same consonant-vowel (*d-a*) pair is an example of reduplicated babbling. (p. 278)
   a. Although *dad* is a word, the child's repetitive use of the consonant-vowel pair *da* is not a word.
   c. Categorical perception is the inability to distinguish between sounds that vary except when those sounds lie on opposite sides of a critical juncture point.
   d. Spectral analysis is a method of analyzing speech sounds by converting them to a visual form.

3. *a. Children differ in the content of their one-word speech. Children who have mostly object labels in their vocabulary exhibit a referential style. (p. 284)
   b. *Expressive style* describes children who primarily have words that direct the behavior of other people, not words for objects.
   c. *Action style* is not a term used to describe aspects of a child's vocabulary.
   d. Pragmatics is the rule for applying language according to social conventions; it is not a term used to describe the type of words in a child's vocabulary.

4. *d. The semantic feature hypothesis emphasizes the use of shared perceptual features of objects to identify unfamiliar objects. (p. 285)
   a. The functional hypothesis states that the child's early concepts are based on the functions of objects. It is unlikely that Abigail is using the functional property of a cat to apply the label *kitty*.
   b. Fast-mapping is the strategy that derives the meaning of an unfamiliar word from the context; Abigail is not deriving the meaning of an unfamiliar word.
   c. There is no expressive hypothesis in the semantic development literature. The expressive style describes the content of one-word speech of some children.

5. *a. The mutual exclusivity bias describes the tendency of children to treat new words as labels for unfamiliar rather than familiar objects. (p. 286)
   b. The semantic feature hypothesis emphasizes the use of shared perceptual features of objects to identify unfamiliar objects.
   c. Referential style describes one-word speech that consists primarily of words for objects.
   d. Expressive style describes one-word speech that consists primarily of words that direct the behavior of others.

6. *b. The child's utterances in the two-word stage are described as telegraphic because the speech omits conjunctions, prepositions, and other modifiers, containing only the essential elements for getting the message across. (p. 287)
   a. Prosodic features include stress and intonation. Brooke's utterance does not indicate any prosodic features.
   c. The term *reflective* is not used to describe aspects of a child's speech.
   d. Metalinguistic refers to the child's ability to think about her use of speech abstractly; it does not refer to a form of speech.

7. *c. Three- to five-year-old children are not usually able to discern semantic ambiguities. In the joke the young child will not understand the ambiguous meaning of the word *butterfly* ("butter fly"). (p. 294)
   a. Phonological ambiguities involve the similarities in the sounds (phonemes) of words; there is no phonological ambiguity in the joke.
   b. The joke does not contain any ambiguity of syntax.
   d. Young children do appreciate humor. The young child's appreciation of humor is usually centered around phonological ambiguities.

8. *d. Damage to Broca's area in the left hemisphere has been associated with the inability to produce fluent speech; therefore, Larissa's grandfather most likely suffered damage to the left hemisphere near Broca's area. (p. 298)
   a. Wernicke's area is involved in the comprehension, not the production, of speech, and in most people Wernicke's area is found in the left hemisphere.
   b. The grandfather had good comprehension of speech but found it difficult to speak. Wernicke's area was probably not damaged because it is involved in the comprehension, not the production, of speech.
   c. Broca's area has been associated with the production of speech, but in most people it is found in the left hemisphere, not the right hemisphere.

9. *c. Piaget argued that once the semiotic function, or the ability to symbolize, emerges, language becomes possible. (p. 303)
   a. Piaget argued that the child must acquire the ability to form mental symbols before language is possible.
   b. The semiotic function *is* the ability to symbolize.
   d. According to Piaget the ability to symbolize occurs before language; therefore, Toshiko should not show telegraphic speech since she has yet to learn her first word.

10. *a. Recent studies show that the more time mothers spend conversing with their infants, the larger the children's vocabularies. Thus, Hannah is likely to have a larger vocabulary than Sheila. (p. 307)
    b. Recent studies show that the more time mothers spend conversing with their infants, the *larger* the children's vocabularies. Thus, Hannah is likely to have a larger, not smaller, vocabulary than Sheila.
    c. Recent studies show that the more time mothers spend conversing with their infants, the *larger* the children's vocabularies. Thus, Hannah is likely to have a larger vocabulary than Sheila.
    d. There is no indication in the text's description of the studies on this subject that there are differences in the comprehension and production of children's speech as a function of the amount of time mothers converse with their children.

CHAPTER 8

COGNITION

LEARNING OBJECTIVES

1. Define cognition and describe Piaget's general ideas concerning cognitive development, including schemes, assimilation, and accommodation. (pp. 318–319)

2. Describe the sensorimotor stage of cognitive development. Identify major features of this stage, including means-end behavior, circular reaction, and object permanence. (pp. 319–321)

3. Describe the features of the preoperational stage and the limitations found during this stage. (pp. 321–322)

4. Describe the major developments in the concrete and formal operational stages of cognitive development. (pp. 322–324)

5. Discuss the implications of Piaget's theory of cognitive growth for education. (pp. 324–325)

6. Describe the evidence suggesting that Piaget may have underestimated the abilities of young children. (pp. 326–327)

7. Discuss the modern criticisms of Piaget's notion of stagelike development of thought and his proposed mechanisms of cognitive development. (pp. 327–328)

8. Describe the major features of the information-processing models of human cognition. (pp. 329–331)

9. Describe and discuss the changes in attention that occur with development. (pp. 331–333)

10. Describe the trends in the development of memory, particularly recognition memory and recall memory. (pp. 333–337)

11. Discuss the importance of memory strategies in aiding recall and describe the development of the spontaneous use of memory strategies. (pp. 337–342)

12. Discuss the issues in the controversy over whether children should provide eyewitness testimony. (pp. 342–343)

13. Discuss the importance of concepts in human thought and describe the development of the concepts of class, number, and space. (pp. 343–349)

14. Describe the achievements in problem-solving abilities such as deductive reasoning and analogical transfer that occur through adolescence. (pp. 349–353)

15. Discuss the importance of the cultural context and the effects of the availability of formal schooling on cognitive development. (pp. 353–355)

16. Discuss the role of parents and teachers in guiding the child's cognitive advancement within a cultural context. (pp. 356–357)

CHAPTER OUTLINE

The study of *cognition*, which includes thinking and other mental states such as attention and memory, is a very large area of research in developmental psychology.

I. **PIAGET'S THEORY OF COGNITIVE DEVELOPMENT** (pp. 318–329)
Piaget's theory was introduced in Chapter 2. We saw that he described the child as actively constructing knowledge and building into already existing knowledge (schemes) through the processes of assimilation and accommodation. Piaget was a stage theorist, maintaining that cognition becomes qualitatively reorganized as the child progresses through four stages.

A. **Stages of Development** (pp. 318–324)
Piaget believed that cognitive development resulted from maturational factors and environmental experiences. He specified four stages that all children progress through in an invariable order. The first stage, the *sensorimotor stage* (zero to two years), is characterized by the child's actions on the environment. The child undergoes three major achievements during this initial stage (which contains six substages). The first accom-

plishment involves a progression from actions that are reflexive to more goal-directed actions called *means-end behavior*. The child often displays *circular reactions*—the repetition of motor acts that produce pleasurable events. A second accomplishment involves the child's gradual changing focus from the self to a greater orientation to the external world. Another accomplishment in this initial stage is the attainment of the *object concept*, also called *object permanence*.

Possession of the object concept is necessary for the development of deferred imitation, the ability to imitate a model who is no longer present, and marks the end of the sensorimotor stage and the beginning of the *preoperational stage*. During this second stage (two to seven years), the child develops his semiotic function, the ability to use a symbol, which is an important prerequisite for language, imagery, fantasy play, and drawing. Preoperational thought, however, has several distinct limitations. The children in this stage are described as *egocentric* because they are unable to separate their own perspective from that of others. Another limitation of the preoperational child is revealed through a series of assessment tasks, called *conservation tasks*, that require the child to make a judgment about the equivalence of two displays following the observation of a transformation of one of the displays (e.g., conservation of liquid task). According to Piaget, conservation errors result from *centration* (focusing on only one aspect of the problem), lack of *reversibility*, and the tendency of the child to *focus on states* rather than on the events that occur between two related states.

The child's ability to solve conservation tasks signals the beginning of the third stage, the *concrete operational stage* (seven to eleven years). The ability to solve conservation tasks results from the child's ability to perform mental activities, or *operations*, such as reversibility.

By stage 4, the *formal operational stage* (eleven to fifteen years), the child is thinking logically and abstractly and can reason *hypothetically*. According to Piaget, no further qualitative changes in cognitive growth occur once the child achieves the formal operational stage, although adult thinking may continue to grow.

B. **Implications for Education** (pp. 324–325)
Piaget's theory of cognitive development has several implications for education. His theory suggests that the educator consider the child's current stage of development and originate plans of instruction that match the child's abilities. For example, a teacher may encourage preoperational children's use of semiotic functions through drawing and pretend play rather than have children use logic to solve problems. Piaget's theory also encourages the active engagement of the child with tasks that are one step beyond the child's current state of knowledge. This strategy requires assessment of the individual child rather than of the class as a whole. Several educational programs based on Piagetian models have emerged, each emphasizing different aspects of Piaget's theory.

C. **Evaluating Piaget's Theory** (pp. 326–329)

Piaget's theory has been enormously successful in generating a large volume of empirical research in developmental psychology. The results of many of these experiments, however, have raised questions about several aspects of Piaget's theory. Piaget may have underestimated the ages at which cognitive skills are attained. Renée Baillargeon demonstrated that infants as young as four months have an elementary understanding of the object concept. Piaget had suggested that the concept of object permanence does not occur until about ten months. Rachel Gelman used the "oddity problem" task to train preoperational children to conserve number, an ability that Piaget argued marked the onset of the concrete operational stage. Piaget thought that preschoolers showed considerable egocentrism, but naturalistic studies of children's communications demonstrate that preschoolers can take the perspective of others since they are often sensitive to the needs of the people they are trying to communicate with.

Piaget saw development as stagelike. This notion posits great consistency in children's performance within a stage of development and predicts a high correlation among various abilities within a stage. Modern research, however, has found greater inconsistencies within a stage than would be expected and has failed to find high correlations among the various abilities within a stage. These results have led many contemporary psychologists to view development more as a continuous process and less as the stagelike process that Piaget envisioned.

Some modern researchers also challenge Piaget's suggestion that the mechanism of development involves the alteration of cognitive structures such as symbolic, logical, and hypothetical thought. Rachel Gelman's study on conservation in four-year-olds, for example, suggests that perhaps the mechanism of cognitive development involves changes in how information is gathered, manipulated, and stored.

The heavy emphasis placed by Piaget on maturation has also been criticized. Researchers have pointed out that not everyone achieves formal operational thinking, including many American adults and members of many non-Western cultures. Moreover, specific cultural experiences have been observed to accelerate the development of formal operational thought. These observations suggest that the child's sociocultural experiences may shape cognitive development to a greater degree than acknowledged by Piaget.

Despite the modern criticisms of Piaget's theory, several of his ideas are well accepted today, such as his view of the child's active role in development and his assumption that the child's knowledge at any given time determines what further knowledge can be acquired.

II. **THE INFORMATION-PROCESSING APPROACH** (pp. 329–353)

Information-processing theorists view human cognition as an information management system with limited space and resources. Two information-processing models are described in the text. The *multistore models* describe information as flowing through sequential structures such as sensory stores, memory stores, a central processor, and a response system; control processes are mental activities assumed to move information from structure to structure. The *limited-resource models* do not place emphasis on mental structures but on various cognitive activities or operations. The resources for operations are limited; thus, a considerable amount of mental activity performed on one operation (such as processing sensory information) will make less available for other operations (such as storage or retrieval of information).

The first stage of information processing takes place in the *sensory store*, in which information is held for a fraction of a second. Then the words move to *working memory*, which holds information for no more than a couple of minutes, or to *long-term memory*, the repository of more enduring information. The multistore models explain cognitive development as increases in the size of structures and in the proficiency of control processes, whereas the limited-resource models describe cognitive growth as increases in the efficiency of operations (as the proficiency of sensory processes improves, more mental activity is available for remembering).

A. The Development of Attention (pp. 331–333)

Before an individual can process information, the relevant informational stimuli must be attended to. Several developmental trends in attention have been observed. There are striking increases in the ability to focus attention on an activity during the first six years of life. This developmental trend results from a maturing central nervous system and from the overall cognitive growth that occurs, as evidenced by the increasing complexities in the things that maintain a child's interest and the child's increasingly more creative ways of playing with objects. The increasing likelihood of *attentional inertia* may also contribute to the developing child's improved ability to focus attention. Older children are more able to deploy their attention effectively and to do so more efficiently. As they grow older, children also show greater selective attention, more easily ignoring irrelevant information. In order for selective attention to develop, the child must first be aware that her attention is limited; thus, gains in *metacognition* occur along with the ability to selectively attend.

B. The Development of Memory (pp. 333–342)

The ability to remember is critical for the execution of cognitive activities. Thus, memory has been a popular and important area of developmental research and has been conceptualized in many different ways. Memory has been described as *episodic* (memories for events that took place at a specific time and place) and as *semantic* (memories for facts and general concepts not related to any specific event). Psychologists have also distinguished between *recognition memory* (the ability to recognize whether a stimulus was previously encountered) and *recall memory* (the ability to reproduce stimuli that have been previously encountered). Recognition memory has been observed very early in development with procedures that utilize the infant's ability to undergo perceptual habituation, such as the paired-comparison procedure. These studies suggest that recognition memory is a rudimentary ability that is necessary for further cognitive growth.

Studies show that the *memory span*, believed to indicate an individual's short-term (working) memory capacity, increases with age. This developmental change in recall appears to be related to the child's improved ability to employ *memory strategies* as he gains experience. Maturation and, more specifically, myelinization of the cerebral cortex also appear to play an important role in the memory span, possibly by increasing the speed of information processing. Older children show greater recall of information than younger children because of their improved memory strategies. For example, when individuals are given a list of words and then asked to recall the words after a brief delay, they usually recall the words at the end and the beginning of the list better than the words in the middle of the list. Better recall of the end words is called the *recency effect* and is believed to reflect what is available in short-term memory, while better recall of beginning words is called the *primacy effect* and is believed to reflect the recall of information that was stored as a result of effective use of memory strategies. Developmental research indicates that children three years of age and older show similar recency effects, but the older children show a stronger primacy effect.

There are many memory strategies that can be used to improve recall, including *rehearsal* and better use of *rehearsal sets* (the nature of the items that are rehearsed). *Organization*, the reordering of items in terms of some higher-order relationship, and *elaboration*, linking items in the form of images or sentences, strengthen memories by imposing meaning on stimuli. The use of *retrieval cues* to aid in the recall of already stored information is also a very effective memory strategy. Developmental studies indicate that these memory strategies are effective in facilitating recall in children of all ages; however, developmental differences emerge when the spontaneous use of memory strategies are examined. The tendency of children to spontaneously use memory strategies increases with age, particularly in children over seven. The failure of young children to employ memory strategies on their own has been referred to as *production deficiency*. The reason for the gradual emergence of memory strategy use in children has been attributed to direct instruction by parents and teachers, an emerging *metamemory* ability that leads to the child's realization of a need for memory strategies, and to the child's expanding general knowledge base.

The importance of general knowledge in recall was demonstrated by Michelene Chi's observation of the effect of *domain-specific knowledge* on the ability to remember. Chi observed superior recall of briefly presented chess positions in children knowledgeable in chess compared to college-educated adults unfamiliar with the game of chess.

Many psychologists are currently interested in determining how knowledge is stored internally. Some describe semantic memory (knowledge about the meaning of words) as *networks* consisting of associations among closely related items, while others describe the attainment of a knowledge base in terms of *scripts*, general frameworks, or organized schemes of knowledge, in which new specific memories are stored.

Controversy: Should Children Provide Eyewitness Testimony? (pp. 342–343)
Although it has been demonstrated that children have impressive memories, some have questioned the accuracy of children's memories when they are called upon to testify in the court. Some studies indicate that young children are more likely to distort their recollection of events as a result of leading questions than are older children.

However, other studies fail to find age differences in susceptibility to leading questions. Several factors may influence children's susceptibility to misleading information, such as the perceived power of the person providing the misinformation and the emotional conditions of the courtroom proceedings.

C. **Concept Development: Class, Number, and Space** (pp. 343–349)

The child's use of *concepts,* or the way in which she organizes information on the basis of some general or abstract principle, increases the efficiency of cognitive processing. Concepts, for example, make possible the classification of pieces of information on the basis of common properties or themes. The study of concept development has indicated that classification can be based on perceptual groupings (objects that look alike), thematic relations (objects that function together or complement each other), or taxonomic groupings (on some abstract principle). Children's earliest concepts (at about twelve months) appear to be largely perceptually based. This reliance on shared perceptual features decreases with age, particularly as children begin to understand hierarchical relations among objects that are perceptually dissimilar. Eleanor Rosch suggests that the initial grouping of objects occurs at a basic level—objects go together when they look alike. By eight or nine years of age, children can begin to categorize items based on superordinate levels that do not necessarily look alike (e.g., clothing that consist of shirts, shoes, and pants). The development of taxonomic classifications may require direct instruction through formal schooling, either by providing instruction on taxonomic classification or by fostering abstract thought.

Piaget argued that preoperational children do not possess numerical concepts, that is, they do not have a full grasp of the meaning of number. Piaget provided the preoperational child's failure to conserve number as evidence for his position. According to Piaget, the preoperational child's failure to conserve number results from the failure to understand the *one-to-one correspondence* that exists between the items of each row in the conservation task and from the failure to attain an understanding of *cardinality* and *ordinality.* Current research, however, suggests that Piaget underestimated the preoperational child's understanding of number concepts. Children as young as three and four years of age understand that number terms include quantitative relations (e.g., smaller and larger), and preoperational children can understand the additive properties of numbers.

Children also organize information in terms of the position that objects take in physical space. Children initially locate objects by relying on the position of their own bodies, particularly if no external environmental cues are available. When *landmarks* or distinct cues are available, preschool-aged children make sufficient use of them to locate objects in large spatial environments. Landmark knowledge leads to *route mapping* as the child begins to use sequential directional changes to represent a spatial environment. The child's eventual integrated use of landmarks and route mapping provides him or her with a sophisticated spatial understanding called *configurational knowledge.*

D. **The Development of Problem-Solving Skills** (pp. 349–352)
Problem-solving skills, which typically involve several steps in analyzing a body of information, have been noted in young children. Investigators have observed children as young as twelve months intentionally combine several subgoals to reach a goal. Nevertheless, considerable growth in problem-solving ability occurs with development. Piaget described the development of problem-solving skills as an abrupt, qualitative shift in thinking. Many contemporary information-processing theorists emphasize the gradual refinement of component skills such as memory and attention rather than changes in logical problem-solving ability. Children as young as four years can solve formal reasoning problems that require transitive inferences (determining the relationship between two objects based on their relationships to other objects), such as in the problem: If A is greater than B and B is greater than C, then what is the relationship between A and C? Formal reasoning abilities that require the use of logic independent of the problem's content (deductive reasoning) do not appear until ten to twelve years. The ability to employ the solution to one problem to other similar problems is called *analogical transfer* and has been observed in children as young as three years. Research suggests that parents and teachers can facilitate analogical transfer in children by pointing out the similarities in the solutions to several problems.

III. **THE CONTEXT OF COGNITIVE DEVELOPMENT** (pp. 353–357)
As discussed in Chapters 2 and 6, the cognitive growth of the child is strongly influenced by interactions with adults and children in the culture in which the child lives.

A. **Cross-Cultural Differences in Cognition** (pp. 353–355)
Cross-cultural studies of cognitive development have found several large differences in children's thinking from culture to culture. For example, unlike American children, the children and adults of the Kpelle tribe of Liberia do not categorize similar items into conceptual groups in their recall. Children and adults of the Yucatán region of Mexico classify objects on the basis of functional similarities rather than taxonomically, as do older American children. These cultural differences appear to be a result of children's experience with formal schooling. Unlike most American children, individuals in the cultures tested do not usually go through formal schooling. Not all cognitive skills depend on the degree of schooling, however. Mayan children in rural Guatemala who had little or no schooling performed similar to American children on a spatial cognitive task. Thus, cross-cultural studies indicate that researchers must consider the skills and abilities that are valued within each culture when investigating the development of cognition. It becomes important, therefore, to understand how the adults of a culture convey the valued skills to children.

B. **The Role of Parents and Teachers** (pp. 356–357)
The cognitive skills and activities that are valued in a given culture are most likely conveyed to children through imitation and direct instruction by parents and teachers. Recent studies clearly document that parents and teachers provide children with direct instruction during problem-solving tasks and reading. Direct instruction is most effective

when both the parent and child are motivated and when the parent is sophisticated enough to be able to work within the child's zone of proximal development.

IV. THEMES IN DEVELOPMENT: COGNITION (pp. 357–358)
What roles do nature and nurture play in cognitive development? Piaget believed that maturation combined with experience was responsible for cognitive growth. Information-processing researchers have found that some cognitive processes are present in early childhood and thus are part of the child's physiological makeup. We have also seen that the experiences of the child can shape or refine emergent cognitive skills.

How does the sociocultural context influence cognitive development? In our Western technological society, adults transmit to children those skills that are highly valued; such cognitive processes become more abstract, planned, and oriented toward problem solving. In cultures that emphasize formalized schooling, children acquire those skills that affect the ways they think and organize their behaviors.

How does the child play an active role in the process of cognitive development? According to Piaget, the child actively organizes cognitive schemes and knowledge to adapt to the environment. The information-processing approach maintains that the child gains increasing control over her own thought processes. Attention, memory, and reasoning are used deliberately and flexibly, depending on the demands of the task at hand.

Is cognitive development continuous or stagelike? Many changes in thinking processes seem to be more gradual than stage theorists like Piaget hypothesized. Yet young children are not as capable of some forms of thought as adolescents are. This issue remains to be resolved.

How does cognitive development interact with development in other domains? The child's cognitive skills interact with almost every other aspect of development. By the same token, development in other domains can influence cognitive growth.

Key Terms Review

1. The young child's realization that objects exist even when they are not within view is called _____ .

2. The tendency for subjects to show good recall for words at the end of a list is called the _____ , while the tendency to show good recall of words at the beginning of a list is called the _____ .

3. The preoperational child who is showing _____ is unable to separate his or her own perspective from that of others.

4. According to Piaget, _____ is the tendency of the child to focus on only one aspect of a problem.

5. _____ memory concerns general concepts and facts without reference to specific events, whereas _____ memory concerns events that took place in a specific time and place.

6. _____ is the principle that the last number in a set of items counted refers to the number of items of the set, while _____ is the principle that a number refers to an item's order within the set.

7. The third stage in Piagetian theory, in which thought is logical when stimuli are physically present, is the _____ stage.

8. A(n) _____ helps extract information that has already been stored in memory.

9. _____ memory is a short-term memory store in which mental operations such as rehearsal can take place, while _____ memory holds information for extended periods of time.

10. The _____ information-processing model describes a sequence of mental structures through which information flows.

11. _____ memory is the ability to reproduce stimuli that have previously been encountered, while _____ memory is the ability to identify whether a presented stimulus has been previously encountered.

12. In Piagetian theory, _____ is the repetition of some behavior or action that produces pleasure.

13. _____ is a cognitive ability to systematically generate and evaluate potential solutions to a problem.

14. The understanding that memory is a cognitive process is called _____ .

15. _____ is a term used in Piagetian theory to describe mental actions such as reversibility.

16. The _____ is the second stage of development in Piagetian theory, in which the child attains symbolic thought.

17. When the child uses sequential directional changes to negotiate or represent a spatial environment, he is using _____ .

18. The _____ is a form of memory that holds information for a very brief period of time in a form that closely resembles the initial input.

19. When an individual employs a solution to one problem in another similar problem, she is demonstrating _____ .

20. _____ is the understanding that two sets are equivalent in number if each element in one set can be mapped onto a unique element of another set with none left over.

21. _____ are used to assess cognitive development by requiring the child to make judgments about the equivalence of two displays, one of which has undergone a transformation.

22. The preoperational child's tendency to treat two or more connected events as unrelated is referred to as a(n) _____ .

23. The knowledge about a specific content area is called _____ .

24. Children under the age of seven show a(n) _____ , which is a failure to spontaneously generate memory strategies.

25. A(n) _____ is the organization of a set of information on the basis of some general or abstract principle.

26. _____ describes continued sustained attention after an initial period of focused attention.

27. A memory strategy in which subjects reorder items to be remembered on the basis of category membership or some higher-order relationship is called _____ ; when subjects link items to be remembered in the form of an image or sentence, they are using the memory strategy called_____ .

28. Organized schemes or frameworks for commonly experienced events are called _____ .

29. The _____ is the first stage in Piagetian theory, in which thought is based primarily on action.

30. A child who is employing a deliberate behavior in order to attain a goal is using _____ .

31. _____ is a term that describes all processes involved in thinking and mental activity.

32. When an individual repeats a list of items to be remembered over and over again, he is using the memory strategy called _____ .

33. The _____ is an information-processing model that emphasizes the allocation of finite energy within the cognitive system.

34. The number of stimulus items that can be recalled after a brief period of time is called the _____ .

35. Rehearsal, organization, and elaboration are examples of _____ that enhance memory performance.

36. Older children can use a distinctive location or _____ to negotiate a spatial environment.

37. Awareness and knowledge of cognitive processes is called _____ .

38. When a child uses landmarks and routes in integrated, holistic ways to represent physical space, he is using _____ .

39. The items that are actually repeated by subjects when they are engaging in rehearsal are called the _____ .

40. _____ is the last of the Piagetian stages, in which thought is abstract and hypothetical.

41. A(n) _____ is a model of semantic memory that consists of associations among closely related items.

42. The ability to conserve becomes possible when _____ emerges, which is the ability to mentally reverse or negate an action or transformation.

Answers to Key Terms Review

1. object permanence (object concept)
2. recency effect, primacy effect
3. egocentrism
4. centration
5. Semantic, episodic
6. Cardinality, ordinality
7. concrete operational
8. retrieval cue
9. Working, long-term
10. multistore
11. Recall, recognition
12. circular reaction
13. Hypothetical reasoning
14. metamemory
15. Operation

16. preoperational stage
17. route mapping
18. sensory store
19. analogical transfer
20. One-to-one correspondence
21. Conservation tasks
22. focus on states
23. domain-specific knowledge
24. production deficiency
25. concept
26. attentional inertia
27. organization, elaboration
28. scripts
29. sensorimotor stage
30. means-end behavior
31. Cognition
32. rehearsal
33. limited-resource model
34. memory span
35. memory strategies
36. landmark
37. metacognition
38. configurational knowledge
39. rehearsal set
40. Formal operational
41. network
42. reversibility

Multiple-Choice Questions

Fact and Concept Questions

1. According to Piaget, development is _____ and thought is _____ at various points in development.
   a. continuous, qualitatively similar
   b. stagelike, quantitatively similar
   c. continuous, quantitatively different
   d. stagelike, qualitatively different

2. Piaget believed that every child will progress through the stages of development
   a. in a different order at different ages.
   b. in the same order, but at different ages.
   c. in the same order at the same ages.
   d. in the order consistent with his or her environmental experiences.

3. The first significant accomplishment of the sensorimotor stage is the infant's deliberate use of an action to achieve a goal, referred to as
   a. a circular reaction.
   b. means-ends behavior.
   c. object permanence.
   d. deferred imitation.

4. According to Piaget, prior to four months of age, the infant
   a. does not possess reflexes.
   b. does not possess an object concept.
   c. possesses a rudimentary object concept.
   d. possesses symbolic thought.

5. Beginning at about two years of age, children's thinking is characterized by
   a. reversibility.
   b. circular reactions.
   c. the ability to conserve.
   d. the semiotic function.

6. If a child can observe a transformation in a physical quantity and reason that the amount remains the same, then the child can solve _____ tasks.
   a. conservation
   b. centration
   c. operational
   d. reversibility

7. At approximately seven years of age, the child becomes capable of solving conservation tasks, indicating the transition to the _____ stage.
   a. preoperational
   b. concrete operational
   c. formal operational
   d. sensorimotor

8. A key feature of formal operational thought is
   a. the inability to take the perspective of another.
   b. the ability to generate hypothetical solutions to a problem.
   c. the ability to think logically only about objects immediately present.
   d. the inability to show reversibility in thinking.

9. One of the criticisms of Piaget's theory of cognitive development is that
   a. he overestimated the abilities of young children.
   b. there appear to be more than four qualitative stages of cognitive growth.
   c. egocentricism is not as prevalent among preschoolers as suggested by Piaget.
   d. cognitive development does not appear to depend on the maturation of the central nervous system, as presumed by Piaget.

10. The limited-resource model accounts for cognitive development in terms of
    a. an increase in the size of working memory.
    b. an increase in the number of control processes.
    c. an increase in the number of mental storage systems.
    d. more efficient allocation of the finite energy available for cognitive activity.

11. According to information-processing models of cognitive development, the first step in the flow of information through the cognitive-processing system is
    a. sensorimotor processing.
    b. attention.
    c. retrieval.
    d. recognition.

12. Modern research on the development of recognition memory indicates that recognition
    a. does not appear until eight to nine months.
    b. marks the end of the sensorimotor stage.
    c. begins at or shortly after birth.
    d. begins to develop after recall memory is established.

13. Working memory, or short-term memory, is believed to be tapped by _____ tasks.
    a. free recall
    b. conservation
    c. recognition
    d. memory span

14. Studies on free recall experiments in children indicate that there are
    a. developmental differences in the primacy effect but not the recency effect.
    b. developmental differences in the recency effect but not the primacy effect.
    c. developmental differences in the primacy and recency effect.
    d. few, if any, developmental differences in the primacy and recency effects.

15. Of the memory strategies discussed in the text, which is the last to appear?
    a. Retrieval cues
    b. Organization
    c. Elaboration
    d. Rehearsal

16. Organizing isolated pieces of information on the basis of some general or abstract principle describes the use of
    a. concepts.
    b. relations.
    c. attention.
    d. memory.

17. The earliest signs of classification skills in children begin toward the end of the first year, when they begin to group objects that
    a. go together functionally.
    b. usually complement each other.
    c. look alike.
    d. belong together based on some abstract principle.

18. Infants as young as nine months have been shown to
    a. classify objects thematically.
    b. use one-to-one correspondence.
    c. conserve quantity.
    d. use landmarks to locate objects.

19. In an experiment on problem solving in twelve-month-olds, Willatts and Rosie found that
    a. the infants in the experimental group could not discover the solution to getting an attractive toy.
    b. the infants in the experimental group could successfully reach the toy by removing the barrier and pulling the string.
    c. the infants in the experimental group removed the barrier but did not pull the string to grasp the toy.
    d. the infants in the control group uncovered the toy by pulling off a cloth.

20. During adolescence, individuals develop the concept of logical necessity. This describes how adolescents and adults can
    a. apply familiar skills to a novel context.
    b. draw conclusions from truthful premises.
    c. draw conclusions from the elements of a problem regardless of the truthfulness of the premises.
    d. decide on the relationship between two objects based on their relationship to other objects.

Application Questions

1. Talia cried when her mother took candy away from her and placed it in her pocket. Talia reached in, trying to retrieve the hidden candy from her mother's pocket. Talia's behavior indicates that she has
   a. circular reactions.
   b. conservation.
   c. object permanence.
   d. egocentrism.

2. Oliver has begun to speak, indicating that he can represent the world symbolically. According to Piaget, Oliver has
   a. reached the formal operational stage.
   b. reached the preoperational stage.
   c. reached the concrete operational stage.
   d. developed deductive reasoning.

3. Salvatore has reached the concrete operational stage, as evidenced by his ability to solve conservation problems. One reason Salvatore can solve conservation problems is that he can perform the mental operation of
   a. reversibility.
   b. centration.
   c. analogical transfer.
   d. deductive reasoning.

4. Cheryl, who is five years older than her brother, is much better than her younger brother at ignoring irrelevant details when engaged in an activity. Cheryl has developed
   a. object permanence.
   b. semantic memory.
   c. selective attention.
   d. metacognition.

5. Twelve-year-old Mandy is better able than her six-year-old sister, Maureen, to
   a. pay attention to two different stimuli at the same time.
   b. recall the irrelevant dimensions of a task.
   c. focus her attention on one dimension and ignore an irrelevant dimension.
   d. recall words at the end of a long list of words.

6. Rebecca has a vivid memory of her fifth birthday party because her dog jumped up on the table and ate her birthday cake. Rebecca's memory is referred to as _____ memory.
   a. semantic
   b. short-term
   c. working
   d. episodic

7. Philip realizes that it is easier for him to remember a short list than a long list of words. Philip is showing
   a. metamemory.
   b. object permanence.
   c. episodic memory.
   d. selective attention.

8. Zachary, who is five years old, has trouble remembering the alphabet but can remember the names and details of dozens of species of birds. Zachary is demonstrating
   a. episodic memory.
   b. metamemory.
   c. configurational knowledge.
   d. domain-specific knowledge.

9. Renee knows that if she is taller than her sister, and her sister is taller than her friend Jessica, then Renee must be taller than Jessica. Renee must have developed
   a. configurational knowledge.
   b. deductive reasoning.
   c. analogical transfer.
   d. metacognition.

10. Maria, who grew up in America, has had much more formal schooling than Pablo, who grew up in Mexico. Which of the following pairs of items is Maria most likely to group together?
    a. Pitchfork and hay
    b. Pitchfork and shovel
    c. Chicken and egg
    d. Chicken and basket

Answers to Multiple-Choice Questions

The correct answer appears first and is preceded by an asterisk.

Answers to Fact and Concept Questions

1. *d. Piaget described development as stagelike, with thought becoming qualitatively reorganized at various times during development. (p. 318)
   a. Piaget was a stage theorist and, therefore, did not describe development as continuous, although he did describe qualitative reorganizations in cognitive development.

b. Although Piaget did describe development as stagelike, he did not describe the transition from stage to stage as quantitative, that is, as a gradual and measurable change.

c. As a stage theorist, Piaget argued against the view that development was a quantitatively continuous process.

2. *b. Piaget believed that development is stagelike, but he also suggested that because of differences in rate of maturation and environmental experiences, children may reach these stages at different ages. (p. 319)

a. Piaget believed that the stages of development were invariant, that they occur in the same order in all children.

c. Piaget believed that development is stagelike, but he also suggested that because of differences in rate of maturation and differences in environmental experiences, children may reach these stages at different ages.

d. Piaget acknowledged the importance of environmental experiences on development, but he believed that such changes could not alter the sequence of the stages.

3. *b. Throughout the first two years, the child gradually learns to produce actions that allow her to attain specific goals; this accomplishment of the sensorimotor stage is known as means-end behavior. (p. 319)

a. Although a circular reaction is a motor response initiated by the young child, it is not a deliberate action to accomplish a goal; a circular reaction usually results from accidentally produced responses that provide some pleasure.

c. Although object permanence is an accomplishment of the sensorimotor stage, it does not refer to the child's deliberate use of an action to achieve a goal.

d. Deferred imitation, the ability to imitate a model who is no longer present, marks the end of the sensorimotor stage and, thus, is not one of the first accomplishments in the first stage of development.

4. *b. Piaget argued that the infant does not have an object concept until four months of age, when he will begin to lift a cloth from a partially covered object. (p. 320)

a. Infants have several reflexes from the time of birth.

c. Piaget was a stage theorist and believed in sudden, qualitative shifts in thought; thus, he argued that the object concept is not present prior to four months.

d. Piaget argued that symbolic thought did not occur until the preoperational stage, when children are about two years old.

5. *d. The ability to use a symbol, called the semiotic function, marks the beginning of the preoperational stage, when the child is about two years old. (p. 321)

a. According to Piaget, reversibility is a mental operation that the preoperational child cannot perform. Because the two-year-old is just entering the preoperational stage, she lacks reversibility.

b. The circular reaction is a characteristic of the young infant in the sensorimotor stage.

c. According to Piaget, the ability to conserve does not occur until the end of the preoperational stage, when the child is about six or seven years old.

6. *a. Conservation tasks are used to assess the child's cognitive development by requiring her or him to make judgments about the equivalence of two displays after one of the displays undergoes a transformation. (p. 322)
   b. Centration is not a task for assessing a child's cognitive development; it is one of several cognitive traits that the child must possess to solve conservation tasks.
   c. Operations are not tasks for assessing a child's cognitive development; *operation* is a term in Piagetian theory for mental actions such as reversibility.
   d. Reversibility is not a task for assessing a child's cognitive development; it is one of several cognitive traits that the child must possess to solve conservation tasks.

7. *b. When children begin to be able to solve conservation tasks, they have entered the concrete operational stage. (p. 322)
   a. Preoperational children cannot solve conservation problems because they have several distinct thought limitations.
   c. The formal operational stage is the final Piagetian stage; the child will have already been able to solve conservation tasks before entering this final stage.
   d. The sensorimotor stage is the first stage of development and ends at about two years.

8. *b. By adolescence the child will most likely be thinking logically and abstractly, and be able to reason hypothetically. (p. 323)
   a. The inability to separate one's own perspective from that of others, called egocentrism, is a characteristic of the preoperational stage. By the formal operational stage, the last stage of development, the individual is no longer egocentric.
   c. A child who is unable to think of an object that is not immediately present lacks on object concept; this thought deficit is a characteristic of the sensorimotor stage.
   d. Children who lack reversibility are unable to conserve, a characteristic of preoperational thought.

9. *c. Modern naturalistic studies of children's communication attempts suggest that preschoolers may not be as egocentric as Piaget presumed. (p. 327)
   a. Many modern experimental results suggest that Piaget underestimated the young child's abilities.
   b. Most of the modern criticisms of Piaget's theory center on the argument that development may be more continuous than presumed by Piaget, not on the number of stages that exist.
   d. Although cognitive development does not appear to be as dependent on the maturation of the central nervous system as presumed by Piaget, it still plays an important role, particularly early in development.

10. *d. The limited-resource models assume that developmental changes in information-processing abilities result from increases in operational efficiency. (p. 330)
  a. The limited-resource model does not emphasize any one particular memory structure like working memory.
  b. It is the multistore model that places emphasis on the control processes that guide information through the various mental structures.
  c. Mental storage systems are some of the structures that the multistore models, not the limited-resource models, assume increase in capacity with development.

11. *b. Before information can be processed it must enter the information-processing system; thus, the individual must first attend to the information that requires processing. (p. 332)
  a. Sensorimotor is a stage of Piaget's theory; it is not a step in an information-processing model of cognitive development.
  c. Information cannot be retrieved from memory until it is first attended to and stored in memory.
  d. Recognition is a type of memory that requires identifying a stimulus that was previously encountered; thus, it cannot be the first step of a cognitive processing system.

12. *c. The use of habituation procedures suggests that recognition occurs very early and may be present at birth. (p. 334)
  a. Studies have observed excellent recognition memory in children as young as five to six months.
  b. The end of the sensorimotor stage is marked by the ability to solve conservation tasks, not by a change in memory.
  d. Recognition memory has been demonstrated to be the earliest form of memory.

13. *d. The memory span, the number of items that can be recalled after a brief period of time, is believed to tap working memory. (p. 336)
  a. Free recall tasks tap long-term memories.
  b. Conservation tasks are used to assess cognitive development, not memory per se.
  c. Recognition tasks are used to determine if an individual can identify whether a stimulus was previously presented—in other words, they test long-term memory.

14. *a. Developmental differences in the primacy effect, better recall of words in the beginning of a list, is most likely a result of differences in the use of memory strategies; developmental differences in the recency effect have not been observed. (p. 337)
  b. Developmental differences were not seen in the recency effect, better recall of words at the end of a list, but were seen in the primacy effect.
  c. Developmental differences were observed in the primacy effect but not the recency effect.
  d. Although developmental differences were not seen in the recency effect, they were observed in the primacy effect.

15. *c. Elaboration as a memory strategy does not occur until adolescence or later. (p. 339)
    a. The spontaneous use of retrieval cues to aid recall emerges in older children at around ten or eleven years, but this is not the last strategy to appear.
    b. The spontaneous use of organization appears in children around ten to eleven years old.
    d. The tendency to rehearse increases with age, with older children showing greater rehearsal than younger children, but rehearsal is not the last memory strategy to develop.

16. *a. When a child is organizing information about the world by employing abstract principles, he is using concepts. (p. 344)
    b. Examining relationships between objects and events is important for learning about the world, but *relations* is not a term used to describe this process.
    c. Attention is a state of alertness or arousal that allows a person to take in information from the environment; it is not a way of organizing incoming information.
    d. Memory is necessary to organize information, but this organization process is not memory itself.

17. *c. Children's tendency to group objects based on similar perceptual characteristics emerges early in development. (p. 344)
    a. When grouping objects that have related functions, children are using thematic relations; this classification begins between one and three years, but it is not the first sign of classification skills.
    b. When grouping objects that complement each other (e.g., spoon and cereal), children are using thematic relations; this classification begins between one and three years, but it is not the first sign of classification skills.
    d. Grouping objects based on some abstract principle is called taxonomic grouping; this type of classification does not occur until after children are capable of perceptually based grouping.

18. *d. Infants as young as nine months have been observed to locate items by using environmental cues or landmarks. (p. 348)
    a. Children do not begin to classify objects thematically until one to three years.
    b. Not understanding one-to-one correspondence is a limitation of the preoperational child, so a nine-month-old child would certainly not understand this numerical concept.
    c. Children cannot conserve quantity until seven to eleven years, when they enter the concrete operational stage.

19. *b. The children in the experimental group were able to solve the problem and reach the toy. (p. 349)
    a. The results of the study showed that infants were capable of intentionally performing several actions to reach an attractive toy.
    c. The children in the control group failed to pull the string; the infants in the experimental group did pull on the string to get the toy.

d. This experiment did not involve the covering of a toy with a cloth.

20. *c. The ability to think abstractly about logical necessity regardless of the truthfulness of the premises does not appear until adolescence. (p. 351)
   a. The ability to apply familiar skills to a new context is called analogical transfer, not logical necessity.
   b. The concept of logical necessity requires drawing a logical conclusion independent of the content of the premises; thus, the premises do not need to be truthful.
   d. The ability to decide on the relationship between two objects based on their relationship to other objects requires an ability in formal reasoning called transitive inference, not the concept of logical necessity.

Answers to Application Questions

1. *c. In order for Talia to continue to search for an object that is no longer visible, she must have an object concept (also called *object permanence*)—the realization that the object still exists even when it is not in view. (p. 320)
   a. Circular reactions refer to the repetition of a behavior. Talia is not displaying this form of behavior.
   b. Conservation requires a judgment concerning the equivalence of two displays after one of the displays undergoes a transformation; the scenario described here is not an example of a conservation task.
   d. This scenario does not describe an example of egocentrism, which is the inability of the preoperational child to separate her own perspective from those of others.

2. *b. The beginning of the preoperational stage is marked by the semiotic function—the ability to use symbols, objects, or words to represent objects or events. (p. 321)
   a. The formal operational stage (the last of Piaget's stages) is marked by more complex forms of abstract and hypothetical thought, and occurs long after the child has learned to speak.
   c. The beginning of the concrete operational stage is indicated by the ability to solve conservation tasks; there is no indication that Oliver can solve conservation tasks.
   d. Deductive reasoning is a form of formal reasoning that does not emerge until the formal operational stage; because Oliver is just beginning to speak, he cannot be in the formal operational stage.

3. *a. One of the reasons that preoperational children cannot solve conservation tasks is that they lack reversibility—the ability to mentally reverse an action or transformation on quantities. Since Salvatore can conserve, he must have reversibility. (p. 322)
   b. Centration, the tendency to focus on only one aspect of a problem, is one of several limitations that hinder children from solving conservation tasks. Because Salvatore can solve conservation problems, he is unlikely to show centration.

c. Analogical transfer is an important cognitive achievement that occurs in the formal operational stage; it is not necessary to solve conservation tasks. There is no indication that Salvatore can show analogical transfer.
d. Deductive reasoning is not evidenced until the formal operational stage.

4. *c. With development, attention becomes selective, so that the child is much more likely to ignore information that is irrelevant or distracts from the focused activity. (p. 333)
a. Knowledge of object permanence is unrelated to the selective ability to focus attention on relevant vs. irrelevant task dimensions.
b. Semantic memory involves memories for general concepts and is not related to selective attention.
d. Metacognition is the achievement of the child's awareness of her own cognitive processes and does not control the selectivity of attention.

5. *c. One of the developmental trends in attention that was described in the text is the increased ability to selectively attend to relevant stimuli. Because Mandy is older than Maureen, she probably shows better selective attention. (p. 333)
a. The ability to attend to two different stimuli simultaneously is a difficult task; no evidence was presented in the text showing developmental change in this ability.
b. No evidence was described in the text indicating that older children show greater recall of a dimension deemed irrelevant.
d. Better recall of words at the end of a list is called the recency effect. Studies have found few developmental differences in the recency effect; therefore, Mandy and Maureen are unlikely to show differences in the recency effect.

6. *d. Because Rebecca is recalling a particular event or episode that she experienced in the past, her memory is classified as episodic memory. (p. 334)
a. Semantic memories are memories of specific facts or concepts with no reference to any specific event. Because Rebecca is recalling a specific event (a previous birthday), her memory is not semantic.
b. Short-term memory (also called working memory) is a temporary form of memory during which operations such as rehearsal and categorization can take place, not a permanently stored memory of a previous event.
c. Working memory is a form of short-term memory and, thus, would not contain long-term memories such as Rebecca's recollection of her fifth birthday.

7. *a. Philip's realization of what is required of him to remember a list of words suggests that he has developed metamemory, an awareness of his memory as a cognitive process. (p. 340)
b. Although memory of objects is necessary to achieve object permanence, object permanence does not define a child's understanding of his own memory processes.
c. Episodic memory defines a specific type of memory, not the individual's realization of memory as a cognitive process.
d. Selective attention, while important for any memory process, does not define the individual's realization of memory as a cognitive process.

8. *d. Zachary's good memory for a specific content area (birds) demonstrates the influence of domain-specific knowledge on memory. (p. 341)
   a. Episodic memory is memory of specific events; Zachary's knowledge of birds involves remembering facts about birds without reference to any specific event.
   b. Metamemory is not a type of memory but an awareness of memory as a cognitive process.
   c. Configurational knowledge is a sophisticated form of spatial understanding, not a form of memory.

9. *b. Renee put two premises together (Renee is taller than her sister, and her sister is taller than Jessica) to draw a logical conclusion (Renee is taller than Jessica); this type of formal reasoning is called deductive reasoning. (p. 351)
   a. Configurational knowledge is a sophisticated form of spatial understanding. Renee's ability displayed in this scenario does not require spatial knowledge.
   c. Analogical transfer involves the ability to employ a solution to one problem to another new, but similar, problem.
   d. Although Renee may have metacognition, the scenario stated in the question is not tapping metacognition.

10. *b. Unlike uneducated children, children with formal education classify objects on the basis of taxonomic relations. Pitchfork and shovel are taxonomically related because they are both farm tools. (p. 353)
   a. Unlike uneducated children, children with formal education classify objects on the basis of taxonomic relations. Pitchfork and hay are functionally, not taxonomically, related.
   c. Unlike uneducated children, children with formal education classify objects on the basis of taxonomic relations. Chicken and egg are thematically, not taxonomically, related because the two naturally "go together."
   d. Unlike uneducated children, children with formal education classify objects on the basis of taxonomic relations. Chicken and basket are not taxonomically related but may be thematically related if, for example, baskets are used to carry chickens.

CHAPTER 9

INTELLIGENCE

LEARNING OBJECTIVES

1. Identify the major issues concerning the nature of intelligence. (pp. 363–364)

2. Describe and discuss the various psychometric approaches to intelligence. (pp. 364–368)

3. Distinguish between the learning models of intelligence and the more traditional psychometric approaches. (pp. 369–371)

4. Describe the information-processing theorists' views of intelligence and discuss the emphasis they place on intelligence as mental processes. (pp. 371–376)

5. Describe the various standardized tests of intelligence that have been developed to assess infants and older children. (pp. 376–384)

6. Discuss the stability of IQ scores in children and intelligence tests in infants. (pp. 384–387)

7. Discuss the predictive utility of IQ tests. (pp. 387–388)

8. Discuss the issues concerning group differences in IQ scores. (pp. 389–391)

9. Identify and discuss which key characteristics of the child's home are related to intellectual development. (pp. 392–394)

10. Discuss the controversy over the importance of birth order on children's IQ. (p. 395)

11. Describe the role of the child's sociocultural environment in the development of intellectual ability. (pp. 395–397)

12. Discuss the effectiveness of early intervention programs on the IQ of disadvantaged children and other children at risk for lower intellectual functioning. (pp. 397–400)

CHAPTER OUTLINE

I. **WHAT IS INTELLIGENCE?** (pp. 363–376)
Is intelligence a general characteristic that appears in many behaviors and activities, or does it consist of separate skills and abilities? Should intelligence be conceptualized in terms of the products that arise from people's activities (emphasized by the psychometric approach) or in terms of the processes people use to solve problems (emphasized by the learning and information-processing approaches)? These two issues are addressed in this chapter.

A. **Psychometric Approaches** (pp. 364–368)
Sir Francis Galton spearheaded the study of individual differences in psychophysical responses, believing that any observed differences were largely a result of genetic influences. James McKean Cattell expanded on Galton's ideas and coined the term *mental test* to suggest that psychophysical measures can provide estimates of intelligence. At the turn of the nineteenth century, Alfred Binet and Theodore Simon, developed the first formal intelligence test and thus established the *psychometric model* of intelligence. Psychometric models test large numbers of individuals in order to quantify and rank-order individual differences in abilities.

Charles Spearman's two-factor theory emphasized a general (or global) intelligence factor that is involved in any cognitive task, although he did acknowledge more specific knowledge and abilities as well. To provide support for his theory Spearman developed and used a statistical procedure, called *factor analysis*, to examine the relationship among a large number of correlations. Louis Thurstone believed that intelligence was comprised of seven independent abilities rather than one general factor. Guilford also posited separate abilities, but he placed his estimate at 150 factors, each factor arising from the unique combination of three basic elements—operations, content, and products. Raymond Cattell and John Horn distinguished between two types of intelligence: *fluid intelligence*, which consists of biologically based mental abilities relatively free of cultural influences, and *crystallized intelligence*, which consists of mental skills acquired through experience in a particular cultural context. Psychometric models have been successful in demonstrating individual differences in various mental tasks but have not resolved the debate about the exact nature of intelligence.

B. **Learning Approaches** (pp. 369–371)

According to learning models, the best approach to understanding the nature of intelligence is to examine the mental processes used during learning. Robert Gagné describes a dynamic model in which intelligence is seen as emerging from an increasingly complex and hierarchical learning process. Joseph Campione and Anne Brown also emphasize the importance of processes, particularly the speed of learning and the ability to transfer what was learned in one context to another context. The latter process is seen as requiring the development of metacognition—each person's ability to monitor his own cognitive abilities. Campione and Brown's transfer theory borrows many of the assumptions of information-processing theories and traditional learning theory.

C. **Information-Processing Approaches** (pp. 371–375)

Like the learning models, the information-processing models focus on mental processes rather than on mental structures. Some of these models have suggested that differences in the speed of cognitive activities, as measured by habituation tasks in infants and reaction times in older children and adults, reflect differences in intelligence. It is important to note, however, that although relationships between speed of processing and intelligence have been observed, processing times may differ among individuals because of motivational, attentional, and cultural factors.

Robert Sternberg's *triarchic theory of intelligence* emphasizes global and specific skills. His theory combines three major subtheories of intelligence to define precisely the large number of cognitive processes and abilities necessary for human intelligence. The three major emphases of the theory are on the individual's ability to adapt to a new environment (contextual subtheory), to deal with novelty and develop automatization of cognitive processes (two-factor subtheory), and to process information effectively and efficiently (componential subtheory). Howard Gardner places greater emphasis on specific skills in his theory of multiple intelligences and stresses the role that culture plays in defining intelligence by specifying the skills that it values.

II. **MEASURING INTELLIGENCE** (pp. 376–388)

The scores on standardized tests of intelligence, such as the IQ test, are assumed to be normally distributed in the population. Because of the statistical nature of normal curves, the percentage of people attaining each possible score can be estimated. For example, less than 3 percent of the population is estimated to have IQ scores lower than 70 (mental retardation) or greater than 130 (gifted).

A. **Standardized Tests of Intelligence** (pp. 378–384)

Psychometricians construct and interpret tests of intelligence. Many different such tests have been developed and are available for use today. Some are administered to individuals, while others are given to groups. The type of test administered also depends on the age of the child. Infant tests of intelligence are administered individually. The Bayley Scales of Infant Mental and Motor Development, which was designed specifically to predict later childhood competence, measures mental and motor abilities. The Fagan Test of Infant Intelligence measures infant recognition memory as determined by the visual fixations of infants to novel stimuli. This test is based on the assumption that depressed responses to novelty indicate an increased risk for intellectual deficits. Individually administered tests include the Stanford-Binet, the Wechsler Intelligence Scale for Children, and the Kaufman Assessment Battery for Children.

The most widely used test for school-aged children is the Stanford-Binet, which has undergone several revisions since it was first developed. Alfred Binet first introduced the concept of *mental age*, which is an expression of a child's mental abilities. Lewis Terman modified and standardized the Binet scales and introduced the *intelligence quotient (IQ)*, which provided an estimate of the child's abilities in four broad areas of mental functioning. In the newest version a *deviation IQ* is provided for each of the four test areas. The Wechsler Intelligence Scale for Children also measures several of the child's mental abilities. The Kaufman Assessment Battery differs from the other two tests in that it focuses on how children process information rather than on the collection of abilities that children display. Group tests are sometimes used because they are more easily administered, are less time consuming, and are easier to score. However, the child who has language difficulties or poor reading skills may be at a disadvantage in a group test. Moreover, group tests don't provide the clinical insights into the child's behavioral characteristics that are possible when the tests are administered on a one-to-one basis. Piagetian tests of intelligence are also available, although not very common. Such tests are based on conservation tasks and are one of the few distinctly developmental tests.

B. **Stability and Prediction: Key Factors in Testing** (pp. 384–388)
Intelligence tests were first developed to predict children's future functioning. Many psychologists believed that intelligence tests administered in early life could be used to predict future performance because the results of such tests were expected to be stable when administered repeatedly with age. Two longitudinal studies, the Berkeley Growth Study and the Fels Longitudinal Study, found that although IQ scores are fairly stable from preschool years to early adulthood, large fluctuations in IQ scores also occur. Shifts in IQ scores result from environmental influences such as the presence or absence of family stress and parents' child-rearing styles. Correlations between some infant measures of intelligence and later childhood measures have been low. Higher correlations are seen when measures of visual attention in infancy are compared with cognitive and language proficiency at three to five years, suggesting that the mental skills tapped by novelty problems may play a role in later cognitive skills. Infant temperament may also be related to later mental functioning.

III. **FACTORS THAT INFLUENCE INTELLIGENCE** (pp. 388–400)

A. **Group Differences in IQ Scores** (pp. 389–391)
The causes of racial and socioeconomic differences in IQ have been debated within the framework of the nature-nurture issue. Arthur Jensen argued that lower IQ scores among African Americans compared with Caucasians was due largely to genetic, or heritability, factors. Jensen's conclusions were criticized on several grounds; the strongest criticism stressed the difficulty of explaining between-group differences in intelligence with

estimates of within-group heritability. *Cross-fostering* studies, which examined the intellectual development of minority children who had been adopted by middle-class white families, have provided considerable support for the strong role of environmental influences on IQ scores of African American children but have also provided support for a role of heredity in intelligence. Some psychologists argue that group differences in IQ are a result of *test bias*. Traditional psychometric tests are seen as not being culturally fair for children of some social and cultural backgrounds. Tests that have been described as culturally fair have yielded mixed results; some have found group differences similar to those seen with more traditional tests, while other tests have yielded smaller group differences than typically observed. Another explanation of observed group differences in IQ scores centers on the differences between minority and majority children in terms of experience with, and attitude toward, test-taking.

B. Experiences in the Child's Home (pp. 392–394)
To determine the role of the environment in intelligence a project called the Home Observation for Measurement of the Environment (HOME) inventory was developed. The HOME inventory was a longitudinal study that examined the quality of caregiver-child interactions in the home and its relationship to later IQ scores and other competencies. This study found significant relationships between certain features of the home environment and later IQ scores, language proficiency, and school achievement. Parental emotional and verbal responsivity to the child and degree of parental involvement with their children were among the important factors identified. Other studies indicate that parents' expectations may also influence their children's later performance on proficiency tests. However, it may be that the direction of the influence is in the other direction, that is, the child's already existing abilities may shape the parent's expectations. An ambitious study by Luis Laosa found that several aspects of parenting practices, particularly by mothers, predicted children's IQ scores. Beneficial practices for the development of verbal skills included reading to their young children and using modeling as a teaching strategy. Moreover, the overall socioeducational value of the mother highly correlated with the child's IQ.

Controversy: Do Birth Order and Sibling Spacing Explain Intelligence? (p. 395)
The *confluence model* proposed by Robert Zajonc and his colleagues hypothesizes that a child's intellectual attainment is influenced by her birth position in the family and by the spacing among the children in the family. According to the model, as the number of children in a family increases, the intellectual environment is weakened, and thus the first-born child should have the greatest intellectual advantages. Several studies have supported these predictions. However, the model also predicts that as the spacing between children in a family increases, the intellectual environment should increase because of the larger number of mature siblings. These predictions have not been generally supported. Nevertheless the debate over the confluence model has stressed the importance of understanding the role of family interactions in intellectual development.

C. **The Child's Sociocultural Environment** (pp. 395–397)

The intellectual abilities displayed by individuals often depend on their cultural background. To better understand the role of culture in the development of various abilities, psychologists have examined various cultures in terms of 1) the activities and behaviors that are essential for adaptation and survival within the culture, 2) parental attitudes toward the role of the child in the culture, and 3) the emphasis the culture places on the formal schooling of its children.

D. **Early Intervention Programs and IQ** (pp. 397–400)

Researchers have addressed the issue of the role of nature and nurture in intellectual development by examining the effect of compensatory education on the IQs of disadvantaged minority children. Project Head Start was designed to place children from lower socioeconomic classes into programs that provided them with the cognitive stimulation that was presumed to be available to the more advantaged middle-class children. If poor performance on IQ tests by children in lower socioeconomic classes was indeed a result of deprived environments, then children in the Head Start program should show increases in IQ scores. Although the initial results found no significant effects on IQ scores, more recent evaluations have established significant positive influences on the intellectual performance of children participating in the program. However, the gains were only transitory, appearing in the first few years and fading in subsequent years. It is unclear why the gains in IQ gradually fade, but researchers have suggested that the poor quality of subsequent school experiences may "undo" the effects of Head Start. Other researchers suggest that Head Start can be shown to have lasting effects if, rather than examining the results of the usual tests of cognitive skills, other areas of intelligence are examined, such as social competence and general success in school.

The Carolina Abecedarian Project aimed to prevent lower intellectual functioning of infants determined to be at risk by providing the infants with medical and nutritional assistance as well as a structured program of day care. As with the Head Start program, initial increases in intellectual functioning waned in some, but not all, children by the time they reached their fifth birthday. A decision on whether early intervention programs are successful depends on one's definition of success. The answer is more optimistic if success is defined within a broad concept of intelligence that includes social competence and success in school than if defined as a permanent increase in IQ scores.

IV. **THEMES IN DEVELOPMENT: INTELLIGENCE** (pp. 400–402)

What roles do nature and nurture play in the development of intelligence? Most psychologists agree that heredity plays a role in the child's intellectual development. Yet research also shows that the child's experiences at home or in educational intervention programs, together with intellectual skills that are touted by the larger culture, modulate how the child's genetic blueprint actually comes to fruition.

How does the sociocultural context influence the development of intelligence? A culture's demands and expectations frame the way in which intelligent behavior will be defined in the first place. On standardized tests, children who have experiences consistent with the knowledge tested will perform well, while others may be at a disadvantage. Other factors associated with social class can also influence IQ test performance.

How does the child play an active role in the development of intelligence? Learning and information-processing approaches have focused on the child's ability to monitor his own cognitive processes and other cognitive activities. Piaget's theory also emphasizes the child's active construction of knowledge.

Is the development of intelligence continuous or stagelike? Many believe that intelligence is a stable, relatively unchanging characteristic that the child is born with. Learning and information-processing theorists, however, see intelligence as a process wherein the child becomes capable of more sophisticated cognitive processing with age. Piaget views intellectual development as stagelike.

Are there sensitive periods in the development of intelligence? Since the results of early intervention programs show that children benefit from participation, early childhood may be the prime time to lay the foundations for intellectual development. However, such findings do not mean that children can't show significant intellectual gains later in development.

How does the development of intelligence interact with development in other domains? Children who obtain high IQ scores are more likely to be successful in school and, as adults, to hold high-status jobs and be successful in them. Also, the child's experiences in various domains can influence intelligence, as defined by newer theoretical perspectives.

Key Terms Review

1. _____ are psychologists who specialize in the construction and interpretation of standardized tests.

2. The _____ is computed by comparing the child's performance on an intelligence test with that of a standardization sample.

3. The _____ was developed by Robert Sternberg; it characterizes intelligence as consisting of three major components.

4. The hypothesis that intellectual attainment is influenced by birth order and spacing among children in a family is known as the _____ .

5. The _____ of a child is expressed as the child's mental abilities relative to the performance of children of various ages.

6. _____ consists of mental skills derived from cultural experience, whereas _____ consists of biologically based mental abilities that are relatively uninfluenced by cultural experiences.

7. Some psychologists argue that traditional standardized tests suffer from _____ because they do not adequately measure the competencies of children from diverse cultural backgrounds.

8. The _____ is a theoretical perspective that quantifies individual differences in test scores in order to establish a rank order of abilities.

9. Psychologists often examine the relationship among a large number of correlations by using the statistical procedure called _____ .

10. The _____ is a numerical score an individual obtains on an intelligence test.

11. A research study that examines children reared in environments that differ from those of their biological parents is referred to as a(n) _____ .

Answers to Key Terms Review

1. Psychometricians
2. deviation IQ
3. triarchic theory
4. confluence model
5. mental age
6. Crystallized intelligence, fluid intelligence
7. test bias
8. psychometric model
9. factor analysis
10. intelligence quotient (IQ)
11. cross-fostering study

Multiple-Choice Questions

Fact and Concept Questions

1. The first person to propose that intelligence is inherited was
   a. Charles Darwin.
   b. Alfred Binet.
   c. Sir Francis Galton.
   d. Louis Thurstone.

2. When psychologists seek to quantify individual differences in intellectual capabilities, they are working in the _____ tradition.
   a. psychophysical
   b. psychometric
   c. learning
   d. process

3. Charles Spearman's view of intelligence is that it
   a. is a composite of several distinct abilities.
   b. is a unitary phenomenon.
   c. cannot be measured.
   d. is based on sensory abilities.

4. The role of social knowledge is important in _____ model of intelligence.
   a. Charles Spearman's
   b. Sir Francis Galton's
   c. Louis Thurstone's
   d. J. P. Guilford's

5. Raymond Cattell and John Horn described a type of intelligence that is acquired through cultural experiences and consists of knowledge about vocabulary, reading comprehension, and information about the world. They called this
   a. crystallized intelligence.
   b. fluid intelligence.
   c. g factor intelligence.
   d. social intelligence.

6. According to Joseph Campione and Ann Brown, an essential component of intelligence is the individual's ability to monitor her own cognitive processes, referred to as _____ skills.
   a. structural
   b. process
   c. fluid
   d. metacognitive

7. In Robert Sternberg's triarchic theory of intelligence, the ability to process novelty and automatize cognitive processes is part of the _____ subtheory.
   a. contextual
   b. two-facet
   c. componential
   d. automatization

8. The population mean on most standardized tests of intelligence is _____ and the standard deviation is _____ .
   a. 50, 100
   b. 100, 50
   c. 100, 15
   d. 68, 15

9. The most widely used standardized infant intelligence test is the
   a. Fagan Test of Infant Intelligence.
   b. Bayley Scales of Infant Mental and Motor Development.
   c. Stanford-Binet Intelligence Test for Infants.
   d. K-ABC.

10. Performance on the Fagan Test of Infant Intelligence
    a. correlates well with IQ scores three years later.
    b. does not correlate with IQ scores after infancy.
    c. is unreliable as a measure of visual attention.
    d. is based on crystallized intelligence.

11. A child's mental age refers to his
    a. age in years.
    b. intellectual ability compared to chronological age mates.
    c. ability to solve novelty problems.
    d. performance on sensory discrimination tasks.

12. A standardized test that is designed according to a Piagetian view of intelligence is the
    a. K-ABC.
    b. WISC-R.
    c. Bayley Scales of Infant Mental and Motor Development.
    d. Concept Assessment Kit.

13. IQ scores are most predictive of
    a. occupational success.
    b. mental health.
    c. school achievement.
    d. annual income.

14. _____ is well known for his view that racial differences in IQ scores are due to heredity.
    a. Louis Thurstone
    b. Jean Piaget
    c. Howard Gardner
    d. Arthur Jensen

15. Sandra Scarr and Richard Weinberg used a method of _____ to determine the influence of the environment on intelligence.
    a. loci
    b. cross-fostering
    c. novelty preference
    d. twins analysis

16. If a test does not assess the knowledge and skills that are adaptive in the child's own culture, then the test suffers from
    a. factor analysis.
    b. factor bias.
    c. test bias.
    d. test fairness.

17. Which of the following culturally fair intelligence tests has revealed smaller differences in test scores between Caucasian and African American children than traditional intelligence tests?
    a. Raven Progressive Matrices
    b. WISC-R
    c. Kaufman Assessment Battery
    d. Stanford-Binet Intelligence Test

18. Characteristics of the child's environment that might be related to later competence are measured in the
    a. WISC-R.
    b. HOME inventory.
    c. Kaufman Assessment Battery.
    d. Triarchic Assessment Scale.

19. Robert Zajonc proposed that the intellectual environment of the child's family can have a great influence on the child's IQ score. This model is called the
    a. confluence model.
    b. triarchic model.
    c. HOME model.
    d. familial context model.

20. Project Head Start is a
    a. high school science program.
    b. program for intellectually gifted children.
    c. community-based athletics program.
    d. preschool enrichment program for underprivileged children.

Application Questions

1. Geraldine has been told that she is very good at "reading" other people, that is, understanding their body language and facial expressions. Geraldine's skill would be recognized in _____ model of intelligence.
   a. Charles Spearman's
   b. Louis Thurstone's
   c. J. P. Guilford's
   d. Alfred Binet's

2. Ten-year-old Bruce scored higher on a test of visual-spatial skills than his thirty-five-year-old mother. The fact that Bruce plays video games often and that his mother has never played them suggests that
   a. Bruce's fluid intelligence is greater than his mother's fluid intelligence.
   b. Bruce's crystallized intelligence is greater than his mother's crystallized intelligence.
   c. Bruce's better performance may be a result of a cohort effect rather than a difference in intelligence.
   d. Bruce's better performance must be a result of greater intelligence since it cannot be a result of a cohort effect.

3. When asked how much time he will need to study a list of twenty words compared to a list of five words, Jacques knows that it will take him much longer to learn the twenty-word list. According to Joseph Campione and Ann Brown, Jacques has developed
   a. crystallized intelligence.
   b. componential knowledge.
   c. metacognitive skills.
   d. two-facet knowledge.

4. Phoebe has been classified as mentally retarded. Her IQ score is likely to be
   a. about 100.
   b. above 110.
   c. above 85.
   d. below 70.

5. Eric is ten months old. Which intelligence test is most likely to be employed to assess his abilities?
   a. WISC-R
   b. Raven Progressive Matrices
   c. HOME
   d. Bayley Scales of Infant Mental and Motor Development

6. Charlene, who is ten years old, is able to perform mental tasks as well as most twelve-year-olds. Charlene is said to have a mental-age score of
   a. 120.
   b. 10.
   c. 12.
   d. 100.

7. Carla is an African American child who was adopted into a Caucasian middle-class family as an infant. Carla's IQ score is likely to be
   a. lower than most Caucasian children's IQ scores.
   b. lower than the IQ scores in the general population.
   c. higher than most African American children's IQ scores.
   d. inherited.

8. Nassir, who was born in Egypt, recently moved to the United States. Although Nassir did well in school in Egypt, he scored low on an intelligence test that he took in his new school in America. Which of the following statements is most likely to be true?
   a. Nassir is below average in intelligence.
   b. The test Nassir took is not culturally fair.
   c. Nassir has poor visual-spatial skills.
   d. Nassir is not motivated to excel in school.

9. Angeline is the middle child in a family with seven closely spaced children. Helena has two younger siblings who are four years apart. All other things being equal, according to Zajonc's confluence model
   a. Angeline is likely to have a higher IQ because she has a larger family.
   b. Helena is likely to have a higher IQ because she has a smaller family.
   c. The two girls will have approximately the same IQ.
   d. Angeline is likely to have a higher IQ because she is a middle child.

10. Jocelyn had been in the Head Start program for two years prior to beginning school. Compared to underprivileged children who did not participate in the Head Start program, Jocelyn will most likely
    a. do better in the first and second grade but will not necessarily maintain this advantage.
    b. show no improvement in intellectual performance.
    c. not show improvement in school skills until the third grade.
    d. maintain an advantage over other underprivileged children through high school.

Answers to Multiple-Choice Questions

The correct answer appears first and is preceded by an asterisk.

Answers to Fact and Concept Questions

1. *c. Sir Francis Galton believed that intelligence, like physical traits, is primarily inherited. (p. 364)
   a. Charles Darwin proposed a theory of evolution that postulates the inheritance of physical characteristics, not intelligence.
   b. Alfred Binet developed the first intelligence test to identify children of lower mental ability.
   d. Louis Thurstone believed that intelligence is composed of several distinct capabilities that can be measured.

2. *b. The psychometric tradition refers to the theoretical perspective that quantifies individual differences in test scores in order to rank-order abilities. (p. 364)
   a. The word *psychophysics* refers to the relationship between physical stimuli and the sensory experiences they produce, not to measures of intelligence.
   c. The learning tradition is concerned with how knowledge is acquired through experience.
   d. Although the term *process tradition* is not used, the processes people use to solve problems are the concern of the learning and information-processing tradition.

3. *b. Spearman claimed that various mental abilities are related to each other because of the presence of a single unitary *g* factor. (p. 365)
   a. Spearman did not believe that intelligence is composed of several distinct abilities.
   c. Spearman operated within the psychometric tradition and did believe that intelligence can be measured.
   d. Spearman did not measure sensory abilities—that was done by Sir Francis Galton—but rather abilities such as verbal and visual-spatial skills.

4. *d. J. P. Guilford proposed 150 factors of intelligence including social knowledge. (p. 366)
   a. Social knowledge was not one of the abilities that Spearman measured in his factor-analysis approach.
   b. Sir Francis Galton measured sensory discrimination, not social knowledge.
   c. Louis Thurstone believed that intelligence is comprised of seven mental abilities, but social knowledge was not one of them.

5. *a. Crystallized intelligence consists of skills that are acquired as a result of living in a specific culture. (p. 367)
   b. Fluid intelligence consists of biologically based mental abilities that are free from cultural influence.

c. The *g* factor is the unitary factor that comprises intelligence according to Spearman.

d. Social intelligence is part of J. P. Guilford's 150 factors of intelligence.

6. *d. Metacognitive skills are the skills that the individual uses to monitor her own cognitive processes. (p. 370)

a. *Structural skill* is not a term used in intelligence research; the structure of intelligence describes what children know at a given point in time.

b. *Process skill* is not an accurate term, although the process of how we acquire knowledge is studied by researchers.

c. *Fluid skill* is not a term used in this field.

7. *b. The two-facet subtheory describes the individual's ability to process novelty and tendency to automatize cognitive processes. (p. 373)

a. The contextual subtheory states that intelligence is an adaptation to the unique environment of the individual.

c. The componential subtheory focuses on the internal mental processes involved in intelligence.

d. There is no automatization subtheory in Sternberg's triarchic theory of intelligence.

8. *c. The average score in the population on most tests of intelligence is 100, and the standard deviation (the average variability of scores around the mean) is 15. (p. 377)

a. The population mean is *not* 50, and the standard deviation is *not* 100.

b. The population mean is 100, but the standard deviation is *not* 50.

d. The population mean is *not* 68, but the standard deviation is 15.

9. *b. The Bayley Scales is the most widely used intelligence test for infants. (p. 378)

a. The Fagan Test of Infant Intelligence is designed for infants under twelve months, but it has not been as widely used as the Bayley Scales.

c. The Stanford-Binet Intelligence Test is designed for use with school-aged children.

d. The K-ABC is a test designed for two- through twelve-year-olds.

10. *a. The Fagan test of Infant Intelligence is based on the infant's tendency to respond to novelty and correlates well with IQ scores three years later. (p. 378)

b. A strong correlation between infant's performance on the Fagan Test of Infant Intelligence and IQ later in development has been observed.

c. The Fagan test measures visual attention. Because this test is reliable, it must be a reliable measure of visual attention.

d. The Fagan test does not measure crystallized intelligence.

11. *b. The child's mental age refers to his ability to solve mental tasks relative to age mates. (p. 379)

a. The child's age in years is his chronological age.

c. The ability to solve novelty problems is not used to determine mental age.

d. Sensory discrimination ability is not used to determine mental age.

12. *d. The Concept Assessment Kit uses Piaget's theory as a guideline and tests children aged four to seven, when the transition from preoperational to concrete-operational thought occurs. (p. 384)
    a. The Kaufman Assessment Battery for Children (K-ABC) is a newer intelligence test that differs from traditional tests in that it emphasizes differences in mental processes, but it is not based on Piagetian tasks.
    b. The revised version of the Wechsler Intelligence Scale for children (WISC-R), the major alternative to the Stanford-Binet, computes the child's score on the basis of the deviation IQ; it is not based on Piagetian tasks.
    c. The Bayley Scales is the most widely used test of infant intelligence based on norms for behaviors expected to occur in the first and second years of life. It is not based on Piagetian tasks.

13. *c. The average correlation between IQ scores and educational achievement is about .50. (p. 387)
    a. Although a relationship between IQ scores and job performance and status has been found, there is a stronger relationship between IQ and school achievement.
    b. IQ tests do not predict mental health.
    d. IQ scores do not predict the amount of money that people will make.

14. *d. Jensen's suggestion that race differences in IQ scores were due to race differences in heritability created a storm of controversy. (p. 389)
    a. Thurstone is well known for his belief that intelligence is comprised of several primary abilities.
    b. Piaget is well known for his theory of cognitive development.
    c. Gardner is well known for his theory of multiple intelligences.

15. *b. In cross-fostering studies children raised in environments markedly different from those of their biological families are used as subjects. (p. 390)
    a. The method of loci is a memory strategy to aid in the recall of information, not a strategy for determining the influence of environment on intelligence.
    c. Novelty preference procedures are used in the Fagan Test of Infant Intelligence to examine infants' mental abilities.
    d. Although twins are often used to study the influence of nature and nurture in intelligence, there is no procedure called twins analysis.

16. *c. Critics of traditional IQ tests argue that these tests are not culturally fair and thus exhibit test bias (p. 391)
    a. Factor analysis is a statistical technique that examines the relationship between a large number of correlations, not a flaw in an intelligence test.
    b. *Factor bias* is not a term used in psychology.
    d. Critics of such tests say that they are *not* fair and therefore are biased.

17. *c. Differences in test scores between Caucasian and African American children are smaller when the Kaufman Assessment Battery, a test designed to be culturally fair, is given than when tests such as the WISC-R are given. (p. 391)

a. Although the Raven Progressive Matrices is assumed to contain minimal cultural bias, Caucasian children still score higher on this test than African American children do.

b. The WISC-R, like the Stanford-Binet, is a traditional test of intelligence and has been criticized as culturally biased.

d. The Stanford-Binet, like the WISC-R, is a traditional test of intelligence that has been criticized as culturally biased.

18. *b. The HOME (Home Observation for Measurement of the Environment) inventory was designed to measure the quality of a child's home environment. (p. 392)

a. The WISC-R is an intelligence test for children; it does not measure characteristics of the child's environment.

c. The Kaufman Assessment Battery is a culturally fair intelligence test; it does not measure characteristics of the child's environment.

d. If you chose this answer you are probably thinking of Sternberg's triarchic theory of intelligence; there is no Triarchic Assessment Scale.

19. *a. In the confluence model the child's intellectual environment is determined by averaging the intellectual maturity of all members of the family. (p. 395)

b. Sternberg's triarchic model does not discuss the effect of birth order or family size on intelligence.

c. The HOME model measures the quality of a child's home environment; it does not describe a relationship between family size and intellectual ability.

d. There is no model called the familial context model.

20. *d. Begun in the 1960s, Project Head Start was designed to enrich the deprived environments of poor children to help raise their levels of intellectual competence. (p. 397)

a. Project Head Start was designed for preschool children, not high school students, and it is not a science education program.

b. Project Head Start is an enrichment program for underprivileged, not intellectually gifted, children.

c. Head Start includes nutritional and medical assistance, but it is not a community-based athletics program.

Answers to Application Questions

1. *c. Guilford proposed 150 factors of intelligence, including knowledge about the mental states or behaviors of others. (p. 366)

a. Spearman believed that intelligence consisted primarily of a general intelligence factor; he did not describe a specific intellectual ability that involved social knowledge like being able to understand body language.

b. Thurstone described intelligence as comprising seven separate abilities, but social knowledge (such as being able to understand body language) was not one of the seven.

    d. Binet helped create the first formal intelligence test, but he did not propose that intelligence included social knowledge.

2. *c. The difference in visual-spatial skills can be explained as a cohort effect—different cultural experiences as a result of age. Bruce's mother did not have video games available to her when she was growing up; therefore, she did not have the same opportunity to develop visual-spatial skills that her son did. (p. 367)

    a. Fluid intelligence consists of biologically based mental abilities that are relatively free from cultural influences. Fluid intelligence is unlikely to be involved here since there is evidence that Bruce benefited from a cultural influence. He was raised in an age of video games but his mother was not; thus his experience may have improved his ability to perform on visual-spatial tests.

    b. Crystallized intelligence consists of skills that are acquired (such as visual-spatial skills) as a result of living in a particular culture. Although it appears that Bruce has greater crystallized intelligence than his mother, this conclusion cannot be made because the difference in performance may be a result of cohort effects.

    d. The fact that Bruce had experience with video games (which are likely to improve visual-spatial skills) and that his mother did not suggests that a cohort effect may account for the observed differences in performance on visual-spatial tasks.

3. *c. Jacques is able to monitor his own thinking processes, a metacognitive skill, well enough to estimate accurately which list will take longer to learn. (p. 370)

    a. Jacques is displaying knowledge of his own cognitive or mental abilities; crystallized intelligence represents general knowledge attained through experience.

    b. In his triarchic theory Sternberg proposed a componential subtheory, which describes how individuals acquire knowledge, not what people know about their own cognitive abilities.

    d. The two-facet subtheory is part of Sternberg's triarchic theory, which explains people's ability to deal with novelty and to automatize cognitive processes.

4. *d. A child who scores lower than 70 on an IQ test is regarded as mentally retarded. (p. 377)

    a. A score of 100 is an average IQ score. Because Phoebe is mentally retarded she cannot have an average IQ.

    b. A score over 110 is an above-average IQ score. Because Phoebe is mentally retarded she cannot have an above-average IQ.

    c. A child who receives an IQ score of 85 is below average in intelligence but has not scored low enough to be classified as mentally retarded.

5. *d. The Bayley Scales is an infant test specifically designed to predict later childhood competence. (p. 378)

    a. The WISC-R is designed for testing children six through sixteen years old.

    b. The Raven Progressive Matrices is not an infant intelligence test but a nonverbal test of cognitive ability that is presumed to have minimal cultural bias.

c. The HOME inventory is not an IQ test but a device used to determine the quality of a child's home environment.

6. *c. Although Charlene's chronological age is ten, she performs as well as the average twelve-year-old; thus Charlene has a mental age of twelve. (p. 379)

a. The score of 120 would be correct if the question asked for Charlene's IQ; however, the question asked for Charlene's mental age.

b. Charlene's chronological age is ten.

d. The score of 100 is too large to be a mental age.

7. *c. African American children adopted into Caucasian middle-class families do not show the typically lower scores seen in African American children, but in fact show higher scores than both African Americans and the general population. (p. 390)

a. Cross-fostering studies found that African American children adopted into Caucasian middle-class families score *higher* than the general population, which includes Caucasian children.

b. Cross-fostering studies found that African American children adopted into Caucasian middle-class families score *higher* than the general population.

d. Although inheritance cannot be ruled out, these cross-fostering studies suggest that environmental influences play an important role in determining IQ test performance.

8. *b. It is likely that because of Nassir's cultural background he was not familiar with the content of the intelligence test and thus scored low; that is, the test may not have been culturally fair. (p. 391)

a. Because Nassir did well in school in his home country, it is unlikely that he is below average in intelligence.

c. Intelligence tests measure much more than visual-spatial skills; thus, his poor performance on the test is unlikely to be largely a result of poor visual-spatial skills.

d. Although low motivation is a possible explanation, the question provides no information about Nassir's motivation.

9. *b. Because Helena has only two siblings spaced farther apart than Angeline's six siblings, Helena should have a less "diluted" intellectual climate and, therefore, she is more likely to have a higher IQ. (p. 395)

a. The confluence model predicts that the family intellectual environment is "diluted" by the presence of young children, particularly if the births are closely spaced. Thus, Angeline should have a lower IQ than Helena.

c. Helena's smaller family size should make her more likely to have a higher IQ.

d. The confluence model predicts that first-born children should have an intellectual edge; thus Helena (who is first born) should have a higher IQ than Angeline.

10. *a. Recent evaluations of the Head Start program indicate that it produces substantial short-term gains, but such gains fade in subsequent years. (p. 398)

b. Head Start children show a gain of about 10 points in their IQ score during the first two years of elementary school.
c. The gains in IQ scores as a result of the Head Start program are seen in the first year or two of elementary school.
d. Although gains in IQ are observed in Head Start children in the first few years of elementary school, these gains fade by the time the children reach high school.

CHAPTER 10

EMOTION

LEARNING OBJECTIVES

1. Define emotions, describe their function, and describe how they are measured. (pp. 406–409)

2. Compare and contrast the historical and contemporary theoretical perspectives on emotion. (pp. 409–413)

3. Discuss the infant's ability to express emotions by smiling, crying, and producing other facial expressions. (pp. 413–417)

4. Describe the infant's ability to discriminate among emotional expressions in others. (pp. 417–418)

5. Describe how emotional expression and recognition regulate the social interactions between infants and others. (pp. 418–420)

6. List and describe the complex emotions that emerge after infancy and explain how children develop an understanding of them. (pp. 420–423)

7. Discuss the sex and cross-cultural differences in children's emotions. (pp. 423–425)

8. Define attachment and compare the theories that have attempted to explain its emergence. (pp. 425–429)

9. Describe the emergence of attachment behaviors. (pp. 429–431)

10. Describe Ainsworth's attachment classifications and discuss the role of mothers and fathers in the development of attachment. (pp. 431–433)

11. Discuss the relationship between temperament and attachment. (pp. 434–435)

12. Describe the stability of attachment classifications and the relationship between early attachment and later social and cognitive outcomes. (pp. 435–437)

13. Discuss the effects of prematurity, adoption, and abuse on the attachment relationship. (pp. 437–440)

14. Describe how variations in cultural expectations for children's behavior affect the attachment relationship between child and caregiver. (pp. 440–442)

15. Discuss the controversial issue concerning the effect of day care on attachment. (pp. 442–444)

CHAPTER OUTLINE

I. **WHAT ARE EMOTIONS?** (pp. 406–409)
Emotions are a complex set of behaviors produced by an internal or external elicitor. Emotions have three components: a physiological component, involving bodily changes; an expressive component, including facial expressions; and an experiential component, the subjective feeling of emotion.

A. **Measuring Emotions** (pp. 407–408)
All three components of emotions must be taken into consideration during the measurement process. Physiological measures include heart rate or EEG patterns. Measurement of facial expressions and vocalizations include detection of changes in the muscles of the face and the loudness, duration, and sound patterns of the child's voice. Self-report measures may be used to assess the child's interpretations of his or her own feelings of emotion. These methods are not without problems. Different emotions may lead to similar physiological responses, the same overt facial expression may indicate different types of emotions, and self-reports of feelings may be biased or difficult to interpret.

B. **The Functions of Emotions** (pp. 408–409)
Emotions appear to organize and regulate the child's behavior. Positive emotional states may motivate the child, whereas negative emotional states may lead to discouragement. Additionally, psychologists have observed a link between emotions and cognition. Cognitive activity is often reflected in the emotional expressions of the child; mastery of task, for example, is expressed as joy or elation. Conversely, emotional states can influence the cognitive processes in which the child is engaged. Children in positive

emotional states perform better and learn faster than children in negative emotional states. Emotions play a key role in initiating, maintaining, or terminating social interactions between the child and others. Moods, a more enduring emotional state, may indicate aspects of the child's personality, such as shyness, dependency, or aggression.

II. THEORIES OF EMOTIONAL DEVELOPMENT: NATURE VERSUS NURTURE (pp. 409–413)

A. The Foundations of Modern Theory: Darwin and Watson (pp. 409–410)
Charles Darwin's theory of evolution led him to propose that emotions are the result of an evolutionary history and serve a survival function. In his investigations of emotions, Darwin found that very young children, animals, and adults from many cultures all had similar emotional expressions and responses to emotional expression. Darwin concluded that emotions and their expression are innate. The founder of the behaviorist tradition, John Watson, suggested that fear, rage, and love were *conditioned emotional responses* to environmental stimuli.

B. Contemporary Perspectives on Emotional Development (pp. 410–413)
Psychologists such as Paul Ekman and Carroll Izard are contemporary supporters of the biological view of the origin of emotions. In cross-cultural research, Ekman has found that people from many cultures express emotions in the same way and interpret emotional expressions similarly. Izard found that young infants make the same facial expressions as adults in response to external stimuli. More importantly, making the facial expression produces a corresponding emotional feeling in the infant.

Michael Lewis and Linda Michalson's cognitive-socialization explanation of emotions emphasizes that the emotions experienced even by the young child are a product of the experiential history of the child, including information from parents and others regarding the appropriate emotional reactions for each situation. Cognitive processes thus act as *mediators* that bridge the gap between environmental stimuli and the emotions they elicit.

III. EXPRESSING, RECOGNIZING, AND UNDERSTANDING EMOTIONS (pp. 413–425)
Research on emotional development has examined the types of emotions that children of various ages can express, their skill in recognizing emotions in others, and their understanding of the events that surround emotional behavior.

A. Early Emotional Development (pp. 413–420)
Studies have shown that newborn infants are capable of making facial expressions that correspond to the emotions of interest, distress, disgust, joy, sadness, and surprise. By four months of age they can also appear angry, and by seven months they can show fear. These emotions are called *basic emotions* because they appear to be innate and do not

require much, if any, learning. Although these basic emotions do not appear to be learned, they do show evidence of being modified with experience over the first few months of life. Smiling in the newborn, for example, occurs most likely in response to a change in physiological state. Later in the first year of life, smiling and laughing occur in response to complex stimuli that the child's increasing cognitive maturity can understand. Crying, like smiling, is initially a reflexive response to an aversive physical state such as hunger or pain. After two months of age the infant's cry becomes more variable and can be voluntarily produced as a request for a desired object, for a change in stimulation, or as a way of communicating distress to the caregiver.

Research has shown that infants are able to imitate adult models making happy, surprised, or sad facial expressions, suggesting that they have an early sensitivity to the emotional expressions of others. By the end of the first year infants begin to show evidence that they understand the meaning of the facial expressions they can discriminate. The phenomenon of *social referencing* indicates that infants make use of others' facial expressions to gain information about the appropriate response to an ambiguous situation, such as whether to cross to the deep side of the visual cliff. Patterns of reciprocal vocalizations and facial expressions between caregiver and infant, called *interactive synchrony*, are evident from about two to three months of age. During this period, the infant learns how to take the initiative in social interactions and how to alter the caregiver's behavior by responding with an appropriate emotional expression. The nature of the emotional exchanges between caregiver and infant influences the emotional bond of attachment between them.

B. Later Emotional Development (pp. 420–423)

Beyond two years of age children begin to show more *complex emotions,* reflecting their growing understanding of social relationships. Emotions such as guilt, envy, shame, and pride require self-understanding and understanding of others' feelings. Basic emotions such as fear undergo developmental changes as well. Initially, fear occurs in response to loud noises or strangers. Later, fear is elicited from many complex events related to the child's advancing cognitive skills.

As their linguistic skills improve, children demonstrate their increased understanding of emotions and the conditions surrounding emotional behavior. Children's knowledge of emotions permits them to respond appropriately in many social situations, such as reacting to the emotional expressions of peers, thus having an impact on their social development. As they enter school, children understand that emotions fade over time and changes in thoughts can lead to changes in feelings. At this time, children also develop emotional skills such as the ability to mask or fake their emotional state. *Display rules*, for example, are the cultural guidelines for when and how to express emotions, such as appearing happy to receive a gift. Young children rely on situational cues to identify their emotional state, whereas adolescents rely on mental states to explain their feelings. Emotional development appears closely tied to advancing cognitive skills that allow children to think in more abstract and complex terms.

C. Variations in Emotional Development (pp. 423–425)
Although there are strong commonalities in emotional behavior across individuals, there are a number of noteworthy differences in individual emotional development. Prior to adolescence few, if any, differences are reported in emotional expression by boys and girls. Observations of parents' behavior, however, suggests that sons and daughters are taught to behave differently with respect to emotional behavior. Researchers have shown that mothers are more expressive with their daughters than their sons, and parents overall encourage girls to show affection and maintain close emotional ties, whereas they instruct boys to control their emotions. These differences in socialization most likely account for many of the stereotypical differences in male and female emotional behavior.

Cultural differences account for differences in frequency of smiling, identification of emotions given the situation, and response to expressions of emotions such as crying. Emotional development thus appears due not only to innate, biological factors that control early infant expressions and recognition of emotions, but also to strong cognitive and socialization factors that refine later emotional development.

IV. ATTACHMENT: EMOTIONAL RELATIONSHIPS WITH OTHERS (pp. 425–442)
Attachment refers to the strong emotional bond that develops between infant and caregivers. Positive attachment relationships are strongly related to successful cognitive, social, and emotional development throughout childhood.

A. The Origins of Attachment: Theoretical Perspectives (pp. 425–429)
According to the psychodynamic view, the infant derives gratification from oral activities such as sucking. The mother becomes associated with the pleasure derived from sucking and, consequently, becomes a source of gratification as well. This relationship with the mother allows the child to develop healthy emotional relationships with others later in life. Learning theory explains that basic biological drives are satisfied by *primary reinforcers* such as food. *Secondary reinforcers* acquire their reinforcing properties by being associated with primary reinforcers. Mother, therefore, becomes rewarding for the infant outside of the feeding context. Thus, both psychodynamic theories and learning theories suggest that the basis for the attachment relationship is related to reduction of biological needs. Harry Harlow and his associates found, however, that infant monkeys who were separated from their mothers and given a choice between a terry cloth surrogate and a wire mesh surrogate spent significantly more time with the terry cloth monkey, even if the cloth surrogate was not equipped to feed the infant. Harlow concluded that "contact comfort" was a more critical factor than biological need reduction in the development of the attachment relationship.

Ethological theories view attachment as the result of innate tendencies in the infant to actively signal the caregiver's attention and the caregiver's innate tendencies to respond to those signals. John Bowlby examined previous researchers' observations that institutionalized infants experienced severe physical, cognitive, and emotional problems. Bowlby believed that attachment progressed in a fixed sequence beginning with the infant's *signaling behaviors*, such as crying and smiling. He observed evidence of the strong attachment bond later in the first year of life in a phenomenon called *separation anxiety*, the visible upset infants experience upon departure of the mother. A related phenomenon, *stranger anxiety*, is the infant's wariness at the approach of an unfamiliar person. Finally, at about three years of age, the attachment relationship becomes more of a partnership, with the child beginning to appreciate the mother's feelings, motives, and goals.

Piaget's cognitive-developmental theory suggests that attachment is related to the acquisition of cognitive capacities such as object permanence.

B. The Developmental Course of Attachment (pp. 429–437)

Attachment behaviors seem to emerge in a reliable sequence, with infants showing preferences for familiar persons, followed by separation and stranger anxiety, and the formation of multiple attachments in addition to the primary attachment to the mother. Mary Ainsworth and her associates developed a standardized task, called the *Strange Situation*, in order to assess the quality of the child's emotional ties to the mother. In this laboratory task, Ainsworth finds that infants who are attached to their mothers use the mother as a *secure base for exploration*. Ainsworth has identified three patterns of attachment in infancy. *Secure attachment* is evidenced by children who feel comfortable in the presence of the mother and distressed in her absence. *Avoidant attachment* is evident in children who avoid their mother and remain in isolated play when they are reunited with her following a brief separation. The *ambivalent attachment* is evident in children who demonstrate tension, excessive clinging, and anger toward the mother following her return. An analysis of the attachment relationship revealed that mothers who accepted the caregiver role, displayed cooperation with their infants, and were accessible to their infants developed secure attachments with their infants. In contrast, mothers of insecurely attached infants were rigid, unresponsive, and demanding of their infants. Critics of Ainsworth's Strange Situation believe that observer bias may contribute to the relationships observed between the mother's behavior and the quality of the attachment. Research on the father-child relationship has revealed that even though fathers spend less time interacting with their children than mothers, children do form close attachments to their fathers.

Stella Chess and Alexander Thomas have found that infants possess different temperaments, biologically based styles of behavior that include moods, distractibility, adaptability, and persistence. These researchers have been able to identify three types of infant temperament—easy, difficult, and slow-to-warm-up—which may affect the attachment relationships they develop with caregivers. The quality of the attachment pattern formed in infancy appears to remain stable over relatively long intervals in the majority of the children tested in a longitudinal study from twelve months to six years of age. Perhaps most importantly, infants found to be securely attached early in infancy show later positive developmental outcomes in both the social and cognitive domains. In contrast, infants classified as anxiously attached displayed many undesirable behaviors in the preschool years. Finally, some research indicates that early infant attachments may predict to adolescent self-esteem and identity and even adult parenting behaviors.

C. **Three Special Cases: Prematurity, Adoption, and Abuse** (pp. 437–440)
Premature birth, adoption, and child abuse are three contexts within which patterns of parent-child attachments may be disrupted. Mothers of premature infants, for example, appear to provide excessive stimulation for their infants in an apparent effort to alter the premature infant's unresponsive behavior. When the quality of attachment at one year of age is assessed, however, no differences are observed between premature and full-term infants and their caregivers. The quality of attachment observed for adopted infants appears to depend on the age at which they were adopted. Infants adopted prior to six months of age show secure patterns of attachment. In contrast, infants separated from their biological parents after six to seven months of age show socioemotional problems later on. Thus, the first few months of life may represent a sensitive period for emotional development. Abused infants and children reveal the most profound incidence of insecure attachments; perhaps as many as 70 to 100 percent of abused infants are insecurely attached. Moreover, abused children have revealed a fourth classification of attachment, *disorganized/disoriented attachment*, in which children exhibit fear of the caregiver, confused facial expressions, and avoidant and ambivalent behavior.

D. **Cross-Cultural Variations in Patterns of Attachment** (pp. 440–442)
Studies of the quality of attachment between infants and caregivers from cultures other than the United States reveal that patterns of attachment may differ depending on the maternal behaviors encouraged within any given culture. For example, in cultures encouraging independence in very young children such as Germany, a greater number of avoidantly attached infants are observed. Isreali infants raised in a kibbutz show ambivalent attachments when compared to American infants, perhaps reflecting their lack of experience with strangers.

Controversy: Does Day Care Affect Attachment? (pp. 442–444)
With the rising percentage of mothers of young children employed outside of the home, more infants than ever are receiving nonparental care beginning early in life. The variables that determine the effects of nonparental care on the emotional development of the young child include the direct effect of the mother's absence, the quality of the substitute care, the age at which nonparental care begins, and the kind of alternative care experienced. Although the majority of studies show no differences in the quality of attachments for day-care vs. home-reared infants, a number of studies have found day-care children to exhibit more avoidant behaviors than home-reared children during the reunion in the Strange Situation. Whether these avoidant behaviors indicate insecure attachments or a move toward independence is unclear. When parents do choose day care for their children it is important for them to select a day-care environment that will provide supportive, responsive substitute caregivers with whom the child can develop secure attachments.

V. THEMES IN DEVELOPMENT: EMOTION (pp. 444–445)

What roles do nature and nurture play in emotional development? Biology assumes a large role in the child's early emotional capacities, but socialization and cognitive development become more prominent as explanations of later emotional expression and understanding, particularly for complex emotions.

How does the sociocultural context influence emotional development? Different cultures place different emphases on emotionality and on those specific emotions considered appropriate to display. A culture's beliefs and values can also influence the child's responses to the Strange Situation.

How does the child play an active role in the process of emotional development? There are numerous ways in which the child plays an active role in emotional development, including the phenomenon of social referencing and the infant's role in producing interactive synchrony with the caregiver.

Are there sensitive periods in emotional development? The development of healthy attachments during infancy forecasts many desirable developmental outcomes later in childhood, so early infancy may indeed be a sensitive period. For example, studies of adopted infants suggest that better outcomes result when infants are adopted prior to the age of six months.

How does emotional development interact with development in other domains? Emotions are closely intertwined with both cognition and social behavior. Cognitive achievements lay the groundwork for advances in attachment and emotional expression. Similarly, children often learn about emotions through social experiences. In addition, successful attachments are associated with positive social and cognitive achievements later in childhood.

Key Terms Review

1. A(n) _____ is an emotional reaction to a previously neutral stimulus that occurs as a result of classical conditioning.

2. A child who looks to his mother for emotional cues in an attempt to interpret an ambiguous event is displaying the phenomenon called _____ .

3. A(n) _____ describes a child's display of close affectional ties to the mother, as measured by the Strange Situation.

4. _____ , such as joy, sadness, and surprise, appear early in infancy.

5. In the Strange Situation the pattern of attachment characterized by tension in the infant, including clinging and avoidance behaviors, is called _____ .

6. A(n) _____ is a cognitive event that bridges the gap between an environmental stimulus and the individual's response.

7. The distress shown by an infant as an unfamiliar person approaches is referred to as _____ .

8. _____ are cultural guidelines about when, how, and to what degree one is to display emotions.

9. The strong emotional bond that occurs between infant and caregiver is called _____ .

10. _____ is displayed by an infant when the caregiver leaves the immediate environment.

11. A(n) _____ attains rewarding properties when it is associated with a(n) _____ such as food.

12. The _____ was developed by Mary Ainsworth to assess the quality of infant-caregiver attachment.

13. The _____ pattern is characterized by the infant's fear of the caregiver and a combination of anxious and resistant attachment behaviors.

14. A child and mother mutually engaging in reciprocal behaviors are displaying _____ .

15. _____ , such as guilt and envy, appear later in childhood and require cognitive and social skills.

16. The _____ pattern of infant-caregiver relations is characterized by neutral emotion in the infant and few affectional behaviors directed toward the caregiver.

17. Ethological theorists describe behaviors such as crying and smiling as examples of _____ , which serve to bring the caregiver physically close to the infant.

18. Mother serves as a(n) _____ when the infant uses her as a reference point during active exploration of a new environment.

19. _____ is a complex set of behaviors that occur in response to an external or internal event.

Answers to Key Terms Review

1. conditioned emotional response
2. social referencing
3. secure attachment
4. Basic emotions
5. ambivalent attachment
6. mediator
7. stranger anxiety
8. Display rules
9. attachment
10. Separation anxiety
11. Secondary reinforcer, primary reinforcer
12. Strange Situation
13. disorganized/disoriented attachment
14. interactive synchrony
15. Complex emotions
16. avoidant attachment
17. signaling behavior
18. secure base for exploration
19. Emotion

Multiple-Choice Questions

Fact and Concept Questions

1. A facial display that signals an emotion makes up the _____ component of the emotion.
   a. physiological
   b. expressive
   c. experiential
   d. elicitor

2. The theory that emotions serve as innate survival functions is consistent with _____ view of emotion.
   a. John Watson's
   b. Michael Lewis's
   c. Sigmund Freud's
   d. Charles Darwin's

3. According to John Watson, conditioned emotional responses are
    a. innate responses to releasing stimuli.
    b. learned responses to stimuli associated with pleasant or aversive consequences.
    c. universal facial expressions.
    d. imitations of facial expressions by infants.

4. Studies of emotional expressions in infancy indicate that
    a. adult observers can reliably identify the facial expressions of young infants.
    b. adult observers can reliably identify the facial expressions of their own infants but
        not of unfamiliar infants.
    c. emotional expressions do not emerge in infants until they have had considerable
        exposure to adults.
    d. unlike crying, smiling is not linked to any physiological state.

5. In the habituation paradigm an infant is repeatedly shown a picture of a smiling face
    until the infant's looking time decreases; the picture is then changed to a frowning
    face. If the infant can detect the change in emotional expression he should show
    a. an increase in looking time when the smiling face is changed to the frowning face.
    b. a decrease in looking time when the smiling face is changed to the frowning face.
    c. no change in looking time when the smiling face is changed to the frowning face.
    d. changes in his own facial expressions that match the expressions of the pictures
        presented.

6. None of the one-year-old infants placed on the shallow side of the visual cliff
    apparatus crossed the deep side when the mother showed a fearful expression. Many
    infants crossed when their mother smiled, however. The infants displayed the
    phenomenon called
    a. conditioned emotional response.
    b. separation anxiety.
    c. anxious attachment.
    d. social referencing.

7. Which of the following is a good example of the child's active involvement in the
    process of emotional development?
    a. A child's display of a conditioned emotional response
    b. A child's use of positive reinforcement to learn appropriate behavior
    c. Smiling in response to changes in physiological state
    d. A child's use of social referencing

8. Infants of clinically depressed mothers
    a. display considerable negative affect when with the mother but not when with
        other, nondepressed adults.

    b. display considerable negative affect when with the mother and with other, nondepressed adults.

    c. display affective responses to mothers and other, nondepressed adults similar to those of infants of nondepressed mothers.

    d. are less likely to form an attachment with their mother than children of nondepressed mothers.

9. Children begin to show complex emotions such as guilt and envy
    a. once their cerebral cortex is fully developed.
    b. as they learn more about the emotional states of others and the social world.
    c. when parents begin consistently to punish inappropriate behavior.
    d. when they first enter school.

10. The basic emotion of fear
    a. emerges early in infancy and shows little if any developmental change.
    b. is not present at birth but emerges as the child's cognitive skills develop.
    c. emerges early in infancy but undergoes changes in terms of the stimuli that elicit it.
    d. is not present at birth but develops after the child has formed an attachment with a caregiver.

11. Studies that have looked for sex differences in emotional development have found that when mothers play with their two-year-old children
    a. the mothers were similarly expressive with boys and girls.
    b. differences in the mother's expressiveness with boys and girls are seen only when the babies are "difficult" babies.
    c. the mothers are more expressive with boys than with girls.
    d. the mothers are more expressive with girls than with boys.

12. Harry Harlow's classic monkey studies provided support for the idea that attachment
    a. is possible because food provided by the first caregivers serves as a powerful primary reinforcer.
    b. results from the security that infants experience from the physical contact with mother.
    c. is a result of an association between mother and gratification through feeding.
    d. is primarily a passive psychological process that infants are inevitably exposed to.

13. Which of the following terms is most closely related to the ethological view of attachment?
    a. Signaling behavior
    b. Secondary reinforcer
    c. Display rules
    d. Object permanence

14. Of the attachment patterns identified by Mary Ainsworth's Strange Situation procedure, the type of attachment seen in our society as most desirable is _____ attachment.
    a. ambivalent
    b. positive
    c. avoidant
    d. secure

15. Attachment patterns between a child and parent are determined by the
    a. temperament of the child.
    b. behavioral characteristics of the parent.
    c. characteristics of the parent and child.
    d. innate characteristics of the child.

16. Studies that have examined the stability of attachment patterns indicate that
    a. the quality of attachment, once established, does not change.
    b. attachment patterns may change from insecurely attached to securely attached, but not vice versa.
    c. the quality of attachment, although usually stable, may change if family stresses occur.
    d. the quality of attachment established in the first year is rarely maintained for relatively long periods of time.

17. Compared to mothers of full-term babies, mothers of premature babies spend _____ time stimulating their infants but become _____ active as the babies get older.
    a. the same, less
    b. less, more
    c. more, less
    d. the same, more

18. Which of the following terms is most likely to characterize the attachment pattern of children from abusive homes?
    a. Passive attachment
    b. Ambivalent attachment
    c. Disorganized/disoriented attachment
    d. Avoidant attachment

19. One recent study showed that Israeli children raised on a kibbutz were
    a. more likely to display ambivalent attachments than American children.
    b. less likely to display insecure attachments than American children.
    c. less likely to display ambivalent attachments than Israeli children raised in cities.
    d. as likely to display insecure attachments as Israeli children raised in cities.

20. As a result of the large number of studies that have examined the effect of day care on attachment, researchers
    a. agree that the effects of day care on children's responses to mothers are minimal or nonexistent.
    b. agree that day care often produces insecure attachments.
    c. agree that day care produces a significant number of disorganized/disoriented attachments.
    d. disagree on the relationship between day care and attachment.

Application Questions

1. Roxanne is three days old. Her parents are amazed to observe her smiling because they didn't think newborns could smile. Roxanne is probably smiling because
   a. her parents are smiling at her.
   b. she has "gas."
   c. she is in REM sleep.
   d. she is happy.

2. Dr. Russo is testing three-month-old infants using the habituation paradigm to see if they can recognize facial expressions. Dr. Russo is likely to find that three-month-olds
   a. can't distinguish among facial expressions.
   b. find it easier to recognize positive than negative facial expressions.
   c. find it easier to recognize negative than positive facial expressions.
   d. find it easier to recognize the facial expressions of strangers compared to their mothers' facial expressions.

3. While his mother is busy preparing dinner, eleven-month-old Todd crawls to the top of the stairs and then stands up. Todd's mother, noticing that Todd has crawled out of her sight, looks for him and finds him perched at the top of the stairs smiling. Todd's mother gasps and looks frightened. Seeing his mother's face, Todd slowly sits down and calls for his mother. Todd's behavior is an example of
   a. signaling behavior.
   b. innate fear of stairs.
   c. social referencing.
   d. attachment.

4. When mother looks sad, her infant, Linda, smiles and coos, causing her mother to smile. Mother and daughter are displaying
   a. separation anxiety.
   b. ambivalent attachment.
   c. interactive synchrony.
   d. an asynchronous interaction.

5. Three-year-old Frieda, who gets upset when her mother attends to her new baby brother, makes repeated attempts to climb into her mother's lap whenever she is feeding the new baby. Frieda's jealousy
   a. is unusual for her age.
   b. indicates a poor quality of attachment with her mother.
   c. demonstrates that she has acquired a complex emotion.
   d. is unrelated to her cognitive level.

6. Jeffrey has substantial knowledge about his emotions, more so than most of his peers. Jeffrey is likely to
   a. be better liked by his peers.
   b. have fewer friends in school.
   c. have poorer cognitive skills than his peers.
   d. be shy and have a limited vocabulary.

7. Whenever twelve-month-old Daria's mother walks out of the room, Daria cries and chases after her. Daria's behavior indicates
   a. separation anxiety.
   b. stranger anxiety.
   c. insecure attachment.
   d. interactive synchrony.

8. Maxine had to leave her fourteen-month-old son, Edward, with a babysitter while she went shopping. Edward cried when his mother left but calmed down after a while. When Maxine returned, Edward ran to her and hugged her. Edward is probably _____ attached to his mother.
   a. insecurely
   b. avoidantly
   c. ambivalently
   d. securely

9. From the day she was born, Alisha has been a content, calm baby who has a regular sleeping and feeding schedule and enjoys new places and people. According to Stella Chess and Alexander Thomas, Alisha probably has a(n) _____ temperament.
   a. secure
   b. slow-to-warm up
   c. easy
   d. calm

10. Lauren frequently experiences her mother leaving for work and subsequently returning but shows little or no separation anxiety even though she is securely attached to her mother. Lauren's response to her mother's absence and return is consistent with Michael Lamb's suggestion that
    a. the attachment patterns identified by the Strange Situation are artifacts of the laboratory situation.
    b. the Strange Situation accurately measures attachment patterns.
    c. the Strange Situation may be examining the influence of other social experiences on attachment rather than the emotional bond between mother and child.
    d. a child's quality of attachment depends on the child's temperament rather than on the mother's caregiving practices.

Answers to Multiple-Choice Questions

The correct answer appears first and is preceded by an asterisk.

Answers to Fact and Concept Questions

1. *b. The expressive component describes the observable component of emotion, such as a facial display. (p. 406)
    a. Physiological components of emotions involve changes in the autonomic nervous system, which are not usually visible to observers.
    c. The experiential component is not a display of emotion but the subjective feeling of having an emotion.
    d. An elicitor is not a component of an emotion but the trigger or invoker of an emotion.

2. *d. The importance of inherited characteristics for the survival of individuals was the major tenet of Darwin's theory of evolution. (p. 410)
    a. John Watson viewed emotion as a product of the child's learning experience, not as an inborn characteristic.
    b. Michael Lewis focuses on the influence of socialization rather than on innate characteristics.
    c. Sigmund Freud would probably agree with the premise of this question, but the role of innate characteristics in an individual's survival was not the major focus of his work.

3. *b. Watson demonstrated (remember his famous case study of little Albert) that through conditioning, negative (and positive) emotional responses can be elicited by a large number of initially neutral stimuli. (p. 410)
    a. Although Watson agreed that a few basic emotions are probably innate or unlearned, conditioned emotional responses was not one of them.

c. Researchers have demonstrated that there are universal facial expressions (suggesting an innate mechanism), but Watson was not one of these researchers.

d. Social learning theorists, not Watson, pointed out the infant's ability to imitate facial expressions.

4. *a. It has been found that observers are able to label the emotions of infants displayed in slides and videotape (p. 413)

b. Not true. The studies described in the text did not look at adult ratings of known and unknown infants.

c. This statement is incorrect. Facial expressions associated with several emotional states have been observed even in newborn infants.

d. Smiling has been linked to emotional states, particularly to *changes* in physiological state.

5. *a. The idea of this procedure is that if the infant detects a change in the stimulus (i.e., a new stimulus), there should be a recovery from habituation; therefore, looking time should increase. (p. 417)

b. If the infant continues to show a decline in looking time it would suggest that the infant is still habituating and therefore may not have detected the change in facial expression.

c. No change in looking time would mean that the infant did not show recovery from habituation and therefore did not detect a change in the picture.

d. This may be true, but it is not what is measured in the habituation paradigm.

6. *d. The infants were able to interpret their mothers' expression to decide whether or not to cross. This phenomenon is called social referencing. (p. 418)

a. It may be true that some infants may be experiencing a conditioned emotional response when they see the facial display of their mothers, but this phenomenon does not completely account for the behavior described in the question, that is, crossing over to the deep side.

b. Some of the infants may be experiencing separation anxiety, but separation anxiety does not explain the infants' behavior in response to the mothers' different expressions.

c. The visual cliff procedure does not measure the quality of child-parent attachment.

7. *d. Social referencing involves the child's active role in looking to others for emotional cues to help interpret a strange or ambiguous event. (p. 418)

a. Conditioned emotional responses are passive since they are triggered by stimuli that the child is exposed to.

b. A child does not actively seek positive reinforcers to learn appropriate behavior; positive reinforcers to shape a child's behavior are usually provided by others.

c. Smiling in infants as a result of changing physiological states is reflexive and therefore passive.

8. *b. A good deal of the negative affect seen in infants of depressed mothers is also seen in face-to-face interactions with nondepressed adults. (p. 420)

a. It is true that infants display negative affect to their depressed mothers, but their negative affect usually extends to other, nondepressed adults as well.

c. Infants of depressed mothers display greater negative affect in face-to-face-interactions than do infants of nondepressed mothers.

d. Although the affective exchanges between mother and child may influence the quality of the attachment, they do not prevent attachment.

9. *b. The young child's emotional states become more complex as she learns more about others' feelings and her relationship with others in the social world. (p. 420)

a. Although a well-developed cerebral cortex is necessary for emotional development, it alone will not ensure that the child develops complex emotions like guilt and envy.

c. Although punishment may play a role in the development of these complex emotions, the child must acquire a broader understanding of her relationship with others in the social world.

d. Mothers report seeing the first sign of these complex emotions at about eighteen months, well before the formal school years.

10. *c. Fear undergoes considerable change with development. Early in infancy fear occurs in response to loud noises or strange people; later in childhood fear is triggered by more complex events. (p. 421)

a. Fear does emerge early in infancy, but it also shows developmental change.

b. Researchers suggest that fear emerges at about seven months of age, but its emergence is not dependent on greater cognitive skills.

d. The development of fear does not depend on the formation of an attachment; for example, fear in infants occurs in response to sudden loud noises.

11. *d. The greater expressiveness exhibited by mothers when with girls may be partly responsible for the greater display of affection seen in girls. (p. 424)

a. Studies show that the degree of a mother's expressiveness depends on whether the child is a boy or girl.

b. This result sounds like a good possibility, but the text does not describe studies on sex differences in emotional development in "difficult" and "easy" babies.

c. Mothers have been observed to be more expressive when playing with girls than with boys.

12. *b. *Contact comfort* is the term Harlow used for the security that infants experience from physically soothing objects. (p. 427)

a. The results of Harlow's monkey studies demonstrated that the availability of food did not play a role in attachment.

c. Harlow presented evidence that contact comfort is more important in attachment than the mother's acquisition of secondary reinforcing characteristics through feeding.

d. The infant monkeys were not passive, as suggested by a conditioning view of attachment, but active since they had to seek out the contact comfort.

13. *a. In ethological theory, signaling behavior is any behavior that brings the caregiver physically close to the baby, such as crying or smiling. (p. 428)
    b. Secondary reinforcers are objects or people that acquire reinforcing properties as a result of their association with a primary reinforcer. This term is most closely related to a learning view of attachment.
    c. *Display rules* is not a term used in ethological theory. Display rules are cultural guidelines about when and how to display emotions.
    d. The importance of object permanence in attachment is discussed in cognitive-developmental views of attachment.

14. *d. Children who are comfortable in their mother's presence and apprehensive in her absence are classified as secure, a desirable characteristic in our society. (p. 432)
    a. Ambivalent attachment is characterized by tension, including extreme passivity, which is not seen as a positive characteristic in our society.
    b. Positive attachment is not one of the attachment patterns identified by Ainsworth.
    c. Avoidant attachment, characterized by avoidance of the caregiver, is seen as undesirable by our society.

15. *c. The characteristics of parent and child, and the synchrony between the behaviors they display, play a major role in the form of attachment that develops. (p. 435)
    a. Although temperament of the child plays a role, it is not the only determinant of attachment patterns.
    b. Although the behavioral characteristics of the parent play a role, they are not the only determinant of attachment patterns.
    d. Innate characteristics of the child, such as temperament, play a role but are not the only determinant of attachment patterns.

16. *c. Stresses in the family have been observed to be associated with shifts from secure to anxious attachments. (p. 436)
    a. Attachment patterns have been observed to change.
    b. There is no evidence indicating that changes in attachment patterns are unidirectional.
    d. Although changes in attachment patterns do occur, attachments established early on typically remain stable for long periods of time.

17. *b. Mothers of premature babies increase their rate of interaction as their babies get older, perhaps in an effort to spur slowed development. (p. 438)
    a. Mothers of premature babies spend *less* time stimulating their infants than mothers of full-term infants.
    c. Mothers of premature babies spend *less* time stimulating their infants than mothers of full-term infants and become *more* active as their babies get older.
    d. Mothers of premature babies spend *less* time stimulating their infants than mothers of full-term infants.

18. *c. According to one study, 80 percent of maltreated children show disorganized/disoriented attachment, which includes avoidant and ambivalent attachment behaviors. (p. 439)
   a. *Passive attachment* is not one of the established terms for patterns of attachment.
   b. Although characteristics seen in ambivalent attachment patterns are also seen in the behaviors of abused children, ambivalent attachment is not the best choice provided.
   d. Although characteristics seen in avoidant attachment patterns are also seen in the behaviors of abused children, ambivalent attachment is not the best choice provided.

19. *a. The experience of being raised in a group setting like a kibbutz is related to a more frequent display of ambivalent attachments compared to American children, who do not have this experience (p. 441)
   b. The display of ambivalent attachment was *greater,* not less, than that seen in American children.
   c. Israeli children raised on a kibbutz displayed *more* ambivalent attachment than Israeli children raised in the city.
   d. Israeli children raised on a kibbutz displayed *more* ambivalent attachment than Israeli children raised in the city.

20. *d. The influence of day care on attachment is a controversial issue among developmental psychology researchers. (p. 442)
   a. This statement is incorrect since some researchers provide evidence they believe demonstrates an effect of day care on attachment.
   b. This statement is incorrect because some researchers argue that no studies convincingly demonstrate the effect of day care on attachment patterns.
   c. Disorganized/disoriented attachment has been associated with abuse, not exposure to day care.

Answers to Application Questions

1. *c. Studies show that smiling in the newborn infant occurs primarily during REM sleep. (p. 415)
   a. Infants begin to respond to visual stimuli (like their mother's face) with a smile at about three months of age. Roxanne is unlikely to be smiling at her parents in return for their smile since she is less than a week old.
   b. It is possible that the parents misinterpreted a facial response to "gas" as a smile, but assuming that the smile was real there is a better answer to choose.
   d. It is unlikely that a three-day-old infant is experiencing the emotion we adults call "happiness."

2. *b. Several studies have shown that infants have an easier time recognizing positive expressions than they do recognizing negative expressions. (p. 418)
   a. Studies show that three- and four-month olds are able to distinguish among several expressions.

 c. Infants can more readily identify positive expressions.

 d. The reverse is true. Infants find it easier to recognize their mothers' facial expressions as opposed to strangers.

3. *c. Being alone on the top of the stairs was probably a new experience for Todd. The emotional cues displayed by his mother made it clear to Todd that he was in potential danger, so he sat down. This is a good example of social referencing. (p. 418)

 a. Todd's mother certainly did send him a signal, but *signaling behavior* is an ethological term that describes a signal elicited by the infant to entice the caregiver to approach him.

 b. If Todd had a fear of stairs he would not have climbed them in the first place.

 d. Todd's attachment to his mother does not adequately explain the sequence of events described in the question; there is a better choice.

4. *c. The mother's reciprocal response to Linda's smile is an example of interactive synchrony between mother and child. (p. 418)

 a. Separation anxiety is the distress that a child experiences when her mother leaves the immediate environment; Linda's mother did not leave.

 b. Linda's positive response to her mother is not consistent with the behavior of ambivalently attached children.

 d. *Asynchronous interaction* would accurately describe the situation if Linda's mother failed to respond to her smiling and coos in a positive manner.

5. *c. Jealousy is one of several complex emotions that children begin to express by their second year. (p. 420)

 a. The expression of complex emotions is evident by the second year in many children, so jealousy in three-year-olds is quite normal.

 b. Jealousy in young children is normal and does not necessarily imply an insecure attachment.

 d. Complex emotions such as jealousy emerge as children's cognitive abilities improve and they understand more about their social world.

6. *a. Children who have a good understanding of their emotions are better liked by their peers (p. 423)

 b. Because children who have a good understanding of their emotions tend to be better liked by peers, Jeffrey is likely to have *more* friends.

 c. Jeffrey is likely to be more advanced cognitively since emotional development is closely related to advances in cognition.

 d. Children who have a good understanding of their emotions are usually proficient verbally and successful with social relationships.

7. *a. Daria's behavior is a classic example of separation anxiety. (p. 428)

 b. A stranger is not described in the question, so this choice is inappropriate.

c. The form of attachment cannot be determined since Daria's behavior is characteristic both of children with secure attachments and of some children with insecure attachments.
d. Interactive synchrony, mutually engaging cycles of caregiver-child behaviors, is not evident in the behavior described.

8. *d. Edward's distress over the departure of his mother and his warm greeting upon her return is a classic example of the securely attached baby. (p. 432)
  a. If Edward was insecurely attached he would not be so enthusiastic when greeting his returning mother.
  b. If Edward was avoidantly attached he would probably avoid or ignore his returning mother.
  c. If Edward was ambivalently attached he would probably show rejecting behavior toward his returning mother.

9. *c. Alisha is most certainly an "easy" baby; she is easy to care for and easy to please. (p. 435)
  a. Chess and Thomas identified three basic types of temperament. A secure temperament was not one of them, although it certainly appears that Alisha is securely attached.
  b. A slow-to-warm-up baby has a somewhat negative mood and tends to withdraw from new stimuli; Alisha does not appear to be a slow-to-warm-up baby.
  d. Alisha is calm but *calm temperament* is not one of the three types of temperament identified by Chess and Thomas.

10. *c. Michael Lamb argues that the behavior of children like Lauren suggests that the Strange Situation does not accurately measure attachment between mother and child, but is influenced by other social and cultural factors. (p. 442)
  a. Michael Lamb argues that the Strange Situation may be a nonoptimal measure of emotional bonds between mother and child, not that the attachment patterns are simple artifacts of the experimental situation.
  b. Lauren's behavior is consistent with Michael Lamb's contention that the Strange Situation does *not* accurately measure attachment between mother and child.
  d. Actually both factors are important. Nevertheless, Lauren's behavior and Michael Lamb's criticism of the Strange Situation do not directly address this issue.

CHAPTER 11

SOCIAL COGNITION

LEARNING OBJECTIVES

1. Define self-regulation and describe how it develops in infancy and early childhood. (pp. 450–452)

2. Describe Vygotsky's view of the development of self-regulatory behavior and compare and contrast his view with programs that stress the role of attention. (pp. 452–456)

3. Describe the patterns observed in the development of self-recognition and self-definition in children. (pp. 456–461)

4. Describe how social comparison influences the self-concept in the developing child. (pp. 461–464)

5. Describe what has been learned about the developing child's understanding of her sense of agency. (pp. 464–465)

6. Define learned helplessness and describe what has been determined concerning its causes and treatments. (pp. 466–468)

7. Describe the development of the child's understanding of himself as a unique individual with stable characteristics and abilities. (pp. 468–471)

8. Describe the factors influencing the development of self-esteem. (pp. 472–474)

9. Discuss the controversy concerning whether or not there is an adolescent identity crisis. (pp. 474–476)

10. Discuss the development of visual and conceptual perspective taking. (pp. 476–479)

11. Compare and contrast John Flavell and Robert Selman's models of perspective taking. (pp. 480–484)

12. Define attribution and discuss the development of attribution skills. (pp. 485–488)

CHAPTER OUTLINE

A socially successful individual must have considerable knowledge of the activities that others engage in, an understanding of the motives and causes of his own behavior, and a command of the rules for interacting in social settings. This broad knowledge of self and others is called *social cognition*.

I. HOW SELF-REGULATION DEVELOPS (pp. 450–456)

A. Self-Regulation in Late Infancy and Early Childhood (pp. 451–452)
As the infant develops from being in a state of total dependence on caregivers into having some ability to be independent, he must learn to show *self-regulation*. That is, he must learn to control his behavior to meet the expectations of caregivers and others. The development of self-regulation undergoes several transitions. At eight to eighteen months infants depend on caregivers to help regulate their behavior. Shortly before their second birthday children can respond to parents' verbal instructions on how and when to regulate their behavior. By two years of age self-regulation is self-initiated, and children can more efficiently inhibit themselves, as is indicated by their performance on *delay-of-gratification* tasks.

B. Factors Influencing Self-Regulation (pp. 452–456)
Lev Vygotsky theorized that language plays a primary role in the regulation of behavior. For the first three years verbal requests of others are effective in controlling a child's behavior. By four or five years the child's own private speech becomes effective in controlling behavior. Private speech is spoken aloud at first, but as a form of self-regulation it gradually becomes silent. Private speech is most likely to occur in situations that are challenging to the child. Studies show that impulsive children can be trained to use silent verbalizations to help regulate their behavior. By late preschool children begin to use their own distracting strategies to help delay gratification. Strategies for redirecting attention become available to children as they develop greater metacognitive abilities.

Stable individual differences in self-regulation have been observed, with some children showing consistent flexibility of behavior when confronted with situations that require flexibility. Individual differences in self-regulation may be due to genetic differences but are also most certainly a result of socialization practices.

II. HOW THE CONCEPT OF SELF DEVELOPS (pp. 457–476)

The subjective sense of *self*, which involves the beliefs, knowledge, and feelings that individuals use to describe themselves, undergoes complex developmental progressions. To study the development of self researchers find it useful to distinguish between the objective self ("me") and the subjective self ("I").

A. Self as Object (pp. 458–464)

Self as object is also called the *self-concept*, a collection of traits and characteristics used to define oneself (a form of self-observation). To have a self-concept an individual must first show self-recognition, an ability that begins to emerge at about eighteen months of age. The development of self-recognition in young children appears to be hastened when observing their own contingent movement. By two years of age the child easily identifies pictures of himself. This self-awareness may lead to self-conscious emotions such as embarrassment and pride. The self-concept also consists of the *categorical self*, classifying oneself in terms of easily observable categories (such as sex and age). Research suggests that preschoolers have considerable knowledge concerning their *inner self*, their private thoughts and feelings, although they might not always be able to verbalize these mental states. At about seven years of age self-descriptions shift from categorical activities ("I run fast") to relational statements (comparisons of qualities with others). Thus, during the elementary school years *social comparison* becomes an important factor in defining the self-concept. Adolescents become more cognizant of the way in which their attributes lead to social interactions with others within the group. More mature adolescents develop self-definitions within the context of a more coherent but abstract personal identity and moral system. How individuals define and evaluate self depends on values of their culture. In some cultures (for example, the Samoan culture) the standing within the group is more important and desirable than individual competencies.

Research designed to determine how social comparison influences self-concept indicates that five- to seven-year olds do not make use of information involving social comparisons when making decisions concerning their abilities. By nine years of age children employ information provided to evaluate their abilities. Young children, when observing others, utilize nonachievement information (what they should be doing) rather than achievement information (how well they are doing). This reliance on nonachievement comparisons explains why young children overestimate their abilities. As children increase the frequency of achievement comparisons their estimates become more realistic.

B. Self as Subject (pp. 464–471)

A component of the subjective self is the sense of agency—the belief that one can influence and control her surroundings. The desire to control the environment, called *effectance motivation*, may be inborn. Preschoolers cite uncontrollable factors when answering questions about themselves. By ten years children acknowledge their own efforts and by thirteen years the contribution of others. Some children have an *internal locus of control*, the sense that what happens to them is under their direct control, which provides them with a strong *mastery orientation*. Children with an *external locus of control* believe that luck or fate is the primary determinant of what happens to them, which may provide them with a sense of *learned helplessness*. In general, internalizers perform better in school and on standardized tests than externalizers. Learned helplessness may arise when children are raised in an environment in which they have little opportunity to master controllable events and are not provided with the appropriate feedback by parents, teachers, and others to attain mastery. Evidence suggests that attribution retraining programs can help children recognize that they can experience greater control of their own behavior.

Other components of the subjective self include the sense of individuality, stability, and reflection. A child's sense of individuality and stability changes over time. The preschooler cites physical characteristics and personal features and qualities. Young adolescents link their individuality and continuity to others through social comparisons. Older adolescents are more likely to cite abstract concepts and unique personal feelings. The sense of reflection may not emerge until late adolescence. It is during this time that adolescents may respond to an imaginary audience and display what David Elkind described as adolescent egocentrism, an excessive preoccupation with themselves as the object of thought. An adolescent who is able to reflect on the self as a capable, unique, and stable individual is on the way to achieving a healthy *personal identity*.

C. **Self-Esteem: Evaluating Self** (pp. 472–474)
An individual who evaluates the self in terms of positive feelings is said to have *self-esteem*, or self-worth. Young children can make global assessments of their sense of self-worth. As children get older, however, they are more likely to give different evaluations for specific domains. The growth of self-esteem depends on the success one achieves in a highly regarded domain and the perceived evaluations of parents, peers, teachers, and others. Children with low self-esteem show greater discrepancies between their perceived confidence and importance of a domain. Whereas children with high self-esteem minimize the importance of those domains in which they are not particularly competent, children with low self-esteem continue to value the domains they are not skilled in. The child with low social support and a high competence/importance discrepancy is likely to have low self-worth. The young child's overall sense of self-worth may be most influenced by her attitudes toward her physical appearance during elementary and middle school; as children get older, social acceptance appears to become more important.

Controversy: Is There Such a Thing as an Adolescent Identity Crisis? (pp. 474–476)
Psychologists disagree on whether an *identity crisis* occurs during adolescence. Some researchers report an overall decrease in self-esteem during the adolescent period that is accompanied by new ways of thinking and behaviors that lead to conflict with family members. Other researchers argue that although conflicts do increase during adolescence, they do not reach a level that should be considered a crisis. Some researchers point out that a large percentage of teenagers are sociable and well-adjusted individuals. Conflicts between adolescents and their parents may reflect a form of adaptation that can lead to shared respect if the conflicts are successfully resolved through negotiations. Nevertheless, 10 to 20 percent of teenagers do experience serious mental health problems that require attention from health professionals.

III. HOW UNDERSTANDING OTHERS DEVELOPS (pp. 476–488)

A. Perspective Taking: Taking the Roles of Others (pp. 477–479)

An important ability necessary to understand and interact with others is *perspective taking*, assuming the visual and conceptual perspective of others. Piaget and Inhelder described four- to six-year-olds as displaying considerable egocentrism when evaluating the visual perspective of others. More recent research suggests that children as young as three to four years of age can do reasonably well at identifying the perspective of others.

John Flavell distinguishes between two levels of visual perspective-taking skill. During the first level (birth to three years) the child realizes that his views do not always match others' views. During the second level, children become increasingly proficient at determining the specific limitations of another's view. Children must also learn that other people may have knowledge about things that is different from their own knowledge. Children's conceptions of the thoughts and cognitions of others are determined in experiments where children are provided with privileged information not available to others and then observed to see if they are aware of the discrepancy. Whereas children under four years usually fail to realize the discrepancy, children over four can make a distinction between what they and others know. Flavell also notes that the child's understanding of the recursive nature of thought develops during the elementary school years and through adolescence, providing more complex perspective-taking abilities.

B. Perspective-taking Approaches (pp. 479–485)

John Flavell's model of perspective taking explains developmental changes in visual and conceptual perspective taking in terms of four cognitive skills that the child must draw upon to carry out effective social interactions: 1) recognizing that others possess different points of view, 2) realizing the need to consider another's perspective, 3) inferring the relevant attributes of others, and 4) applying these inferences and monitoring their successful application during social interchange.

Robert Selman's model of perspective taking emphasizes qualitative changes in development. Selman used children's responses to social dilemmas to distinguish among five stages of role-taking ability. These invariant stagelike advances range from the inability or unwillingness to maintain a distinction between one's own perspective of a situation and another's perspective (three to six years) to the ability to consider several points of view (ten- to twelve-year-olds) and the consideration of the larger society (young adolescents). Flavell's and Selman's models of perspective taking suggest that cognitive skills have an important role in perspective taking. However, social factors most certainly play an influential role as well, since many changes (such as going to school) take place in a child's life during the time that perspective taking is developing.

C. How Attribution Skills Develop (pp. 485–488)

Understanding self and others also involves *attribution*, inferences about the characteristics that cause others' and our own behaviors. In many situations preschoolers are as capable as adults of attributing the actions of others to inner qualities such as motives and beliefs. Preschoolers, however, tend to overattribute intentionality compared to adults. Piaget suggested that overattribution of intentionality was a result of the preschoolers' egocentrism. Other research suggests that overattribution in young children is more complex and may depend on the information available to the preschoolers and on their familiarity with the situation. By six years of age attributions of intention match adult levels.

Psychologists often distinguish between internal attributions (based on factors within a person such as attitude and interest) and external attributions (based on situational factors such as parental and school pressures). Despite the observed overattribution of intentions (an internal factor) in preschoolers, young children are often described as relying on external rather than internal attributions of others' behavior. Pat Miller and Patricia Aloise suggest that this conclusion is largely based on the clinical methods used to obtain information about children's beliefs of the causes of behavior.

Recent studies indicate that when alternate methods are used even very young children prefer to use internal attributions. The process by which internal attributions are used to form descriptions or conceptualizations of someone's personality is called *person perception* and includes the understanding that people have *dispositions,* enduring tendencies and competencies. Studies of the development of person perception indicate that it parallels changes observed in understanding the self. In early childhood physical characteristics such as place of residence are highlighted. During the elementary school years children increasingly infer global personality and dispositional traits despite the variability in the behaviors of others.

IV. THEMES IN DEVELOPMENT: SOCIAL COGNITION (pp. 489–490)

What roles do nature and nurture play in the development of social cognition? Children learn strategies from caregivers, teachers, and others for instructing themselves, controlling their attention, and planning. Children also rely on people in their environment for learning about themselves and others. Some competencies, however, may build upon children's innate nature.

How does the sociocultural context influence the development of social cognition? The evaluations children place on themselves will depend on whether their culture stresses autonomy, loyalty, cooperation, or some other qualities and how closely they measure up to them. The value a society places on social etiquette, effective communication, and other interpersonal skills may also have a significant impact.

How does the child play an active role in the development of social cognition? As children gain cognitive and social skills, they initiate their own efforts to control their activities. They actively search out information from others, perhaps at first to "fit in" and learn how to behave in a specific situation. Comparison becomes important in middle childhood, while in adolescence a personal identity becomes an important goal.

Is the development of social cognition continuous or stagelike? Selman's analysis of perspective taking provides an example of how the development of social cognition can be viewed as stagelike. Others, such as Flavell, see perspective taking as continuously improving and expanding. Evidence that developmental changes represent stagelike changes remains limited.

How does the development of social cognition interact with development in other domains? With development, cognitive resources and socialization practices intersect to permit children to take charge of their own lives. Cognitive, linguistic, emotional, and physical aspects of development, along with the social environment, all contribute to the development of social cognition.

Key Terms Review

1. _____ is the process of describing and conceptualizing someone's personality.

2. _____ tasks are used by psychologists to evaluate a child's ability to regulate his own behavior.

3. The realization that one is an independent, unique, stable, and self-reflective entity is described as the _____ .

4. When an individual makes an inference about the causes of another person's behavior he is making a(n) _____ .

5. When in the absence of an adult a child shows control over her own behavior in accordance with the standards of the community she is displaying _____ .

6. The _____ is a private and unobservable aspect of the self that is associated with the mind.

7. Individuals who see their successes and failures as primarily resulting from outside factors such as luck have a(n) _____ .

8. _____ refers to an individual's knowledge of humans and the activities in which they engage.

9. Because of inconsistent outcomes individuals may develop _____ , a sense that one has little control over situations.

10. The multitude of perceptions, conceptions, and values one holds about oneself is called the _____ .

11. A(n) _____ consists of those enduring tendencies and competencies that characterize an individual.

12. A(n) _____ is a period in which an individual experiences considerable uncertainty about himself and his role in society.

13. The child's efforts to master and gain control of the environment is theorized to be a result of an inborn desire called _____ .

14. A child who defines himself in relation to the skills, attributes, and qualities of others is using a process called _____ .

15. _____ is the ability to take the role of another person and to understand what that person is thinking, feeling, or knows.

16. A person who has a coherent view of who he is and wants to be has established a(n) _____ .

17. An individual who believes that her own efforts and activities influence success and failure has a(n) _____ .

18. _____ is the child's feelings of worth.

19. A(n) _____ is a belief that achievements are based on one's own efforts rather than luck or other factors beyond one's control.

20. The _____ is a conceptual process in which a child classifies herself according to easily observable categories that can be used to distinguish people.

Answers to Key Terms Review

1. Person perception
2. Delay-of-gratification
3. self
4. attribution
5. self-regulation
6. inner self
7. external locus of control
8. Social cognition
9. learned helplessness
10. self-concept
11. disposition
12. identity crisis
13. effectance motivation
14. social comparison
15. Perspective taking or role taking
16. personal identity
17. internal locus of control
18. Self-esteem

19. mastery orientation
20. categorical self

Multiple-Choice Questions

Fact and Concept Questions

1. The broad knowledge that individuals acquire about the motives, feelings, capacities, and thoughts about themselves and others is called
   a. self-regulation.
   b. social cognition.
   c. attribution.
   d. disposition.

2. Caregivers play an important role in helping young children to organize their activities so that dangerous and inappropriate behaviors are kept to a minimum. This process is referred to as
   a. self-regulation.
   b. social cognition.
   c. co-regulation.
   d. delay of gratification.

3. If a child can demonstrate delay of gratification, then the child will
   a. be unable to regulate her own behavior.
   b. be able to regulate her own behavior.
   c. be unable to wait to perform a tempting activity.
   d. be unable to comply with instructions concerning her behavior.

4. According to Sigmund Freud, which structure of the personality is involved in self-regulation?
   a. The id
   b. The ego
   c. The self
   d. Private speech

5. According to Lev Vygotsky, which of the following describes the four- or five-year-old child's ability regarding self-regulation?
   a. The child is unable to regulate his own behavior.
   b. The child relies solely on his parents' verbal control over his behavior.
   c. The child uses private speech, usually spoken out loud, to regulate his own behavior.
   d. The child uses private speech, usually expressed silently in his mind, to regulate his own behavior.

6. Research with mothers of preschool-aged children has found that
   a. mothers who use physical restraint most often do best at regulating their children's behavior.
   b. mothers who do not respond to their children's repeated requests are most successful at regulating their children's behavior.
   c. mothers who divert their children's attention away from potential conflicts are most effective in regulating their children's behavior.
   d. mothers' behavior had little impact on regulating their children's behavior.

7. According to William James, the self-concept is part of the
   a. subjective self.
   b. objective self.
   c. superego.
   d. self-esteem.

8. The development of self-recognition appears to be related to the appearance of emotions such as
   a. sadness.
   b. joy.
   c. fear.
   d. embarrassment.

9. When children make statements that define who they are based on distinguishing characteristics, they are exhibiting their
   a. egocentrism.
   b. categorical self.
   c. metacognitive skill.
   d. inner self.

10. When evaluating their own achievement, younger children do not take into account information about others' performance. This indicates that
    a. they do not make social comparisons when evaluating their own abilities.
    b. they are sensitive to the feelings of others.
    c. they have excellent metacognitive skills.
    d. they have a well-developed self-concept.

11. Children with an internal locus of control
    a. feel that others control the positive or negative outcomes that occur in their lives.
    b. feel that luck or fate is responsible for their successes or failures.
    c. frequently defer to others for assistance or validation.
    d. feel that what happens to them is a direct result of their own efforts and actions.

12. Children can avoid the pitfalls of learned helplessness by
    a. becoming dependent on others for help in school.
    b. having an external locus of control.
    c. gaining mastery over aspects of their environment.
    d. being exposed to conflicting and inconsistent environmental experiences.

13. According to David Elkind, adolescents have an exaggerated sense of being observed by others. This is referred to as
    a. personal identity.
    b. categorical self.
    c. sense of reflection.
    d. imaginary audience.

14. Research on children's self-esteem suggests that
    a. unconscious factors influence self-esteem.
    b. children's perception of how others see them influences their self-esteem.
    c. a large discrepancy between perceived competence and importance of a particular domain leads to greater self-esteem.
    d. perceived social support is unrelated to the child's self-esteem.

15. During the adolescent period self-esteem tends to
    a. decrease.
    b. increase.
    c. remain the same.
    d. be unaffected by the identity crisis.

16. John Flavell has identified two levels of visual perspective taking. Children under three years of age _____ , whereas children older than four or five years of age _____ .
    a. do not distinguish between their own views and those of another person; realize their own view differs from another's view.
    b. distinguish between their own views and those of another person; do not distinguish between their own views and those of another person.
    c. do not distinguish between their own views and those of another person; do not distinguish between their own views and those of another person until they enter school.
    d. distinguish between their own views and those of another person; can specify precisely the differences between their own viewpoint and that of another person.

17. In thinking about others, John Flavell suggests that children develop recursive thought. This is
    a. the ability to think reflectively about what others are thinking.
    b. the limited use of visual perspective taking.
    c. the ability to think abstractly and hypothetically.
    d. also known as adolescent egocentrism.

18. Robert Selman's model of perspective taking differs from John Flavell's model primarily because
    a. Selman's model is not developmental.
    b. Selman's model postulates qualitative differences in role taking from one developmental stage to the next.
    c. Selman's model hypothesizes quantitative changes in the amount of information a child can process about others.
    d. children may regress to earlier role-taking abilities once they reach adolescence.

19. Preschoolers have been found to
    a. overattribute intentionality for all behaviors and events.
    b. overattribute to accidental causes all intentional behaviors they observe.
    c. be unable to understand the connection between motives and behavior.
    d. make few errors when determining attributions of behavior.

20. When a child provides a reason for behavior that is based on some intrinsic or psychological attribute, the reason is referred to as a(n) _____ attribution.
    a. external
    b. internal
    c. accidental
    d. situational

Application Questions

1. Alaina has begun to crawl around and get into dangerous situations such as touching electrical outlets and pulling on lamp cords that hang down to her level. Alaina's parents realize they must do some "childproofing" so she doesn't get into trouble. Alaina's parents are serving to
    a. inhibit Alaina's development.
    b. co-regulate Alaina's behavior.
    c. self-regulate Alaina's behavior.
    d. delay Alaina's gratification.

2. Dion is told that he has to wait to eat the lollipop his grandmother gave him until after dinner. Dion has no trouble complying with this self-regulation of his behavior, indicating that he
    a. is about one year old.
    b. does not like lollipops.
    c. has an external locus of control.
    d. can delay gratification.

3. Marcia was shopping in a toy store for a birthday present for a friend of her three-year-old son, Chris. Her son began repeatedly asking her if he could also get a toy. Marcia will be most successful at getting Chris to stop asking for a toy if she says
   a. "Don't ask me again; I said you may not have a toy."
   b. "If you ask again, then you may not have dessert after dinner tonight."
   c. "Let's talk about what you're going to do at your friend's birthday party."
   d. nothing; that is, she ignores Chris's repeated questions.

4. Sasha, who is one year old, is in the park with her father feeding the ducks in the pond. As she reaches out over the water's edge to throw bread to the ducks, Sasha notices her reflection in the water. She points to her reflection and says, "Baby." Her dad smiles and says, "Yes, Sasha." Sasha most likely
   a. has self-recognition.
   b. thinks the reflection is another baby, not herself.
   c. has established an inner self.
   d. has established a categorical self.

5. Andrea told her nursery school teacher, "I'm a girl and Vanessa is my best friend." Andrea appears to have a good sense of her
   a. locus of control.
   b. categorical self.
   c. attribution.
   d. self-regulation.

6. Roger, who is two years old, has learned that if he presses the buttons on the TV remote control the pictures on the screen change. Roger takes great delight in this activity and apparently enjoys having control over the images on the TV screen. According to Robert White, Roger is demonstrating
   a. locus of control.
   b. attribution.
   c. delay of gratification.
   d. effectance motivation.

7. Bobby does not do very well in music class. Bobby is likely to have
   a. low self-esteem if he thinks music is not that important in his life.
   b. high self-esteem if he thinks music is not that important in his life.
   c. low self-esteem if he succeeds in all other academic areas.
   d. high self-esteem if he performs poorly in many other academic areas.

8. Larisa has had a happy childhood and has had few problems adjusting to adolescence. She appears to be coping very effectively with the demands placed on her by her family, friends, and society in general. Larisa
   a. is a very unusual adolescent.
   b. is typical of the vast majority of adolescents.
   c. is probably covering up some underlying crisis.
   d. has not developed a personal identity.

9. Feodor, who is two and a half, is sitting in his car seat in the back seat of his mother's car while she is driving. Looking at a picture book, he asks his mother, "What is this cow doing?" According to John Flavell, Feodor is likely to
   a. continue to ask his mother the question even though she cannot see the picture book.
   b. turn the book around to help his mother see the picture in the book more easily.
   c. describe additional details of the picture in the book so that his mother can answer his question.
   d. realize that his mother is driving and stop asking the question.

10. Kim is nine years old. While trying to get a glass from the kitchen cabinet she accidentally knocks down her mother's favorite pitcher and it breaks. Kim is upset because she thinks that her mother will think she was being careless and that's why the pitcher broke. Kim's thinking is consistent with Selman's concept of
    a. one-loop recursive thought.
    b. two-loop recursive thought.
    c. egocentric role taking.
    d. in-depth role taking.

Answers to Multiple-Choice Questions

The correct answer appears first and is preceded by an asterisk.

Answers to Fact and Concept Questions

1. *b. Social cognition is the broad knowledge that individuals acquire about themselves and others and the activities in which they engage. (p. 450)
   a. Self-regulation means controlling one's behavior in order to conform to the expectations of caregivers and the community.
   c. An attribution is an inference that an individual makes about the causes of another person's behavior or the causes of her own behavior.
   d. A disposition consists of the enduring tendencies and competencies that characterize an individual.

2. *c. Co-regulation includes the involvement of caregivers, who help the child refrain from dangerous or inappropriate behaviors. (p. 451)
   a. Self-regulation requires children to control their own behavior in the absence of other adults.
   b. Social cognition is the individual's knowledge of people and their activities, as well as knowledge of the self and how we interact with others.
   d. Delay of gratification is the capacity to wait for highly desirable activities or outcomes and appears to be related to the development of self-regulation.

3. *b. If a child can delay gratification this indicates that she has developed self-restraint, an important component of self-regulation. (p. 452)
   a. Delay of gratification has been shown to be directly related to self-regulation.
   c. Delay of gratification is specifically defined as the ability to wait to perform some tempting or desirable activity.
   d. If a child can delay gratification then she has developed the self-restraint necessary to comply with instructions concerning her own behavior.

4. *b. The ego is the mental structure that, according to Freud, controls perceptual and cognitive processes that are rational and responsive to social constraints on behavior. (p. 452)
   a. According to Freud, the id is the part of the personality that is unconscious and requires immediate gratification without thought of social acceptability.
   c. The self is not part of Freud's theorized structure of the personality.
   d. Private speech is part of Vygotsky's theory of self-regulation, not Freud's.

5. *c. Vygotsky claims that four- or five-year-olds do have the ability to regulate their own behavior through the use of private speech. Their private speech, however, must be spoken aloud as a form of narrative in order to effectively control their behavior. (p. 453)
   a. Vygotsky believes that by age four or five, children do demonstrate the ability to regulate their own behavior.
   b. Children under three years of age rely solely on their parents' verbal control over their behavior.
   d. Over the years following age five, Vygotsky claims that children internalize this private speech and it is expressed silently in their mind to regulate their own behavior.

6. *c. Holden found that mothers of preschoolers who diverted their children's attention from desired objects were most effective in regulating their children's behavior. (p. 454)
   a. Research has found that physical restraint is not as effective as when caregivers distract children's attention away from desired objects.
   b. Ignoring a child's request does not effectively regulate his behavior.
   d. In the research study by Holden, mothers' behavior did have differential impact on their children's behavior, with diverting children's attention from conflicts being most effective at controlling behavior.

7. *b. The objective self consists of all of the traits and characteristics that the individual believes she possesses, or her self-concept. (p. 458)
   a. The subjective self consists of one's own realizations about the self with respect to how one initiates, organizes, and interprets experience.
   c. The superego is part of Freud's theory of the structure of the personality and has no part in James's description of the self-concept.
   d. Self-esteem refers to an individual's feelings of worth, her sense of whether she is good and valued as an individual.

8. *d. Embarrassment has been linked to the development of self-recognition and self-awareness at about fifteen to eighteen months of age. (p. 459)
   a. Sadness is a basic emotion that appears in infancy, long before self-recognition appears.
   b. Joy is a basic emotion that appears in infancy, long before self-recognition appears.
   c. Fear is a basic emotion that appears in infancy, long before self-recognition appears.

9. *b. The categorical self is part of the child's self-concept in which a child classifies himself according to observable characteristics such as gender, age, skills, where he lives, and who his friends are. (p. 459)
   a. Egocentrism is a Piagetian concept concerning the preschool child's inability to take the perspective of another.
   c. Metacognition refers to the child's knowledge of his own cognitive ability.
   d. The inner self is composed of private thoughts and feelings associated with the mind and unobservable by others.

10. *a. In her research, Diane Ruble found that children under seven years old did not make use of information about other children's performance when asked to evaluate their own performance. (p. 462)
    b. Although young children may be sensitive to others' emotional distress, they do not make social comparisons when evaluating their achievement abilities.
    c. Research cited in the text indicates that young children do not have very good metacognitive skills.
    d. Although the self-concept begins to form in early childhood it does not become well developed until much later.

11. *d. Children with an internal locus of control believe that their actions and efforts are responsible for the positive and negative outcomes in their lives. (p. 465)
    a. Children with an external locus of control would be most likely to feel that others control the positive or negative outcomes in their lives.
    b. Feeling that luck or fate is responsible for success or failure is typical of individuals with an external locus of control.
    c. Children with an internal locus of control are more likely to rely on themselves than on validation from others.

12. *c. Children who gain mastery and competence over their environment are least likely to fall into a pattern of learned helplessness. (p. 467)
    a. Children who depend on others for their school success are not likely to see their own efforts as effective; they are therefore more susceptible to learned helplessness.
    b. Children with an external locus of control are not likely to see their own efforts as effective in their school success; they are therefore more likely to develop a pattern of learned helplessness.

    d. When children are exposed to conflicting and inconsistent environmental experiences they are more likely to experience failure and feel helpless, which creates a vicious cycle of learned helplessness.

13. *d. The imaginary audience stems from adolescents' exaggerated self-consciousness about who they are; they have a sense of always being observed. (p. 470)
    a. Personal identity is a coherent, internalized view of who one is and who one wants to be.
    b. The categorical self is a conceptual process in which a child classifies herself according to observable characteristics such as gender, age, skills, where she lives, and who her friends are.
    c. The sense of reflection refers to the individual's ability to contemplate the self.

14. *b. Research suggests that the "generalized other," the combined evaluation of others, may contribute to the sense of worth. (p. 472)
    a. Research on self-esteem has focused on the positive and negative feelings one grants to oneself; such feelings are conscious, not unconscious.
    c. A discrepancy between perceived competence and the importance of a particular domain is linked to lower, not higher, self-esteem.
    d. Research strongly suggests that among other things improved self-esteem requires a supportive social milieu.

15. *a. Although there is some debate concerning the existence of an identity crisis, research suggests that children entering adolescence tend to show a decline in self-esteem, especially girls. (p. 475)
    b. No studies have been reviewed indicating that there is an increase in self-esteem during adolescence.
    c. Although some researchers argue that the conflict during the adolescent period is not as frequent and traumatic as believed by most people, there still is some research showing that self-esteem decreases during this period.
    d. The identity crisis, whether or not it exists to the extent implied by the term *crisis*, most certainly has an influence on children's self-esteem.

16. *d. These two levels of visual perspective-taking skills described by Flavell reflect cognitive gains in differentiating oneself from others and in knowledge of space and spatial relationships. (p. 477)
    a. According to Flavell, children under three can distinguish between their views and those of another person.
    b. According to Flavell, children learn that their own views are different from others by late infancy. This perspective-taking ability is further refined, not lost, with development.
    c. According to Flavell, children begin to distinguish between their views and those of another person by late infancy without the need of formal schooling.

17. *a. The recursive nature of thought involves one or more levels of "you're thinking that I'm thinking . . ." (p. 479)

b. Visual perspective taking is concerned with the issue of how we understand what others see, not what others think.

c. Recursive thought does not refer to abstract and hypothetical thought, although it may depend on the more abstract and hypothetical reasoning associated with formal operational thought.

d. Adolescent egocentrism is an adolescent's belief that she is unlike any other person.

18. *b. Unlike Flavell, Selman believes that role taking undergoes qualitative changes from one age to the next. (p. 481)
a. Both Flavell and Selman's models are developmental.
c. Selman's developmental model is a stage theory, not a quantitative theory.
d. Selman's model, like other stage models of development, predicts that children do not regress to lower levels.

19. *a. Many researchers have reported preschoolers' tendency to overattribute intentionality, although researchers disagree on the reasons for this overattribution. (p. 485)
b. The reverse is true—preschoolers are actually overzealous in their attributions of intentions.
c. Studies suggest that young children understand motives that are closely linked to behavior.
d. Preschoolers do make errors because they tend to overattribute intentionality.

20. *b. An internal attribution is made when an intrinsic cause such as interest is provided as an explanation for behavior. (p. 487)
a. An external attribution is made when an external cause such as parental pressure is provided as an explanation for behavior.
c. There is nothing accidental about children's attributions of behavior.
d. Intrinsic or psychological attributes are not situational.

Answers to Application Questions

1. *b. Alaina's parents, like most parents, play an important role in co-regulating their children's behavior. (p. 451)
a. Alaina needs to practice her motor skills and satisfy her growing curiosity, but her parents must provide a safe environment to help ensure that Alaina develops into an adult.
c. Alaina's parents' actions to "childproof" their home are a good example of how young children's self-regulation is more appropriately labeled co-regulation.
d. The actions of Alaina's parents are unlikely to delay Alaina's gratification because she most likely has other gratifying activities to engage in.

2. *d. Asking a child to wait for some time before attaining a highly desired outcome is a classic example of a delay-of-gratification task; Dion can clearly delay gratification. (p. 452)

    a. Dion is probably at least two because children do not begin to show reasonable ability to inhibit their behavior until two years of age.

    b. The fact that Dion was asked to wait to eat the lollipop indicates that he desired the treat.

    c. External locus of control is not related to the ability to inhibit one's behavior.

3. *c. Marcia is trying to start an interesting conversation with her son. Mothers who anticipate conflict by engaging their child in an interesting conversation are more successful in preventing conflict. (p. 454)

    a. Verbal restraint has been found to be less effective than diverting children's attention when attempting to prevent conflicts.

    b. This response is an example of a parent being forced to respond to a child's demands, which often leads to continued conflict.

    d. Marcia is not likely to reduce her son's demands by ignoring him.

4. *b. Because Sasha is unlikely to show self-recognition, her response probably reflects her belief that she is looking at another baby. (p. 458)

    a. Babies younger than fifteen to eighteen months of age show little evidence of self-recognition; therefore it is unlikely that twelve-month-old Sasha recognizes herself.

    c. Young children like Sasha have difficulty establishing an inner self, the aspect of the self that is associated with the mind.

    d. The categorical self, a conceptual process by which a child classifies herself according to easily observable categories, begins in the early preschool years.

5. *b. Andrea is classifying herself in terms of the easily observable category of gender, which suggests that she has established a categorical self. (p. 459)

    a. Locus of control describes an individual's sense of control, which can be either internal or external; Andrea's response is not related to her sense of control.

    c. Andrea is not making an attribution, which is an inference about another person's characteristics that cause that person's behavior.

    d. Self-regulation is trying to control one's own behavior in accordance with the caregiver's or community standards. Andrea is not demonstrating self-regulation.

6. *d. Roger is demonstrating effectance motivation, an intrinsic desire to gain control over the environment. (p. 464)

    a. Locus of control requires some knowledge on the child's part of whether what happens to him is dependent on his own efforts or is a result of luck or fate.

    b. If Roger were making an attribution he would be making an inference about his own characteristics that cause his behavior, but Roger is not making an inference about the cause of his behavior.

    c. Roger is not delaying gratification by playing with the remote control.

7. *b. Bobby's self-esteem is not likely to be lowered by his poor performance if he does not perceive music as important in his life. (p. 473)

a. If Bobby perceives little discrepancy between his performance and the importance of the task, his self-esteem is not likely to be lowered.
c. Bobby is not likely to have low self-esteem if he does not perceive music as an important area of his life.
d. If Bobby performs poorly in many areas he is more likely to have low, not high, self-esteem.

8. *b. The vast majority of adolescents are sociable, adjusted individuals who effectively cope with the pressures and demands placed on them by society. (p. 475)
   a. Most adolescents adjust to this time in their life fairly well and do not experience extreme emotional stress.
   c. There is no evidence that Larisa is covering up any underlying crisis.
   d. Most individuals develop a sense of personal identity during adolescence.

9. *b. Flavell would suggest that Feodor probably understands that his mother's view is different from his own. Therefore Feodor is likely to adjust the book to help his mother look at the picture. (p. 477)
   a. According to Flavell, children begin to understand in late infancy that their own view and others' views are not identical. Because Feodor is two and a half years old he probably understands that his mother cannot see the book and is less likely to continue asking the question without improving his mother's view of the book.
   c. Young Feodor is unlikely to be able to describe the picture in much detail.
   d. Flavell was concerned with visual perspective-taking skills; thus the appropriate answer to this question should be related to such skills. Feodor's realization that his mother was driving is not relevant to visual perspective-taking.

10. *a. According to Selman, one-loop recursions in thought emerge around eight to ten years old and indicate anticipations of how others will think about the individual's actions. (p. 481)
    b. Selman does not refer to the next stage as two-loop recursive thought, but mutual role taking, which would imply knowledge of the embedded nature of recursive thought, emerges between ten and twelve years of age.
    c. Egocentric role taking is characteristic of children between the ages of three and six years and does not involve recursive thought.
    d. In-depth role taking does not emerge until adolescence and involves knowledge of societal views of the individual's behavior.

CHAPTER 12

SEX ROLES

LEARNING OBJECTIVES

1. Identify and describe sex-role stereotypes. (pp. 494–496)

2. Describe and discuss the actual differences observed between the sexes. (pp. 496–501)

3. Describe the biological explanations of sex differences, specifying the roles of chromosomes, hormones, and brain differences on behavior. (pp. 501–504)

4. Discuss the cross-cultural research findings concerning sex differences. (pp. 504–505)

5. Describe the psychodynamic explanation of the sexual identification process. (pp. 505–506)

6. Discuss the influence of parents, peers, and others on sex-role development according to social learning theory. (pp. 506–508)

7. Describe the cognitive-developmental explanations of gender identity, gender constancy, and gender schemas. (pp. 508–510)

8. List and describe developmental changes in what children know about sex roles. (pp. 511–516)

9. Describe the influence of parents on the child's sex-role development. (pp. 516–520)

10. Describe the influence of peers on the child's sex-role development. (pp. 520–523)

11. Describe the influence of teachers and schools on the child's sex-role development. (pp. 524–527)

12. Discuss the research examining why boys may be better at certain mathematics skills than girls. (pp. 527–528)

13. Define androgyny and discuss the relationships among masculinity, femininity, androgyny, and psychological well-being. (pp. 528–530)

CHAPTER OUTLINE

Individuals within a given culture hold expectations and beliefs about the behaviors characteristic of males and females called *sex-role stereotypes*. The process by which these stereotypes develop is called *sex typing* and depends on biological, cognitive, and socialization factors.

I. SEX DIFFERENCES: REAL OR IMAGINED? (pp. 494–501)

A. The Stereotypes: What Are They? (pp. 494–496)
Although some differences in sex-role stereotypes are seen across cultures, there are many cross-cultural similarities. Men are often described in terms of *instrumental personality characteristics* such as assertiveness and independence, whereas women are described in terms of *expressive personality characteristics* associated with emotions.

B. What Sex Differences Actually Exist? (pp. 496–500)
Despite the pervasiveness of sex-role stereotypes, research suggests that males and females are more alike than different; that is, there is greater variability in several characteristics within the sexes than between the sexes. Although sex differences in physical attributes appear very early, differences in cognition and social behavior are less obvious. Early studies suggested that girls are more skilled than boys in verbal ability, but a recent meta-analysis did not detect any sex differences in verbal skills. Overall sex differences in math skills also failed to appear in a recent meta-analytical study. These studies suggest that sex differences in verbal and mathematical skills are diminishing. The only cognitive skill in which sex differences are still revealed is mental rotation and spatial perception, where males outperform females. Although few sex differences exist in social behavior, males are more aggressive than females, particularly among preschoolers. This difference decreases through the college years. Sex differences have also been observed in empathy and identification of facial expressions, where females outperform males.

II. THEORIES OF SEX-ROLE DEVELOPMENT (pp. 501–511)

A. Biological Theories (pp. 501–505)
Biological theories focus on the interactions between behavior and chromosomal and hormonal influences. During initial sexual differentiation of the fetus, XY chromosomes lead to the growth of the testes and the secretion of male hormones called *androgens*. The lack of a Y chromosome (XX pair) leads to the growth of ovaries. The presence of the testes leads to the production of *testosterone,* an androgen that is actually present in both sexes, but in greater amounts in males.

The androgens also influence the organization of the structure of some areas of the central nervous system. Such differences in brain structure may account for greater aggressive behavior in males. Consistent with this possibility is the finding that females exposed to excess levels of androgens during prenatal development are more likely to engage in rough-and-tumble play than unexposed females. The relationship between testosterone and aggression is not clear, however, since it may be that aggression increases testosterone levels rather than that higher testosterone levels increase aggression.

Some investigators suggest that sex differences in visual-spatial skills result from differences in lateralization of the brain. According to this view the later maturity in males produces greater brain lateralization compared to girls, who mature earlier and more quickly. Other researchers suggest that sex differences in visual-spatial skills result from differences in the play experiences of boys and girls, with boys more likely to play with toys that encourage visual-spatial skills. Further evidence suggesting that sex typing is not simply a result of biological influences comes from cross-cultural patterns of sex differences. Margaret Mead's classic study of three New Guinea tribes showed that patterns of sex typing are not universal but vary according to the needs of diverse cultures.

B. Psychodynamic Theories (pp. 505–506)
Psychodynamic theorists (Sigmund Freud and neo-Freudians) emphasize the role of unconscious processes in sex-role development. Gender differences in sex-role socialization are assumed to emerge during the phallic stage as boys resolve their Oedipal complex and girls their Electra complex by identifying with the same-sex parent. A major weakness of psychoanalytic theory is that the identification process does not appear to be an important factor in sex-role development since considerable differences between father and son or mother and daughter are often observed.

C. Social Learning Theories (pp. 506–508)
According to social learning theory, behavioral differences between the sexes result primarily from differential reinforcement and punishment of sex-typed behavior and imitation or modeling of these behaviors. Social learning theory has also incorporated the importance of attention, recognition, and motivation in explaining how sex roles are learned through modeling. Children are more likely to attend to and imitate and display *sex-typical* rather than *sex-atypical* behavior.

D. **Cognitive-Developmental Theories** (pp. 508–510)
Cognitive-developmental theories are based on Piagetian ideas emphasizing the ways in which children understand sex roles and their own gender.

In Lawrence Kohlberg's theory, sex-role development is described as emerging as a result of cognitive development. An important cognitive milestone is *gender identity*, the knowledge that one is male or female, which occurs at about thirty months. At about the fourth year of age the child develops *gender stability*, the knowledge that gender does not change over time. The understanding that sex is not determined by external factors such as clothing or behaviors or desires is called *gender constancy*, and occurs at about seven years.

Gender schema theory also stresses the importance of gender identity and intrinsic motivations to display sex-typical behavior, but unlike Kohlberg's theory does not place importance on the attainment of gender constancy. Gender schema theorists such as Carol Martin and Charles Halverson argue that once children acquire gender identity they actively construct *gender schemas* to organize information relevant to sex typing and their social world.

Cognitive-developmental theories have been useful in understanding sex typing, imitation of modeled behavior, and particularly in explaining children's distortion of information inconsistent with sex stereotypes. Cognitive-developmental theories, however, do not adequately explain certain differential behavioral patterns seen between the sexes.

III. **HOW CHILDREN'S KNOWLEDGE OF SEX ROLES DEVELOPS** (pp. 511–516)

A. **Gender Identity** (pp. 511–512)
Most children label themselves correctly as female or male and begin to show a preference for toys consistent with their own gender between the ages of two and three. Once formed, gender identity is unlikely to change. Children who develop gender identity before the age of twenty-eight months engage in more sex-typical play than children who develop gender identity after twenty-eight months.

B. **Gender Constancy** (p. 512)
The role of gender constancy, or children's knowledge of gender as a fixed characteristic, is less clear. Inconsistent relationships between gender constancy and imitation of same-sex and opposite-sex models have been observed. Gender constancy is not related to other aspects of sexed-typed behavior.

C. **Gender Schemas** (pp. 513–514)
Children vary in their use of gender to categorize social information. Gender-schematic children have a strong gender schema and show more consistent sex-typing behavior than gender-aschematic children, who have a weaker gender schema. Gender schemas also influence how children process sex-typed information. Gender-schematic children are less likely to remember information about sex-atypical activities and are more likely to distort the information to fit more closely their beliefs about gender. Thus, gender-

schematic children are less likely than gender-aschematic children to see sex stereotypes as flexible. Sandra Bem suggests that children become gender schematic when gender is used as an important classification schema by the people that children are exposed to—parents, teachers, and peers.

D. **Sex-Role Stereotypes** (pp. 514–516)
Consistent sex-role stereotypes emerge by thirty months of age as indicated by children's consistent preference for "same-sex" over "opposite-sex" objects. The observation that twenty-four-month old children show considerable accuracy in identifying sex-role stereotypes suggests that knowledge of sex-role stereotypes begins at an early age. Even the young preschooler is likely to identify aggressive behavior as a male characteristic and interest in dolls as a female characteristic. As children get older they begin to recognize that sex stereotypes are flexible, although they may not necessarily view sex-atypical behavior as acceptable.

IV. **THE SOCIALIZATION OF SEX ROLES** (pp. 516–528)
Sex roles are assumed to be taught to children by others in their social environment, first parents and other family members and then peers and others in their school experiences.

A. **The Influence of Parents** (pp. 516–520)
Parents provide their children with sex-typing information in subtle ways (for example, by providing the toys to play with) and in more direct ways, such as playing more aggressively with their sons than with their daughters. One study showed that how adults respond to infants or interpret their behavior is influenced by the perceived sex rather than the actual sex of the baby. Parents also provide sex-typing information by delivering direct reinforcement for sex-typical behavior in their children and punishing sex-atypical behavior.

Parental attitudes are another indirect way in which parents influence sex-typing in their children. In elementary school parents have higher academic achievement expectations for their daughters, but by adolescence parents are more likely to encourage academic achievement in their sons.

Studies of sex typing in nontraditional families (for example, single-parent families and families with working mothers) suggest that the sex-typing information provided in nontraditional families may differ from the sex-typing information provided by the traditional family. Children of employed mothers, for example, are more likely to have flexible conceptions of sex roles. Daughters of working mothers have higher achievement motivation and are more likely to have female-typed and male-typed behavioral traits. Changing attitudes toward sex-role socialization has led many to advocate the raising of children in a nonsexist fashion.

Sandra Bem suggests that to minimize sex typing in children parents should: 1) provide their children with information about the biological basis of gender at about the time that the children are forming gender identities, 2) provide reading and viewing materials that exemplify sex-typical and sex-atypical activities, and 3) provide their children with a "sexism schema," explaining that others may hold beliefs about the sexes that are different from their own.

B. **The Influence of Peers** (pp. 520–523)
The peer group also has a large influence on children's sex-role development. In one study, play behavior between pairs of unacquainted two-year-olds in sex-neutral clothing was very different when the pair were of the same sex than when they were of the opposite sex. In preschool and kindergarten, children reliably reward the behavior of boys if it is sex-typical but punish behavior if it is sex-atypical. Girls, while rewarded by their peers for sex-typical behaviors, are not punished for sex-atypical behavior. Pressures exerted by the peer group, particularly from same-sex peers, are very effective in influencing most children's play behavior.

Children who exhibit *cross-gender behavior*, persistent behaviors characteristic of the opposite sex, fail to respond to the pressures of their peers. Children's negative attitudes toward cross-gender behavior (particularly in boys) increases with age. Thus, cross-gender boys are more likely to become social isolates over time than cross-gender girls.

Sex segregation, the clustering of individuals in same-sex groups, enhances the peer group's influence on sex-typing by fostering different social interactions in boys (aggressive play) and girls (cooperative play). Sex segregation becomes less pronounced by adolescence as children begin heterosexual interactions. Interestingly, such interactions enhance conformity to sex-role norms in males and females.

In adolescence behaviors other than sex-typed behaviors, such as politeness and leadership abilities, become important in determining popularity. Adolescents are also more likely to tolerate sex-atypical personality characteristics.

C. **The Influence of Teachers and Schools** (pp. 524–527)
Teachers display attitudes that reflect sex-role stereotypes. For example, teachers are likely to see males as more skilled in mathematics and females as more skilled in language, even though sex differences in these abilities are minimal or nonexistent. Teachers are also more likely to dispense disapproval to boys than to girls. Studies show that teachers can use their influence to reduce sex segregation in preschoolers and kindergartners by reinforcing cross-sex play.

Like parents and teachers, students also view some subjects as masculine and others as feminine. Math, for example, is seen as masculine by children of many cultures. Girls perceive themselves as less competent in math and are less willing to take math courses than boys despite the fact that girls do as well as boys on classroom and standardized math tests. One factor that may influence children's expectancies for academic success may be sex-typing in the school curriculum content. One study found that children prefer computerized tutorial material that is designed for their own sex.

The nature of evaluative feedback may also influence children's academic expectancies. Females are more likely to receive discriminate feedback (directed at academic work) from their teachers than nondiscriminate feedback (directed at academic and social behavior). Males are more likely to be the recipients of indiscriminate feedback that is directed primarily at nonacademic behavior. Girls' lowered achievement expectancies and greater self-criticism of their academic work, therefore, may result partly from the evaluations they receive, since discriminate criticisms are more likely to result in feelings of incompetence and lowered expectations than indiscriminate criticisms.

Controversy: Why Are Boys Better at Certain Mathematics Skills Than Girls? (pp. 527–528)
In a recent longitudinal study of intellectually gifted adolescents, males were observed to score better in mathematics than girls, prompting the authors to suggest a biological basis for sex differences in mathematics ability. Critics pointed out that girls' lowered achievement expectations in mathematics and parental attitudes may account for the sex differences in scores rather than genetic differences. When mathematics scores of boys and girls of all abilities are compared, reliable sex differences do not emerge. Thus, it appears that sex differences in an academic area such as mathematics are unlikely to be due to genetic factors alone.

V. ANDROGYNY: A PSYCHOLOGICAL CONCEPT (pp. 528–530)
Early theorists viewed sex-atypical behavior as undesirable. Recent views of sex-role development recognize that psychologically *androgynous* individuals, people who possess high levels of masculine and feminine characteristics, are more adaptive than traditional masculine or feminine individuals. According to Sandra Bem's classification scheme, androgynous people exhibit high levels of masculine and feminine personality characteristics, while people who have few masculine or feminine characteristics are defined as undifferentiated. Bem provided evidence that androgynous individuals show greater behavioral adaptability than masculine, feminine, or undifferentiated individuals. Psychological androgyny is also associated with psychological health and popularity with peers.

What factors determine whether someone becomes androgynous is unclear. Parental characteristics may play a role, but few studies have examined this possibility. Eccles suggests that androgyny emerges during adolescence as children develop abilities to conceptualize sex roles in more complex, abstract terms, rather than through modeling.

VI. THEMES IN DEVELOPMENT: SEX ROLES (pp. 530–532)
What roles do nature and nurture play in sex-role development? Although biological factors such as hormones and brain lateralization can influence behavior, so too can behavior influence levels of hormones. Research also shows that parents, peers, and teachers treat boys and girls differently, providing support for the nurture position.

How does the sociocultural context influence sex-role development? Most cultures hold stereotypical beliefs about sex roles, although the specific characteristics associated with each sex can vary.

How does the child play an active role in sex-role development? The child's active role is emphasized in cognitive-developmental theories of sex-role development. For example, many children construct gender schemas, which in turn influence how they process information and how they themselves behave.

Is sex-role development continuous or stagelike? Theorists like Freud and Kohlberg believe sex-role development occurs in stages. On the other hand, social learning theorists emphasize the cumulative and incremental effects of reinforcement and modeling on sex-role development.

Are there sensitive periods in sex-role development? Little empirical research supports Freud's theory of the critical period in which the Oedipal and Electra complexes are resolved. The first three or four years of life may be a sensitive period, since children may have psychological difficulties if they are classified as a different sex after this time.

How does sex-role development interact with development in other domains? Bandura describes cognitive processes that influence which models, male or female, children will imitate. Kohlberg suggests that cognitive advances precede gender knowledge such as gender constancy. The child's state of sex-role development can also influence cognitive processing.

Key Terms Review

1. The knowledge that gender does not change as a result of an alteration in appearance or behavior is known as _____ .

2. Testosterone belongs to the class of masculinizing hormones called _____ .

3. Characteristics associated with acting on the world are described as _____ personality characteristics.

4. Individuals acquire the characteristics and behaviors prescribed by their culture for their sex through the process of _____ .

5. A(n) _____ is a cognitive organizing structure utilized to make sense of information relevant to sex typing.

6. _____ are expectations or beliefs that individuals hold about the characteristic behaviors of males and females.

7. _____ refers to behaviors usually associated with one sex, while _____ are those that are inconsistent with the norm for a particular sex.

8. A child who persistently behaves in ways that are characteristic of the opposite sex is said to be displaying _____ .

9. _____ refers to the phenomenon where individuals cluster into same-sex groups.

10. An individual who possesses high levels of personality characteristics associated with both sexes is said to be _____ .

11. Characteristics associated with emotions or relationships with people and usually considered to be feminine are described as _____ personality characteristics.

12. _____ refers to the knowledge that one is male or female, whereas the knowledge that one's gender does not change over time is called _____ .

Answers to Key Terms Review

1. gender constancy
2. androgens
3. instrumental
4. sex typing
5. gender schema
6. Sex-role stereotypes
7. Sex-typical behavior, sex-atypical behaviors
8. cross-gender behavior
9. Sex segregation
10. androgynous
11. expressive
12. Gender identity, gender stability

Multiple-Choice Questions

Fact and Concept Questions

1. The acquisition of sex-role stereotypes
   a. is primarily an American phenomenon.
   b. begins before the age of five in most cultures.
   c. begins when children enter formal schooling in most cultures.
   d. is the same across all cultures examined, suggesting a strong biological influence.

2. Which of the following statements does *not* accurately describe observed sex differences?
   a. Recent studies find no substantial sex differences in verbal skills.
   b. Sex differences in mathematical skills are much less significant than they used to be.
   c. Males are generally better at mental rotation tasks than females.
   d. Females are more likely to be miscarried or to die in infancy than males.

3. Studies of the hormonal influences on sexual development indicate that
   a. excessive levels of androgens can change an XX chromosomal configuration into a XY chromosomal configuration.
   b. prenatally administered androgens can produce female genitalia in individuals with an XY chromosomal pattern.
   c. prenatally administered androgens increase aggressive behaviors such as rough-and-tumble play.
   d. prenatally administered estrogen can produce female genitalia in an individual with an XY chromosomal pattern.

4. The suggestion that sex differences in verbal and visual-spatial skills are caused by differences in brain lateralization is supported by the finding that
   a. regardless of sex, children who mature early score better on verbal tasks than on spatial tasks.
   b. boys are more likely to play with toys that facilitate the development of visual-spatial skills than are girls.
   c. sex-role differentiation does not occur in all cultures.
   d. males and females differ in the levels of hormones involved in sexual development.

5. The _____ theory emphasizes that sex-role development is closely tied to personality development.
   a. psychodynamic
   b. social learning
   c. gender schema
   d. information-processing

6. According to the text, the best explanation for the roles that parents, peers, and others play in sex-role development is provided by _____ theories.
   a. biological
   b. cognitive-developmental
   c. social learning
   d. psychodynamic

7. A child who shows sex-atypical behavior
   a. displays behavior that is uncharacteristic of either sex.
   b. displays behavior that is inconsistent with the norm of his or her sex.
   c. most likely has ambiguous genitalia.
   d. most likely has a hormonal pattern that is inconsistent with his or her sex.

8. The attainment of gender constancy is a milestone that is stressed in _____ theory.
   a. social learning
   b. gender schema
   c. Kohlberg's cognitive-developmental
   d. psychodynamic

9. Most two-and-a-half-year-old children
   a. can apply appropriate gender labels to pictures of others but not to themselves.
   b. can apply appropriate gender labels to pictures of others and to themselves.
   c. cannot apply appropriate gender labels to pictures of others but can apply the labels to themselves.
   d. cannot apply appropriate gender labels either to pictures of others or to themselves.

10. Children who are regularly exposed to gender as a relevant social category are likely to become
    a. gender schematic.
    b. gender aschematic.
    c. gender atypical.
    d. gender typical.

11. Studies reviewed in the text indicate that children have already begun to develop knowledge of sex-role stereotypes by the age of two. How was knowledge of sex-role stereotypes assessed in children two years and older?
    a. By observing the children's choice of toys while playing
    b. By interviewing the parents of the children
    c. By asking the children to sort photographs of "boy things" and "girl things"
    d. By interviewing children with the use of hand puppets

12. Research on the interaction pattern between adults and their infants has shown that parents tend to treat boys and girls
    a. similarly during early infancy but differently by late infancy.
    b. differently during early and late infancy.
    c. similarly during early and late infancy.
    d. differently during early infancy but similarly by late infancy.

13. In a study of preschoolers and their parents, mothers were found to
    a. consistently enforce sex-role stereotypes with their girls but not with their boys.
    b. consistently enforce sex-role stereotypes with their girls and boys.
    c. consistently enforce sex-role stereotypes with their boys but not with their girls.
    d. be more consistent than fathers in enforcing sex-role stereotypes in their children.

14. Advocates of nonsexist child rearing point out that
    a. to raise nonsexist children, parents should minimize discussion of the biological basis of gender identity.
    b. raising children to be nonsexist should not be difficult if parents are committed to nonsexist views.
    c. to raise children to be nonsexist, parents should minimize the use of a "sexism schema."
    d. traditional sex typing narrows the number of choices that children can make in their lives.

15. Studies suggest that the influence of peers on sex typing in children is apparent as early as
    a. two years of age in boys and girls.
    b. three years of age if the child attends preschool.
    c. three years in boys and four years in girls.
    d. three years in girls and four years in boys.

16. Children's adoption of sex-typed behavior is enhanced by the phenomenon known as
    a. androgyny.
    b. gender stability.
    c. sex segregation.
    d. cross-gender comparison.

17. Some academic subjects, such as mathematics, are generally seen as masculine and others as feminine by
    a. students, but not parents or teachers.
    b. students and parents, but not teachers.
    c. students and teachers, but not parents.
    d. students, parents, and teachers.

18. Jacquelynne Eccles conducted a study in which attitudes toward academic subjects were measured in fifth- through twelfth-graders. Which of the following was *not* observed in Eccles's study?
    a. Males performed better than females on standardized mathematics tests.
    b. Girls perceived themselves as less competent at mathematics.
    c. Girls were less willing to take mathematics courses than boys.
    d. Girls viewed mathematics as less valuable than did boys.

19. According to Carol Dweck, feelings of incompetence and lowered academic expectations are more likely to occur in children if teachers use _____ criticism.
    a. indiscriminate evaluative
    b. discriminate evaluative
    c. discriminate nonevaluative
    d. indiscriminate nonevaluative

20. _____ introduced the concept of androgyny to challenge the traditional view of masculinity and femininity as opposite ends of a bipolar dimension.
    a. Lawrence Kohlberg
    b. Carol Dweck
    c. Sandra Bem
    d. Beverly Fagot

Application Questions

1. Frank was asked to choose one word to describe a characteristic of the typical high school girl. Which of the following terms is he most likely to choose?
    a. Outspoken
    b. Assertive
    c. Understanding
    d. Independent

2. Deborah attends the same high school that her mother attended twenty years ago. If we were to compare Deborah's verbal performance on a standardized test with her mother's verbal performance when she was in high school we would probably find that
    a. both Deborah and her mother scored similar to the boys in their classes.
    b. both Deborah and her mother outperformed the boys in their classes.
    c. Deborah's mother outperformed most boys in her class but Deborah scored similar to the boys in her class.
    d. Deborah outperformed most boys in her class but her mother scored similar to the boys in her class.

3. Camille was born with masculinized genitalia and as a toddler engaged in more rough physical play than other girls her age. Camille most likely was born with a condition known as
    a. androgyny.
    b. adrenogenital syndrome.
    c. sex segregation.
    d. gender reversal.

4. Calida is a very verbal toddler. One day she asked her mother, "When you were small like me were you a little boy or a little girl?" Calida's question indicates that she has not yet developed
   a. gender stability.
   b. gender identity.
   c. sex-typical behavior
   d. gender awareness.

5. When Jake's toddler friend Leora suggested that they both play house by pretending to wash dishes Jake responded, "Girls wash dishes. I'm a boy. I'm gonna pretend to fix the dishwasher." Jake's reaction suggests that he has constructed
   a. androgynous schemas.
   b. cross-gender behavior.
   c. sex-atypical behavior.
   d. gender schemas.

6. Meredith has a three-year-old son and a four-year-old daughter. Although her children have their own sex-typical toys they occasionally play with each other's toys. Meredith is
   a. more likely to punish her son for playing with sex-atypical toys than she is likely to punish her daughter.
   b. likely to punish both son and daughter for playing with sex-atypical toys.
   c. more likely to punish her daughter for playing with sex-atypical toys than she is likely to punish her son.
   d. likely to reinforce both son and daughter for playing with sex-atypical toys.

7. Elissa's mother works at a full-time accounting job, whereas Dotty's mother does not work outside the home. With respect to sex typing
   a. Elissa probably exhibits greater flexibility than Dotty.
   b. Dotty probably exhibits greater flexibility than Elissa.
   c. both Elissa and Dotty are likely to show adherence to traditional sex-role norms.
   d. both Elissa and Dotty are likely to show similar flexibility in sex typing.

8. At preschool, Allen occasionally likes to play at the kitchen center and Lizzy occasionally likes to play with the trucks. Recent studies suggest that Allen and Lizzy's peers are likely to
   a. be indifferent to their sex-atypical play behavior.
   b. punish their sex-atypical play behavior.
   c. punish Lizzy's sex-atypical play but not Allen's sex-atypical play.
   d. punish Allen's sex-atypical play but not Lizzy's sex-atypical play.

9. When his best friend asked Stuart how he did on his English paper, Stuart said, "I got a D again. I'm never gonna pass this class because the English teacher hates me." Stuart is
   a. making an internal attribution.
   b. making an external attribution.
   c. displaying a gender schema.
   d. displaying adolescent egocentrism.

10. While examining Leroy's psychological profile report, the school counselor read a notation indicating that Leroy has strong "androgynous characteristics." This means that
   a. Leroy's physical characteristics are neither distinctly male nor distinctly female.
   b. Leroy displays primarily feminine personality characteristics.
   c. Leroy displays very low levels of feminine personality characteristics.
   d. Leroy displays high levels of masculine and feminine personality characteristics.

Answers to Multiple-Choice Questions

The correct answer appears first and is preceded by an asterisk.

Answers to Fact and Concept Questions

1. *b. Children from all the countries studied have been found to have some knowledge of sex-role stereotypes before the age of five. (p. 494)
   a. Sex-role stereotypes are not limited to our society; they have been observed in cultures all over the world.
   c. Children display sex-role stereotypes before they begin formal schooling.
   d. Cross-cultural studies conducted by Margaret Mead suggest that the sex roles seen in our society are neither natural nor universal.

2. *d. This statement is false. Males show greater physical vulnerability during delivery and infancy. (p. 497)
   a. This statement is true. Meta-analyses of cognitive sex differences find no substantial differences in verbal skills.
   b. This statement is true. Although some studies continue to show sex differences in mathematics, this difference is much smaller than it used to be.
   c. This statement is true. The superior performance of boys in visual-spatial skills is the only reliable sex difference in cognitive skills.

3. *c. Animal studies and observations of children with adrenogenital syndrome show that androgens increase aggressive behavior such as rough-and-tumble play. (p. 502)

a. The level of androgens present depends on the chromosomal pattern inherited; hormonal influences cannot alter chromosomal patterns.
b. Androgens are masculinizing hormones; they cannot produce female genitalia.
d. Estrogen does not cause the development of female genitalia; it is the lack of androgens that permits the development of female genitalia.

4. *a. According to the lateralization hypothesis, girls have greater verbal skills and lower visual-spatial skills because on average their brains mature more quickly than those of boys. If rate of maturity is the important factor, then the fastest-maturing brains in either sex should show greater verbal abilities and poorer visual-spatial skills. (p. 503)
b. This statement is true, but it is not relevant to the brain-lateralization hypothesis, which emphasizes biological sex differences rather than social differences.
c. This statement is true, but it is not relevant to the brain-lateralization hypothesis.
d. This statement is true, but the level of hormones is not an important factor in the brain-lateralization hypothesis of sex differences in cognitive skills.

5. *a. Sigmund Freud, the father of psychodynamic theory, believed that children's adoption of differing masculine and feminine roles is closely tied to events that occur during personality development. (p. 506)
b. Social learning theory emphasizes the role that others play by reinforcing or punishing children's behaviors in sex-typed ways.
c. Gender schema theory is a cognitive-developmental theory that emphasizes the importance of children's intrinsic motivation to behave sex-typically.
d. Information-processing theories do not consider the role of personality development.

6. *c. Social learning theory is valuable for understanding how children learn sex-typed behavior by interacting with family members and others in their social world. (p. 506)
a. The biological theories are valuable for understanding the physiological factors that might influence masculinity and femininity.
b. Cognitive-developmental theories are valuable for understanding how concepts of gender are integrated in children's minds.
d. Psychodynamic theory stresses the importance of personality development in sex-role development, particularly the importance of the identification process.

7. *b. Sex-atypical behaviors are behaviors that are inconsistent with the behaviors of same-sex peers and more consistent with opposite-sex peers. (p. 508)
a. A child's sex-atypical behavior is consistent with the behavior of the opposite sex.
c. Sex-atypical behavior is not related to ambiguous genitalia.
d. There is no indication that there is a relationship between hormonal levels and sex-atypical behavior. Evidence suggests that children use complex sources of information to decide whether to imitate a model.

8. *c. According to Kohlberg's theory, gender constancy is acquired after the development of gender stability at about seven years of age. (p. 509)
   a. The emergence of milestones implies a stage theory of development; social learning theory is not a stage theory and does not include the concept of gender constancy.
   b. Although gender schema is a stage theory that adopts Piagetian concepts, it does not stress the attainment of gender constancy.
   d. Psychodynamic theory does not stress cognitive processes such as gender constancy.

9. *b. Children show the ability to categorize social information on the basis of gender as early as two years of age. (p. 511)
   a. Most children can apply gender labels to themselves by two years of age.
   c. Most children can apply appropriate gender labels to others by two years of age.
   d. Most children can apply appropriate gender labels to themselves and others by two years of age.

10. *a. Children who are frequently reminded of differences between males and females by people in their social world are more likely to develop and use gender schemas to classify social information. (p. 514)
    b. Gender-aschematic children do not experience gender as a social category as frequently as gender-schematic children and therefore are more likely to believe that gender stereotypes are flexible.
    c. *Gender atypical* is not a term used to describe sex-role stereotypes.
    d. *Gender typical* is not a term used to describe sex-role stereotypes.

11. *c. In one study two-year-olds were able to identify accurately 61 percent of the stereotypical "boy things" and "girl things" in the photographs. (p. 514)
    a. Although an examination of the choice of toys can provide information on sex-typed preferences, this procedure was not used to determine children's knowledge of sex-role stereotypes.
    b. Interviewing parents can be useful in sex-role stereotype research, but this approach was not used to determine children's knowledge of sex-role stereotypes.
    d. This sounds like an interesting approach, but it was not the one used in the studies reviewed in the chapter.

12. *b. Throughout infancy and childhood, parents are more likely to be protective of their girls and more likely to play roughly with their boys. (p. 516)
    a. Parents play more roughly with their male children throughout infancy.
    c. Parents are more protective of their girls and more likely to play roughly with their boys throughout infancy.
    d. Parents play more roughly with their male children throughout infancy.

13. *a. Although mothers are consistent with their daughters, their responses to their sons' behavior are more mixed (p. 517)

b. Mothers are not as consistent with their sons; for example, they alternately punish and reinforce sex-atypical play.
c. Mothers consistently reinforce their daughters' play with sex-typical toys and punish play with sex-atypical toys.
d. Fathers are more consistent than mothers in enforcing sex-role norms with their sons and daughters.

14. *d. Advocates argue that sex typing limits the choices that children can make to a small number of the total possible behaviors available. (p. 519)
a. Advocates of this view (such as Sandra Bem) argue that parents should teach their children the biological bases of gender.
b. Advocates are aware of the difficulty of raising nonsexist children in a modern society that strongly emphasizes gender.
c. Bem suggests that parents provide their children with a sexism schema in order to teach children that other people may hold beliefs about the sexes that are different from their own.

15. *a. The influence of peers on sex typing behavior can be seen in very young children of both sexes. (p. 520)
b. Peer influences on sex typing behavior in very young children are not associated with participation in a preschool program.
c. Peer influences on sex-typing behavior have been observed in girls and boys as young as two years of age.
d. Peer influences on sex-typing behavior have been observed in girls and boys as young as two years of age.

16. *c. Sex segregation refers to the clustering of individuals into same-sex groups, a phenomenon that enhances sex typing. (p. 523)
a. Androgyny refers to an individual with high levels of characteristics of both sexes; an androgynous orientation would not enhance sex typing but most likely would reduce it.
b. Gender stability, the knowledge that gender does not change over time, is usually attained by age four.
d. *Cross-gender comparison* is not a term discussed in this chapter.

17. *d. Research indicates that students, parents, and teachers view some subjects as masculine and others as feminine. (p. 525)
a. Research indicates that, like students, parents and teachers view some subjects as masculine and others as feminine.
b. Research indicates that, like students and parents, teachers view some subjects as masculine and others as feminine.
c. Research indicates that, like students and teachers, parents view some subjects as masculine and others as feminine.

18. *a. This statement is false. Eccles found no sex differences in children's classroom or standardized mathematics test scores. (p. 525)

b. This statement is true. Even though there were no sex differences in test scores, girls perceived themselves as less competent in mathematics.

c. This statement is true. Even though there were no differences in test scores, girls were less willing to take mathematics courses in the future.

d. This statement is true. Even though there were no differences in test scores, girls saw mathematics as less valuable than did boys.

19. *b. Dweck proposed that discriminate evaluative feedback, which is directed primarily at academic work, is more likely to result in feelings of incompetence and lowered expectations. (p. 526)

a. Dweck proposed that indiscriminate evaluative feedback, which is directed at both academic and social behavior, is less likely to result in feelings of incompetence and lowered expectations.

c. Dweck examined the influence of evaluative, not nonevaluative, criticism on children's academic expectancies.

d. Dweck examined the influence of evaluative, not nonevaluative, criticism on children's academic expectancies.

20. *c. Bem argued that masculinity and femininity are not mutually exclusive. (p. 528)

a. Kohlberg proposed that sex roles emerge as a consequence of stagelike developments in cognition. He did not introduce the concept of androgyny.

b. Dweck studied children's academic expectancies.

d. Fagot studied peer enforcement of sex roles and cross-gender children. She did not introduce the concept of androgyny

Answers to Application Questions

1. *c. Being understanding is one of the expressive characteristics that are seen as feminine in our society. (p. 495)

a. Outspokenness is one of the instrumental characteristics that are perceived as masculine in our society.

b. Assertiveness is one of the instrumental characteristics that are perceived as masculine in our society.

d. Independence is one of the instrumental characteristics that are perceived as masculine in our society.

2. *c. Prior to 1974, girls outperformed boys; therefore, Deborah's mother probably outscored the boys in her class. Beginning in 1974, sex differences in verbal skills disappeared; therefore, Deborah probably did not outperform most of the boys in her class. (p. 498)

a. Prior to 1974, girls outperformed boys; therefore, Deborah's mother probably outscored the boys in her class.

b. Beginning in 1974, sex differences in verbal skills disappeared; therefore, Deborah probably did not outperform most of the boys in her class.

d. The observed disappearance of sex differences in verbal ability suggests that Deborah probably did not outperform the boys in her class.

3. *b. In adrenogenital syndrome excess androgens are produced by a malfunctioning adrenocortical gland. The increased level of androgens masculinizes the genitalia and increases rough-and-tumble play. (p. 502)
   a. Although *androgyny* refers to personality characteristics associated with both sexes, androgyny is not a result of the hormonal influences that are suggested by Camille's masculinized genitalia.
   c. Sex segregation describes a phenomenon in which individuals cluster into same-sex groups.
   d. Camille's gender was not reversed; she is still a female with greater than usual masculine characteristics.

4. *a. Clearly, Calida does not understand that gender does not change over time, so she lacks gender stability. (p. 509)
   b. Calida appears to understand that one can be either a boy or a girl; therefore she has gender identity.
   c. Sex-typical behavior is a behavior that is usually associated with one sex. Sex-role behaviors are not described in the question.
   d. *Gender awareness* is not a term introduced in the textbook; nevertheless, Calida certainly is aware that gender is a social factor.

5. *d. Jake has developed a gender schema that helps him decide what is appropriate behavior for a boy and what is appropriate behavior for a girl. (p. 510)
   a. Jake is not displaying androgynous behavior by refusing to engage in a girl's activity.
   b. Because Jake refuses to take part in behavior that is usually seen as feminine he is resisting cross-gender behavior.
   c. Jake is displaying sex-typical behavior and refusing to engage in sex-atypical behavior.

6. *c. Mothers consistently punish their daughters for playing with sex-atypical toys, whereas they alternately punish and reinforce their sons' play with sex-atypical toys. (p. 517)
   a. Mothers are less consistent with their sons when it comes to punishing play with atypical toys; therefore Meredith is less likely to punish her son.
   b. Mothers consistently punish their daughters for playing with sex-atypical toys and are inconsistent with their sons; therefore Meredith is more likely to punish her daughter.
   d. Mothers occasionally reinforce their sons' play with sex-atypical toys but are less likely to reinforce their daughters.

7. *a. Studies show that maternal employment facilitates flexibility in children's conception of sex roles; therefore Elissa is more likely to exhibit flexibility. (p. 518)
   b. Because Dotty's mother does not work outside the home and Elissa's mother does, Elissa is more likely to exhibit flexibility.
   c. Because maternal employment is associated with greater flexibility in sex typing, Elissa is more likely to show flexible sex typing.

    d. Because maternal employment is associated with greater flexibility in sex typing, Elissa is more likely to show flexible sex typing.

8. *d. Boys are more likely to be punished by their peers for sex-atypical play; therefore Allen is more likely to be punished than Lizzy is. (p. 521)

    a. Although there are sex differences in peer influences, in general, peers have a strong influence on children's adoption of sex-typed behaviors. It would be surprising if Allen and Lizzy's friends were indifferent.

    b. Boys are more likely to be punished by their peers for sex-atypical play; therefore Allen will probably be punished but not Lizzy.

    c. Boys are more likely to be punished by their peers for sex-atypical play; therefore Lizzy is less likely to be punished than Allen is.

9. *b. Stuart is explaining his poor performance by attributing it to his teacher's attitude toward him, an external attribution. (p. 526)

    a. Internal attributions deal with personality characteristics such as intelligence; Stuart is blaming his performance on his teacher, not on one of his personality characteristics.

    c. There is no indication that Stuart is concerned with a gender issue.

    d. Adolescent egocentrism is the belief than one is unlike other people in many ways; Stuart's response does not suggest adolescent egocentrism.

10. *d. Bem called people with high levels of masculine and feminine behaviors androgynous. (p. 529)

    a. Androgyny is not associated with the physical characteristics of an individual.

    b. Androgynous individuals display a high degree of behaviors of both sexes, not only of the opposite sex.

    c. Androgynous individuals display a high degree of behaviors of both sexes.

CHAPTER 13

MORAL JUDGMENT AND BEHAVIOR

LEARNING OBJECTIVES

1. Define moral development and describe how various psychological theories have tried to explain moral development. (pp. 535–536)

2. Describe Freud's psychodynamic view of moral development. (pp. 536–537)

3. Describe and discuss the distinctive features of moral development as formulated by social learning theory. (pp. 537–540)

4. Describe Piaget's theory of moral development and discuss the results of empirical research evaluating his theory. (pp. 540–543)

5. Describe Kohlberg's theory of moral development and discuss the results of empirical research evaluating his theory. (pp. 543–549)

6. Discuss the issues and research findings concerning whether there are sex differences in moral development. (pp. 549–550)

7. Discuss Turiel's view of moral development as domain-specific knowledge. (pp. 550–551)

8. Compare and contrast the major theories of moral development. (pp. 551–552)

9. Define altruism and discuss the development of altruistic behavior. (pp. 552–554)

10. Describe the sex and cross-cultural differences in altruism and moral reasoning that have been revealed by researchers. (pp. 554–557)

11. List and discuss all of the factors that have been found to influence altruistic behavior and moral reasoning. (pp. 558–564)

12. Define aggression and discuss the development of aggressive behavior. (pp. 564–565)

13. List and discuss all of the factors that have been found to influence aggressive behavior and its control. (pp. 565–570)

CHAPTER OUTLINE

I. **PSYCHOLOGICAL THEORIES OF MORAL DEVELOPMENT** (pp. 536–552)
   The primary goal of socialization is to have children develop a sense of morality. Without this morality social groups would suffer from an inability to control aggression and foster behaviors that benefit group members. Psychologists studying moral development are primarily interested in how children acquire aggressive and prosocial behaviors.

A. **Psychodynamic Theory** (pp. 536–537)
   According to Sigmund Freud, the child acquires morality through the process of identification with the same-sex parent following resolution of the phallic stage conflict (Oedipal or Electra complex). When the five- or six-year-old child identifies with the same-sex parent, he internalizes the moral standards of the parent. It is at this point in psychosexual development that the child's superego emerges, which acts as both conscience (what not to do) and ego ideal (appropriate and desirable behaviors).

   One controversial aspect of the psychodynamic explanation of moral development is its position that girls develop weaker superegos than boys because the Electra complex is not as emotionally intense as the Oedipal complex. In addition, there has been little empirical support for Freud's theory that guilt over phallic stage desires results in an internalization of moral standards. Furthermore, children begin to show evidence of moral behavior prior to five or six years of age.

B. **Social Learning Theory** (pp. 537–540)
   Social learning theory proposes that children acquire moral behavior through the processes of reinforcement and observational learning. Parents and others either reward or punish the child's behavior as well as provide models that the child can observe and imitate. Thus, the child learns moral behavior in the same way any other behavior is learned. Moral development is viewed as the gradual acquisition of specific behaviors.

   Social learning theories focus on the child's observable behavior and not on moral reasoning or judgment. Empirical support for social learning theory is found in studies demonstrating that children who observe models committing a prohibited act, or resisting the temptation to misbehave, are more likely to either misbehave or resist temptation themselves. Some research, however, has revealed that children are more likely to imitate a model's deviant behavior than his compliant behavior. Reinforcement or punishment of the model's behavior has also been shown to influence the child's behavior accordingly.

Critics of social learning theory point out that this theory does not adequately consider the child's thinking or reasoning about moral issues. More recently, Albert Bandura's social cognitive theory addresses the role of cognitive processes in the development of morality.

C. Cognitive-Development Theories (pp. 540–551)

Piaget suggests that children progress through a series of stages of moral reasoning that reflects their underlying stage shifts in cognitive ability. Children's understanding of rules progresses from an initial stage when they do not understand rules, to a comprehension at about age six that rules are sacred and cannot be violated, to a final stage at about age ten when they understand that rules are the result of mutual consent among the participants of a game.

In his research on how children reason about moral dilemmas, Piaget found that when children are in a stage of *moral realism*, or *heteronomy*, they judge the act by the objective and visible consequences, not by the intentions of the transgressor. They also have a belief in *immanent justice*, that some punishment must follow the transgression, and *expiatory punishment*, that punishments are not necessarily related to the wrongful act. After age ten, children enter a stage of *moral relativism*, or *autonomy*, which is evidenced by their ability to take into account the motives of the transgressor. Punishment should follow only if the act was an intentional violation. In this stage *punishment by reciprocity* indicates that the punishment should be related to violation.

Piaget believes that as the child reaches the stage of concrete operations, she is less likely to rely on adult authority and more likely to exhibit moral reasoning based on the principle of reciprocity. Counterevidence for Piaget's theory indicates that not all children show internal consistency in their moral reasoning and that some very young children can be sensitive to the intentions of a given act.

Lawrence Kohlberg's theory was heavily influenced by Piaget's work. Kohlberg hypothesized three levels of moral reasoning, with two substages at each level. Kohlberg asserted that the stages occur in a universal progression. At the *preconventional level* the child's behavior is motivated by external pressures, avoiding punishment (stage 1) and gaining rewards (stage 2). At the *conventional level* the child is concerned with being good and avoiding the disapproval of others (stage 3) and not violating rules (stage 4). Finally, children at the *postconventional level* develop an understanding of the basis for laws and rules. Children are concerned with self-respect and maintaining the social contract (stage 5) and ultimately show concern for general moral principles whether or not they violate the laws of society (stage 6). Kohlberg emphasized changes in the child's perspective-taking ability as the basis for stage changes in moral reasoning.

Even though many empirical studies have confirmed the existence of transitions in moral reasoning with age, some specific aspects of Kohlberg's theory have not been supported, such as the relationship between perspective-taking ability and advances in moral reasoning. In addition, Kohlberg's theory may be biased by Western philosophies of moral principles; individuals from some other cultures do not reason about some of the dilemmas as individuals from Western cultures do.

Controversy: Are There Sex Differences in Moral Development? (pp. 549–550)
In his research, Kohlberg found that most males reason at the Stage 4 level of moral development, whereas females reason at the Stage 3 level. Other psychologists have found, however, that females reason differently than males, but not at a more immature level. Carol Gilligan found that females develop a *morality of care and responsibility* in contrast to the *morality of justice* that describes the more typical pattern of moral reasoning by males. Of the large number of studies that have used Kohlberg's tasks to study moral reasoning, only a few have found reliable sex differences in the level at which males and females reason about morality.

Psychologists such as Elliot Turiel have proposed that moral development is independent of cognitive development in other domains. Turiel believes that the moral domain of social-cognitive development consists of rules that regulate the individual's rights or welfare, whereas the societal domain consists of knowledge about *social conventions*, and the psychological domain consists of knowledge of inner thought and feelings about the self and others. Turiel has found that children as young as three years old make distinctions between transgressions in the societal domain.

Although all three theorists propose age-related changes in moral reasoning, Turiel suggests that these changes reflect quantitative transitions based on the child's experiences, whereas Piaget and Kohlberg propose stagelike qualitative changes that reflect the underlying maturation of cognitive structures.

II. PROSOCIAL BEHAVIOR: ALTRUISM (pp. 552–564)
Prosocial behavior is any positive action performed to benefit others. *Altruism* is a specific prosocial behavior carried out to benefit others without expectations of reward.

A. The Development of Altruism (pp. 552–557)
Even young infants demonstrate a rudimentary form of *empathy*, a response to the feelings of others that includes sympathetic concern. By the time children are ten to fourteen months old they display a wide range of empathic reactions to the distress of another. They will cry, attend to the other individual, or soothe themselves by sucking their thumb or seeking the parent. Between one and two years of age children begin touching or patting the person in distress, or seek to provide a comforting object such as a blanket or toy; verbal expression of another's distress also emerges at this time. Preschoolers are more varied in their empathic responses and will help the victim, punish

the agent of the child's distress, protect the victim, and ask for adult help. From school age to adolescence altruistic behavior is less clear. Although some children show greater empathy with age, others may actually help or share less.

Psychologists have found few reliable sex differences in altruism. The only apparent difference seems to be that girls are more likely to verbalize their sympathy than boys, but both showed the same amount of assistance.

Using a series of "prosocial dilemmas," Nancy Eisenberg found that American children demonstrate a developmental progression in their prosocial reasoning. During the preschool years, children reason *hedonistically*, agreeing to help in order to obtain affection or material rewards. From school age to high school, children demonstrate *needs-oriented reasoning*, expression of concern for the physical or psychological needs of others. During the high school years, children develop an *empathic* style of reasoning, by trying to imagine how the other person feels. In non-Western cultures where the societal norms and values are different, variations in this prosocial reasoning sequence occur.

Some research has found that children in urban settings behave less altruistically than children in rural settings. Thus, altruism is more likely to occur in societies where the predominant ethic is one of interdependence and group cooperation, rather than in cultures that emphasize individualism and self-reliance.

B. **Factors Influencing Altruism** (pp. 557–562)
Several theorists believe that the most important factor influencing altruistic behavior is empathy. When the child feels empathic distress at another's distress, for example, the child will be motivated to relieve the other's distress, thereby alleviating her own distress. Other researchers, however, have found that young children show positive empathy and prosocial behavior as well, and therefore must not be responding simply to eliminate their own negative feelings.

Some studies have revealed a positive relationship between the degree of altruism exhibited and the child's level of prosocial reasoning. Children who reason hedonistically help others less frequently than children who reason empathically. The child's level of prosocial reasoning does not always predict his altruistic behavior because in some cases even though the child understands the importance of helping others, he may not have the skills or resources necessary to help.

The child's socialization experience also influences altruism. Parental reward, either material or social, and parents' own behavior, which provides a model for the child's behavior, are both major factors in the development of altruism. Parental rationale for altruistic behavior also plays a role. When parents use *induction*, that is, reason with children about the consequences of their altruistic or lack of altruistic behavior, children are encouraged to be empathic and consequently show more helping behavior. Children whose parents use *power assertion*, that is, forceful commands or physical punishment to promote altruism, are less empathic and less altruistic in their behavior.

C. **Moral Education** (pp. 552–564)
With the alarming decline of moral values of children, many public officials, educators, and parents have expressed a need to train moral values beginning in elementary school. These training programs have involved children discussing moral dilemmas similar to Kohlberg's, under the guidance of a trained instructor who does not tell the children what to think but rather encourages their discussion and alternative points of view. Children in programs such as this have scored higher on tests of moral reasoning than children not in the programs. Other programs have employed *cooperative learning*, small peer groups that are formed to work on joint educational projects. In these small groups children are encouraged to listen to each other and assist each other in completion of the task. In addition to the academic benefits of these programs, results have indicated that children who participate in cooperative learning are more likely to help others when asked to do so than are children who did not participate in the cooperative learning program.

III. **AGGRESSION** (pp. 564–570)
Aggression is physical or verbal behavior that is intended to harm to irritate someone else. The more aggressive the behavior of the child, the more likely that child is to be rejected from peer groups. In its most extreme form aggression can lead to juvenile delinquency and antisocial behavior.

A. **The Development of Aggression** (pp. 564–565)
Beginning at age one or two years children show aggressive behavior in the form of struggles over desired objects. During the preschool years physical aggression declines and verbal aggression increases. Instrumental aggression, aggression aimed at acquiring an object, decreases, whereas hostile aggression, aggression aimed at another person, increases. Prior to age six boys display more physical and verbal aggression than girls. After early childhood boys continue to show more physical aggression than girls, but the findings on verbal aggression are mixed. There are reliable correlations between aggressive behavior in childhood and aggressive behavior in adulthood.

B. **Factors Influencing Aggression** (pp. 565–569)
Biological explanations of aggressive behavior suggest that hormones such as testosterone are linked to aggression in many species. Furthermore, aggression may have survival consequences that ensure that aggressive traits are passed along genetically.

The *frustration-aggression hypothesis* states that aggression follows any event in which the individual's goals are blocked. Social learning theorists propose that aggression is learned behavior acquired by reinforcement history and observation of aggressive models. Cognitive models of aggression suggest that the child's understanding and interpretation of the intentions of another will affect whether the child responds aggressively. In addition, there may be a tendency for aggressive children to attribute hostility to another's behavior and consequently respond aggressively to that person.

Parenting practices may also influence the child's aggressive behavior. Parents who display warmth and nurturance toward their children have children who are less aggressive. Conversely, aggressive children tend to have parents who lack warmth and positive emotional regard, and who severely punish their children's aggressive behavior. Punishment increases children's physical acting-out and provides powerful modeling of aggressive behavior. On the other hand, overly permissive parents also have children who are more aggressive than parents who adopt a more warm and nurturant style with their children.

C. **Controlling Aggression** (pp. 569–570)

Although aggression is not always easily controlled, some research suggests that intervening in parents' interactions with their children may help. Teaching parents to use more induction and less power assertion when they discipline their children should lead to less aggressive behavior. Also, instructing children on the consequences of their actions, thereby changing the child's understanding of aggressive behavior, has been found to increase the amount of prosocial behavior and decrease the amount of aggressive behavior the child exhibits.

IV. **THEMES IN DEVELOPMENT: MORAL JUDGMENT AND BEHAVIOR** (pp. 570–571)

What roles do nature and nurture play in moral development? Although there may be early, biologically based tendencies for children to display empathy and aggression, most researchers have described how the child's subsequent cognitions and socialization experiences shape morality.

How does the sociocultural context influence moral development? Children's moral reasoning and behavior often reflect the values of the larger cultural group. Children's responses to moral dilemmas often reflect their culture's beliefs.

How does the child play an active role in the process of moral development? Most theorists hypothesize that children internalize the moral norms of the larger society. Children actively construct moral standards based on their experience with others, and they often influence the disciplinary techniques that their parents use.

Is moral development stagelike or continuous? The theories of Freud, Piaget, and Kohlberg all propose that moral development is stagelike. However, although stage theories are still popular, viewpoints that emphasize continuous growth are gaining more and more attention.

How does moral development interact with development in other domains? Emotions such as empathy are an important element in moral development. Cognitive skills, such as reasoning about the intentions of others, are also involved. Moral development also influences other domains, as altruistic children tend to have healthy peer relationships while aggressive children tend to have poor ones.

Key Terms Review

1. The _____ hypothesis suggests that aggression results from the blocking of an organism's goals.

2. The tendency to make moral judgments on the basis of reason and abstract principles of equity is called _____ .

3. _____ is a vicarious response to the feelings of others.

4. A child who expresses the belief that punishment should be related to the transgression believes in _____ .

5. A parent who relies on reasoning and explanation to discipline his child is using _____ , whereas a parent who relies on the use of forceful commands and physical punishment is using _____ .

6. Kohlberg's second level of moral reasoning is the _____ , in which the child conforms to the norms of the majority and wishes to preserve the social order.

7. _____ is physical or verbal behavior intended to harm someone else, while _____ is behavior carried out to help another without expectation of reward.

8. _____ is the young child's belief that punishment will inevitably follow a transgression.

9. _____ is the second stage of Piaget's theory of moral development, in which moral judgments are made on the basis of an actor's intentions.

10. _____ is a form of prosocial reasoning in which children attempt to put themselves in another's place and understand that person's feelings.

11. The tendency to make moral judgments on the basis of preserving relationships with others is referred to as _____ .

12. _____ are behavioral rules that regulate social interactions.

13. _____ is positive social action performed to benefit others.

14. The first stage in Piaget's theory of moral development is _____ , in which moral judgments are made on the basis of the consequences of an act.

15. The first level of Kohlberg's theory of moral reasoning is the _____ , in which morality is motivated by the avoidance of punishments and attainment of rewards.

16. _____ is an educational experience that involves collaborative efforts by a group of peers.

17. A form of prosocial reasoning in which children say they will help in order to obtain material rewards is called _____ .

18. When children express a concern for the physical or psychological needs of others they are showing a form of prosocial reasoning called _____ .

19. _____ describes the young child's belief that punishment need not be related to a transgression as long as the punishment is severe enough to prevent its recurrence.

20. The _____ is the third level of Kohlberg's developmental theory of moral reasoning.

Answers to Key Terms Review

1. frustration-aggression
2. morality of justice
3. Empathy
4. punishment by reciprocity
5. induction, power assertion
6. conventional level
7. Aggression, altruism
8. Immanent justice
9. Moral relativism (*or* autonomy)
10. Empathic reasoning
11. morality of care and responsibility
12. Social conventions
13. Prosocial behavior
14. moral realism (*or* heteronomy)
15. preconventional level
16. Cooperative learning
17. hedonistic reasoning
18. needs-oriented reasoning
19. Expiatory punishment
20. postconventional level

Multiple-Choice Questions

Fact and Concept Questions

1. Cognitive-developmental theories of moral development emphasize
   a. moral behavior.
   b. affect.
   c. moral reasoning.
   d. speed of processing.

2. Which of the following is *not* emphasized by social learning theories of moral development?
   a. The child's active role
   b. The role of parents as primary sources of reward and punishment
   c. Morality as a process of incremental growth
   d. The child's overt observable behavior

3. Bandura has contributed to social learning theory by
   a. emphasizing the importance of the timing of punishment and reinforcement for teaching moral development.
   b. introducing the use of delay-of-gratification tasks to measure moral behavior in young children.
   c. introducing to social learning theory the role of cognitive processes in the emergence of morality.
   d. emphasizing the powerful influence of parents' disciplinary strategies on children's moral development.

4. According to Piaget's view of moral development, very young children
   a. do not incorporate rules into their play because they are unaware of the existence of rules.
   b. may be aware of the existence of rules but do not incorporate them into their play.
   c. are aware of the existence of rules and respect them unquestionably.
   d. are aware of the existence of rules and understand that they result from mutual consent.

5. Which of the following beliefs about moral issues is a factor in Piaget's stage of moral relativism?
   a. Immanent justice
   b. Heteronomy
   c. Expiatory punishment
   d. Punishment by reciprocity

6. Piaget's assertion that cognitive growth underlies changes in moral reasoning
   a. has not been supported by modern research.
   b. has received support from modern research.
   c. has received mixed support from modern research.
   d. has not been adequately tested as of yet.

7. According to Kohlberg, in the preconventional level of moral development children's behavior is motivated by
   a. the need to conform to the norms of the majority.
   b. the need to maintain certain principles and values.
   c. the need to be responsible and uphold the laws of the societal group.
   d. the avoidance of punishment and preservation of their own self-interest.

8. _____ is a substage of Kohlberg's conventional level of moral reasoning.
   a. Good boy morality
   b. Morality of contract and democracy
   c. Naive instrumental hedonism
   d. Punishment and obedience orientation

9. Kohlberg and Piaget differ in their explanations of moral development in that
   a. Piaget saw moral development as a stagelike process and Kohlberg did not.
   b. Kohlberg placed less emphasis on the role of adult authority in young children's moral development.
   c. Kohlberg placed less emphasis on social experience in promoting advances in moral reasoning.
   d. Kohlberg believed that movement toward autonomy occurs much earlier than Piaget envisioned.

10. Which of the following statements concerning gender differences in moral development is true?
    a. Research indicates that there are no gender differences in moral development.
    b. Gilligan provided strong support for Kohlberg's initial observation of differences in moral development between the sexes.
    c. Research suggests that sex differences are found only in non-Western cultures.
    d. Debate centers around what constitutes moral reasoning and how or if it differs in males and females.

11. Turiel describes moral reasoning as domain-specific knowledge. In his view the _____ domain consists of rules that regulate one's own or another's rights, whereas the _____ domain is the child's knowledge of the social world.
    a. social, moral
    b. psychological, moral
    c. moral, social
    d. moral, psychological

12. A shortcoming of cognitive-developmental theories of moral development is that
    a. moral reasoning is not always clearly related to moral behavior.
    b. consistent age-related changes in moral reasoning have not been observed.
    c. changes in moral reasoning do not parallel changes in cognitive ability.
    d. it is not possible to test experimentally the ideas proposed by such theories.

13. Eisenberg's work on prosocial reasoning suggests that _____ reasoning emerges during the late elementary and high school years.
    a. needs-oriented
    b. hedonistic
    c. empathic
    d. altruistic

14. Cross-cultural studies on moral reasoning have observed
    a. consistent, universal patterns of prosocial reasoning and altruistic behavior.
    b. cross-cultural differences in prosocial reasoning and altruistic behavior.
    c. cross-cultural differences in prosocial reasoning but no differences in altruistic behavior.
    d. cross-cultural differences in altruistic behavior but no differences in prosocial reasoning.

15. Studies that have examined the relationship between empathy and altruism have found that
    a. empathy always precedes altruistic behavior.
    b. empathy always leads to altruistic behavior.
    c. empathy sometimes precedes and sometimes leads to altruistic behavior.
    d. there is no relationship between empathy and altruistic behavior.

16. _____ is a child-rearing technique in which parents promote more helping behavior in children by encouraging them to be empathic.
    a. Power assertion
    b. Punishment by reciprocity
    c. Expiatory punishment
    d. Induction

17. Moral education programs that utilize cooperative learning indicate that
    a. specific moral principles can be taught without explicit instruction on moral principles.
    b. moral reasoning and moral behavior cannot be taught in a classroom situation.
    c. moral reasoning and moral behavior can be taught only through explicit instruction on moral principles.
    d. moral reasoning can be taught, but the changes in moral reasoning are not accompanied by changes in moral behavior.

18. Which of the following statements concerning the development of aggression is *not* true?
    a. The first signs of aggression among peers emerge between one and two years of age.
    b. Young children often resolve a dispute with a peer without the intervention of an adult.
    c. During the preschool years physical aggression decreases and verbal aggression increases.
    d. During the preschool years instrumental aggression increases and hostile aggression decreases.

19. The frustration-aggression hypothesis of aggressive behavior is rooted in the _____ view of development.
    a. social learning
    b. ethological
    c. psychoanalytic
    d. cognitive

20. Research on the factors influencing the development of aggression has revealed that aggressive behavior
    a. is primarily a result of biologically based predispositions.
    b. is relatively unaffected by children's cognitive processes.
    c. is related to unique patterns of cognition and socialization history.
    d. is primarily a result of the parent's child-rearing practices.

Application Questions

1. Perry and Gwen helped their mother bake chocolate chip cookies. After putting the freshly baked cookies in the cookie jar their mother said, "I'm going downstairs for a few minutes. Don't eat any of the cookies. When I get back you can have some." When the mother returned she found three cookies missing. When she asked who misbehaved and ate the cookies Perry responded, "Gwen was badder. She had two cookies and I only had one." Perry appears to be in the stage of moral development called
    a. immanent justice.
    b. moral relativism.
    c. expiatory punishment.
    d. moral realism.

2. Twelve-year-old Terrence was assisting a camp counselor in teaching second-graders how to play baseball. One of the second-graders picked up the bat and began swinging it over his head as he ran among the rest of the children. Terrence quickly ran to the boy with the bat and removed it from his hands. The children watching are likely to
   a. interpret Terrence's behavior as hostile.
   b. interpret Terrence's behavior as forceful but prosocial.
   c. imitate the boy's potentially harmful bat-swinging behavior.
   d. fear Terrence.

3. Kyle and Lester went to Bill's house to look at his baseball card collection. When Bill went to the bathroom Kyle suggested that they take a card while Bill was not there to see them. Lester did not want to steal the card, saying, "When he finds the card is missing he'll realize we took it and he will think we're crooks." Lester is most likely in Kohlberg's
   a. stage 1: punishment and obedience orientation.
   b. stage 2: naive instrumental hedonism.
   c. stage 3: good boy morality.
   d. stage 4: authority-maintaining morality.

4. During snack time at nursery school, Alice saw one playmate pull the hair of another playmate; she also saw her friend Pedro throw his half-eaten pretzel on the floor. Alice is
   a. more likely to react to the hair-pulling incident than to the pretzel-throwing incident.
   b. more likely to react to the pretzel-throwing incident than to the hair-pulling incident.
   c. unlikely to react to either the hair-pulling or the pretzel-throwing incident.
   d. equally likely to react to the hair-pulling incident and the pretzel-throwing incident

5. Jim made it very clear that he knew cheating was wrong. Yet one day Jim was caught cheating on an English test. Jim's behavior suggests that
   a. Jim is probably a liar as well as a cheater.
   b. moral reasoning is not always related to moral behavior.
   c. it is not possible to study moral reasoning in children.
   d. children cannot distinguish between moral and social conventional rules.

6. Three-year-old Lyssa saw her five-year-old cousin fall and begin to cry. Lyssa is most likely to
   a. soothe herself by sucking her thumb.
   b. provide solace to her cousin by patting her.
   c. express verbal concern and provide reassurance.
   d. be indifferent to her cousin's distress.

7. Colleen wants to raise her son to be altruistic and empathetic. According to social learning research Colleen should
   a. reward her son's helping behavior with social rewards such as saying, "You're a good boy."
   b. reward her son's helping behavior with material rewards such as candy or toys.
   c. repeatedly discuss with her son the importance of helping and sharing with others.
   d. punish her son for instances of selfish behavior.

8. Like most parents, Faye disciplines her children often. Which of the following responses is most likely to encourage the development of altruistic behavior?
   a. "Didn't I tell you to share that popcorn with your sister? That's it, mister. You're not playing with your video games today."
   b. "Don't you listen? I told you not to take your brother's toy without asking first."
   c. "If you share your candy bar with your little sister, I'll buy you a pack of baseball cards on my way home from work."
   d. "I guess you're a very good helper and a good big brother."

9. Timothy's mother took away a cookie that he had picked up from the table. Timothy began to scream and hit his mother. Timothy's aggressive behavior upon removal of the cookie can be best explained by
   a. his innate aggressive tendencies.
   b. social learning theory.
   c. cognitive-developmental theory.
   d. the frustration-aggression hypothesis.

10. Alex has always been an aggressive boy. At a friend's birthday party another boy accidently bumped into Alex while they were approaching the table to get a piece of the birthday cake. Alex is likely to
   a. view the other boy's behavior as aggressive.
   b. view the other boy's behavior as unintentional.
   c. ignore the boy's action.
   d. attribute the boy's action to the party situation.

Answers to Multiple-Choice Questions

The correct answer appears first and is preceded by an asterisk.

Answers to Fact and Concept Questions

1. *c. Moral reasoning—how the child thinks about moral problems—is central to cognitive-developmental theory. (p. 536)
   a. The child's acquisition of moral behavior is emphasized by social learning theory.
   b. Psychodynamic theory focuses on affective dimensions of moral development.

d. Speed of processing is often studied in cognitive psychology but not as a measure of moral development.

2. *a. Social learning theory does not emphasize the child's active role in moral development. According to social learning theory children play a passive role, absorbing the moral perspectives of the social group. (p. 538)

   b. The role of parents *is* emphasized by social learning theory. Social learning theory assumes parents are important sources of rewards and punishments.

   c. Growth of morality *is* emphasized by social learning theory. Because social learning theory is not a stage theory, moral development is seen as a gradual process of growth.

   d. Social learning theory does emphasize the child's observable behavior. Social learning theory posits that moral behavior is learned like any other observable behavior.

3. *c. Bandura argued that children's moral behavior is influenced by cognitive representations that they derive by observing others. (p. 540)

   a. The timing of punishment and reward is an important factor described by social learning theory, but it was not emphasized by Bandura.

   b. Delay of gratification is emphasized by social learning theory, but it was not introduced by Bandura.

   d. Bandura placed greater emphasis on parents as models, not as dispensers of rewards and punishment.

4. *b. Despite their awareness of some rules, young children do not incorporate them into their play. (p. 541)

   a. Piaget suggested that preschool-aged children may become aware of the existence of rules by watching older children play.

   c. Young children may be aware of the existence of rules, but they do not respect them unquestionably until about six years of age.

   d. The understanding that rules often arise through mutual consent usually begins at the age of ten.

5. *d. In the stage of moral relativism, children believe in punishment by reciprocity: that punishments should be related to the wrongful act. (p. 542)

   a. Immanent justice, the view that punishment is inevitable, is seen during the stage of development called moral realism.

   b. *Heteronomy* is another term for the stage of moral realism in which moral judgments are made on the basis of the consequences of an act.

   c. Expiatory punishment, the notion that punishments severe enough to teach a lesson need not be related to a wrongful act, is seen during the stage of moral realism.

6. *b. Support for this assertion includes the observation that moral thought is related to IQ and to Piagetian stages of cognitive development. (p. 543)

   a. Piaget's assertion that cognitive growth underlies changes in moral reasoning has received considerable experimental support.

   c. Support for Piaget's assertion that cognitive growth underlies changes in moral reasoning is not mixed.

   d. There has been considerable research on Piaget's ideas on development, including his ideas on moral development.

7. *d. The preconventional child is motivated by external pressures such as punishment and rewards. (p. 544)

   a. The child who has a need to conform to the rules of the majority is in the conventional level.

   b. The individual in the postconventional level recognizes the need to maintain certain principles.

   c. The child who understands the need to uphold the laws of the societal group is in the conventional level.

8. *a. Good boy morality is the first of the two substages of Kohlberg's conventional level. (p. 545)

   b. Morality of contract and democracy is the first of two substages in Kohlberg's postconventional level.

   c. Naive instrumental hedonism is the second of two substages in Kohlberg's preconventional level.

   d. Punishment and obedience orientation is the first of two substages in Kohlberg's preconventional level.

9. *b. Kohlberg placed greater emphasis on rewards and punishments doled out by adults than on adult authority per se. (p. 546)

   a. Like Piaget, Kohlberg viewed development as a stagelike process.

   c. Social reasoning was central to the development of moral reasoning for both Piaget and Kohlberg.

   d. Kohlberg believed that movement toward autonomy occurs toward the end of adolescence, later than Piaget thought.

10. *d. Gilligan's criticism of Kohlberg's views has provided a larger forum for discussing what constitutes moral reasoning. (p. 550)

   a. Sex differences in moral reasoning have been identified, but the interpretation of these differences is a matter of debate.

   b. Gilligan criticized Kohlberg's view of women as inferior compared to males in moral reasoning and suggested that women's moral reasoning was different, not inferior.

   c. Research examining moral reasoning has been conducted primarily in Western cultures.

11. *c. The moral domain consists of rules that regulate behavior. The societal domain is the child's knowledge of the social world. (p. 550)

   a. These are the correct terms, but they are in the wrong order.

b. The psychological domain consists of knowledge of the inner thoughts and feelings of the self and others, not rules that regulate behavior.
d. *Moral domain* is the correct term; *psychological domain* is incorrect because it is not the knowledge of the social world but knowledge of inner thoughts and feelings.

12. *a. The relationship between subjects' scores on moral reasoning tests and moral behavior is not always strong. (p. 551)
b. There is considerable evidence that there are age-related changes in how children reason about moral problems.
c. Changes in moral reasoning parallel more general changes in cognitive abilities.
d. Cognitive-developmental theories are testable and have led to an enormous body of experimental research findings.

13. *c. Empathic reasoning is a form of prosocial reasoning that emerges in older elementary school children and becomes more prevalent in the high school years. (p. 556)
a. Needs-orienting reasoning, where one expresses a concern for the physical and psychological needs of others, prevails in preschoolers and elementary school children up to seven or eight years of age.
b. Hedonistic reasoning, a form of prosocial reasoning in which children say they will help to obtain rewards, is prevalent in preschoolers and young elementary school children.
d. Altruistic reasoning is not one of Eisenberg's levels of prosocial reasoning.

14. *b. Children from different cultures have been observed to differ in their tendency to reason about prosocial matters. Differences in altruism have also been observed, particularly when urban and rural children are compared. (p. 557)
a. In some cultures where societal values are different from those in Western cultures, variations in moral reasoning are seen.
c. Differences in altruistic behaviors have been observed; altruistic behavior is more likely to occur in societies where the predominant ethic is that of interdependence and group orientation.
d. Studies of children raised on an Israeli kibbutz and of children from a New Guinea coastal village indicate that there are cross-cultural differences in moral reasoning.

15. *c. There is some relationship between empathic reactions and altruistic behavior. This relationship between empathy and altruism is stronger later in childhood (p. 559)
a. Perhaps because of the methodological difficulties of measuring empathic reactions, a consistent relationship between altruism and empathy has not always been found.
b. Even though a child may be showing an empathic reaction, altruistic behavior does not necessarily follow, partly because the child may not know when or how to provide assistance.

d. Although not perfect there is some relationship between empathic reactions and altruistic behavior.

16. *d. Induction, which involves parental use of reasoning, often arouses empathic feelings in children (p. 561)
   a. Power assertion, which involves the use of forceful commands and punishment, is less likely to encourage children to be empathic.
   b. Punishment by reciprocity is not a child-rearing technique.
   c. Expiatory punishment is not a child-rearing technique.

17. *a. In one study, children learned moral principles by participating in experiential learning and group endeavors, not by being trained in specific moral principles. (p. 564)
   b. Studies show that prosocial development is encouraged in cooperative learning situations.
   c. Cooperative learning influences prosocial behavior without the use of specific instruction.
   d. Although moral reasoning is not always clearly related to moral behavior, there is no indication that moral reasoning encouraged by training programs always fails to lead to moral behavior.

18. *d. During the preschool years instrumental aggression *decreases* and hostile aggression *increases*. (p. 565)
   a. This statement is true. Conflict among peers, usually over toys, emerges between one and two years of age.
   b. This statement is true. Conflicts between peers are usually resolved when one child yields to the other child.
   c. This statement is true. During the preschool years hitting, kicking, and other physically aggressive acts decline, while hostile aggression or person-oriented aggression increases.

19. *b. In the ethological model, aggression is seen as a form of energy that builds in the individual and is released when the individual is frustrated because attainment of a desired goal is blocked. (p. 566)
   a. Social learning theory, not the buildup of energy, emphasizes the child's reinforcement history.
   c. The psychoanalytic approach views aggression in terms of unconscious processes.
   d. Cognitive theories suggest that whether or not a child acts aggressively depends on how the child understands the intentions of a partner in a social situation.

20. *c. Children with persistent aggressive styles judge the intentions of others as hostile and do not think of the negative consequences of their aggressive acts. These children are also more likely to have been raised by parents who encouraged aggressive behavior. (p. 567)

a. Although children may show a biologically based predisposition toward aggressive behavior, studies strongly suggest that aggression is also related to socialization factors.
b. Studies show that children's aggression is related to unique patterns of cognition.
d. Although parenting style plays an important role, aggressive behavior is also strongly influenced by patterns of cognition.

Answers to Application Questions

1. *d. Children in the moral realism stage judge rightness and wrongness by objective, visible consequences such as how many cookies were taken. (p. 542)
   a. Immanent justice is not a stage; it is the belief that punishment will inevitably follow a transgression.
   b. A child in the moral relativism stage makes judgments on the basis of intentions. Perry is not comparing motives for taking the cookies.
   c. Expiatory punishment is not a stage; it is a belief that punishment need not be related to a wrongful act.

2. *b. Although Terrence's behavior was forceful, second-graders are very likely to understand that his behavior was for the benefit of all the children. (p. 543)
   a. Even very young children are sensitive to the intentions behind a given act. Therefore, they are likely to understand that Terrence had good intentions when he stopped the boy's dangerous behavior.
   c. The children are not likely to imitate the bat-swinging behavior of the boy since the boy's behavior was punished (stopped) by the camp counselor's assistant.
   d. Because even young children are sensitive to intentions behind a given act, they are unlikely to fear Terrence because of his action.

3. *c. Lester wants to avoid disapproval by his friend Bill. Striving to avoid the disapproval of others is the motive for action in stage 3. (p. 545)
   a. The primary motive for action in stage 1 is the avoidance of punishment. Lester did not express a fear of being punished.
   b. The primary motive for action in stage 2 is the desire for rewards. Lester did not indicate a desire for reward.
   d. In stage 4 an act is considered wrong if it violates a rule or does harm to others. Lester does not indicate a concern that stealing is wrong or that Bill will suffer from the theft of his card.

4. *a. Young children are more likely to react to behavior violating a moral rule (such as hurting someone by pulling hair) than to a behavior violating a social norm (such as throwing uneaten food on the floor). (p. 550)
   b. The pretzel-throwing incident is a violation of a social norm, whereas hair-pulling is a violation of a moral rule; preschoolers are more likely to react to violations of a moral rule.

    c. Preschoolers are likely to react to violation of both rules, but particularly to the violation of the moral rule.

    d. Preschoolers are more likely to react to the violation of the moral rule.

5. *b. Moral reasoning is not always strongly related to moral behavior. The lack of correlation between Jim's position on cheating and his observed cheating behavior is an example of the less than perfect relationship between moral reasoning and moral behavior. (p. 551)

    a. Although Jim may have lied about his views on cheating, there is no way of knowing this; there is a better choice for this question.

    c. Not only is the study of moral development possible, it is a very important area of study in child development.

    d. Studies show that children as young as three years distinguish between moral and social conventional rules.

6. *c. Lyssa is a preschool-aged child. Preschoolers are likely to provide verbal comfort and reassurance to a victim. (p. 554)

    a. Babies under one year of age are likely to soothe themselves.

    b. Children one to two years of age are likely to touch or pat a victim to provide solace.

    d. Young children display varied and complex responses to the needs of others, so Lyssa is unlikely to be indifferent.

7. *a. Children reinforced with social rewards are more likely to report helping another child or sharing because of concern for the welfare of the other child. (p. 560)

    b. Children who receive material rewards are more likely to report helping another child simply to obtain rewards.

    c. Social learning studies on altruistic behavior show that observing what models do is more effective than simply hearing what models say; thus, simply talking to children about the importance of being altruistic is likely to be less effective.

    d. Punishing instances of selfish behavior may decrease the frequency of such behavior but is unlikely to develop altruism and empathy.

8. *d. In this statement Faye makes an attribution about her child's prosocial behaviors. Such attributions are more likely to cause children to behave altruistically. (p. 562)

    a. A statement like this is an example of power assertion, which is less likely to foster altruistic behavior.

    b. A statement like this is an example of power assertion, which is less likely to foster altruistic behavior.

    c. Providing children with material rewards may increase altruistic behavior, but the behavior is more likely a result of the desire to obtain rewards than of an internal motive for altruism.

9. *d. Timothy's goal of eating the cookie was frustrated by his mother's actions. According to frustration-aggression hypothesis, it was the frustration that led to Timothy's aggression. (p. 566)

a. There is nothing in the description of Timothy's behavior to suggest that his aggressive tendencies are innate.
b. Social learning theory emphasizes the role of reinforcement, punishment, and modeling in shaping behaviors such as aggression, but there are no indications that Timothy's aggressive behavior was reinforced or is a result of modeling others.
c. Cognitive-developmental theories stress the importance of cognitive factors such as attributions; there are no indications of cognitive mediators of aggression in the description of Timothy's behavior.

10. *a. Studies show that aggressive boys are more biased toward making hostile attributions about the actions of peers than nonaggressive boys. Alex is quite likely to see the other boy's action as hostile. (p. 566)
b. Because aggressive boys are biased toward making hostile attributions, Alex is likely to see the other boy's actions as hostile rather than unintentional.
c. Because aggressive boys are biased toward making hostile attributions, Alex is less likely to ignore the boy's action.
d. Because aggressive boys are biased toward making hostile attributions, Alex is more likely to attribute the unintentional bumping to an internal hostile attribution rather than an external attribution such as the situation at the party.

CHAPTER 14

THE INFLUENCE OF THE FAMILY

LEARNING OBJECTIVES

1. Describe the American family of today and explain how it differs from American families of the past. (pp. 576–577)

2. Describe the system approach to understanding the family. (pp. 577–579)

3. Describe the influence of the parent in the child's socialization, particularly the influence of different parenting styles. (pp. 579–583)

4. Describe the various approaches used by parents to control their children's behavior and the effects of such control procedures on children's behavioral and emotional development. (pp. 583–587)

5. Discuss the controversy concerning the use of punishment to control a child's behavior and describe the time-out procedure as an alternative to punishment. (pp. 587–589)

6. Discuss how attributions and children's behavior can influence how they interact with parents and other children. (pp. 589–591)

7. Describe and discuss the various maladaptive styles of parenting that may lead to dysfunctional and abusive families. (pp. 591–595)

8. Compare and contrast the parenting styles observed in different cultures and different socioeconomic groups. (pp. 595–597)

9. Compare and contrast the influence of mothers and fathers on the child's social, emotional, and cognitive development. (pp. 597–601)

10. Describe the influence of siblings on the overall development of the child and the nature of sibling relationships throughout development. (pp. 601–605)

11. Describe the influence of maternal employment and day care on the child. (pp. 605–609)

12. Describe the impact of divorce and the relationships that children develop with their stepparents. (pp. 609–613)

CHAPTER OUTLINE

Families play a major role in children's *socialization*, the process by which children acquire the social knowledge, behaviors, and attitudes valued by the larger society.

I. **UNDERSTANDING THE FAMILY** (pp. 576–579)
The structure and function of the family has changed over the years as a result of economic, political, and cultural factors. In recent history the American family has shifted from the *extended family* (grandparents, aunts, uncles, and parents) to the *nuclear family* (parents and offspring).

A. **The Demographics of the American Family** (pp. 576–577)
No one structure characterizes the American family. The dominant family structure is the two-parent family, but the percentage of two-parent families has decreased since the 1950s, and the percentage of one-parent homes has increased.

B. **A Systems Approach** (pp. 577–579)
Systems theory examines the relationships among family members rather than the structure of the family. This approach views the family as a dynamic, self-regulating social unit in which all members influence each other simultaneously. Systems theory regards a single family member as belonging to several subsystems at once: the microlevel (between parent and child), the family environment, and larger social contexts (school and peers). Within the family members are seen as having reciprocal influences on one another. Parents socialize their children through direct training, by serving as a model, and by choosing many other aspects of their children's life. The child's own behavior influences how the parent responds and is partially responsible for the gradual move away from a parental supervisory role.

II. PARENTS AND SOCIALIZATION (pp. 579–597)

A. Styles of Parenting (pp. 580–583)

Diana Baumrind identified several styles that parents adopt in interacting with their children. The *authoritarian parent* is strict, valuing respect for authority and regulating the child's behavior with threats and punishment. The *authoritative parent* also regulates the child's behavior but does so by using rewards more than punishment. Authoritative parents also set limits on the child's behavior, providing explanations for the requests asked of the child. Authoritative parents are supportive and warm in their interactions with their children. The *permissive parent* places few demands on the children, allowing him to make many of his own decisions. Authoritative parents are responsive and nurturant, while permissive parents are moderately nurturant or uninvolved. The authoritarian parent is less nurturant and more rejecting.

The children of authoritative parents tend to have the most desirable characteristics, such as *instrumental competence*, the display of independence, self-control, and cooperation. Children of authoritarian and permissive parents do not exhibit instrumental competence. Authoritarian parenting in particular is associated with aggressive behavior in boys, overreliance on others in girls, and less advanced moral reasoning in both.

The *uninvolved parent* is a recently identified parenting style in which the parent is emotionally detached from the child and uncommitted to her parental role. Children of these parents have low self-esteem and increased aggression.

B. Strategies of Parental Control (pp. 583–591)

The strategies used by parents to control their children's behavior include induction (reasoning and explanation), power assertion, and love withdrawal. Induction is related to the most desirable child behaviors, whereas power assertion is associated with greater aggression and love withdrawal with avoidance of the parent. In general the parent's mode of discipline shifts in the first three years of the child's life from power assertion to induction. With older children middle-class parents use a variety of control strategies depending on the situation. When the parent desires an immediate impact he issues commands. When long-term consequences are desired he uses self-oriented induction. The need for parental control diminishes with age as children learn to regulate their own behavior.

Punishment is a form of power assertion in which the frequency of an undesired behavior is reduced by presenting an aversive stimulus or by removing a desired stimulus. In one study Ross Parke utilized the forbidden-toy paradigm to examine the influence of several variables on the effectiveness of punishment. Induction was observed to be much more effective than punishment for controlling a child's behavior. Punishment is more effective when provided consistently among caregivers (*interagent consistency*) and from situation to situation by the same caregiver (*intra-agent consistency*). Timing and the intensity of the punishing stimulus also influence the effectiveness of punishment.

Controversy: Spare the Rod and Spoil the Child? (pp. 587–588)
Although it is effective in reducing behaviors in the short term, punishment (particularly physical punishment) is also associated with long-term negative consequences. Children who are frequently punished show greater aggression and are more likely to avoid the punishing agents. Increased aggression may be the result of modeling the aggressive behavior of the punisher; the aggressive behavior may be positively reinforced by the attention that the behavior usually attracts. Thus, the best approach to controlling a child's behavior is to use reasoning and to focus on reinforcing the child's positive behaviors and avoid reinforcing their transgressions.

Time-out is an effective alternative to physical punishment. With this technique, when the child behaves in an inappropriate manner he is physically removed from the situation and placed in a quiet, neutral place for a two- to five-minute period. Time-out has been demonstrated to be quite effective in reducing or eliminating troublesome behaviors in children. Time-out procedures are believed to be effective because they remove the child from any potential rewards for inappropriate behavior and because they allow the child and caregiver the opportunity to "cool down" following an incident.

The type of parenting strategies a parent chooses to control her child's behavior is influenced by the kinds of attributions that the parent makes about the child's behavior. In Theodore Dix and Joan Grusec's attribution model of socialization the parent first observes the child's behavior and then makes a causal attribution about the child's intentions. The parent then responds to the child based on the attribution made. If the attribution is correct then the parent will be effective in controlling the child's behavior. If the attribution is inaccurate, attempts at behavioral control may be ineffective and negative emotions may arise.

Richard Bell's *control theory* suggests that the parent-child relationship is also influenced by the child's behavioral style. Control theory views individuals as having upper and lower limits of tolerance for each others' behaviors. A child who frequently tests the "upper limits" of tolerance is more likely to precipitate an authoritarian, power-assertive parenting style.

C. **Problems in Parenting** (pp. 591–595)
Observational studies of dysfunctional families suggest that maladaptive behavioral patterns are learned from day-to-day family interactions that result from poor child-management strategies. Children raised in a family with a *coercive style* of reciprocal aggression between parent and child become out of control and violent in situations outside of the home.

When parents of aggressive families are trained to employ discipline effectively and consistently, the children's rate of deviant behavior decreases. The attentional deficit model of dysfunctional parenting suggests that parents may have knowledge of good parenting skills or can easily learn proper parenting skills, but other family or social stresses prevent them from applying them.

Children from abusive homes are more likely to be anxiously attached, to show low self-esteem, to have learning problems in school, to have emotional problems, and are at greater risk for delinquency and violent criminal behavior. Parents in abusive families tend to rely on a coercive parenting style and on power-assertive techniques and are less consistent in their use of positive reinforcement. The members of such abusive families interact with each other infrequently, often experience greater life stress than nonabusive families, and tend to be isolated from the outside world, providing fewer possibilities for social support. Characteristics of the child also contribute to the dynamics of abusive family interaction; for example, premature children are at special risk for abuse because they tend to have high-pitched cries and an unattractive appearance.

D. **Cultural and Social Class Variations in Parenting** (pp. 595–597)
Some parental socialization patterns are seen across varied cultures. Infants and toddlers, for example, are universally nurtured by parents. By the time children reach school age, parental nurturance has shifted to concern with training their children to behave in ways valued by the cultural group.

Sociocultural beliefs and values play a significant role in parental socialization practices. In cultures that depend on children as an important part of the work force (for example, in Kenya and Liberia) parents stress the importance of obedience and the training of children to do chores responsibly. In contrast, middle-class American parents do not stress training since most children are not required to work for economic survival.

Evidence that culture affects parenting styles comes from studies examining parent-child relationships. For example, in order to control children's behavior, Japanese mothers use less physical punishment and more verbal reasoning than do American mothers.

Social class differences within a culture also influence parenting styles. Middle-class mothers are more likely to use induction as a discipline strategy, whereas lower-class mothers are more likely to employ power-assertive techniques. Several factors associated with social class may account for the observed differences in parenting styles. Lower-class families, for example, are more likely to experience psychological distress and therefore are more likely to experience parenting as difficult. However, economic stress may encourage alternative family structures (such as the extended family) and socialization processes (the fostering of interdependence and cooperation) that help meet the needs of the growing children.

III. **RELATIONSHIPS WITH MOTHERS, FATHERS, AND SIBLINGS** (pp. 597–605)

A. **Mothering versus Fathering: Are There Differences?** (pp. 598–601)
Although mothers continue to carry the majority of the child-care responsibilities in modern American society, research indicates that fathers also play a significant role in their children's development. Mothers and fathers interact with their newborn infants in similar ways, but shortly after the newborn period fathers tend to be more physical and "idiosyncratic" when playing with their infants, and mothers tend to be more caring and

comforting. Most fathers spend less time with their children than mothers do, even when mothers are employed outside the home. The fathers' relative uninvolvement with caregiving duties is not due to their inability to engage in responsive parenting, but may result partly from a lack of confidence in their caregiving skills and from the mothers' reluctance to relinquish the caregiving duties to the fathers.

Early studies showing that boys raised without fathers were more likely to have academic and behavioral difficulties were interpreted as evidence in favor of the importance of the identification process. Recent research, however, suggests that the absence of a father as a model or identification figure is not as important as the loss of a father as a source of emotional and financial support.

Fathers and mothers most likely contribute to child development in similar ways. Thus when fathers are highly involved in caregiving activities they are providing their children with more responsive parenting and more cognitively stimulating activities than those experienced by children whose fathers are not involved. Consequently, children of highly involved fathers show less sex-role beliefs and score higher on tests of cognitive competence. In many cultures, fathers are becoming increasingly involved in the care of their children. The Swedish government, for example, has established social policies to encourage parental participation. However, some societies continue to have low parental involvement, largely because of cultural beliefs concerning the roles of the father and the mother in the family.

B. **Siblings** (pp. 601–605)
The role that siblings play in a child's development is apparent when examining the characteristics of the only child. Only children show higher achievement and intelligence scores and have more positive relationships with their parents than do children with siblings. These advantages are also seen in first-born children and probably result from the increased time that only children and first-borns spend with their parents. The fact that smaller families have higher intelligence scores and show higher self-esteem is consistent with the view that parents in larger families spend less time interacting with their children.

The birth of a sibling also has a large impact, particularly on a first-born child, often leading to sibling rivalry. Sibling conflict is most likely to develop and persist if the older child perceives a sharp decrease in parental attention.

Interactions among siblings change with age. Preschool-aged siblings engage in considerable prosocial and aggressive behaviors; brothers are more likely to initiate aggressive behaviors, while sisters are more likely to engage in prosocial actions. During adolescence siblings are more dominant and nurturant toward younger siblings, but this relationship becomes more egalitarian with the passage of time.

IV. FAMILIES IN TRANSITION (pp. 605–613)

A. Maternal Employment (pp. 606–609)
The increase in the number of mothers working in the labor force has stimulated interest in the effects of maternal employment on child development. Children of working mothers, particularly girls, have higher levels of achievement and self-esteem and hold fewer stereotypical beliefs about sex roles than children of nonworking mothers. It is not maternal employment per se that leads to these positive qualities in their children, but the interactive style of the mother. Although working mothers spend less time caring for their children, they compensate for mother-child interaction time by setting aside more quality time during evenings and weekends.

Another important factor is the mother's attitude toward mothering, work, and staying at home. A mother who prefers the situation she is in (either working or staying at home) is more likely to provide positive family interactions and have well-adjusted children.

Because many mothers must work to survive economically, many children are placed in alternate child-care situations. Recent research shows that quality day care produces no negative effects on overall development and may improve children's performance on cognitive competence tests during the preschool years. Children with day-care experience also tend to be more socially competent. Preliminary studies on children enrolled in low-quality day-care centers prior to one year of age show that children displayed several negative effects in kindergarten, such as difficulty with peers. In general, a high-quality day-care center is one that mirrors the qualities of good parenting.

B. The Impact of Divorce (pp. 609–613)
The impact of divorce on children is usually negative, especially in the first year following the divorce. Many of the negative effects diminish two years after the divorce, especially in girls. Boys are more likely to continue to show negative effects such as increased aggression, noncompliance, and academic difficulties. Negative interaction patterns usually develop as a result of the mother's adoption of an authoritarian parenting style, which along with decreasing compliance in the children leads to a coercive cycle of parent-child interactions.

Young children (six to eight years) have the most difficult time adjusting to divorce, although adolescents also are likely to suffer negative psychological consequences. Some children show recovery from the stress of divorce and become well adapted to the new family situation. A healthy adaptation to divorce is associated with the parent's adoption of the authoritative parental style, which usually means reduced stress on the family. Children, particularly adolescents, also have difficulty adjusting to stepparents, perhaps because stepparents are less likely to adopt an authoritative parental style with their stepchildren. However, boys are more likely to benefit from a stepfather than are girls.

The negative consequences of divorce are related to increased family conflict associated with the transition from a two-parent home to a one-parent home. But if an intact two-parent family is fraught with conflict and maladaptive patterns of interaction, divorce may actually lead to a better situation in the long run.

V. THEMES IN DEVELOPMENT: THE INFLUENCE OF THE FAMILY (pp. 613–614)

How does the sociocultural context influence family processes? Many of the goals parents have for their children are influenced by their culture's beliefs and values. Culture also influences who will participate in child care and to what extent. Other factors, such as family size, maternal employment, and divorce, can alter family structures.

How does the child play an active role in family processes? Children can have significant effects on interactions with parents, siblings, and others. Parents and siblings react to the child's growing independence and competence by displaying less dominance and regulation. The child's behaviors may also influence the parents' choice of discipline style.

How do family processes interact with other domains of development? The style of parenting a child is exposed to has a significant impact on the child's development in other domains. A child with authoritarian parents, for example, tends to have relatively low self-esteem, poor relations with peers, and high levels of aggression. Interactions with siblings provide children with opportunities to develop social skills. Transitions in families can affect children's emotional, social, and cognitive development.

Key Terms Review

1. The _____ consists solely of parents and children.

2. When a parent disciplines a child by removing him from all sources of reinforcement, the parent is making use of the procedure called _____ .

3. The _____ is a pattern of reciprocal aggression between parent and child.

4. A child who displays _____ has self-control and is independent, achievement oriented, and cooperative.

5. The _____ parent relies on coercive techniques to discipline the child.

6. _____ refers to a single caregiver's application of discipline from one situation to another.

7. The _____ includes secondary relations such as grandparents, aunts, uncles, and cousins as well as parents and siblings.

8. The _____ parent is emotionally detached from the child and focuses on her own needs as opposed to the child's.

9. _____ posits that during parent-child interactions the intensity of one partner's behavior affects the intensity of the other's response.

10. _____ refers to the consistency of disciplinary strategies among different caregivers.

11. The _____ parent sets few limits on the child's behavior.

12. _____ is a theory of family functioning that emphasizes the reciprocal interactions among various members.

13. The _____ parent sets limits on a child's behavior by using the technique of induction.

14. Children acquire the social knowledge, skills, and attitudes valued by the larger society through the process of _____ .

Answers to Key Terms Review

1. nuclear family
2. time-out
3. coercive cycle
4. instrumental competence
5. authoritarian
6. Intra-agent consistency
7. extended family
8. uninvolved
9. Control theory
10. Interagent consistency
11. permissive
12. Systems theory
13. authoritative
14. socialization

Multiple-Choice Questions

Fact and Concept Questions

1. Whereas the _____ family includes relatives such as grandparents, aunts, and cousins, the _____ family consists only of parents and their children.
   a. nuclear, modern
   b. extended, nuclear
   c. traditional, modern
   d. modern, nuclear

2. According to current census statistics, approximately _____ percent of marriages end in divorce.
   a. 25
   b. 30
   c. 50
   d. 75

3. Systems theory assumes that
   a. development is a product of the complex interactions taking place among family members.
   b. development is a maturational process that takes place regardless of family dynamics.
   c. biological factors play no role in the dynamics of family life.
   d. families are stable entities that undergo little change over long periods of time.

4. The primary agents of a child's socialization are
   a. peers.
   b. teachers.
   c. parents.
   d. maturational factors.

5. According to Baumrind, parents who use reasoning and explanation, rather than physical punishment, to regulate their children's behavior are
   a. permissive.
   b. authoritative.
   c. authoritarian.
   d. instrumental.

6. _____ parents are likely to use induction as a disciplinary method, whereas _____ parents are more likely to use power assertion.
   a. Permissive, authoritative
   b. Authoritarian, authoritative
   c. Permissive, authoritarian
   d. Authoritative, authoritarian

7. Studies on the effects of various techniques for controlling children's behavior have found that
   a. intense punishment is the most effective way of eliminating unwanted behavior.
   b. reasoning, or induction, is the most effective way of eliminating unwanted behavior.
   c. less nurturant parents give more effective punishment.
   d. the timing of punishments is not a factor in their effectiveness.

8. The assumption that parents and children have upper and lower limits of tolerance for the types of behaviors that each shows is known as
   a. control theory.
   b. systems theory.
   c. interagent consistency.
   d. coercive style.

9. Families of antisocial boys are usually characterized by
   a. parents who use reasoning and consistently employ discipline.
   b. parents who are divorced.
   c. high levels of reciprocal aggression between parent and child.
   d. parents who both work outside the home.

10. According to the attentional deficit model of dysfunctional parenting
    a. families become dysfunctional because of the stress of caring for a child who has an attentional disorder.
    b. stressed parents do not apply good parenting practices because they fail to learn them.
    c. stressed parents use a large variety of child management techniques, which often leads to confused children.
    d. stressed parents develop a limited repertoire of responses, often coercive, to discipline their children.

11. Studies on the effects of child abuse have found that
    a. abused infants are likely to be securely attached to their mothers.
    b. child abuse does not affect cognitive development.
    c. abused children are at great risk for emotional and behavioral problems.
    d. abused children make deliberate attempts not to maltreat their own children when they become parents.

12. Parenting in various cultures around the world has been found to be
    a. very similar in terms of the strategies used to control children.
    b. markedly different from culture to culture.
    c. similar in many fundamental ways but with different emphases on the techniques and goals of parenting.
    d. impossible to compare because of different belief systems.

13. Observed differences in parenting practices among various socioeconomic classes within a culture reveal that lower-class mothers are more likely to use _____ than middle-class mothers.
    a. power assertion
    b. induction
    c. positive reinforcement
    d. verbal reasoning

14. A majority of research evidence suggests that
    a. fathers are not as responsive to their infants as mothers.
    b. fathers and mothers are equally responsive to their infants.
    c. fathers and mothers spend equal time with their children.
    d. fathers are likely to feel as competent as mothers in caring for their children.

15. Boys growing up without fathers are more likely to have problems in school achievement and control of aggression. According to contemporary views the reason for this effect is that
    a. there is no opportunity to undergo identification with the father.
    b. mothers have less effective parenting strategies than fathers.
    c. the absence of the father results in a loss of a source of emotional and financial support for the whole family.
    d. the absence of the father results in a loss of an appropriate masculine role model.

16. The only child is likely to be
    a. spoiled.
    b. lonely.
    c. intelligent.
    d. immature.

17. The conflict that frequently exists between brothers and sisters within a family is referred to as
    a. a coercive cycle.
    b. sibling rivalry.
    c. sibling confluence.
    d. birth order effects.

18. Daughters of mothers who work outside of the home are more likely to _____ than daughters of mothers who do not work.
    a. be dependent and have low self-esteem
    b. have problems in school
    c. have low IQ scores
    d. have high self-esteem and show greater independence

19. Research on the effects of day care on child development has found that
    a. day care has a severe negative impact on children's development.
    b. day-care children have lower IQ scores than home-reared children.
    c. day-care children show greater IQ scores and language development than home-reared children.
    d. day-care children are withdrawn and dependent, and show emotional problems later on.

20. With respect to the effects of divorce on children, studies have demonstrated that
    a. the negative effects typically diminish two years following the divorce.
    b. the effects are inconsequential.
    c. the negative effects are not obvious until two years following the divorce.
    d. girls have greater difficulty adjusting to the divorce than boys.

Application Questions

1. Sharona's parents have always permitted her to have a say in family decisions, and they provide explanations whenever they set rules or limits on her behavior. Sharona's parents are probably _____ parents.
    a. authoritarian
    b. permissive
    c. authoritative
    d. uninvolved

2. When Walter was two his mother was likely to use _____ as a method of controlling his behavior. Now that he is four his mother uses _____ as a way of disciplining him.
    a. induction, power assertion
    b. power assertion, induction
    c. induction, love withdrawal
    d. love withdrawal, power assertion

3. Gloria, who is four years old, went to a restaurant for dinner with her parents. During the meal Gloria began misbehaving at the table so her father took her out to the car and waited quietly there with her until she calmed down. Gloria's parents have found this technique of removing Gloria from the situation, called _____ , very effective in controlling their child's behavior.
    a. love withdrawal
    b. induction
    c. physical punishment
    d. time-out

4. Yoshio is Japanese. When controlling his behavior Yoshio's mother is most likely to use
   a. power assertion.
   b. punishment.
   c. verbal reasoning.
   d. physical abuse.

5. Tai is six months old. Her father is a stay-at-home dad and therefore her primary caregiver. Tai's father probably
   a. is less responsive to her than her mother is.
   b. is just as likely as Tai's mother to hold, touch, and talk to Tai.
   c. spends less time playing with her than her mother does.
   d. has less influence on her cognitive development than her mother does.

6. Brian is an only child. He is likely to
   a. be lonely.
   b. be an underachiever.
   c. do poorly on standardized IQ tests.
   d. show higher IQ scores than children with siblings.

7. Magda is three years old and her mother just had another baby. Over time Magda is likely to develop a _____ relationship with her brother if she experiences a(n) _____ in maternal contact.
   a. friendly and positive, increase
   b. friendly and positive, drop
   c. hostile and aggressive, increase
   d. hostile and aggressive, drop

8. Jonah is the son of middle-class parents, both of whom have full-time jobs outside of the home. It is probably true that Jonah will
   a. exhibit delinquent behavior.
   b. see his mother as an incompetent housewife and mother.
   c. develop egalitarian views about male and female social roles.
   d. have views about male and female social roles that are similar to Jack's, whose mother has never worked outside the home.

9. According to current research findings, which of the following women is likely to have the best attitude toward mothering?
   a. Norma, who stays at home with her children because she chooses to do so
   b. Jackie, who for financial reasons has to work at a full-time job while her children are in day care
   c. Kathy, who is reluctantly staying home with her two children because her husband believes it will be best for the children
   d. Rafaela, who has two small children and had to return to work following her divorce

10. Donald's parents were divorced last year. It is likely that Donald
    a. has not completely adjusted to the divorce.
    b. has completely adjusted to the divorce.
    c. is having problems at home but not in school.
    d. will be even more upset when his mother remarries this year.

Answers to Multiple-Choice Questions

The correct answer appears first and is preceded by an asterisk.

Answers to Fact and Concept Questions

1. *b. The extended family was typical of American family life prior to the nineteenth century, when grandparents, aunts, uncles, and cousins often lived together with the primary family. The nuclear family, more typical of postindustrial America, consists solely of parents and their children. (p. 576)
   a. The term *nuclear family* refers to parents and their offspring. The term *modern family* implies many types of family arrangements, including single parents, dual-career parents, and stepparents.
   c. The text does not define any family style as "traditional." It does refer to modern families as those made up of nuclear families, single-parent families, dual-career families, and step families.
   d. The modern family does not typically include grandparents, aunts, and cousins.

2. *c. As of 1990, statistics indicate that approximately 50 percent of marriages end in divorce. (p. 576)
   a. According to statistics, approximately 50 percent of marriages end in divorce.
   b. According to statistics, approximately 50 percent of marriages end in divorce.
   d. According to statistics, approximately 50 percent of marriages end in divorce.

3. *a. Systems theory proposes that a child's development is the result of the interactions that take place among all family members. (p. 577)
   b. This statement is consistent with a biological model of development, not a systems theory approach.
   c. Systems theory regards all aspects of family life, including biological factors, as important for family interactions.
   d. Systems theory assumes that families are in a continual state of change as family members have reciprocal influences on one another.

4. *c. Parents are regarded as the primary agents in the child's socialization; they have the greatest impact on the child's development. (p. 579)
   a. Although peers play a role in the child's socialization, parents are the primary socializing agents for the child.

b. Teachers also play a role in the child's socialization, but parents are the primary socializing agents for the child.

d. Certainly maturational factors play an important role in development, but without the interactions with parents and the environment the child would not develop normally.

5. *b. Authoritative parents regulate their children's behavior through the use of clearly communicated expectations and by providing reasons for their restrictions. (p. 580)

a. Permissive parents place few restrictions on their children's behavior and tend to be uninvolved with their children.

c. Authoritarian parents demand unquestioned obedience from their children and use threats or physical punishment to regulate their children's behavior.

d. Baumrind did not describe a category of parenting called instrumental.

6. *d. Induction includes the use of reasoning and explanation in disciplining children, characteristics of authoritative parenting styles. Power assertion includes physical punishment and is the primary disciplinary approach used by authoritarian parents. (p. 583)

a. Permissive parents infrequently regulate their children's behavior; authoritative parents tend to use induction, not power assertion.

b. Authoritarian parents demand obedience through power assertion, not induction; authoritative parents more often use induction.

c. Permissive parents place few demands on their children and therefore do not make use of induction.

7. *b. Providing an explanation for the need to control one's behavior (induction) has been observed to be the most important factor in influencing children's behavior. (p. 586)

a. Induction is more effective than punishment for controlling behavior.

c. Some studies suggest that nurturant adults are more effective in controlling their children's behavior.

d. Early punishment is more effective than late punishment in controlling children's behavior.

8. *a. According to control theory, when a child's misbehavior pushes parents to their "upper limits," parents will respond with more forceful disciplinary techniques; if the child's behavior approaches the parent's "lower limits," the parent will attempt to stimulate the child. (p. 590)

b. Systems theory is a model for understanding reciprocal interactions among family members.

c. Interagent consistency describes a single caregiver's consistent use of discipline.

d. The coercive cycle describes a pattern of reciprocal aggression between parent and child.

9. *c. Families of antisocial boys are characterized by high levels of aggression between parents and child (coercive cycle). (p. 591)

a. Families of antisocial boys are unlikely to be characterized by an inductive parenting style.

b. Although divorce represents a difficult transition for children, it does not necessarily lead to antisocial behavior in the children.

d. Although some studies report a link between maternal employment and lower achievement scores in boys, there is no evidence of a link to antisocial behavior.

10. *d. According to the attentional deficit model, stressed parents often are limited in terms of the child management techniques that they try and frequently rely on the same coercive styles. (p. 593)

a. According to the attentional deficit model, the attentional deficit is with the stressed parent, not the child.

b. According to the attentional deficit model, stressed parents may have knowledge of good parenting skills, but they do not apply them because they are distracted by other family problems.

c. According to the attentional deficit model, stressed parents use a limited number of child management techniques.

11. *c. Children with a history of abuse are more likely to display extreme emotional characteristics such as withdrawal or aggressive patterns of behavior. (p. 594)

a. Abused children are likely to be anxiously attached to their mothers.

b. Children with a history of abuse score lower on tests of cognitive maturity and manifest school learning problems.

d. Abused children are more likely to become abusive parents than children with no history of abuse.

12. *c. Although many similarities in parenting patterns have been observed across cultures, the specific demands and socialization goals of different cultures play a role in shaping parenting patterns. (p. 596)

a. Although many cross-cultural similarities in parenting patterns have been found, there are notable differences between some cultures.

b. Despite very different economic, social, and political differences among the cultures studied, many strong similarities in parenting patterns have been observed.

d. Considerable empirical work on cross-cultural variations in parenting patterns has been successfully conducted.

13. *a. Lower-class mothers are more likely to use power-assertive techniques, such as uttering the command "Do it because I say so!" (p. 596)

b. Middle-class mothers are more likely to employ induction in their parenting practices.

c. Lower-class mothers dispense fewer positive reinforcers than middle-class mothers.

d. Middle-class mothers are more likely to employ verbal reasoning than lower-class mothers.

14. *b. Fathers are just as likely as mothers to hold, touch, and vocalize to their babies. (p. 598)
 a. Fathers are as responsive to their infants as are mothers.
 c. Although fathers are as responsive to their infants as are mothers, fathers spend less time with their children.
 d. Fathers are less likely to feel confident of their caregiving skills.

15. *c. The contemporary view describes good fathering as resembling good mothering. Thus any child (particularly boys) who loses a parent loses a source of emotional and financial support. (p. 600)
 a. Contemporary views on the influence of the father place less emphasis on his importance as an identification figure.
 b. There is no evidence suggesting that fathers have better parenting skills than mothers.
 d. Contemporary views of the influence of the father place less emphasis on his importance as a masculine role model and more on his importance as a supportive parent.

16. *c. Only children show higher achievement and intelligence scores than children with siblings. (p. 601)
 a. The stereotype of only child as a spoiled brat is a myth, unsubstantiated by research.
 b. No differences in sociability between only children and children with siblings have been observed; therefore, only children are not likely to be lonely.
 d. Only children show higher maturity than children with siblings.

17. *b. *Sibling rivalry* is the term commonly used to describe the conflict that often exists between siblings, particularly upon the arrival of a new sibling. (p. 603)
 a. The coercive cycle refers to the pattern of conflict between parent and child, not between siblings.
 c. *Sibling confluence* is not a term used to describe the relationship between rival siblings.
 d. The term *birth order effects* describes the influence of birth order on a child's intellectual and personality development, not the conflict that may exist between siblings.

18. *d. Daughters of employed mothers are more likely to be independent and to have high self-esteem. (p. 606)
 a. Daughters of employed mothers are less likely to be dependent and less likely to have low self-esteem.
 b. Daughters of employed mothers are more likely to show greater achievement.
 c. No differences in IQ have been observed when comparing daughters of employed and stay-at-home mothers.

19. *c. Some researchers report that day-care children outperform children raised at home on tests of IQ and language ability. (p. 608)

a. Day care does not have a severe negative impact on a child's development. In fact, few differences between children raised in day care and children raised at home have been found.

b. One area in which day-care children have been observed to differ from children reared at home is in performance on standardized IQ tests, but the day-care children do better, not worse.

d. Day care has few negative effects on children. Day-care children are socially competent and show greater self-confidence and independence.

20. *a. Many of the negative effects of divorce diminish two years after the divorce, particularly for girls. (p. 610)

b. Divorce has substantial negative effects on children, especially during the first year after the divorce and particularly in boys.

c. The negative effects of divorce are most pronounced during the first year and diminish after two years.

d. Boys appear to have more difficulty adjusting to divorce than do girls.

Answers to Application Questions

1. *c. Sharona's parents expect her to behave in a mature fashion and communicate their expectations clearly; these are characteristics of an authoritative parenting style. (p. 580)

a. Authoritarian parents demand obedience to commands and often rely on coercive techniques. Sharona's parents are clearly not authoritarian.

b. Permissive parents place few demands on their children. Because Sharona's parents set rules and limits, they clearly are not permissive.

d. Uninvolved parents are uncommitted to their parental role and emotionally detached from their children. Sharona's parents are clearly not uninvolved parents.

2. *b. With young preschoolers most parents use power assertion techniques to control defiant behaviors, but as the children get older and become more autonomous parents use induction techniques more frequently. (p. 583)

a. Most mothers tend to use physical means, not induction, to control their young preschoolers. As children get older, mothers use induction more often.

c. Most mothers tend to use physical means, not induction, to control their young preschoolers. Love withdrawal as a control technique is infrequently used by mothers of young children.

d. Love withdrawal as a control technique is infrequently used by mothers of young children.

3. *d. Gloria's father used the disciplinary strategy called time-out, which involves removing the child from all possible reinforcements (in this case, from the table in the restaurant) after committing a transgression. (p. 588)

a. Gloria's father did not use love withdrawal, which is a form of punishment that involves temporary coldness or rejection by a parent.

b. Gloria's father did not use induction, which involves the use of reasoning, explanation, and communication of the standards of behavior.

c. There is no indication that Gloria's father used physical punishment to control her behavior.

4. *c. Japanese rely more often on induction techniques than on power-assertion techniques. (p. 596)

a. Mothers in the Japanese culture are less likely to use power-assertion techniques.

b. Japanese mothers emphasize responsibility and commitment to others, and thus are less likely to use punishment to control their children's behavior.

d. Because Japanese mothers do not rely on power-assertion techniques to control their children's behavior they are less likely to physically abuse their children.

5. *b. Studies show that fathers are as likely as mothers to hold, touch, and vocalize to their infants. (p. 598)

a. Fathers are as responsive to their infants as are mothers.

c. Because Tai's father is the primary caregiver, it is unlikely that he spends less time with Tai than does her mother.

d. Like mothers, fathers have significant influences on many aspects of their children's development, particularly if the father is the primary caregiver.

6. *d. Only children appear to have several benefits over children with siblings, some of which lead to better performance on IQ tests. (p. 601)

a. There is little reason to expect Brian to be lonely since only children have their parents' exclusive attention and are not deficient in sociability.

b. Only children show higher achievement than children with siblings; thus, Brian is probably not an underachiever.

c. Only children show higher intelligence scores than children with siblings; thus, Brian probably would perform average or better than average on IQ tests.

7. *d. Negative relationships between siblings are likely to develop if the older sibling experiences a sharp drop in maternal contact. (p. 604)

a. A child's contact with the mother is highly unlikely to increase following the birth of a sibling.

b. A drop in maternal contact is most likely to lead to a hostile and aggressive pattern of interaction.

c. A hostile and aggressive pattern of interaction is most likely to occur following a drop in maternal contact. Moreover, a child's contact with the mother is highly unlikely to increase following the birth of a sibling.

8. *c. Because both of Jonah's parents work he has the opportunity to see both parents in multiple roles and therefore is more likely to develop egalitarian beliefs. (p. 606)

a. Although some studies report a link between maternal employment and lower achievement scores in boys, there is no evidence of a link to delinquent behavior.

b. Boys whose mothers work outside the home are likely to see both sexes as competent.

d. Studies show a strong effect of maternal employment on sex-role attitudes of sons and daughters; thus Jonah's views are likely to be different from Jack's views.

9. *a. Research has found that a woman's attitude toward mothering is best when she is satisfied with her choice of working or staying at home. Norma appears to have a preference for staying home with her children and therefore is likely to have the most positive attitude toward mothering and interacting with her children. (p. 607)
   b. Women who are forced to work when they would prefer to be at home with children experience great stress, which leads to negative maternal attitudes and family interactions.
   c. Mothers who stay at home but would prefer to be working outside the home tend to be depressed and find mothering stressful.
   d. Mothers who must be employed because of divorce or other financial hardships experience stress, which leads to negative maternal attitudes and a negative family climate.

10. *a. Research indicates that the worst period for children following the divorce of parents is the first year. Therefore, it is likely that Donald has not yet adjusted to his parents' divorce. (p. 610)
   b. The effects of divorce on children typically begin to diminish *two* years following the divorce.
   c. In some studies, boys of divorced parents were found to have problems at home and in school for a number of years following the divorce.
   d. Boys have been found to benefit from their mother's remarriage because the addition of a stepfather may disrupt the coercive cycle that sometimes develops between mothers and sons.

CHAPTER 15

THE INFLUENCE OF PEERS

LEARNING OBJECTIVES

1. Describe the developmental changes in peer relationships through adolescence. (pp. 618–623)

2. Discuss the different positions concerning whether children should be permitted to engage in rough-and-tumble play. (pp. 623–624)

3. Describe and discuss the functions of peer groups and how they form. (pp. 624–627)

4. Describe and discuss the joint and conflicting pressures to conform that are placed on children by parents and peers. (pp. 628–629)

5. Describe how peers help socialize the child by serving as models and reinforcers within a culture or society. (pp. 629–633)

6. Describe how psychologists measure peer acceptance and what has been learned about the characteristics of popular and unpopular children. (pp. 633–639)

7. Discuss the various factors that are believed to play a role in the development of social competence. (pp. 639–643)

8. Describe and discuss the different procedures that have been successful in training social skills in children. (pp. 643–646)

9. Discuss children's patterns of friendship, their understanding of the concept of friendship, and how their understanding is linked to advances in social cognition. (pp. 646–651)

10. Discuss the function of friendship and describe how children become friends. (pp. 651–652)

CHAPTER OUTLINE

I. DEVELOPMENTAL CHANGES IN PEER RELATIONS (pp. 618–624)
Peers are companions who are approximately the same age and developmental level. Peers often function as equals.

A. Early Peer Exchanges and Play (pp. 619–620)
Infants as young as three months of age recognize and respond to peers differently from caregivers and other adults. During the first year of life interactions with peers are brief. By the second year peer interactions become longer as children begin to engage in play. By the third year peer interactions become more frequent.

Young children have been observed to engage in three forms of play: (1) *solitary play*, where children play alone, apart from other children, (2) *parallel play*, where children play alone but beside other children, and (3) *cooperative play*, where children interact during play. Preschoolers begin to engage in "make-believe" play called *social pretend play*, which requires symbolic capabilities and the understanding of the rules of social dialogue and communication.

B. The School Years and Adolescence (pp. 621–623)
When children start elementary school they begin to engage in group activities. *Rough-and-tumble play*, which emerges at around two years of age, becomes more prominent during elementary school years, particularly in boys.

The activities that school-aged children engage in are diverse. In one survey of fifth- and sixth-graders the most cited activities involved talking to each other and playing sports.

By adolescence many children form *cliques*, groups of five to ten children who frequently interact with one another, and identify with a *crowd*, a large group of peers who share a specific trait or reputation. The influence of cliques and crowds can be strong, providing a child with prescriptions on how to dress and behave. In adolescence increased interest in the opposite sex adds the element of sexuality to peer relations.

By early adulthood most individuals lose interest in cliques and crowds and become more independent and secure with their self-identities.

Controversy: Should Children's Rough-and-Tumble Play Be Discouraged? (pp. 623–624)
Preschool and elementary school children engage in considerable physical play, including rough-and-tumble play. Some concerns have been expressed concerning

rough-and-tumble play. In one study this form of play was observed to lead often to intense aggression. Other studies indicate that rough-and-tumble play can escalate into intense aggression when unpopular children are involved. But among popular children rough-and-tumble play often leads to organized games with rules, therefore providing a context for learning.

II. PEER GROUP DYNAMICS (pp. 624–629)

A. Peer Group Formation (pp. 625–627)
Peer groups form as children who share backgrounds, interests, and activities interact. Peer group formation and operation were described in the classic experience known as the Robber's Cave Study. In this experiment fifth-graders who did not know each other were placed in one of two groups. The interactions among the children within each group (intragroup) and between the two groups (intergroup) were examined throughout the period of the study and yielded the following observations. Groups form when individuals share activities and have similar goals. As a group is taking shape some individuals assume a more dominant role than others. A group's identity strengthens when there is competition with other groups, although intergroup conflict often rises. Animosity between peer groups is reduced when the two groups are made to work together to achieve some common goals.

B. Dominance Hierarchies (p. 627)
Very early in the process of peer group formation children establish *dominance hierarchies:* some children are more active and aggressive, while others more passive and submissive. These dominance hierarchies remain stable for the first few months but usually change as children begin to know each other better and as they approach adolescence. The use of physical power as a form of dominance shifts to other characteristics, such as interpersonal skills. Dominance hierarchies may serve to improve a group's chances of meeting certain objectives, to make social relationships more predictable, and to provide greater control over the aggressive tendencies of members of the group.

C. Peer Pressure and Conformity (pp. 628–629)
When children in the seventh through twelfth grades were asked about peer pressure they reported they felt the greatest pressure to spend time with peers and to excel in school and the least amount of pressure to engage in misconduct. Older adolescents, however, did report greater pressure toward misconduct than younger adolescents. Children's tendency to conform to peer pressure peaks in early adolescence (between sixth and ninth grade) but declines by late adolescence. Young adolescents' increased vulnerability to conform to peer pressure may be partly a result of greater independence from their parents and partly a result of adjusting to a new school setting, which many young adolescents experience as they move from elementary school to junior high.

Peers exert pressures by rewarding behaviors that conform to the group's norms and by reacting negatively to an individual's resistance to conformity. Some of the pressures provided by peers and adults are similar (such as pressure to achieve in school), while other pressures are conflicting (such as drinking or smoking). Adolescents who place value on adult norms are less popular with their peers, whereas adolescents who place less value on conforming to adult norms are more popular.

III. PEERS AS AGENTS OF SOCIALIZATION (pp. 629–633)

A. Peers as Models (p. 630)
Social learning theory argues that peers serve as an important model of behavior. Peer models, particularly models viewed as competent, can promote negative behaviors such as aggression as well as positive behaviors such as sharing.

B. Peers as Reinforcers (pp. 630–631)
Peers reinforce their friends' behaviors. In one study 75 percent of aggressive behavior was reinforced by the victim's submission. When aggressive acts led to counteraggression, the aggressive act was less likely to be repeated.

C. Peers as Transmitters of Cultural Values (pp. 631–633)
Urie Bronfenbrenner's observations of peer relations in the Soviet Union demonstrate the important role that peers play in transmitting to children the values of the cultural group. Compared to American children, Soviet children are less likely to behave anti-socially and more likely to conform to a group—traits consistent with the ideals of Soviet society. The development of these traits in Soviet children is encouraged by the collective child-rearing practices in the Soviet Union. From early in life most children are placed in group child care and encouraged to engage in group cooperation. During the formal school years each class is divided into subgroups called links. Members of each link must cooperate in order to succeed in competition with other links. Altruistic behavior is encouraged by having each class "adopt" lower class.

IV. PEER POPULARITY AND SOCIAL COMPETENCE (pp. 633–646)

A. Measuring Peer Acceptance (pp. 633–635)
Several approaches have been used to measure peer acceptance. *Sociometric nomination* involves having children name the peers who fit a certain criterion, such as "the classmates you especially like." The number of positive or negative nominations that a child receives from her peers is then used as a measure of peer status.

With the *sociometric rating scale* children are asked to rate a peer on several items; the average rating for each child provides a measure of the child's popularity. Researchers also rely on teacher ratings and on objective behavioral observations of children in various social activities.

Studies have indicated that peer status remains quite stable over several years, particularly if the child is classified as rejected.

B. **Characteristics of Popular and Unpopular Children** (pp. 635–639)
Peer popularity is influenced by many factors. A child is more likely to be popular if he is attractive. Children rate attractive children as more friendly, intelligent, and social than unattractive children. A child's name is also likely to influence peer acceptance; children with unique names are less likely to be popular. Children who are proficient in motor skills are also more likely to have greater peer acceptance.

The most important factor in determining popularity appears to be social skills. Popular children show more social skills than rejected and neglected children, who often behave in socially inappropriate ways. In one study popular children were observed to have larger social networks and were more likely to engage in cooperative play and conversation. Rejected children interacted with smaller groups and were more likely to engage in aggressive and other antagonistic behaviors. In another study neglected children were observed to be the least aggressive and were more likely to engage in isolated activities.

Researchers often examine social competence by observing a child's behavior as she enters an unfamiliar group of children at play. While rejected children tend to disrupt the ongoing activity of the group by drawing attention to themselves, popular children are more likely to integrate themselves into the group gradually by making appropriate statements that do not divert attention from the group's activities. Neglected children tend to watch passively and therefore are less likely to be incorporated into the group's play.

Whether a child's social status is caused by the social skills displayed by the child or whether the child's social status leads to the development of social skills is a question that must be addressed. Several studies suggest that children's social behavior precedes their social status.

C. **The Origins of Social Competence** (pp. 639–643)
What factors are important for the development of social skills? Parents have a major impact on their children's social behaviors by serving as models and by providing explicit instructions on how to behave. The behaviors of children often resemble the behaviors of the parents. When introducing their children to a play group of peers, mothers of unpopular children tend to interrupt the activities of a play group, while mothers of popular children tend to encourage their children to join the activities of the group without disruption. Mothers of popular children are also less disagreeable and demanding when at play with their children. The greater the number of peer contacts initiated by the parent the higher the child's popularity.

Kenneth Dodge's five-stage model of social competence is an information-processing model that describes the cognitive and behavioral skills required of a child to enter a group of children successfully. The child must first perceive the group's cues correctly (stage 1: encoding process) and correctly interpret the signals (stage 2: representative process). The child must then generate one or more potential behavior responses (stage 3: response search process), evaluate the possible consequences of each behavior, and choose a response (stage 4: response decision process). Once the behavior is performed the child must monitor the outcome and modify his behavior, if necessary, before repeating the cycle (stage 5: enactment process). Popular children are better than unpopular children at each step of the model.

Popular children are better at identifying the emotions depicted by pictures of children's faces and are less likely to misinterpret the intentions of children's overt behavior and emotional responses of peers. Popular children are also less likely to choose inappropriate ways to solve a social problem and are more likely to change behavioral strategies deemed ineffective. Thus popular children have greater knowledge of social skills and put this knowledge to good use in the behavior they manifest. Unpopular children have limited knowledge, which is reflected in their behavior and contributes to continuing unpopularity.

D. **Training Social Skills** (pp. 643–646)
Several intervention programs have been implemented to help socially unskilled children gain greater peer acceptance. Modeling can be effective in improving social interactions in socially withdrawn children. In one study withdrawn children who watched videotapes of children playing together showed increased numbers of social interactions and experienced more positive social responses from peers. Reinforcement of appropriate social behaviors is also effective in increasing their frequency. Direct instruction in social skills, called *coaching*, is also a very effective training technique. The coaching technique usually involves children in role playing or in activities with socially accepted classmates. Evaluations of these training programs indicate that modeling, reinforcement, and coaching are very effective in enhancing social skills. Their long-term impact, however, has not yet been assessed.

V. **CHILDREN'S FRIENDSHIPS** (pp. 646–652)

A. **Children's Patterns and Conceptions of Friendship** (pp. 646–649)
Most children spend considerable time with at least one peer. To preschoolers a peer or friend is seen as a playmate, someone to play and share objects with. In the middle school years children are more concerned with peer acceptance. Cross-sex friendships are rare, and children begin to spend more time with same-sex friends than with either parent. Friendship interactions include cooperation and conflicts, with gossip as a major instrument to assess the attitudes and beliefs of their peers. Middle childhood is also a time when children begin to instill intimacy and trust into friendships, particularly girls.

Sex differences in friendship networks become clearly evident by the middle school years. Boys' friendships are usually extensive, while girls' circles of friends are smaller but more intense. These sex differences may be a result of the types of games that the sexes play; boys are encouraged to play group games like baseball, while girls play games that promote intimacy, such as "house." By adolescence same-sex friendships continue to be seen as important providers of intimacy and trust, and the frequency of opposite-sex interactions increases as well.

B. **Friendship and Social Cognition** (pp. 649–650)
In his five-stage model of friendship development, Robert Selman suggests that the changes in children's conceptions of friendship are accompanied by changes in social cognition. For example, children can begin to respect others' needs and desires only after they have lost their egocentricity. Older children's more abstract reasoning abilities are presumed to underlie their more complex views of friendship.

C. **How Children Become Friends** (pp. 650–651)
Children become friends when they are successful in exchanging information, particularly if the exchange occurs in the initial interaction. The friendship is likely to be maintained if they actively search for activities that can be shared and if they successfully resolve conflicts that arise. At older ages friendships are maintained by clarity of communication and self-disclosure. Thus, making friends requires attending and properly interpreting social cues and having knowledge of the appropriate way to behave during positive and negative episodes in an interaction.

D. **The Functions of Friendship** (pp. 651–652)
Friendship forms a basis of emotional support, protecting children from anxiety and stress and increasing self-esteem. Availability of friends also provides opportunities to learn and practice social skills, such as cooperation and conflict resolution. In one study pairs of four- and five-year-olds were observed to be more cooperative and effective in winning a game if the pair were friends. In another study, children were more likely to resolve a conflict if the conflict occurred with a friend. Childhood friendship also provides children with the opportunity to learn about the benefits of intimacy.

VI. **THEMES IN DEVELOPMENT: THE INFLUENCE OF PEERS** (pp. 652–654)
How does the sociocultural context influence peer relations? Cultures vary in the amount of peer experience they encourage for children. In most societies, peers pressure each other to conform to specific cultural values, such as sex-typed behaviors. The child's culture can also influence the standards that shape peer acceptance; in the United States, for example, athletic ability and social skill are highly valued.

How does the child play an active role in peer relations? Attractiveness, body build, and athletic skill, as well as social skills, all affect how peers react to a child. Children who can read others' emotions, gauge the consequences of their own behavior, and know the strategies for good social interaction tend to be popular with their peers.

Are developmental changes in peer relations continuous or stagelike? Parten and Selman both believe that development in peer relations occurs in stages. However, research now shows that preschoolers often concurrently display several types of play and that children's interactions suggest more complexity than Selman's model shows.

How do peer relations interact with other domains of development? Popular children do well in school, have high levels of self-esteem, and suffer fewer emotional difficulties than unpopular children. The ability to interact with peers is related to developments in social knowledge, cognitive capabilities, and communication skills.

Key Terms Review

1. A(n) _____ is a companion of approximately the same age and developmental level.

2. The _____ is an assessment measure in which children rate peers on a number of social dimensions.

3. A(n) _____ consists of five to ten peers who frequently interact with each other.

4. In _____ a child plays without regard for what others are doing.

5. During _____ children engage in active, physical play but do not intend to impose harm.

6. _____ is interactive play in which children's actions are reciprocal.

7. A researcher who asks children to name a specified number of peers who fit a certain criterion is using an assessment measure called _____ .

8. When children make use of imaginary and symbolic objects and social roles in their play behavior they are displaying _____ .

9. A(n) _____ is a group's organized infrastructure that is based on power relationships.

10. A large group of peers that is characterized by specific traits or a specific reputation is called a(n) _____ .

11. _____ consists of side-by-side, noninteractive play.

Answers to Key Terms Review

1. peer
2. sociometric rating scale
3. clique
4. solitary play
5. rough-and-tumble play
6. Cooperative play
7. sociometric nomination

8. social pretend play (*or* sociodramatic play)
9. dominance hierarchy
10. crowd
11. Parallel play

Multiple-Choice Questions

Fact and Concept Questions

1. Boys who have good peer relationships
   a. enjoy school more.
   b. are more likely to experience academic difficulties.
   c. are more likely to commit delinquent acts.
   d. experience fewer physical illnesses.

2. A peer is a companion
   a. who shares similar interests.
   b. of the same socioeconomic background.
   c. of the same sex.
   d. who is approximately the same age and developmental level.

3. Compared to peer interactions among toddlers, infants
   a. show no evidence of peer exchanges.
   b. show greater frequencies of peer interactions.
   c. show briefer periods of peer interactions.
   d. show more frequent negative social exchanges.

4. Studies of rough-and-tumble play among preschool and elementary school–aged children suggest that episodes of rough-and-tumble play
   a. are not as frequent among children as commonly believed.
   b. invariably lead to intense aggressive actions in most children.
   c. may promote prosocial behaviors in most children.
   d. should be discouraged by parents and teachers.

5. The Robber's Cave Study examined
   a. the origins of social competence.
   b. peer group formation.
   c. children's conception of friendship.
   d. peers as transmitters of cultural values.

6. Studies of peer group formation suggest that
   a. structured situations that encourage cooperation strengthen group identity.
   b. unsuccessful performance in competitive contests with other groups invariably weakens intragroup identity.
   c. forcing rival groups to share activities reduces intergroup hostilities.
   d. participation in competitive contests usually weakens intergroup hostilities.

7. Peer pressure
   a. as a phenomenon is accepted by the general public, but evidence suggests that it is not a real phenomenon.
   b. peeks prior to adolescence and begins to decrease late in adolescence.
   c. to misbehave is the greatest pressure reported by adolescent children.
   d. toward misconduct is greater among older adolescents than younger adolescents.

8. Young school-aged children are usually exposed to
   a. very different pressures from parents and peers.
   b. similar pressures from parents and peers.
   c. pressures from their parents but not from their peers.
   d. pressures from their peers but not from their parents.

9. The _____ is a peer assessment technique in which children are asked to name a number of peers who fit a certain criterion.
   a. dominance hierarchy
   b. sociometric rating scale
   c. sociometric nomination
   d. peer status scale

10. Which of the following best characterizes a neglected child?
    a. Few positive nominations and few negative nominations
    b. Few positive nominations and many negative nominations
    c. Many positive nominations and few negative nominations
    d. Many positive nominations and many negative nominations

11. Which of the following characteristics is the most important factor in peer acceptance?
    a. The child's name
    b. The physical attractiveness of the child
    c. The child's proficiency in motor activities
    d. The child's social skills

12. In one study young neglected children were observed
    a. to be as successful as popular children in entering a play group.
    b. to be more likely to engage in isolated activities than popular children.
    c. to keep the focus of attention on the peer group rather than themselves when trying to join a play group.
    d. to restrict their conversation with acquaintances to relevant comments.

13. When a popular child tries to join a play group of unfamiliar children she is likely to
    a. begin with low-risk activities but move toward high-risk activities as she receives positive feedback.
    b. begin with low-risk activities but move toward high-risk activities regardless of the feedback that she receives.
    c. begin with and maintain high-risk activities throughout the play-group period.
    d. begin with high-risk activities but move toward low-risk activities as she receives positive feedback.

14. Mothers of unpopular children
    a. are less disagreeable and demanding when playing with their children.
    b. are more likely to initiate peer contacts than mothers of popular children.
    c. display behaviors that are similar to their children's behavior.
    d. are more likely to focus on feelings when interacting with their children.

15. Which of the following experiences during the preschool years is more likely to lead to greater social competence in children?
    a. Being reared at home with parents and no siblings
    b. Being reared at home with parents and siblings
    c. Being enrolled in day care for more than one year
    d. Being enrolled in day care with the same peers for more than one year

16. In studies of children's processing of social information it has been observed that
    a. popular children are more skillful than unpopular children at interpreting social cues.
    b. popular children are less skillful than unpopular children at interpreting social cues.
    c. popular and unpopular children interpret social cues with equal proficiency but differ in their ability to generate potential behavioral responses.
    d. popular and unpopular children interpret social cues with equal proficiency but differ in their ability to select the appropriate response.

17. Which of the following is *not* a way in which peers socialize their age mates?
    a. By serving as models
    b. By providing positive reinforcers
    c. By coaching
    d. By providing negative reinforcers

18. A researcher who examines children's views of friendship is likely to find
    a. few sex differences in concepts of friendship.
    b. sex differences in friendship patterns among children in the middle school years.
    c. concern for acceptance by peers among children in the preschool years.
    d. a large increase in cross-sex friendships in the middle school years.

19. According to Selman's model young children's conception of friendship is limited to concrete, self-oriented situations because of
    a. their age.
    b. their egocentricity.
    c. their history of reinforcement.
    d. peer pressure.

20. Correlational studies that have examined the function of friendship suggest that
    a. arguments are more likely to escalate among friends than among casual acquaintances.
    b. children who have close and intimate friendships are more likely to have conflicts with family members.
    c. friendships play an important role in protecting children from anxiety and stress.
    d. friends provide surprisingly little support for a child's social and emotional development.

Application Questions

1. Three-year-old Andujar recently was enrolled in a preschool. Andujar is likely to engage in
   a. solitary play
   b. parallel play.
   c. cooperative play.
   d. solitary, parallel, and cooperative play.

2. Irving and Craig are both sophomores in the same high school. Although they know each other and take some of the same classes, they do not spend much time together. Irving and Craig are described by most of their peers as two of the "brains" of the school. Irving and Craig are members of the same
   a. clique.
   b. crowd.
   c. gang.
   d. link.

3. Scott runs a large summer camp for boys. Two weeks into the camp season Scott learned that the boys had formed two groups with unique identities and that the two groups were not getting along. To reduce the possibility of increasing conflict Scott should
   a. demand that the two groups share activities with each other.
   b. arrange for the two groups to participate in an organized series of competitive games.
   c. demand that the groups break up and form new groups for the remainder of the summer.
   d. arrange for the two groups to participate in the building of a new playground near the lake.

4. Yvette is a high school senior who has values very consistent with the values conveyed by her parents. According to recent studies Yvette is probably
   a. more popular with her peers than adolescents who place less value on adult norms.
   b. less popular with her peers than adolescents who place less value on adult norms.
   c. likely to give in to peer pressure and experiment with some risky behaviors.
   d. a loner with few friends.

5. Jo Anne is very popular in her school. In a sociometric nomination study Jo Anne is most likely to receive
   a. more positive nominations than negative nominations.
   b. a high number of positive and negative nominations.
   c. a high ranking of peer status by her teachers.
   d. a high ranking of peer status by a researcher making objective behavioral observations of Jo Anne's social activities.

6. Willie was a rejected child when he was in the second grade. Now that Willie is in the seventh grade he is likely to be
   a. popular.
   b. rejected.
   c. controversial.
   d. unaffected by his peers.

7. Who is more likely to have a popular peer status?
   a. An average boy named Christopher
   b. Harry, a shy but very attractive boy
   c. Norman, a klutzy boy who is not very good in sports
   d. David, a very verbal and cooperative boy

8. Four preschoolers are discussing how they will play house. One of these children is an unpopular child. Which of the following statements is most likely to come from the unpopular child?
   a. "I don't want to be the daddy, I want to be the baby."
   b. "We can pretend that we are going out to dinner."
   c. "My mommy said that we are going to Disney World for our summer vacation."
   d. "I can wear my mom's high heels, so I'll pretend to be the mommy."

9. Eleanor and Earl have a seven-year-old son who can be described as unpopular. Studies of the parental influences on children's social competence suggest that
   a. Eleanor and Earl probably have a minimal influence on their child's social competence.
   b. Eleanor probably has a greater influence on her child's social competence than Earl does.
   c. Eleanor's behavior probably resembles the behavior of her child.
   d. Eleanor's behavior is likely to be very different from her child's behavior.

10. Larry was upset when his older brother suggested that Larry's best friend was Jennifer. Larry is most likely a
    a. preschooler.
    b. first-grader.
    c. fifth-grader.
    d. tenth-grader.

Answers to Multiple-Choice Questions

The correct answer appears first and is preceded by an asterisk.

Answers to Fact and Concept Questions

1. *a. Children who have good peer relationships are more likely to enjoy school than children with poor peer relationships. (p. 617)
   b. Children who have good peer relationships are less likely to experience academic difficulties.
   c. Children who have good peer relationships are less likely to commit delinquent acts.
   d. The text does not report any research suggesting a relationship between peer relationships and physical illnesses.

2. *d. Peers often function as equals; they are approximately of the same age and developmental level, but may differ in sex and socioeconomic background and do not necessarily have common interests. (p. 618)
   a. Although peers may share an interest, a common interest is not a necessary characteristic of peers.
   b. Similar socioeconomic backgrounds is not a necessary characteristic of peers.
   c. Peers can be of the same sex or of the opposite sex.

3. *c. Most peer interactions among infants last for briefer periods than peer exchanges among toddlers. (p. 619)
   a. Infants, like toddlers, show a reaction to the sight of another baby.
   b. Peer interactions are more frequent during toddlerhood.
   d. There is no indication that peer exchanges are more negative among infants than among toddlers.

4. *c. Some studies suggest that rough-and-tumble play, particularly among popular children, often promotes prosocial behaviors. (p. 623)
   a. Physical play among preschool children, including rough-and-tumble play, often occurs spontaneously, especially among boys, and thus is a normal part of development.

b. Rough-and-tumble play sometimes escalates into intense aggression, particularly among unpopular boys, but this is not always the case, and it does not occur in most children.
d. Although the topic of rough-and-tumble play is controversial, some researchers suggest that rough-and-tumble play has a positive role in the child's development and therefore should not necessarily be discouraged by parents.

5. *b. The Robber's Cave Study invited fifth-grade boys to a summer camp program in order to examine how peer groups form and operate. (p. 625)
a. The Robber's Cave Study did not examine the origins of social competence.
c. The Robber's Cave Study did not examine children's concept of friendship.
d. Although the cultural transmission of values very likely occurred in the Robber's Cave Study, the experiment was not specifically designed to examine peers as transmitters of cultural values.

6. *a. The results of the Robber's Cave Study suggest that when antagonistic groups work together to achieve a common goal, hostilities decrease. (p. 626)
b. The results of the Robber's Cave Study suggest that although losing in competitive activities may initially lead to intragroup conflict, group identity eventually becomes stronger.
c. The results of the Robber's Cave Study suggest that forcing rival groups to share activities does not reduce intergroup hostilities.
d. The results of the Robber's Cave Study suggest that participation in competitive contests usually increases intergroup hostilities.

7. *d. Although adolescents reported the least peer pressure toward misconduct, older adolescents did report more pressure to misbehave than younger adolescents. (p. 628)
a. Peer pressure is a real and robust phenomenon.
b. Vulnerability to peer pressure peaks in early adolescence.
c. Adolescents reported pressure to engage in misconduct to be the least of the pressures exerted by their peers.

8. *b. Some of the pressures provided by parents and peers are similar, such as pressures to be competent and to achieve in school. (p. 629)
a. Although the pressures from parents and peers are not identical, parents and peers do share some of the same goals.
c. Parents and peers both place pressure on the growing child.
d. Peers and parents both place pressure on the growing child.

9. *c. With sociometric nomination measures children are asked to name peers who fit a certain criterion, such as "peers you would like to play video games with." (p. 633)
a. Dominance hierarchy is a group's organized infrastructure that is based on power relationships. It is not a measure of peer relationships.

b. A sociometric rating scale is a peer assessment measure, but it does not ask a child to name a number of peers. Instead, children are asked to rate peers on several dimensions.

d. The peer status scale is not a peer assessment measure.

10. *a. Few positive nominations and few negative nominations are characteristic of a neglected child. (p. 634)

b. Few positive nominations and many negative nominations are characteristic of a rejected child.

c. Many positive nominations and few negative nominations are characteristic of a popular child.

d. Many positive nominations and many negative nominations are characteristic of a controversial child.

11. *d. The child's social skills appear to be the most important factor in peer acceptance. (p. 636)

a. The child's name plays a role in peer acceptance, but it is not the most important factor.

b. The child's physical attractiveness plays a role in peer acceptance, but it is not the most important factor.

c. The child's motor skills play a role in peer acceptance but are not the most important factor.

12. *b. In one study neglected children tended to engage in isolated activities and had low visibility with peers. (p. 637)

a. Neglected children, like most unpopular children, are not as successful in entering a play group as are popular children.

c. Popular children keep the focus of attention on the peer group rather than on themselves. Unpopular children, on the other hand, disrupt the group's activities by bringing attention to themselves.

d. Popular children tend to restrict their conversation with acquaintances to relevant comments. Unpopular children, on the other hand, often make irrelevant comments when they speak with acquaintances.

13. *a. Popular children first make statements about the peers in the group (a low-risk activity). As they receive positive feedback they engage in more high risk activities. (p. 638)

b. A popular child is sensitive to the reactions of peers and is likely to proceed cautiously to ensure acceptance in the group.

c. Popular children first make statements about the peers in the group (a low-risk activity); they do not begin with high-risk activities.

d. Popular children first make statements about the peers in the group (a low-risk activity); they do not begin with high-risk activities.

14. *c. Mothers of unpopular children display behaviors very similar to their children, such as using their authority to disrupt the ongoing play of a group their child is attempting to join. (p. 639)
   a. Mothers of *popular* children are less disagreeable and demanding when playing with their children.
   b. Mothers of unpopular children are *less* likely to initiate peer contacts.
   d. Mothers of *popular* children are more likely to focus on feelings when interacting with their children.

15. *d. Toddlers who spend a year or more with the *same* peers in day care show the greatest social competence. (p. 641)
   a. Social competence appears to increase as children have more experience with peers. A child reared at home with no siblings has few opportunities to interact with peers.
   b. A child reared at home with siblings has greater experiences with other children than a child raised home without siblings, but not as much as a child who attends day care.
   c. Peer interactions in day care appear to increase social competence in children, but there are other important factors that improve social competence, such as the stability of the peer group.

16. *a. Popular children are better able than unpopular children to interpret social cues. (p. 642)
   b. Popular children are *more* skillful than unpopular children at interpreting social cues.
   c. Not only are popular children more skillful at interpreting social cues, but they are also better at generating several potential behavioral responses.
   d. Not only are popular children more skillful at interpreting social cues, but they are also better at selecting appropriate responses.

17. *c. Coaching is not a way in which peers socialize their age mates, but a method of training social skills. (p. 644)
   a. Peers do socialize their age mates by serving as models. Peer imitation is an important socialization process, particularly in young children.
   b. Peers do socialize their age mates by providing positive reinforcers. Peers actively positively reinforce their friends' behavior.
   d. Peers do socialize their age mates by providing negative reinforcers. Peers also negatively reinforce their friends' behavior.

18. *b. During the middle school years friendships in boys are usually extensive, while in girls they tend to be intensive. (p. 648)
   a. Considerable sex differences in children's view of friendship have been observed.
   c. Children become concerned with being accepted by their peers in the middle school years, not during preschool.
   d. Cross-sex friendships are rare in the middle school years, but increase in the adolescent years.

19. *b. According to Selman, it is the young child's egocentricity that limits her concept of friendship. (p. 650)
    a. Children's conceptions of friendship do change with age, but it is not age per se that determines a child's concept of friendship.
    c. Selman's theory emphasizes the child's social perspective-taking ability, not the child's history of reinforcement.
    d. Selman's theory emphasizes the child's social perspective-taking ability, not the child's exposure to peer pressure.

20. *c. The sharing of affection and emotional support among friends appears to serve to protect children from anxiety and stress. (p. 651)
    a. When children are in a conflict with friends they are more likely to resolve the conflict than to let it escalate.
    b. Children who have close and intimate friendships have higher self-esteem and are more sociable; thus there is no reason to expect that conflict with family members will increase.
    d. Friendships provide strong social and emotional support.

Answers to Application Questions

1. *d. Recent research suggests that preschoolers engage in solitary, parallel, and cooperative play. (p. 619)
    a. Solitary play (playing alone, apart from other children) does occur in preschoolers, but it is not the only form of play that they engage in.
    b. Parallel play (playing independent of, but alongside, other children) does occur in preschoolers, but it is not the only form of play that they engage in.
    c. Cooperative play (interacting with other children during play) does occur in preschoolers, but it is not the only form of play that they engage in.

2. *b. A crowd is a large group of peers that is characterized by specific traits or reputation. Because Irving and Craig are both described as "brains," it can be said that they belong to the same crowd. (p. 622)
    a. A clique is a group of five to ten children who frequently interact with each other. Because Irving and Craig do not spend much time together they are not part of the same clique.
    c. *Gang* is not a psychological term. Moreover, Irving and Craig do not spend time together, like gang members do.
    d. A link is a cooperative group experience in the Soviet Union. Irving and Craig are not a part of a link.

3. *d. Studies suggest that intergroup hostilities are reduced when the feuding groups are made to work together to achieve a common goal such as building a new playground. (p. 626)
    a. Studies suggest that intergroup hostilities are not reduced when the two groups are forced to share activities.
    b. Studies suggest that organized competitions increase intergroup hostilities.

c. Although this may appear to be a plausible solution, it is unclear how the camp counselors can assure that the original groups remain apart.

4. *b. Adolescents, like Yvette, who strongly value conforming to adult norms are less popular with their peers. (p. 629)
   a. Because Yvette's values are very similar to her parents', she most likely values conforming to adult norms. However, adolescents who strongly value conforming to adult norms are *less* popular with their peers.
   c. Adolescents, like Yvette, who strongly value conforming to adult norms are less likely to experiment with behaviors that are considered risky.
   d. Although Yvette's desire to conform to adult norms makes her less popular than adolescents who place less value on adult norms, it does not necessarily mean that she is a loner and has few friends.

5. *a. Jo Anne, like most popular children, is likely to receive more positive nominations than negative nominations. (p. 634)
   b. Jo Anne would receive a high number of positive and negative nominations if she were a controversial child.
   c. Teacher rankings are not determined in sociometric nominations.
   d. Behavioral observations are not made in sociometric nominations.

6. *b. A child's peer status remains stable over a period of years, especially a child who is classified as rejected. Because Willie was rejected in the second grade he is likely to be rejected in the seventh grade. (p. 635)
   a. The child's peer status remains stable over a period of years. Because Willie was not popular in the second grade he is unlikely to be popular in the seventh grade.
   c. The child's peer status remains stable over a period of years. Because Willie was not controversial in the second grade he is unlikely to be controversial in the seventh grade.
   d. Willie, like any child, is certainly influenced by peers.

7. *d. The most important factor that determines peer popularity is the child's social skills. Because David is very verbal and cooperative he, most likely, engages in prosocial behaviors, which, very likely, make him the most popular. (p. 636)
   a. Although a child's name is a factor in determining the popularity of a child, it is not the most important factor; there is a better answer.
   b. Although a child's physical appearance is a factor in determining the popularity of a child, it is not the most important factor; there is a better answer.
   c. Norman has at least two characteristics that are likely to make him unpopular, an uncommon name and poor motor abilities.

8. *c. Unpopular children are more likely to make irrelevant comments. Because this statement is unrelated to playing house, it suggests that an unpopular child said it. (p. 638)
   a. Although this statement is somewhat confrontational, it does not necessarily suggest that the child is unpopular.

b. This statement is relevant to the task at hand, playing house; therefore, it does not suggest that an unpopular child said it.
d. This statement is relevant to the task at hand, playing house; therefore, it does not suggest that an unpopular child said it.

9. *c. Studies that have examined mother and child interactions suggest that mothers of unpopular children have behaviors that resemble their children's behavior. (p. 639)
a. Studies suggest that parents have important influences on children's social competence.
b. There are no indications that mothers influence children's social competence more than fathers.
d. Mothers of unpopular children display behaviors that resemble their children's behavior.

10. *c. Cross-sex friendships in fifth-graders are rare. Moreover, fifth-graders often openly resist the idea that they may have an opposite-sex friend. (p. 647)
a. Although preschoolers usually spend more time with same-sex peers than opposite-sex peers, they do not resist the idea that they may have a friend of the opposite sex.
b. Although first-graders usually spend more time with same-sex peers than opposite-sex peers, they do not resist the idea that they may have a friend of the opposite sex.
d. Cross-sex friendships increase in high school; therefore, tenth-graders are less likely to resist the idea that they may have an opposite sex friend.

CHAPTER 16

THE INFLUENCE OF SCHOOL AND TELEVISION

LEARNING OBJECTIVES

1. Describe the effects of schooling on the developing child's academic achievement and self-concept. (pp. 658–661)

2. Describe the physical characteristics of the school environment that play a role in the child's development. (pp. 661–662)

3. Describe and discuss the different approaches to educating children in the classroom. (pp. 662–667)

4. Discuss the controversy concerning whether students should be grouped according to academic ability. (pp. 667–668)

5. Describe the difficulties that children may experience as they go through transitions in schooling and how their transitions can be eased by parents and teachers. (pp. 668–671)

6. Describe how the teacher's expectations and classroom management strategies influence students' self-esteem and performance in the classroom. (pp. 671–674)

7. Describe the various explanations that have been proposed to account for differences in school achievement that are seen across different cultural groups. Discuss the effectiveness of intervention programs such as the KEEP model. (pp. 674–675)

8. Discuss how cultural attitudes and beliefs influence academic achievement among African American and Asian children. (pp. 675–678)

9. Describe the impact of computers on the cognitive and social development of male and female children. (pp. 678–684)

10. Describe the pattern of television viewing among children and their ability to comprehend television programs. (pp. 684–687)

11. Describe the impact television has on children's cognitive and language development. (pp. 687–689)

12. Describe television's impact on the child's social development, including a discussion of aggression, prosocial behavior, and sex-role stereotypes. (pp. 689–695)

CHAPTER OUTLINE

I. **SCHOOL** (pp. 658–684)
The main aim of education is to provide children with academic skills, but the child's numerous hours in school can also have a profound impact on self-concept and psychological well-being.

A. **What Are the Effects of School on the Developing Child?** (pp. 658–661)
One of the most important outcomes of schooling is literacy, the ability to read and write. Most young adults complete high school, but national surveys suggest that the achievement of American students in reading, writing, and science has declined or does not compare favorably with students from other industrialized countries.

There is a positive correlation between academic achievement and self-esteem. High self-esteem appears to lead to greater academic achievement, and, conversely, high achievement fosters greater self-esteem. In one study high-achieving students who were made to believe that they had failed a test showed a decline in self-esteem.

B. **The Physical Environment of the School** (pp. 661–662)
School size and class size influence the child's development. Students from smaller schools tend to participate more in school activities, feel more competent, and say they are more challenged. Smaller class size is associated with greater academic success among students. For example, among first-graders assigned to different size classes, children from the smaller classes showed greater improvements on standardized tests of reading and mathematics.

The physical layout of the classroom influences the relationships among students and between teachers and students. When desks in the classroom are arranged in rows facing the teacher, more student-teacher exchanges occur with children seated in the front row and center aisle. When desks are arranged in a circle, a greater number of students have the opportunity to participate.

C. **Philosophies of Education** (pp. 662–667)
The traditional approach in education views the teacher as an authority figure and transmitter of information and the students as individual learners. Alternative models of education view the teacher-student relationship in nontraditional ways. One nontraditional educational approach is the *open classroom*, where peer interaction, movement of students around activity centers, and "discovery"-based learning are emphasized. Although children from open classrooms show no overall advantage over children from traditional classrooms in academic achievement, they do show gains in social development, such as being more cooperative and developing broad networks of relationships with peers.

In *cooperative learning* approaches, such as Robert Slavin's Student Teams–Achievement Divisions (STAD) method, students work in groups on academic tasks, with teams often competing against each other. Students show greater achievement in academic subjects, greater self-esteem, more favorable attitudes toward academics, and more cross-racial friendships after participating in STAD.

Peer collaboration involves pairs of students working on academic problems without competition. In one study with fourth-graders peer collaboration improved formal reasoning on math and spatial problems and reduced sex differences in these types of tasks. The positive effects of peer learning are consistent with Piaget's and Vygotsky's suggestions that peer interaction encourage the advancement of cognitive skills.

Controversy: Should Students Be Grouped According to Academic Ability? (pp. 667–668)
Proponents of academic tracking argue that grouping students according to academic ability allows bright children to be challenged and motivated, and spares slower learners the embarrassment of continual failure. Critics argue, however, that academic tracking lowers the self expectations of slower learners, diminishes the quality of their educational experience, and may serve to limit the access of children from different economic and ethnic/racial backgrounds to educational resources.

D. **School Transitions** (pp. 668–671)
One important transition is the start of school. Children who are cooperative and have extensive positive social contacts are more likely to make a smooth adjustment. The presence of familiar peers also helps with transitions by facilitating peer acceptance, possibly by providing a "secure base" from which to develop additional social relationships.

The transition to middle school or junior high school is also important since it adds to the stresses that many preadolescents are already experiencing. Students often show a decline in school satisfaction, a drop in self-esteem (particularly in girls), and more physical complaints at this time. When teachers provide greater social support and when students take most of their classes with the same peer group, many of the negative effects associated with the transition to junior high school decline.

E. **Teachers: Key Agents of Influence** (pp. 671–674)
The expectations that teachers have of their students can create a self-fulfilling prophecy. The classic study by Robert Rosenthal and Lenore Jacobson documented how students' achievement levels rise or decline to the level expected by teachers. Subsequent studies indicated that high-achieving students are given more opportunities to participate, more time to answer questions, and receive more praise and less criticism than low-achieving students.

Teachers' classroom-management strategies can influence academic and other outcomes for students. Effective teachers keep classroom time focused on instruction and are personally involved in every phase of the learning process. Teachers who continually provide opportunities for students to compare themselves (by assigning similar tasks to all students, organizing tasks according to student ability level, and by providing public grade announcements) may set the stage for lower self-esteem among some students. Teachers who set limits on students' behaviors but also deliver frequent praise and provide a pleasant, comfortable environment foster the greatest academic and personal gains among students. An especially important dimension is the degree to which teachers promote student autonomy within the classroom. Children who experience greater responsibility in the classroom have higher self-esteem than children whose teachers are perceived as controlling and directive.

F. **Cultural Differences in School Achievement** (pp. 674–678)
Children respond differently to the school experience because each child brings with him attitudes and beliefs that were acquired in his family and cultural environment. A consistent finding is that children from African American backgrounds score lower than Caucasian children on many measures of academic performance. The explanation for greater school difficulties among certain cultural minority groups has been debated by psychologists and educators.

The *cultural compatibility hypothesis* has replaced the cultural deficit hypothesis as an explanation for the lower academic achievement of children from minority groups. It asserts that minority children are culturally different, not culturally deficient, and argues that these children will achieve more if their educational experiences are consistent with the practices of their background culture. The Kamehameha Early Education Program (KEEP) is an example of an educational intervention program designed within the framework of the cultural compatibility hypothesis to help improve academic achievement among minority Hawaiian children in the state of Hawaii.

African American children are often confronted with an educational experience that conflicts with their background culture, with racism, and with economic hardship, all of which can interfere with school achievement. Asian children show a pattern of higher achievement in reading and mathematics compared to American children. These differing patterns of achievement are not a result of superior cognitive skills in any one group. Asian children spend a greater proportion of classroom time in academic activities, have a longer school year, and do more homework compared to American children.

G. **Computers** (pp. 678–684)
Most schools provide students with the opportunity to use computers, although the way students use computers varies with age; younger schoolchildren engage in more drill-and-practice routines, while high school students tend to do more programming.

Computer-assisted instruction (CAI) involves the use of computers to supply tutorial information and drill-and-practice routines. CAI approaches generally improve students' academic achievement scores, particularly among elementary school and special needs children. CAI experience also increases children's positive attitudes toward computers and the subject area they are studying. Interactive software that requires creative problem solving or encourages comprehension strategies can also promote academic learning, especially the development of *heuristic strategies* (problem-solving approaches that involve higher-order analyses).

Experiences with computer programming, such as the Logo program, have produced conflicting results. Some researchers report that children show few cognitive gains, while others find that children using Logo show gains on several measures of cognitive competence, including classification skill, self-monitoring, creativity, spatial cognitive skill, enhanced rule learning, and the ability to analyze the process of problem solving.

Computer activities often promote opportunities for social interaction among students, especially when teachers encourage group problem solving. Boys are more likely than girls to use computers, perhaps because of societal stereotypes about activities that are appropriate for each sex. When girls use computers or enroll in computer courses their performance is similar to their male classmates.

II. **TELEVISION** (pp. 684–695)
Most American households have at least one television, and it is estimated that children spend about one-third of their waking hours watching television.

A. **Patterns of Television Viewing among Children** (pp. 684–685)
Infants as young as six months of age watch television. The time spent viewing increases dramatically in the preschool years, peaks at age ten to twelve, then declines in adolescence. Preschoolers prefer to watch nonanimated informative programs designed especially for children; at three to five years, they prefer cartoons; older children watch programs for general audiences.

B. **Children's TV Viewing: Active or Passive?** (pp. 685–686)

The fact that children have preferences for certain types of programs and that these preferences change with age indicates that television viewing is not always a passive process. Formal features of television, such as sound effects, capture children's attention, while other features, such as visual cuts, maintain attention. Children actively direct their attention to the portions of programs they most readily understand.

C. **Children's Comprehension of Television Programs** (pp. 686–687)

Preschoolers understand short story segments that are aimed at children (such as the short segments found on "Sesame Street"). When they watch programs for general audiences, they are less likely to remember the explicit and implicit content than are older children. Advances in cognitive skills, such as the ability to integrate information separated by time, are linked to children's comprehension of television. Increases in general knowledge and advances in verbal skills also enhance children's comprehension of television shows. Another developmental change is related to children's understanding of what is real and fabricated on television. Older children are better able than younger children to recognize that most television programs depict fabricated as opposed to real events.

D. **Television's Impact on Cognitive and Language Development** (pp. 687–689)

Studies have shown that children from disadvantaged backgrounds show gains in several school readiness skills after viewing "Sesame Street" for one season. Some investigators have argued that these gains, although significant, are small. "Sesame Street" has also been criticized on other points, such as its fast-paced format, but such criticisms have not been empirically tested.

Television may provide children with opportunities to learn new words, especially since many shows developed for children contain the elements of "motherese."

E. **Television's Impact on Social Development** (pp. 689–695)

Social learning theory predicts that the high levels of violence depicted on television provide children with numerous models for aggression. In contrast, according to the *catharsis hypothesis,* viewing televised violence reduces aggression by releasing pent-up frustrations. There is little evidence in support of the catharsis hypothesis.

Several studies suggest a causal relationship between television and aggression. Albert Bandura's classic laboratory study of children observing models behave aggressively toward a Bobo doll suggested that models on film are as powerful as "live" models in eliciting aggression. Critics of this study question whether punching a Bobo doll can be considered an aggressive behavior. Field experiments and large-scale correlational studies also provide evidence linking violence on television with aggression.

Investigators suggest that to reduce the potentially harmful consequences of violent television programs, parents should limit children's exposure to them and discuss the programs with their children.

Some research suggests that when children view prosocial television programs, their own tendency to behave prosocially increases.

Children who watch more television tend to have more stereotyped ideas about sex roles, possibly because most television shows display traditional sex-role stereotypes.

Children are the targets of a large number of television commercials. Children who watch a lot of television respond to the messages of commercials but are not always able to evaluate critically the information presented in commercials.

III. THEMES IN DEVELOPMENT: THE INFLUENCE OF SCHOOL AND TELEVISION (pp. 695–696)
How does the sociocultural context influence the child's experiences with school and television? Not all cultures emphasize formal schooling, and not all children have access to television or computers. Various elements of the child's cultural background may either harmonize or conflict with the predominant values of the educational system. Children's academic performance is better when educational practices are compatible with their background.

How does the child play an active role in experiences with school and television? When children are encouraged to participate in school, they show greater academic achievement and higher self-esteem. Techniques such as peer collaboration, classroom autonomy, and computer activities promote the child's active involvement. In television viewing, children actively direct their attention to programs they understand, although sometimes they are passively exposed to programs selected by others.

How do the child's experiences with school and television interact with the various domains of development? Children who have good peer relations and social skills are more likely to adjust easily to school. In school, children have opportunities for intellectual development, peer relations, and promotion of their self-concept. Experiences with computers can also encourage cognitive and social development. Educational television programs can enhance cognitive growth. Television can also influence social behavior by its portrayal of violence, prosocial acts, and sex-role stereotypes.

Key Terms Review

1. _____ is a peer-centered learning experience in which pairs of students work together on academic problems, usually without competing against other students.

2. _____ utilizes computers to provide tutorial information and drill-and-practice routines.

3. According to the _____ , school instruction is most effective if it is consistent with the practices of the child's background culture.

4. The suggestion that viewing television violence reduces tendencies to behave aggressively by releasing built-up frustrations or hostilities is called the _____ .

5. In the _____ structured opportunities are provided for students to "discover" knowledge, and peer interaction is encouraged.

6. _____ are problem-solving methods that involve higher-order analyses, such as subdividing a problem into smaller parts.

7. In _____ students of different abilities work together in small groups to solve academic problems.

Answers to Key Terms Review

1. Peer collaboration
2. Computer-assisted instruction
3. cultural compatibility hypothesis
4. catharsis hypothesis
5. open classroom
6. Heuristic strategies
7. cooperative learning

Multiple-Choice Questions

Fact and Concept Questions

1. An original goal of compulsory education in the United States was to
   a. teach religious beliefs.
   b. teach vocational skills.
   c. teach morality and citizenship.
   d. separate the wealthy from the poorer classes.

2. Measures of academic achievement among American students within the last decade reveal that
   a. scores on standardized tests of achievement are higher than they were thirty years ago.
   b. approximately 50 percent of seventeen-year-olds are functionally illiterate.
   c. 75 percent of thirteen-year-olds can read complicated written information.
   d. less than 20 percent of eighth-graders can write adequately.

3. Studies of the effects of the physical arrangement of a classroom on active student participation show that
   a. student participation is greatest when students' desks are aligned in rows and columns.
   b. student participation is greatest when students are placed in assigned seats.
   c. student participation is greatest when students' desks are placed in a circle.
   d. physical arrangement of the classroom has no effect on student participation.

4. In the open classroom, students
   a. sit in assigned seats arranged in rows and columns facing the teacher.
   b. are encouraged to collaborate by working in activity centers with less formally structured lessons.
   c. are encouraged to be competitive with one another.
   d. are not given any instruction by the teacher.

5. The theoretical models of development proposed by both Piaget and Vygotsky would favor which of the following classroom practices?
   a. Traditional classroom learning
   b. Cooperative learning
   c. Dependent learning
   d. Experimental learning

6. The practice of grouping children in classes according to academic ability is called
   a. tracking.
   b. collaboration.
   c. cooperation.
   d. scaffolding.

7. The transition from elementary to secondary school is typically associated with a(n)
   a. increase in self-esteem.
   b. decline in stress and peer pressure.
   c. increase in academic achievement and extracurricular activities.
   d. decline in academic achievement and extracurricular activities.

8. According to Rosenthal and Jacobson, the Pygmalian effect is the
   a. tendency for teachers' expectations to affect students' academic performance.
   b. effect of small class size on increased academic performance.
   c. benefits of cooperative learning over traditional learning.
   d. tendency for teachers to show favoritism toward physically attractive children.

9. With respect to the climate of the classroom, teachers who _____ have the most positive influence on student achievement and behavior.
   a. are controlling and directive
   b. set limits but provide praise and feedback
   c. use verbal punishment and reasoning
   d. make few attempts to set limits on children

10. The KEEP program was designed to
    a. keep minority children off the streets.
    b. train minority children in test-taking skills.
    c. provide an early education experience compatible with Hawaiian culture.
    d. train African American children in academic skills.

11. Which of the following is *not* true of computer-assisted instruction?
    a. Children work at their own pace.
    b. Children receive immediate feedback for correct or incorrect answers.
    c. Children who use computers show academic advantages over children who do not use computers.
    d. Computer programs make use of sound effects and graphics to capture the child's attention.

12. The computer language Logo was designed to facilitate children's
    a. mastery of theoretical and abstract knowledge.
    b. understanding of physics.
    c. use of verbal language skills.
    d. social interactions.

13. Research indicates that boys like computers _____ than girls and that girls perform _____ boys in computer programming classes.
    a. more, worse than
    b. more, as well as
    c. less, worse than
    d. less, as well as

14. On average, American children spend nearly as much time watching TV as they do
    a. eating.
    b. reading.
    c. playing.
    d. sleeping.

15. Research with preschool children indicates that _____ will be most influential in whether or not the child pays attention to the TV.
    a. sound effects
    b. colorful displays
    c. comprehensibility
    d. time of day

16. Studies suggest that the children's TV program "Sesame Street"
    a. has little effect on children's cognitive development, but does influence children's prosocial behavior.
    b. improves children's cognitive skills as well as their prosocial attitudes.
    c. results in reducing the amount of time children spend practicing prereading skills such as learning letters and numbers and writing their own name.
    d. creates a negative attitude toward school in children from disadvantaged backgrounds.

17. Although not empirically tested, one criticism of "Sesame Street" has been that
    a. the program does not result in improved cognitive skills for preschoolers who watch it.
    b. the fast-paced format of the show makes it difficult for preschoolers to comprehend its content.
    c. the fast-paced format of the show prevents children from adopting reflective, sustained learning strategies in school.
    d. women and ethnic minorities are not represented equally with white male characters on the program.

18. Research on the impact of TV on children's social development suggests that
    a. violence on TV does not affect children's aggressive behavior.
    b. the catharsis hypothesis is correct with regard to televised aggression and children's behavior.
    c. children ignore the behavior of aggressive models on TV.
    d. social learning accounts of the effects of modeled aggression on children's behavior are more accurate.

19. In one research study, children who viewed a TV program called "Freestyle"
    a. modified their acceptance of nontraditional sex roles and activities.
    b. modified their view of the intent of televised commercials.
    c. were unable to realize that commercials are designed to influence consumer buying practices.
    d. behaved more aggressively after they watched the program.

20. Children who watch a lot of television
    a. are less likely to request the products they see advertised in commercials.
    b. are more likely to request the products they see advertised in commercials.
    c. do not respond to educational messages concerning the truthfulness of commercials.
    d. are more likely to be skeptical about the product claims in commercials.

Application Questions

1. Philip attends a high school with approximately 2,000 students. Philip is likely to
    a. have high self-esteem.
    b. feel competent and challenged.
    c. participate in many school activities.
    d. have less access to leadership roles.

2. Desiree's teacher encourages collaboration among students and structures lessons such that shared problem solving and creativity are considered important goals. Desiree's class is typical of the _____ classroom.
    a. traditional
    b. open
    c. authoritarian
    d. competitive

3. Ryan was placed in the slow track class in the first grade. Where is Ryan most likely to be when he is in the fourth grade?
    a. Ryan will very likely be in the advanced track class.
    b. Ryan will very likely be in the slow track class.
    c. Ryan will definitely be in the slow track class.
    d. It is impossible to predict which track Ryan will be in.

4. Fred, an African American child, is likely to have more difficulties in school than James, a Caucasian child. The _____ hypothesis suggests this may be so because Fred has had family experiences that did not prepare him for the demands of school.
    a. KEEP
    b. cultural compatibility
    c. cultural deficit
    d. cultural bias

5. Liza has had a computer in her classroom for a number of years. As a high school student, Liza will most likely use the computer for
    a. drill-and-practice lessons.
    b. programming.
    c. computer-assisted instruction.
    d. assistance with memorization.

6. Diana has mastered the computer program Logo. Consequently, she likely has knowledge of
    a. the geography of the countries of the world.
    b. the mathematical rules of geometry.
    c. the musical scale.
    d. the process of planning, executing, and debugging computer programs.

7. José is a teenager. Compared to a few years ago, he probably
   a. spends more time watching television.
   b. spends less time watching television.
   c. spends the same amount of time watching television.
   d. does not watch television.

8. When nine-year-old Marcy watches cartoons she is likely to
   a. be unable to understand the actions of the cartoon characters.
   b. believe that the cartoon characters are really experiencing the events portrayed.
   c. understand that the cartoons do not depict reality.
   d. be unable to integrate information across scenes.

9. Daryl watches a large number of violent television programs. _____ predicts that Daryl is likely to behave aggressively, whereas _____ predicts that Daryl will not behave aggressively.
   a. The frustration-aggression hypothesis, the catharsis hypothesis
   b. The catharsis hypothesis, the frustration-aggression hypothesis
   c. The catharsis hypothesis, social learning theory
   d. Social learning theory, the catharsis hypothesis

10. Which of the following children is most likely to be affected by the sexist content of television?
    a. Madeleine, a girl from a low socioeconomic background
    b. Lynn, a girl from a middle-class background
    c. Bernie, a boy with below-average intelligence
    d. Steve, a boy from a low socioeconomic background

Answers to Multiple-Choice Questions

The correct answer appears first and is preceded by an asterisk.

Answers to Fact and Concept Questions

1. *c. A major emphasis of compulsory education in the mid- and late nineteenth century was to produce honest, hard-working contributors to society through moral development and character training. (p. 658)
   a. The original emphasis in public education was not religious training, but producing honest and hard-working contributors to society.
   b. The early emphasis of public education was on moral development and character training, not on vocational training.
   d. Free education for all American children was seen as a socioeconomic equalizer, not as a form of socioeconomic segregation.

2. *d.   In a recent study only 13 percent of eighth-graders wrote "adequately." (p. 659)
   a.   American high school students score lower on most standardized tests than they did three decades ago.
   b.   About 13 percent of seventeen-year-olds are functionally illiterate because they cannot read or write.
   c.   Approximately 11 percent of thirteen-year-olds can read complicated written material.

3. *c.   When students are arranged in a circle in the classroom they raise their hands more frequently and make more spontaneous comments about the lesson. (p. 662)
   a.   The traditional classroom with rows and columns of desks yields clear differences in student participation, with the students in the front row and center aisle most likely to interact with the teacher.
   b.   There is no indication that assigning students to seats influences active student participation.
   d.   Studies show that the way in which a classroom is physically arranged influences student-teacher interactions as well as student-student interactions.

4. *b.   In the open classroom the students are encouraged to engage in cooperative learning experiences, and the teacher is often considered a collaborator in the learning experience. (p. 663)
   a.   Rows and columns of desks facing the teacher is the characteristic physical layout of the traditional classroom.
   c.   The open classroom encourages inquisitiveness and socialization. Competition is discouraged.
   d.   Although the open classroom is less structured than the traditional classroom, the teacher in the open classroom gives some structured lessons that provide opportunities for sharing and cooperative discovery.

5. *b.   Both Piaget and Vygotsky favor cooperative learning. According to Piaget, peer interactions during cooperative learning provide conflicts and disequilibrium, which produce reorganizations in the child's thinking. According to Vygotsky, peers facilitate cognitive growth when they have similar abilities (by operating within similar *zones of proximal development*) and when they have different abilities (by providing *scaffolding*). (p. 666)
   a.   Piaget and Vygotsky believe that peer interaction encourages advancement of cognitive skills. Because the traditional classroom discourages interaction between children, Piaget and Vygotsky are unlikely to favor the traditional classroom.
   c.   Dependent learning is not a classroom practice.
   d.   Experimental learning is not a classroom practice.

6. *a.   Although it is controversial, tracking students in terms of academic ability is a common practice in the American educational system. (p. 667)
   b.   Collaboration refers to working together to solve an academic problem. It is not a classroom structure.

c. Children placed in different groups would not have the opportunity to cooperate with each other.

d. Scaffolding describes the temporary support provided by an adult or peer to encourage further development of skills in a lesser-skilled person. It is not a classroom structure.

7. *d. A decline in school satisfaction, grades, and participation in extracurricular activities has been observed during the transition from elementary to secondary school. (p. 669)

a. Some researchers have found a decrease in self-esteem, especially among preadolescent girls.

b. The many life changes that occur during this time encourage stress in preadolescents. The transition from elementary to secondary school compounds the stress.

c. Many studies report a drop in grades and participation in extracurricular activities during this transition.

8. *a. In the Pygmalian effect teachers create a self-fulfilling prophecy by treating students differently based on their beliefs about the children's intellectual performance. (p. 671)

b. The Pygmalian effect does not deal with class size, but with teacher expectations of student performance.

c. The Pygmalian effect does not describe effects of different educational models, but the effects of teacher expectations on student performance.

d. Although the Pygmalian effect describes differential treatment of students, such treatment is based on teachers' beliefs about children's intellectual performance (which may be partly influenced by the physical characteristics of the child), not simply the physical attractiveness of the students.

9. *b. Teachers who control children in the classroom with positive reinforcement, reasoning, and positive emotions provide the children with a pleasant, comfortable environment that fosters academic and personal gains. (p. 672)

a. Teachers who are controlling and directive do make the classroom run smoothly, but they do not foster the greatest academic and personal gains among their students.

c. Children who are targets of frequent verbal punishment from their teacher are less likely to achieve than children who receive positive reinforcement for acceptable behavior.

d. It is important for teachers to set limits on students' behavior, but teachers who use reasoning and positive reinforcement to set these limits are more likely to foster academic and personal growth than teachers who use punishment to set them.

10. *c. The KEEP program structured the classroom of minority Hawaiian children to emphasize collaboration and cooperation, characteristics that are highly valued in the Hawaiian culture. (p. 675)

a. The KEEP program did not take minority children out of the street and place them in a classroom. The program restructured the classroom experience to make it compatible with the practices of the children's culture.

b. The KEEP program encouraged learning through cooperation and collaboration; it did not train children in traditional test-taking skills.

d. The KEEP program was designed for minority Hawaiian children, not African American children.

11. *c. Computer-assisted instruction is primarily used to supplement, not replace, traditional classroom instruction. (p. 679)

a. The statement is true. A major advantage of CAI over traditional classroom instruction is that the child can work at his own pace.

b. This statement is true. Computers permit students to receive immediate feedback on their performance.

d. This statement is true. Computer programs often make use of interesting sounds and graphics to help keep the young child's attention.

12. *a. Seymour Papert, creator of Logo, believes that Logo is an ideal setting for children to test their own theories and therefore master abstract concepts and ideas more quickly. (p. 680)

b. Logo is a programming language, not a program that teaches physics.

c. Logo is a programming language, not a program that teaches verbal language skills.

d. Although Logo may precipitate peer interaction, the program was not designed with this purpose in mind.

13. *b. Boys like computers more than girls, but boys and girls perform equally well in computer classes. (p. 684)

a. Boys do like computers more than girls, but they do not perform worse than girls in computer classes.

c. Boys do not like computers less than girls, nor do they perform more poorly than girls in computer classes.

d. Boys do not like computers less than girls, and they perform as well as girls in computer classes.

14. *d. One third of the child's life is spent watching TV, which is more time than anything children do except sleeping. (p. 684)

a. Children spend more time watching TV than eating.

b. Children spend more time watching TV than reading.

c. Children spend more time watching TV than playing.

15. *c. TV viewing is often an active process; thus, comprehensibility is the most influential factor because children actively direct their attention to the portion of the TV program they understand. (p. 686)

a. Although children are influenced by sound effects in TV programs, sound is not the most influential factor.

b. Although children are influenced by color displays in TV programs, color is not the most influential factor.

d. Although children's TV-viewing activities may be influenced by the time of day, it is not the most influential factor.

16. *b. Children who watch "Sesame Street" show gains on several cognitive skills, such as knowing letters and numbers, and show more positive attitudes toward people of other races. (p. 688)

a. Some studies have found cognitive gains, such as higher scores in standardized vocabulary tests, in children who watch "Sesame Street."

c. There is no evidence of a reduction in the practice of prereading skills in children viewing "Sesame Street." In fact, children who watch "Sesame Street" show gains in prereading skills.

d. Children from various social and ethnic backgrounds, as well as from disadvantaged backgrounds, show cognitive gains and more positive attitudes toward school after watching "Sesame Street."

17. *c. Some critics of "Sesame Street" argue that children who watch the program may come to expect equally fast-paced learning experiences in school and thereby fail to develop reflective learning strategies. (p. 689)

a. Cognitive gains have been observed in preschoolers who regularly watch "Sesame Street."

b. Although some researchers have criticized the fast-paced action of "Sesame Street," the criticism was not directed at the inability of children to comprehend the program's content.

d. "Sesame Street" deliberately includes characters of both genders and of various racial and ethnic backgrounds.

18. *d. Laboratory studies and field experiments provide considerable support for the social learning theory position that viewing aggressive models increases aggressive behavior in children. (p. 690)

a. Research findings suggest that there is a causal relationship between watching violence on TV and aggressive behavior in children.

b. There is little evidence to support the catharsis hypothesis.

c. Several studies provide evidence that children often imitate the behavior of an aggressive model.

19. *a. Recent studies indicate that the TV series "Freestyle" successfully counteracts children's stereotypical beliefs about sex-typed characteristics and behaviors. (p. 694)

b. The TV series "Freestyle" was developed to counteract sex-role stereotypes, not to educate children about commercials.

c. The TV series "Freestyle" was developed to counteract sex-role stereotypes, not to educate children about commercials.

d. The TV series "Freestyle" was developed to counteract sex-role stereotypes, not to study modeling of aggressive behavior.

20. *b. Children who are heavy TV viewers respond to the messages of commercials and therefore are more likely to request the products in the commercials. (p. 695)
   a. Children who are heavy TV viewers are *more* likely to request the products in the commercials.
   c. Children who are heavy viewers of TV do respond to educational messages concerning the intent of commercials and the fact that commercials are not always truthful.
   d. Children who are heavy TV viewers respond to commercials; therefore, they do not appear to be skeptical of the claims made by commercials.

Answers to Application Questions

1. *d. Students who attend a large high school are less likely to have opportunities to engage in leadership roles than students who attend a small high school. (p. 661)
   a. Students who attend a small high school are more likely to feel competent and thus have greater self-esteem than students who attend a large high school.
   b. Students who attend a small high school are more likely to feel competent and challenged than students who attend a large high school.
   c. Students who attend a small high school are more likely to participate in school activities than students who attend a large high school.

2. *b. Desiree's class is an example of the open classroom, where the teacher provides some structure but encourages frequent collaboration among students. (p. 663)
   a. In the traditional classroom the major interaction is between the teacher and students, not among the students; Desiree is not in a traditional classroom.
   c. The authoritarian classroom is not a type of classroom that has been identified. Moreover, the term *authoritarian* implies a strict and inflexible teaching style.
   d. A classroom structure that encourages collaborative learning rarely compares children's accomplishments and thus would not be very competitive.

3. *b. Once students are placed in a given academic track it is very difficult for them to switch to another group; therefore, Ryan will most likely remain in the slow track. (p. 668)
   a. It is unlikely that Ryan will be in the advanced track, because once students are placed in a given academic track it is very difficult for them to switch to another group.
   c. Although Ryan will very likely be in the slow track class, we cannot assume that he *definitely* will not switch to a higher track class.
   d. It is impossible to know for certain what track Ryan will be in when in the fourth grade, but given the consequences of tracking that have been observed by psychologists and educators, we have good reason to expect that Ryan will remain in the slow track class.

4. *c. The cultural deficit hypothesis emphasizes deficiencies in the backgrounds of minority children. The suggestion that Fred's family experiences did not prepare him adequately for school is consistent with the view of this hypothesis. (p. 674)

a. The KEEP model was designed to be compatible with the child's cultural background and thus is based on the cultural compatibility model, not the cultural deficit model.
b. The cultural compatibility hypothesis views the minority child as culturally different rather than culturally deficient. The suggestion that Fred was not adequately prepared for school implies the cultural deficit hypothesis.
d. Cultural bias is a criticism of standardized tests of intelligence, not a hypothesis explaining the school performance of minority children.

5. *b. High school students tend to use the computer primarily to write their own programs. (p. 678)
a. Elementary school children tend to use more drill-and-practice software, whereas high school students tend to use the computer for programming.
c. Computer-assisted instruction is more common and more effective with elementary and special needs children.
d. Computers are not generally used as an aid in memorizing information.

6. *d. Logo is a programming language designed to teach children programming and to help them master abstract concepts and ideas. Diana, therefore, most likely learned to program and debug Logo programs. (p. 681)
a. Logo is a programming language. It does not teach geography.
b. Logo is a programming language. Although it can be used to teach some aspects of geometry, Logo was not designed to teach geometry.
c. Logo is a programming language. It does not teach music.

7. *b. TV viewing peaks at around ten to twelve years of age and declines during adolescence, so José probably watches less TV than he did a few years ago. (p. 685)
a. Adolescents spend less time watching television than younger children.
c. Adolescents spend less time watching television than younger children, so José's TV-viewing time has probably decreased.
d. Although television watching declines during adolescence, it is unlikely to stop altogether.

8. *c. Children as young as five understand that cartoons are fantasy, so Marcy most certainly understands as well. (p. 687)
a. Children as young as preschool age can understand some of the actions of cartoon characters, so Marcy most certainly can as well.
b. Children as young as five understand that cartoons are fantasy, so Marcy most certainly understands as well.
d. Even young children can integrate simple story plots, but they get increasingly better at integrating information across scenes as they mature cognitively.

9. *d. Social learning theory would predict an increase in Daryl's aggressive behavior as a result of imitation of the acts of aggression portrayed on television. In contrast, the catharsis hypothesis would predict a reduction in Daryl's aggressive behavior,

suggesting that as the child watches the aggressive acts portrayed, he will release vicariously any stored-up hostilities. (p. 690)

a. The frustration-aggression hypothesis predicts that individuals will become aggressive when they are prevented from reaching a desired goal, not from watching violent TV programs. The second part of this answer is correct. The catharsis hypothesis would predict that Daryl's aggressive behavior will be reduced by watching violent TV programs.

b. The catharsis hypothesis would predict a reduction in Daryl's aggressive behavior. The frustration-aggression hypothesis predicts that individuals will become more aggressive when they are prevented from reaching a desired goal, not by watching TV.

c. The catharsis hypothesis would predict a reduction, not an increase, in Daryl's aggressive behavior. Social learning theory would predict an increase in Daryl's aggressive behavior as a result of modeling the aggressive acts portrayed on television.

10. *b. Correlational studies suggest that girls from middle-class families are more likely to be influenced by the sex-role stereotypes displayed in TV programs. (p. 694)

a. Girls from middle-class families, not lower-class families, are more likely to be influenced by stereotyped sex roles portrayed in TV programs.

c. Boys are less likely than girls to be influenced by the sexist content of TV programs.

d. Boys are less likely than girls to be influenced by the sexist content of TV programs.